Border Crossings

A BEDFORD SPOTLIGHT READER

Border Crossings

A BEDFORD SPOTLIGHT READER

Catherine Cucinella
California State University, San Marcos

Bedford/St. Martin's

A Macmillan Education Imprint

Boston • New York

For Bedford/St. Martin's
Vice President, Editorial, Macmillan Higher Education Humanities: Edwin Hill
Editorial Director, English and Music: Karen S. Henry
Senior Publisher for Composition, Business and Technical Writing,
  Developmental Writing: Leasa Burton
Executive Editor: John E. Sullivan III
Developmental Editor: Jonathan Douglas
Publishing Services Manager: Andrea Cava
Production Supervisor: Carolyn Quimby
Marketing Manager: Joy Fisher Williams
Project Management: Books By Design, Inc.
Director of Rights and Permissions: Hilary Newman
Senior Art Director: Anna Palchik
Text Design: Castle Design; Janis Owens, Books By Design, Inc.
Cover Design: John Callahan
Cover Art: danielvfung/Getty Images
Composition: Achorn International, Inc.
Printing and Binding: RR Donnelley and Sons

Manufactured in the United States of America.

0 9 8 7 6 5
f e d c b a

For information, write: Bedford/St. Martin's, 75 Arlington Street, Boston,
  MA 02116   (617-399-4000)

ISBN 978-1-319-02014-9

Acknowledgments
Text acknowledgments and copyrights appear at the back of the book on pages 330–32, which constitute an extension of the copyright page. Art acknowledgments and copyrights appear on the same page as the art selections they cover. It is a violation of the law to reproduce these selections by any means whatsoever without the written permission of the copyright holder.

The Bedford Spotlight Reader Series is a line of single-theme readers, each featuring Bedford's trademark care and quality. The readers in the series collect thoughtfully chosen readings sufficient for an entire writing course—about thirty selections—to allow instructors to provide carefully developed, high-quality instruction at an affordable price. Bedford Spotlight Readers are designed to help students make inquiries from multiple perspectives, opening up topics such as borders, food, gender, happiness, money, monsters, and sustainability to critical analysis. An editorial board of more than a dozen compositionists whose programs focus on specific themes have assisted in the development of the series.

Spotlight Readers offer plenty of material for a composition course while keeping the price low. Each volume in the series includes multiple perspectives on the topic and its effects on individuals and society. Chapters are built around central questions such as "Does Creativity Transcend Borders?" and "What Rituals Shape Our Gender?" and so offer numerous entry points for inquiry and discussion. High-interest readings, chosen for their suitability in the classroom, represent a mix of genres and disciplines as well as a choice of accessible and challenging selections to allow instructors to tailor their approach. Each chapter thus brings to light related—even surprising—questions and ideas.

A rich editorial apparatus provides a sound pedagogical foundation. A general introduction, chapter introductions, and headnotes supply context. Following each selection, writing prompts provide avenues of inquiry tuned to different levels of engagement, from reading comprehension ("Understanding the Text"), to critical analysis ("Reflection and Response"), to the kind of integrative analysis appropriate to the research paper ("Making Connections"). A Web site for the series offers support for teaching, with sample syllabi, additional assignments, Web links, and more; visit **macmillanhighered.com/spotlight**.

Preface for Instructors

The subjects of borders and border crossings are particularly relevant for today's students and therefore make useful topics of exploration in a writing course. Borders matter in the lives of our students, and they play a significant role in shaping who they are and how they act. With travel becoming more common and Internet access more essential than ever, many students are continually negotiating physical and linguistic border lines. Moreover, these students often have a fluency with technology and online communication that transcends and challenges traditional boundaries in new ways. Students entering first-year composition classrooms face expectations about their college writing that differ from those they encounter in their personal writing or in the writing they did in high school. Although many have learned to respond effectively to these expectations, many have not. Thus, the politics of linguistic borders—where, when, and by whom specific language can or cannot be used—resonates strongly with students in most composition courses. As topics of discussion and inquiry, border crossings like these allow students and instructors to question the ways in which all of us confront and challenge the limits of these borders, while simultaneously finding the possibilities and opportunities that border spaces allow.

Border Crossings gives students the opportunity to raise and answer questions about the various borders that they encounter, inhabit, and cross. The book begins this investigation by placing the concept of *borders* in a larger context. The readings in Chapter 1 encourage students to define the nature of borders and identify the various borders that exist in our world. The readings in the remaining chapters then ask students to examine the limits of those borders. As students consider those limits, they will also think about who or what defines and controls those boundaries. This line of inquiry leads to other, deeper questions: What effects do borders have on individuals and communities? When are borders necessary? Who are border crossers? What is involved in the process of border crossing? How have the Internet, social media, and technology changed borders and our understanding of borders? Will or should borders become obsolete? What is the relationship between bordered spaces and our sense of self? How do geographical borders create cultural and conceptual ones? These and other questions provide points of entry for students to think and write critically about this topic. However, these questions also leave room for you to nudge students toward areas of inquiry beyond the scope of this book.

While this book provides many questions, options, and perspectives from which to choose, it also covers the essential topics surrounding traditional geographical borders and their impact. One area of inquiry that will feature prominently in most American discussions of borders is the U.S.-Mexico border, and this book includes many readings addressing this issue, particularly in Chapters 2 and 3. Less frequently noted, however, is the expansion of the U.S.-Mexico border's influence, which reaches far beyond its geographical location in the Southwest. For example, "Borders, Border-Crossing, and Political Art in North Carolina," a reading in Chapter 4, looks at how the work of Mexican artist Cornelio Campos has been received far from the U.S.-Mexico border. This reading offers instructors a way to introduce the idea that border cultures exist in multiple locations, often distant from our international borders. It also provides students an opportunity to write about other types of border communities with which they may be familiar—such as migrants or refugees who have crossed borders and formed new communities while retaining a "migrant imaginary," or the aspirations, ideals, and knowledge that migrants have developed in response to moving across the border. *Border Crossings* also includes readings dealing with the U.S.-Canada border and U.S. state borders. To give students some sense of the history of the lines that we see on maps, I have included excerpts from Mark Stein's *How the States Got Their Shapes* as well as readings about the debates on the Mason-Dixon Line and the consequences of the Missouri Compromise.

At the same time, one of *Border Crossings'* greatest strengths is that its scope extends beyond geographical boundaries and asks students to consider conceptual, linguistic, and cultural ones, making the book a valuable resource in a writing classroom. As students consider the effect that borders have on writing and speaking, they begin to realize the power of developing confidence in their own writing and speaking. Many of the readings reinforce the power of words and the links among language, culture, and identity. This text offers students a topic that allows them to join critical conversations about these issues and situate themselves within a larger context of the "real" world.

As a thriving multidisciplinary field, border studies has generated numerous articles, books, and artwork on the subject. Although *Border Crossings* cannot address every aspect of this rich field, this very richness does offer both students and instructors a way into the subject of borders, and this book includes diverse readings that represent a variety of disciplines (anthropology, sociology, linguistics, political science, geography, border studies) in a variety of genres (blogs, op-ed pieces, historical documents, book chapters, scholarly articles, interviews, poetry, fiction). This variety allows instructors to engage in their own border crossings, through a more interdisciplinary approach, and also to call attention to the decisions writers make and the strategies they employ in order to convey their ideas, arguments, and observations to their readers. In addition, each chapter is organized to highlight the interaction among the various authors and their varied perspectives on borders. The introductions, headnotes, and questions are intended to stimulate thoughtful discussion and critical engagement, to put students in active conversation with the authors in these pages. I have included extra materials to enhance your class, and I encourage you to visit **macmillanhighered.com/spotlight** for links to a variety of free instructor's resources, including a list of additional videos, Web sites, and readings on borders, as well as sample syllabi and assignments that you may find useful as you prepare your own class with *Border Crossings*.

All of these readings, questions, and additional materials have been included to encourage your students to explore how political, geographical, conceptual, real, and imagined borders construct the spaces that we inhabit. I hope that your students, through reading this book actively, will begin to uncover how borders affect who we are and how we interact with our world.

Acknowledgments

I offer my sincerest thanks to the many people who helped shape this book and to those who always support my projects. First, *Border Crossings* would not have happened without the enthusiasm and encouragement of Amy Shefferd, Senior Sales Representative, and Lauren Arrant, Product and Technology Specialist, at Macmillan Education. I am also grateful to John Sullivan, Executive Editor, for his enthusiasm in embracing this project and for his guidance in clarifying its focus. Both Barbara Hernandez and Sheri Blaney were adept at handling the thorny issues of permissions. Thank you! Working with Jonathan Douglas, Developmental Editor, has made this project absolutely joyous. His comments, suggestions, and revisions always aligned with my vision for *Border Crossings*, and I thank him for this truly collaborative experience.

I also want to thank the following instructors who took time out of their very busy lives to review an early version of this book: Jayne Braman, California State University, San Marcos; Erica Duran, California State University, San Marcos; Mark Herlihy, Endicott College; Elizabeth Kessler, University of Houston; and Jim Shimkus, University of North Georgia.

Thank you to my colleagues at California State University who generously inquired about this project and listened patiently as I explained my ideas: Erica Duran, Melanie James, Janette Larson, Carrie Morrow, Jake Strona, Staci Beavers, Dawn Formo, Scott Greenwood, and David Avalos.

I thank the many, many students who daily cross borders in my classroom and in classrooms everywhere.

I also wish to acknowledge two incredible women who have helped me negotiate the border crossing necessary to finish this project: Mei-I Chang and Dale Metcalfe—my gratitude.

And to my family who endured months of hearing me say, "I have to meet a deadline": my daughters, Carrie Chacon and Nicki Fiocco, and my sister, Leslie DeFrancesco—when's the next party?

Finally, thank you, Chris, for, well . . . you know.

Catherine Cucinella

Get the Most Out of Your Course with *Border Crossings*

Bedford/St. Martin's offers resources and format choices that help you and your students get even more out of your book and course. To learn more about or to order any of the following products, contact your Bedford/St. Martin's sales representative, e-mail sales support (**sales_support@bfwpub.com**), or visit the Web site at **macmillanhighered.com/spotlight**.

Select Value Packages

Add value to your text by packaging one of the following resources with *Border Crossings*. To learn more about package options for any of the following products, contact your Bedford/St. Martin's sales representative or visit **macmillanhighered.com/spotlight**.

Writer's Help 2.0 is a powerful online writing resource that helps students find answers whether they are searching for writing advice on their own or as part of an assignment.

- **Smart search**
  Built on research with more than 1,600 student writers, the smart search in *Writer's Help 2.0* provides reliable results even when students use novice terms, such as *flow* and *unstuck*.

- **Trusted content from our best-selling handbooks**
  Choose *Writer's Help 2.0 for Hacker Handbooks* or *Writer's Help 2.0 for Lunsford Handbooks* and ensure that students have clear advice and examples for all of their writing questions.

- **Adaptive exercises that engage students**
  Writer's Help 2.0 includes LearningCurve, game-like online quizzing that adapts to what students already know and helps them focus on what they need to learn.

Student access can be packaged with *Border Crossings* at a significant discount. Contact your sales representative to order a package ISBN for *Writer's Help 2.0 for Hacker Handbooks* or *Writer's Help 2.0 for Lunsford Handbooks* to ensure that your students have easy access to online writing support. Students who rent a book or buy a used book can purchase access to *Writer's Help 2.0* at **macmillanhighered.com/writershelp2**.

Instructors may request free access by registering as an instructor at **macmillanhighered.com/writershelp2**. For technical support, visit **macmillanhighered.com/getsupport**.

LaunchPad Solo for Readers and Writers allows students to work on whatever they need help with the most. At home or in class, students learn at their own pace, with instruction tailored to each student's unique needs. *LaunchPad Solo for Readers and Writers* features:

- **Pre-built units that support a learning arc**
  Each easy-to-assign unit includes a pre-test check, multimedia instruction and assessment, and a post-test that assesses what students have learned about critical reading, the writing process, using sources, grammar, style, mechanics, and help for multilingual writers.

- **A video introduction to many topics**
  Introductions offer an overview of the unit's topic, and many include a brief, accessible video to illustrate the concepts at hand.

- **Adaptive quizzing for targeted learning**
  Most units include LearningCurve, game-like adaptive quizzing that focuses on the areas in which each student needs the most help.

- **The ability to monitor student progress**
  Use our Gradebook to see which students are on track and which need additional help with specific topics.

LaunchPad Solo for Readers and Writers can be **packaged at a significant discount**. Contact your local Bedford/St. Martin's sales representative for a package ISBN to ensure that your students can take full advantage. Visit **macmillanhighered.com/catalog/readwrite** for more information.

Critical Reading and Writing: A Bedford Spotlight Rhetoric, **by Jeff Ousborne**, is a brief supplement that provides coverage of critical reading, thinking, writing, and research. It is designed to work with any of the books in the Bedford Spotlight Reader Series. *Critical Reading and Writing: A Bedford Spotlight Rhetoric* (a $10 value!) can be packaged for **free** with your book. Contact your sales representative for a package ISBN.

Portfolio Keeping, **Third Edition, by Nedra Reynolds and Elizabeth Davis**, provides all the information students need to use the portfolio method successfully in a writing course. *Portfolio Teaching*, a companion guide for instructors, provides the practical information instructors and writing program administrators need to use the portfolio method successfully in a writing course. To order *Portfolio Keeping* packaged with this text, contact your sales representative for a package ISBN.

Make Learning Fun with *Re:Writing 3*

Bedford's free and open online resource includes videos and interactive elements to engage students in new ways of writing. You'll find tutorials about using common digital writing tools, an interactive peer review game, Extreme Paragraph Makeover, and more. Visit **macmillanhighered.com/rewriting**.

Instructor Resources

You have a lot to do in your course. Bedford/St. Martin's wants to make it easy for you to find the support you need—and to get it quickly.

The additional instructor's resources for *Border Crossings* are available as downloadable files from the Bedford/St. Martin's online catalog at **macmillanhighered.com/spotlight**. In addition to sample syllabi, the instructor's resources include a list of additional readings, Web sites, videos, and other resources on borders and border crossings to assign with the book.

TeachingCentral offers the entire list of Bedford/St. Martin's print and online professional resources in one place. You'll find landmark reference works, sourcebooks on pedagogical issues, award-winning collections, and practical advice for the classroom—all free for instructors. Visit **macmillanhighered.com/teachingcentral**.

Bedford *Bits* collects creative ideas for teaching a range of composition topics in a frequently updated blog. A community of teachers—leading scholars, authors, and editors such as Andrea Lunsford, Elizabeth Losh, Jack Solomon, and Elizabeth Wardle—discuss assignments, activities, revision, research, grammar and style, multimodal composition, technology, peer review, and much more. Take, use, adapt, and pass the ideas around. Then come back to the site to comment or share your own suggestions. Visit **community.macmillan.com**.

Contents

Chapter 2   Why Do Geographical Borders Matter?   51

Chapter 3   How Do Borders Influence the Ways We Write and Speak? 139

Chapter 5   Can We Rethink a World without Borders?   269

Contents by Discipline

Economics

Education

Geography

History

Journalism

Literature

Political Science

Psychology

Contents by Theme

Gender and Women's Experiences

Global Flows and Movement

History and Interpreting the Past

Home and Sense of Place

Identity and Sense of Self

The Power of Language

Race

The U.S.-Mexico Border

Introduction for Students

What Is College Writing?

When we write in college, or anywhere, we need something to write about, something that will excite our interest and engage others, too. All writers need a topic — novelists, poets, historians, journalists, teachers, and students like you. This book, *Border Crossings*, provides that topic and invites you to read, think, and write critically about one subject — borders. However, you will not do so from a single approach, perspective, or context. As you read, think, and write, you will encounter questions about the role of borders in your life and in society; their influence on identity and language; their effects on politics, culture, and art; and the plausibility of a "borderless world." By offering a wide range of authors and asking you to engage with their various ideas about borders, this book both provides you with a thought-provoking topic and helps you develop your writing and thinking skills.

The readings and questions in this book reinforce the hallmarks of college writing: critical reading, critical thinking, and writing. Writing in college involves more than just simple communication and unstructured thought. It requires you to engage actively and critically with your ideas and those of others. This engagement means reading closely and critically a range of texts and understanding, analyzing, and synthesizing complicated ideas presented by diverse writers. Reading critically demands that you make sense of complex material by asking questions of the text as you read, by talking back to it, and by marking it up. Thinking critically means recognizing and understanding logical connections among ideas, identifying and evaluating arguments, determining the relevance and significance of ideas, uncovering assumptions and biases in your claims and arguments as well as in those of others, considering ideas and arguments from multiple perspectives, and contemplating your own beliefs and values. Reading and writing about borders sparks discussions and debates, thus offering you many areas of exploration, topics of discovery, and subjects about which to write.

Why Borders?

We live in a world of borders, and all of us, on some level, depend on those borders to order our world and help us make sense of our surroundings and our place in them. Part of what borders do, of course, involves separation — making differences clearly visible for us: "I am here because I am not there." Borders also involve ownership; they mark distinctions between what is mine and what is not mine — hence fences and walls, designed to keep "my" property safe and "others" out. In both of these cases, this ordering of space marks off territory: "I am located on this side; I own this space." From an early age, we have all had some experience with trying to create a space for ourselves, to claim ownership of it, to border it. For example, perhaps as a child you put a sign on your bedroom door: "Do not enter" or "No adults." Or maybe you used string to mark off your side of a room that you shared with a sibling and hung a sign that read: "Do not cross this line or else!" Even at a very young age, we feel the need to claim space, and in the process we create borders. As you can see, whether you have given much thought to borders or not, you already know a lot about them. However, thinking and writing about borders require recognizing borders' complexities, aspects that reach beyond demarcating physical or geographical space.

The borders that mark our lives and that influence society are wide-ranging: geographical (national, regional, state, local), political, economic, legal, medical, religious, social, environmental, linguistic (personal, familial, social, academic), and sexual. These borders affect how we think about who we are and where we are. Because borders define nations and determine politics, they also influence how we think about and interact with others. Therefore, investigating what borders are and how they function offers you an opportunity to ask crucial questions about what it means to need bordered spaces and to cross border lines.

All of us cross borders on a daily basis, whether or not we realize that we do so. When you leave the private space of your home or dorm room and travel to the public space of school or work, you cross borders. You may negotiate that crossing relatively easily; however, someone else may find traveling from home to school a perilous border crossing. The ease or difficulty depends on the types of borders crossed — formal or informal, marked or invisible, cultural or political. Long after physical borders disappear, individuals may still carry an internal sense of those barriers. For example, professional writer and author Patrick Radden Keefe, writing for the *New Yorker*, tells of a time when he was in Belfast, Ireland, where walls separating the city's Catholic neighborhoods from the Protestant ones remain. While driving with a young Irishman, Keefe found himself on a street with no wall, with "a Catholic neighborhood on the left and a Protestant one on the right." He saw a Subway sandwich shop on the Catholic side and asked his companion "if local Protestants might cross the street to buy a sandwich." The answer: "Not a chance" (Keefe 53).[1] No wall or fence blocked the way, yet in a city defined by its bordered neighborhoods, individuals see borders where no formal walls exist.

As this example illustrates, borders exert powerful influences on us, and they do so in many ways. Studying borders allows you to discover which borders affect you most directly. Thinking critically on this subject, however, also means considering how borders affect others. This line of inquiry begins with understanding what borders are, who creates them, whom they benefit, and whom they harm.

As you address these key ideas, at times you will be entering the academic discourse (conventions, language, and codes within a specific field) of border studies. This field of study within academia also includes scholars from geography, sociology, anthropology, economics, political science, history, environmental science, environmental psychology, and environmental history. Many other individuals both inside and outside academia contribute to this discourse as well, such as those in literature, art, Chicano/a studies, human rights, and law. *Border Crossings* invites you to join these conversations and raise questions about the role of borders in our rapidly changing world.

---

[1]Keefe, Patrick Radden. "Where the Bodies Are Buried." *The New Yorker* 16 Mar. 2015: 42–69.

To join these conversations, we need to ask questions about our relationship to borders. We need to question the value that we, as a society, place on borders. We also need to recognize how we collectively view borders. Do we see them as natural, fixed, and unchanging? Or do we view them as socially constructed, fluid, and changeable? While you may have difficulty finding definitive answers to these questions, this difficulty makes studying borders work well as a subject in your writing course. It allows *you* to identify which aspect of the topic interests *you*, which is most relevant to *your* goals, and which most affects *your* community. To figure out our relationships to borders, you will first have to consider your own personal understanding of and relationship to borders.

One of the most fundamental questions that you will encounter concerns the range of borders that crisscross our lives both physically and conceptually. On closer inspection, the notion of borders proves slippery. It encompasses the borders we can see, the communities that surround them (the "borderlands" with their languages and customs), the people who cross borders (documented and undocumented), refugees, and tourists. It includes art, culture, identity, and politics. These are just some of the issues around borders that are presented in this book — though all are worth thinking and writing about.

The Organization of This Book

To give this book a shape, I had to create some boundaries between chapters. Each chapter title presents a framing question that the readings in the chapter address and that you will consider as you read. As you approach each chapter, however, I want you to think of the "borders" between them as porous. The chapters themselves and the questions exist as only one suggested organization among many. You may, and should, freely cross these borders because to "answer" the framing questions is to ask and answer many more.

Chapter 1, "What Are Borders?," is at the philosophical core of this inquiry. Presenting the writings of a poet, a novelist, and scholars, this chapter introduces you to the concept of borders and the associated elements of territoriality and sovereignty. Each reading provides another facet in the multifaceted nature of borders, and taken together, they reveal that we cannot simply ask what borders are. Instead, we must ask a multitude of other questions regarding their history, their function, and their relationship to us. As you formulate your answer to what borders are, you will confront arguments regarding their constructed nature and their symbolic function.

Chapter 2, "Why Do Geographical Borders Matter?," broadens the discussion by asking you to consider the everyday realities of people living in international border communities and about what other physical spaces borders create. The stories, ideas, and arguments in this chapter use various approaches to address the significance of borders in our lives. Several writers situate their own personal experiences of living in a border region within larger historical, cultural, and sociological contexts in order to reveal how borders affect individuals and communities. Some writers conduct research in border communities, asking the inhabitants of these regions to tell their stories. Others move beyond borderlands and focus on cultural borders. Almost all of the writers, however, see cultural and conceptual boundaries as extensions of geographical ones.

Chapter 3, "How Do Borders Influence the Ways We Write and Speak?," asks how boundaries affect our interactions with others. Generally, writing and talking involve others. We use these activities to communicate our thoughts, ideas, beliefs, and desires to those around us. If you apply a border-studies lens to how and when you use certain languages, you can begin to ask crucial questions about the link among borders, language, culture, and identity. The writers in this chapter investigate this link, as they challenge us to broaden our conception of what it means to cross linguistic barriers. The readings here, like those in Chapter 2, extend the meaning of *borders* beyond that of physical, geographical ones. In doing so, the writers open several paths for you to explore the many ways that borders affect language and, by extension, identity and culture. When you consider how borders influence writing and speaking, your own experiences with language — your language behaviors — will be a crucial starting point to help you become more aware of linguistic borders and conventions.

Chapter 4, "Does Creativity Transcend Borders?," explores the relationship between artistic creation and borders. It asks you to consider whether art, music, literature, film, technology, and dance stop at borders or whether these creative activities and productions cross cultural and geographical barriers. As the poets, scholars, artists, and musicians in this chapter convey their perspectives on this subject, they suggest the promise — and the price — of trying to cross borders in this way. While some are hopeful, other readings reinforce the need to understand the pain that boundaries can cause, their influence on the lives of those living in their shadows, and their sometimes harsh effects on the experiences of border crossers.

Chapter 5, "Can We Rethink a World without Borders?," brings us into the realm of possibility and plausibility. It asks you to reexamine what you know about borders and then to reconfigure that knowledge and imagine a new world. On the one hand, the readings in this chapter reintroduce familiar concepts, such as sovereignty, territoriality, and the existence of different types of borders. They also remind us that many types of border crossings already occur in our world today, as money, goods, people, labor, art, technology, and culture constantly flow between borders in our heavily bordered world. On the other hand, the writers challenge us to reimagine the role borders play in our lives today, and ask us to consider what a borderless world might look like and what ethical consequences — both good and bad — this may have on a global scale.

Each chapter focuses on a specific aspect of borders and border crossings and includes a range of viewpoints. The authors come from diverse backgrounds — sociologists, economists, novelists, historians, poets, political theorists, musicians, geographers, travel writers, artists, and anthropologists. They use a variety of genres and approaches — academic essays, newspaper articles, blogs, op-eds, images, interviews, historical documents, personal narratives, studies, and poems. However, despite their diverse fields and backgrounds, all the authors and their ideas are connected. This book, along with the questions that follow each reading, puts these writers in a conversation with one another and with you, the reader.

A Note on the Questions

To participate fully in this conversation with the writers in this book, you will need to engage with each writer's ideas. With this goal in mind, I have designed sets of questions following each reading: "Understanding the Text," "Reflection and Response," and "Making Connections." "Understanding the Text" questions direct you back to the reading and to the writer's specific points — his or her key ideas, arguments, evidence, and examples. These questions might ask you to identify and explain a main argument or to clarify how the writer uses key terms. "Reflection and Response" questions ask that you interact with the reading by bringing your own ideas, experiences, and examples to the text, putting you in direct conversation with the writer. Finally, "Making Connections" questions lead to writing tasks that urge you to consider several readings either from one chapter or from several, and encourage you to read beyond the "borders" of *Border Crossings*. The prompts in this section require you to think and write critically about the ideas you encounter, forcing you to place yourself within the discourse of borders by staking out a position.

How you use this book and these questions will, of course, depend on your instructor. He or she will decide which chapters and readings to assign and in what order. Your instructor may use some, all, or none of the questions following each reading. However, I have designed this book with you, the student, in mind, and I hope that whatever approach your instructor uses, you will find that the subject of borders offers numerous areas of exploration, discovery, and inquiry to encourage the practice and development of your writing skills. On a more fundamental level, writing about borders matters because the very act of existing in a world with other living beings involves choosing to cross a border or refusing to do so — thus opting either to remain within the confines of walls, fences, and borders or to cross these boundaries into the unknown and experience new cultures, languages, and landscapes.

danielvfung/Getty Images

1 | What Are Borders?

W hat do we mean when we talk about borders? What *is* a border? These questions are much more complicated than they first appear. The *New Oxford Dictionary* defines a border as a "line separating two political or geographical areas" or "the edge or boundary of something, or the part near it." These definitions, however, only raise further questions about the nature of borders. For example, what constitutes a proper border line? Is this line always visible and fixed? If a border is not fixed, how do we know when we are near a border's edge? Can the areas on each side of the line be both political *and* geographical?

As we try to define borders and answer these questions, we quickly realize that our understanding of borders extends beyond what the dictionary offers because we all encounter them every day — in the form of fences, walls, and doors and in the current debates on immigration, technology, and security. The questions we ask, the terms we use to talk about borders, and the contexts in which we do so continually expand as we reflect on the types of borders we experience. Therefore, to fully explain what borders are, we must think critically about all the borders we experience on a daily basis. The authors in this chapter invite us to ask questions, to contemplate the different types of borders, and to reflect on the many concepts associated with borders.

Individually and collectively, these writers make clear that as we work through the defining question of this chapter, we are not simply *defining* a word; rather, we are investigating a dynamic concept. In "Mending Wall," Robert Frost poses crucial questions regarding what exactly walls do and why they "make good neighbors." To explain what something is, we often explain how that thing functions and identify other concepts associated with it. Thus, in "A Very Bordered World," Alexander Diener and Joshua Hagen highlight the complicated nature of borders and identify us as "geographic beings" who rely on "borders as organizing principles." However, as these writers remind us, we cannot understand borders without exam-

photo: danielvfung/Getty Images

ining the concepts of territoriality, sovereignty, and, of course, power. The notion of territory and its relation to borders most interests Stuart Elden in "Territory without Borders," as he challenges us to rethink this relationship in light of the ever-changing landscape of borders.

Next, in "Building Walls," Reed Karaim provides historical insights on a few famous walls that nations have built. Yet, like other writers in this chapter, he reveals that confronting the "what" of borders leads to the "why" and, ultimately, to the realization that answering either question is a messy process. Finally, in excerpts from *How the States Got Their Shapes*, Mark Stein underscores the value in knowing why states have their particular shapes and highlights the malleable history of the United States' interior borders.

For all the writers in this chapter, investigating the nature of borders — explaining what they are, why they exist, and what they do — involves examining an array of critical issues, such as how borders shape the histories, struggles, and experiences of real people and how those histories, struggles, and experiences shape borders. We are, quite significantly, molded by our borders as much as we mold them. As you read this chapter, consider the ways that we define borders and how these definitions shape our understanding of borders and our shifting relationships to them.

Mending Wall

Robert Frost

Often described as one of the great, quintessentially American poets, Robert Frost (1874–1963) was the first poet to read at a presidential inauguration, that of John F. Kennedy in 1961. Frost won four Pulitzer Prizes for his collections of poetry, and on his seventy-fifth birthday the U.S. Senate passed a resolution in his honor, naming him "America's great poet-philosopher." In "Mending Wall," which appeared in his second volume of poetry, *North of Boston* (1914), Frost does, indeed, philosophize about our desire for and rejection of walls. As you read, pay particular attention to the questions Frost's speaker asks about walls and the justifications for building barriers that the poem offers.

Something there is that doesn't love a wall,
That sends the frozen-ground-swell under it,
And spills the upper boulders in the sun;
And makes gaps even two can pass abreast.
The work of hunters is another thing: 5
I have come after them and made repair
Where they have left not one stone on a stone,
But they would have the rabbit out of hiding,
To please the yelping dogs. The gaps I mean,
No one has seen them made or heard them made,   10
But at spring mending-time we find them there.
I let my neighbor know beyond the hill;
And on a day we meet to walk the line
And set the wall between us once again.
We keep the wall between us as we go.   15
To each the boulders that have fallen to each.
And some are loaves and some so nearly balls
We have to use a spell to make them balance:
"Stay where you are until our backs are turned!"
We wear our fingers rough with handling them.   20
Oh, just another kind of out-door game,
One on a side. It comes to little more:
There where it is we do not need the wall:
He is all pine and I am apple orchard.
My apple trees will never get across   25
And eat the cones under his pines, I tell him.
He only says, "Good fences make good neighbors."

Walls and fences between houses are common sights in many neighborhoods.
JTB Photo/Contributor/Getty Images

Spring is the mischief in me, and I wonder
If I could put a notion in his head:
"*Why* do they make good neighbors? Isn't it   30
Where there are cows? But here there are no cows.
Before I built a wall I'd ask to know
What I was walling in or walling out,
And to whom I was like to give offense.
Something there is that doesn't love a wall,   35
That wants it down." I could say "Elves" to him,
But it's not elves exactly, and I'd rather
He said it for himself. I see him there
Bringing a stone grasped firmly by the top
In each hand, like an old-stone savage armed.   40
He moves in darkness as it seems to me,
Not of woods only and the shade of trees.
He will not go behind his father's saying,
And he likes having thought of it so well
He says again, "Good fences make good neighbors."   45

Understanding the Text

1. What specifically is the speaker of "Mending Wall" describing?

2. What explicit and implicit questions about walls does the speaker ask? How does the poem answer those questions?

3. Tone and repetition are important aspects of poetry. Identify both of these elements in this poem, and explain how they contribute to the poem's message.

Reflection and Response

4. What justifications for — and challenges with — building walls does Frost offer? Respond to the speaker's question about why walls "make good neighbors."

5. Reread "Mending Wall," paying careful attention to the poem's tone, descriptive language, and connotative meanings. In addition to the tangible barriers that demarcate property, what other kinds of walls do you think Frost alludes to in this poem? What elements in the poem support your response?

Making Connections

6. In "A Very Bordered World" (p. 15), Alexander Diener and Joshua Hagen state that "borders are *not* themselves strictly natural phenomena." After reading their piece carefully, note where their ideas intersect with those in Frost's poem. Then write an essay in which you explain what the poem reveals about the nature of borders and our relationship to them. Use specific examples from the readings to illustrate your points and support your interpretation.

7. In lines 27 and 45, the speaker's neighbor repeats the saying "Good fences make good neighbors." What reasons does Frost mention to justify this claim? Can you think of other reasons that Frost doesn't mention, such as those you may have read in the news or encountered personally?

A Very Bordered World

Alexander C. Diener
and Joshua Hagen

Alexander Diener teaches in the geography department at the University of Kansas. While he explores political, social, and cultural geography in general, Diener specifically focuses on border studies, geographies of nationalism and transnationalism, and geopolitics. Joshua Hagen, who teaches geography at Marshall University, writes primarily about international borders, urban planning, and historic preservation. Together, Hagen and Diener are the coeditors of *Borderlines and Borderlands: Political Oddities at the Edge of the Nation-State* (2010) and the coauthors of *Borders: A Very Short Introduction* (2012), from which "A Very Bordered World" is excerpted.

In this selection, Diener and Hagen introduce readers to their argument regarding the constructed nature of borders and the terms critical to understanding the complicated subject of borders. As you read, consider the authors' claim that "borders are not 'natural' phenomena," and note what evidence they use to support their argument.

W e live in a very bordered world. The daily news is filled with controversies concerning the political, cultural, and economic borders that crisscross the Earth's surface. Borders are central features in current international disputes relating to security, migration, trade, and natural resources. They also factor prominently into local debates over land use and property rights. Regardless of the scale, it is clear that humans draw lines that divide the world into specific places, territories, and categories. We are "geographic beings" for whom the creation of places, and by consequence the process of bordering, seems natural. But borders are not "natural" phenomena; they exist in the world only to the extent that humans regard them as meaningful. Truth be told, most people cross hundreds of geographic boundaries on a daily basis. Some are formal borders demarcating ownership or the limits of governmental authority, while others are symbolic or informal associations of places with social groups or ideas.

Our daily routines provide a simple example. Typical mornings involve spaces specifically designed to limit access, such as bedrooms and bathrooms, as well as more open spaces like kitchens and dining areas. A trip to work usually requires leaving private property and passing through various public spaces, neighborhoods, or municipalities. Workplaces are also divided into spaces designated for specific purposes (offices, lunchrooms, factory floors, etc.). The borders that define these various spaces, whether familial, social, economic, or political, address issues of access, mobility, and belonging in different ways. For example, a factory gate is intended to restrict access to certain people, whereas the entrance of a retail store is designed to lure people inside. This highlights the seemingly contradictory role of borders as bridges, gateways, and meeting points or barriers, obstacles, and points of separation.

In addition to influencing movement, geographic borders also define spaces of differing laws and social norms. In this way, borders create and signify varied legal obligations, social categories, and behavioral expectations for different areas. Returning to our example, some work spaces might require a hardhat or hearing protection, while lowered voices and business attire are expected in other areas. Signs restricting access to employees or paying customers signal authority over space and differentiate between groups of people. These mundane examples reveal the diverse role of borders as dividers of space, symbolic markers of control, and social processes of daily life. Reflecting their significance, borders have become a focus of study across the social sciences and humanities.

"We are 'geographic beings' for whom the creation of places, and by consequence the process of bordering, seems natural. But borders are not 'natural' phenomena; they exist in the world only to the extent that humans regard them as meaningful."

Beginning as fuzzy zones between tribal groups, the phenomenon of "frontiers" eventually evolved to encompass the transitional spaces between walled cities or imperial realms. Following Europe's wars of religion during the sixteenth century culminating in the Peace of Westphalia in 1648,° frontiers across Europe were gradually morphed into seemingly rigid lines dividing nation-states. This model of organizing political space was subsequently exported to the rest of the world through European colonial conquest, most prominently during the eighteenth and nineteenth centuries. Efforts at bureaucratic control within these states, and at times ethnic, cultural, or religious differences, compelled the further division of space into provinces, counties, townships, cities, reservations, and other administrative districts. In addition to these formal governmental structures, countless informal social boundaries, such as gendered spaces, gang territories, gated communities, and ethnic neigh-

Peace of Westphalia in 1648: a European peace treaty that ended the Eighty Years' War between the Netherlands and Spain. Under the terms of the treaty, many countries received new territories or were granted sovereignty over territories.

borhoods, are also expressed spatially. *All* of these have some type of formal or informal border marking them apart from other political and social spaces.

Ultimately, the world has become crisscrossed with such a variety of geographic boundaries that they often appear natural and timeless. Yet reality is more complicated. Although the bounding of space may be common in human social organization, borders are *not* themselves strictly natural phenomena. Or put another way, humans may be geographic beings predisposed to spatial organization, but how we structure territory, and to what end, has evolved quite radically over time reflecting changing political, social, and economic contexts. The theoretical foundations of bounded space encompass a wide range of scholarly perspectives.

Territory, Sovereignty, and Borders

The primary function of geographic borders is to create and differentiate places. In other words, borders separate the social, political, economic, or cultural meanings of one geographic space from another. While the world is replete with various geographic boundaries, the institutional phenomenon of borders is most commonly associated with the idea of territory.

Territoriality is the means by which humans create, communicate, and control geographical spaces, either individually or through some social or political entity. Modes of territoriality have varied significantly over time and across space resulting in diverse practices of bordering. These range from the placement of permanent markers to the performance of intermittent ceremonies and from the precise demarcation of sharp lines to the broad definition of transitional zones. Therefore, territoriality and practices of bordering are neither constant nor consistent but rather highly contingent and adaptable. Though pervasive throughout recorded history, the root causes of territoriality have been long debated by scholars. Some have favored sociobiology or primordialist approaches° believing that territoriality stems from an *a priori* instinct. In this view, social groups instinctively seek territorial control to secure resources necessary for survival. This suggests humans are subject to perpetual "survival of the fittest" contests as groups seek to control territory, secure resources, and deny access to competing groups. Such a perspective is highly problematic. Although animals exhibit territoriality, for example, in marking out hunting ranges, attempts to link human

---

primordialist approach: a view in anthropology that sees nations and ethnic groups as natural phenomena that form because of inherent biological and territorial factors.

territoriality to mere instinct unduly reduces a far more complex process to a natural reflex. Human place-making and territoriality differ from that of animals in two distinct ways.

First, territorial control is not, nor has it ever been, the sole means by which humans enact political power. Countless forms of de-territorialized "authority" (the legitimate exercise of power) have existed throughout history and continue to exist today. Contemporary examples include various religious and social movements, as well as nongovernmental organizations relating to environmentalism, human rights, and feminism that propagate their ideologies as universal and claim authority across space, class, and various forms of identity. The global influence of certain businesses, such as microprocessor giant Intel, could also be considered a form of de-territorialized authority since these technologies clearly transcend territorial boundaries.

The second manner in which human territoriality differs from that of animals relates to the evolution of human territoriality. Unlike animals, human spatial thinking has manifested in very different ways over time. For example, frontiers, or zones of limited rule of law, were once commonplace in the world but today are conspicuous and rare. Also, some human communities did not develop a conception of land "ownership" until forced to do so by groups that had done so. While territoriality existed among both groups, it is clear that the phenomenon manifested very differently.

Consideration of the evolution of human spatial thinking has cata- 10 lyzed alternative theories as to the causes of territoriality. Some scholars favor a constructivist approach that rejects the environmental determinist notions of primordialists. Constructivists° contend that territoriality results from historical contexts, practical needs, and geopolitical contingencies. These scholars suggest that determinations of "us" and "them," "insiders" and "outsiders," and "in place" and "out of place" are not related to what we commonly identify as innate categories such as race and ethnicity, or even cultural characteristics such as language or religion, but are formed through unequal power relations within and between social systems. Territoriality thereby serves as a social mechanism for this control, driving the process of defining what is "ours" in opposition to what is "theirs." By demarcating and defending territory, groups control specific spaces and resources in an effort to regulate extraterritorial practices, such as entry and exit, and intraterritorial practices, such as

---

constructivists: a group of scholars who argue that humans generate knowledge and meaning from social interactions and relationships.

social hierarchies and governance. Regardless of its origin, territoriality has become institutionalized in the modern era with the effect of naturalizing the overtly social processes of bordering.

As manifestations of territoriality, borders provide a means to assign things to particular spaces and regulate access into and/or out of specific areas. This innately social and political process links to the idea of ownership or rightful and permanent possession of land. Over recent centuries, the development of dramatic disparities in power within and between human groups has given rise to the concepts of sovereignty and jurisdiction. Though rather recent inventions, these concepts were central to defining the limits of a nation's power and establishing borders as the organizing principles for the modern state system.

Sovereignty can be defined as the exercise of supreme authority and control over a distinct territory and its corresponding population and resources. Jurisdiction refers to a bounded area within which the authority of a particular person, group, or institution is legally recognized. Though similar in form and function, jurisdiction generally relates to a smaller area of authority within a higher-order sovereign entity. Both are very complex ideas that help define the spatiality of governance (state, ethnic territory, province, municipality, etc.) and the nature of that control. In some cases, control may be benign or beneficial by offering sanctuary and security. In other cases, the control may be oppressive or violent, constituting a prison to those within or a fortress against those outside.

Sovereignty and jurisdiction signify at least some form of popularly recognized authority over a bounded territory while also disguising the often violent origins of such rule. They mask the processes by which other "spatialities," or modes of human interaction with space, and identities were plowed under. Because identity is not static and spatial patterns of interaction and exchange are fluid, complete territorial sovereignty and jurisdiction (an "air-tight seal") are never fully achievable. Not even the famed Iron Curtain completely blocked out external ideas and goods. As such, territorial sovereignty and jurisdiction remain, in conjunction with national territoriality, both causes and responses to much intra- and interstate tension and conflict. For example, Israeli settlers have moved beyond the margins of their sovereign state territory in an effort to claim land they believe to be theirs and enhance security for the country's core. These acts serve to mobilize Palestinian resistance and countermeasures to express sovereignty and enhance their own security. In this example, and many others, borders are active forces helping constitute dynamics of order and disorder across varied global and local landscapes.

The Field of Border Studies

Reflecting their centrality to human social interaction and the exercise of power, borders have become hot research topics across a number of disciplines. Since the late 1960s, geographers, sociologists, anthropologists, economists, environmental psychologists, political scientists, legal scholars, and historians have challenged prior scholarship presuming borders play rather passive roles in international and intrastate relations. Rather than simple pretexts for conflict or impediments to mobility, border scholars began to consider the lines that divide human groups as key processes of multiscalar geopolitics worthy of deeper and more textured consideration. There are many reasons for the relative neglect that border studies endured through much of the twentieth century, but the most important was the assumption of a fixed relationship between power and territory inherent in the nation-state° system.

Despite the efforts of the growing border studies community, this as-   15
sumption has only recently come to be questioned by politicians, the broader academy, and the general public. Few fully appreciate that very different modes of territorial organization existed merely three centuries ago. The sociopolitical order resulting from the transition of monarchical rule by hereditary nobility to democratic governments of elected representatives, along with urbanization, industrialization, and the dissemination of "enlightenment values," is a relatively recent and spatially uneven phenomenon. Nevertheless, these events gave rise to new territorial assumptions and practices that had a profound effect on the way people perceive themselves and their respective places in the world.

The replacement of frontiers with clearly delineated borders reframed human identity and most social processes by ensnaring them in what political geographers commonly refer to as the "territorial trap." This concept derives from three interrelated assumptions. The first is that states are the exclusive arbiters of power within their territories. In other words, states are invested with sovereignty. The second assumption holds that domestic (internal) and foreign (external) affairs are different realms of political and social activity. Therefore, each realm operates with fundamentally different standards of legality and morality. The third assumption views the boundaries of the state as matching the boundaries of the society. In other words, states act as rigid containers that neatly partition global space into nation-state territories corresponding to distinct societies.

nation-state: a form of political organization in which a group of people share the same history, tradition, or language and live in a particular area under one government.

In short, throughout much of the twentieth century, the territorial trap relegated research on geographic boundaries to subfields like political anthropology, political geography, or regional politics, economics, and sociology. Nevertheless, beginning slowly in the 1960–70s with decolonization,° gaining momentum through the 1980s with the lessening of Soviet global power, and booming in the 1990s with the (re)emergence of new states from the collapsed USSR,° the topic of borders edged back into academic writing as scholars questioned the overt emphasis on "security" rather than "opportunity." Border studies gained even greater popularity with the advance of neoliberal economic thought,° the consolidation of the European Union,° and the resurgence of protectionist ideologies in reaction to the spate of terrorist attacks in the early 2000s.

We are, nevertheless, experiencing a transition of human spatiality and borders. Contradictory border processes generate great anxiety among those tasked with adapting to this evolving spatial reality. Policymakers struggle to strike a precarious balance between facilitating cross-border trade and investment, and managing the post-9/11 security environment. It seems that for every initiative seeking to "soften" borders, facilitating a freer flow of people and materials, there are an equal number intended to "harden" borders, requiring new forms of documentation and constructing new physical barriers. These movements toward the physical materialization of borders must also contend with the new realities of cyberspace that facilitate novel human connections by reducing the friction of distance while simultaneously providing a forum for confrontation, discrimination, and hatred. The human capacity to employ borders to filter flows into and out of territory is central to this new era of shifting spatiality.

A Very Short Introduction to Borders

Borders are integral components of human activity and organization. As such, we are compelled to deepen our understanding of their role as areas of opportunity and insecurity, zones of contact and conflict, sites of

---

1960s–70s with decolonization: a period during which a number of countries achieved autonomy or independence from their colonial rulers, particularly in Asia and Africa.
new states from the collapsed USSR: In the early 1990s, the Union of Soviet Socialist Republics collapsed and became fifteen separate countries.
neoliberal economic thought: an approach associated with laissez-faire economic theory, whose advocates support extensive economic liberalization, free trade, and reduced government interference.
the consolidation of the European Union: the economic and political partnership among twenty-eight European countries, which promoted a standardized system of laws and looser policies on trade and travel among member countries.

cooperation and competition, places of ambivalent identities and aggressive assertions of difference. These dichotomies may alternate with time and place, but more interestingly, they often coexist. We must come to terms with the means by which borders structure our lives, while simultaneously lessening their perpetuation of antagonistic difference and apathetic indifference. We must find a way to harness their ability to catalyze belonging and identity but diminish their propensity for exclusion and the creation of "others." We must confront the increasingly transportable and multiscalar nature of territory and engage the multilayered role of borders in a variety of social settings. We must tackle ethical questions—For whom are borders constructed? By whom? And to what ends?

Borders require further study both from the top down and from the bottom up, from the state scale and from the local scale, as they are perhaps the most obvious political geographic entities in our lives. Ultimately, the lived experience of borders reminds us that their opacity is as important as their transparency. We must be mindful of borders' capacity to evolve in role and change in nature. Sites of cooperation can become sites of contestation, and vice versa. Yet it is for these reasons that borders are and will remain such important factors shaping our world. 20

Understanding the Text

1. Explain the two kinds of geographical boundaries most of us cross every day. What are the implications and functions of these borders and border crossings?

2. What is *territoriality*? In your own words, describe the approaches to territoriality that Diener and Hagen identify.

3. How do Diener and Hagen define *sovereignty* and *jurisdiction*? What similarities and differences do they point out between the two concepts?

4. Explain "the 'territorial trap'" (par. 16) and the three assumptions on which it rests.

Reflection and Response

5. Diener and Hagen claim that "borders are not 'natural' phenomena; they exist in the world only to the extent that humans regard them as meaningful" (par. 1). In what ways or when are borders meaningful in your life? As you think about this question, consider the personal spaces that are important to you, your family, and your friends. Then you may want to broaden your ideas — to your community, city, state, country, or hemisphere. How do Diener and Hagen's views about spatiality, territory, and us versus them influence your response? What other elements or concepts do you believe give borders meaning?

6. In their discussion on sovereignty and jurisdiction, Diener and Hagen make the following claim: "Because identity is not static and spatial patterns of interaction and exchange are fluid, complete territorial sovereignty and jurisdiction (an 'air-tight seal') are never fully achievable" (par. 13). Do you agree? Why or why not?

Making Connections

7. Diener and Hagen argue that borders very often serve as "active forces helping constitute dynamics of order and disorder across varied global and local landscapes" (par. 13). Norma Cantú also writes about the paradoxes and contradictions of border regions (p. 58). What does Cantú's essay add to your understanding of Diener and Hagen's argument? How do these authors explain what borders are and how they function? In your response, compare and contrast Cantú's ideas with yours and with those of Diener and Hagen.

8. Read the Missouri Compromise on page 132. Then, drawing on Diener and Hagen's explanations and arguments about borders, territoriality, sovereignty, and jurisdiction, explain and analyze the Missouri Compromise. You may want to make connections to additional research and other readings in this book. For example, Stuart Elden's "Territory without Borders" (p. 24) might prove helpful.

Territory without Borders

Stuart Elden

Stuart Elden is a professor of political theory and geography at the University of Warwick in Coventry, England. He also edits the journal *Environment and Planning D: Society and Space* and publishes in the areas of geopolitics, spatial theory, globalization, territory, terrorism, and place. He is the author of five books, including *The Birth of Territory* (2013), which won the Association of American Geographers Meridian Book Award, and *Terror and Territory: The Spatial Extent of Sovereignty* (2009), which garnered the Association of American Geographers Globe Award.

In his work, Elden challenges us to rethink our ideas about place, space, territory, and borders — what they are and what they do. In the following selection, which originally appeared in the *Harvard International Review*, a student-run publication encouraging academic debate, he reveals the importance of thinking differently about the relationship between territory and borders. As you read, notice how Elden defines "territory with borders" by first describing its opposite, "territory without borders."

What does it mean to speak of "territory without borders"? Let me say immediately that this is not the same as the "borderless world" argument, nor in agreement with the idea that geography no longer matters. While borders are less important in some places, such as within much of Europe, in others they continue to be crucial. The US-Mexico border, the external border policing of Europe, and the Israeli wall in the West Bank are only the most striking examples of the continual importance of borders. I am not suggesting that we should comprehend the modern world through a lens that understands globalization as de-territorialization. Indeed, it is the concomitant° processes of re-territorialization—the constant making and remaking of territories— that should perhaps be more of the focus in our empirical and political studies.

Nor am I using the phrase as a way of describing modes of political organizations such as Schengenland,° which seeks to dispense with border controls. Schengenland has indeed been described as a "territory without borders"; it would be more accurate to describe it as an area with uneven borders. While it is true that mobility in Schengenland is much

concomitant: naturally accompanied or associated with something else.
Schengenland: a borderless region near the town of Schengen in Luxembourg.

24

easier for those individuals whose status is good and whose papers are in order, mobility is restricted and strictly monitored through transnational security and policing for those who fail to meet these characteristics.

In addition, it is essential to note attempts to do away with borders within Europe have applied to its internal divisions, and have resulted in a stronger assertion of external borders. The patrols in the Mediterranean represent one such example, especially given recent events in northern Africa. A similar tension runs through the European project more generally, and attempts to frame an "area of freedom, security and justice" remain juxtaposed to a hardening of borders in other respects, especially around security and migration.

Rather, what I want to do here is to raise the question of whether we can *think* territory without dependence on borders. This does not mean we should conceive of a territory without borders, an imagined space which has neither limit nor end. Instead, we should stop using a notion of "border," "boundary," or "boundedness" as the key element to *define* territory, as a *concept*. I want to suggest that the standard definition of territory as a bordered, bounded, or defined space is actually an impediment to understandings of geopolitical relations. In short, I think we need a better theory of territory. We should not take the standard definition of territory as a bounded space under the control of a group, perhaps a state, straight-forwardly or unproblematically. As I look back through history to trace the emergence of modern territorial notions, I hope to address two key questions. How did a singular conception of territory emerge out of the divergent systems of organization that have historically characterized global political culture? And how does that definition inform the modern understanding of global political relations?

The Evolution of the Concept of Territory

The concept of territory within Western political thought is a relatively 5 new one. In classical Latin the term *territorium* is used very sparingly and means the land surrounding a political settlement such as a town. It is used that way, for example, by Cicero, Varro, and Seneca.° Only later did the term begin to be used in a broader sense to describe the lands belonging to a single political unit. Even then it was used to characterize the vague notion of an area over which power might extend rather than a tightly circumscribed region. Similarly, when the Romans discussed political control of land they were more likely to use terms relating to the

---

Cicero, Varro, and Seneca: ancient Roman philosophers, writers, and scholars.

idea of *finis*, a border or limit. Again, the Romans used such terms in a looser sense than we would today. Cicero tells us in *De re publica*, for instance, that the Spartans claimed ownership over all the lands that they could touch with a spear.

The key area of Roman thinking that employed notions of *territorium* was law. Roman law was further developed in the later Middle Ages, with its rediscovery and incorporation into political-legal systems across Europe. It was at this time that jurisdiction became tied to territory in an explicit way. This was a crucial development. Rather than territory being simply the land owned or controlled by the ruler, it now became the limit or extent of the ruler's political power. Since power became exercised over territory and as a consequence over the people and the actions within it, territory was both the object of political rule and its extent. Particular kinds of rule were exercised thus within territory, but did not extend beyond it.

This late fourteenth century idea was only slowly picked up in political theory more generally, especially by German writers in the seventeenth century trying to make sense of the multiple and conflicting powers within the Holy Roman Empire. Alongside these political-legal developments there was also a set of innovations in a more political-technical register which enabled polities or nascent states to survey, map, defend, catalogue, and control their lands in new ways. Developments in a whole range of political techniques are therefore important in this broader story. Notions of limitation are instrumental in understanding these developing theories of territory, and many of these arguments and practices looked to assert or reinforce them. But borders were not ultimately the defining notion of a territory or of the territories belonging to or subject to a political unit. Many of the borders to these historic polities were very loosely defined and were marked informally with ditches, fences, rivers, and even lines drawn on the ground: These borders were often of an unspecified width, and were more akin to a zone. They represented a kind of fortification, a temporary stopping point into an empire with a theoretically limitless extent. Only rarely were these borders seen as fixed and static. It is often claimed that the first boundary in a modern sense, as a defined line of zero width, was the one through the Pyrenees which separated France and Spain following the 1659 Treaty of the Pyrenees.° That boundary was only made possible because of the legal practices and technical ability that were available at that time.

1659 Treaty of the Pyrenees: a peace treaty between France and Spain that ended the Franco-Spanish War of 1648–59.

Territory, then, in this modern sense, should not be understood as defined by borders, in that putting a border around something is sufficient to demarcate it as a territory. Rather, territory is a multi-faceted concept and practice, one which encompasses economic, strategic, legal, and technical aspects, and can perhaps better be understood as the political counterpart of the homogeneous,° measured, and mathematicized notion of space that emerged with the scientific revolution. In that way of thinking, the political rendering of that sense of space is the condition of possibility for the demarcation of such modern boundaries as the one through the Pyrenees. The geometric basis of surveying and cartography° was simply not present before. It is the understanding of political space that is fundamental, and the idea of boundaries a secondary aspect, dependent on the first.

> "Territory, then, in this modern sense, should not be understood as defined by borders, in that putting a border around something is sufficient to demarcate it as a territory."

As the French writer Paul Alliès suggests in his book *L'invention du territoire*, "To define territory, we are told, one delimits borders. Or to think the border, must we not already have an idea of homogeneous territory?" To put this more forcefully, since Alliès' doubt is well-judged: borders only become possible in their modern sense, as boundaries, through a notion of space, rather than the other way round. Focusing on the determination of space that makes boundaries possible, and in particular the role of calculation in determining space opens up the idea of seeing boundaries not as a primary distinction that separates "territory" from other ways of understanding political control of land; but as a second-order problem founded upon a particular sense of calculation and its consequent grasp of space. Space, in this modern understanding, is often something bounded and exclusive, but more crucially is something calculable, extended in three dimensions.

In the early modern period, particularly, we see a whole range of strategies applied to the lands controlled by political entities such as the newly emerging states. Land is mapped, ordered, measured, divided, and controlled in various ways, with attempts at making it more homogeneous, with movement of goods and people allowed, prevented, or regulated, and internal order imposed. These kinds of political rationalities or techniques are calculative like those applied at a similar time to the

10

homogeneous: alike or uniform in composition; consisting of parts that are the same.
cartography: the study and practice of mapmaking.

population. Political arithmetic, or population statistics, impact on land too. Territory, on this reading, is thus a rendering of the emergent concept of "space" as a political-legal category, made possible by a range of techniques.

The modern notion of territory is certainly partly about boundaries and impermeability,° but more as a particular form that it took in certain times and places. For a variety of reasons, the idea of a tightly circumscribed area, with networks of rule and reinforced boundaries, fitted the aim of rulers across Europe in the seventeenth and eighteenth centuries. At that time the notion that those borders might be fixed was not seriously considered—land could still be conquered, bought, exchanged, or otherwise gained through alliances or marriage, or removed through punitive° peace settlements. Colonialism saw many of these ideas extended beyond Europe itself, though it should be stressed that many of these techniques were actually trialed first in colonial settings and only later brought back to Europe. Gaining territory through conquest or losing it when defeated remained common into the twentieth century—the Treaty of Versailles, or the wider Peace of Paris, for instance. Yet from the sixteenth century on there was a strong assertion of the rights of the sovereign power within those borders. Territory increasingly became associated with exclusive forms of sovereignty.

Challenging the still prevailing myth that the origin of the modern concept of territory is with the modern state system in the Peace of Westphalia, this more historically nuanced understanding of the emergence of this concept helps to shed light on more than simply Europe's history. Understanding territory in this broader sense, as the political control of a calculative space, as a political technology, allows us to account for a range of modern phenomena. The purpose here is less to offer a better single definition of territory, which can be contrasted with other ones, than to raise the kinds of questions we would need to ask to understand how territory has been understood and practiced in a range of different times and places. Conceiving of territory as the bringing together of a range of different political phenomena—economic, strategic, legal, and technical—does more than simply offer a historically sensitive account of the concept and its emergence. It allows us to understand that while borders are extremely important, they are not a defining element of territory but rather its consequence. Territory as a political counterpart of calculative space makes possible the delimitation and demarcation of

---

impermeability: the degree to which something does not permit passage or is unable to be broken through.
punitive: intended to punish someone or something; extremely or unfairly severe.

borders as boundaries, rather than borders making territory. While it might take on a strictly bordered form at particular times, looser, over-lapping, and multiple arrangements are also possible. We can then understand the plurality of different political-spatial arrangements that take place.

Contemporary Developments

Much has been written, in this symposium from the *Harvard International Review* and elsewhere, about a whole range of important political changes that are taking place concerning borders. As the example of Schengenland shows, the "borderless" world is, at best, profoundly uneven. Some people are able to cross international borders with ease, while others are delayed or prevented from crossing them, or even imprisoned within their logics. Many borders are now no longer located at the physical limits of a state, but taken to other places. For example, it is common to clear immigration to enter the US while still within the confines of a Canadian airport, and many European states have taken their immigration processing off-shore. Some Australian islands are declared non-territorial for this very purpose.

Non-recognized borders, such as that between the Republic of Cyprus and the Turkish Republic of Northern Cyprus, perform many of the ritu-als of border crossing; this example most clearly shows how any modern border, while nominally a boundary line of zero width, is actually a zone. The wall in the West Bank is another anomaly, because Israel's legally recognized sovereignty ends someway before the wall itself is reached; but the effective sovereignty of its projection of political power extends to the Jordan valley.

Many other contemporary political geographical issues similarly com- 15 plicate the straightforward idea of a state exercising exclusive sovereignty within tightly defined borders. The most pressing border disputes today are often over maritime boundaries, with the strategic and economic im-portance of laying legal claim to rocks or small islands, allowing the tech-nical exploitation of vast expanses of sea and seabed. Rich states lease land for various purposes from neighbors, such as the Bintan Resorts on an Indonesian island, which are owned, regulated, and controlled by neigh-boring Singapore. China is using its economic might to use land in Africa for agriculture and to extract minerals. Embassies and military bases often have complicated jurisdictional status. Most notoriously, Guantánamo bay, leased from Cuba following a 1903 treaty, is legally considered not to be part of the United States territory, and therefore outside US law, while remaining under its effective control.

In the wider context of the "war on terror," we have seen a shift in the relation between territorial preservation—the fixing of borders and the rejection of ideas that territory can be gained or lost—and territorial sovereignty, where a state is able to exercise exclusive internal sovereignty within those borders. In states such as Afghanistan or Iraq, the actions of the rulers of those states within their borders were deemed to legitimatize external intervention. This co-opted longer-standing ideas of humanitarian intervention or the responsibility to protect civilian populations in relation to other challenges—in these instances the harboring of terrorists or the pursuit of weapons of mass destruction. Yet at the same time, the international community was unwilling to allow either of these states to fragment along ethnic or religious lines or to countenance the wider redrawing of borders within their regions. In early modern Europe, sovereignty was claimed to be absolute but the borders within which it was exercised were continually mutable; today we are seeing the reverse: an attempt to have borders fixed but sovereignty within them contingent. The fracturing of the Soviet Union and Yugoslavia along the lines of their constituent republics led to ethnic conflicts and still enduring border disputes. Even though sovereignty had been directly challenged by the 1999 NATO war in Kosovo, there was a strong reluctance in the international community to allow an independent state to emerge. The independence of South Sudan will be a fascinating process to watch. As I argued in my book *Terror and Territory: The Spatial Extent of Sovereignty*, what we were seeing in these and other instances such as Lebanon, Pakistan, and Somalia was a challenge to the existing relations among territory, borders, and sovereignty, but not the end of their importance. Similar arguments could be made about ongoing events in Libya.

The historically informed and conceptually developed way of thinking about territory, outlined above, allows us to grasp the changes that are taking place in the world today. Thinking territory without borders provides us a better understanding of the borders of territory.

Understanding the Text

1. What does Elden identify as "a crucial development" (par. 6) in the evolution of the concept of *territory*? In your own words, explain why he thinks this development was so important.

2. How does Elden support his claim that "[t]erritory, then, in this modern sense, should not be understood as defined by borders, in that putting a border around something is sufficient to demarcate it as a territory" (par. 8)?

3. What does Elden mean when he defines territory as "the political control of a calculative space" (par. 12)? According to Elden, why is it so important to understand territory in this way?

Reflection and Response

4. Elden identifies the following elements as critical for understanding territory: economic, strategic, legal, and technical. Do you think these elements are equally important in order to define territory? If so, why? If not, which ones do you believe are most crucial? Explain and support your position.

5. When he discusses contemporary issues, Elden notes many political changes involving borders. In so doing, he also reveals the complicated relationship among territory, borders, and sovereignty. Using textual evidence from Elden's essay, explain the nature of that relationship. In your response, consider if or how our understanding of each term has changed. You may want to discuss more recent political changes in relation to borders, territory, or sovereignty, as well as your own experiences.

Making Connections

6. In paragraphs 13–16, Elden includes many modern-day examples to illustrate the changing nature of borders, territories, and sovereignty. Choose one of the examples he provides or choose your own example, and do some additional research on it. Then write an essay explaining what your case reveals about borders, territory, or sovereignty.

7. At the beginning of his essay, Elden asserts that his argument regarding "territory without borders" differs from a "borderless world" argument, which the readings in Chapter 5 address. Choose one or two of those readings to explain what a "borderless world" argument is. Using your understanding of this argument and Elden's argument in "Territory without Borders," explain the differences and similarities between the two. As you craft your explanation, you will need to summarize and synthesize the various writers' ideas and include textual evidence from the readings.

Building Walls

Reed Karaim

A freelance writer and novelist, Reed Karaim won the Robin Goldstein Award for Outstanding Regional Reporting. Based in Tucson, Arizona, he writes for many publications, including *National Geographic*, *Smithsonian*, *American Scholar*, and *Congressional Quarterly Researcher* (*CQ Researcher*). He is also the author of the novel *If Men Were Angels* (1999).

"Building Walls" first appeared in the September 19, 2008, issue of *CQ Researcher*, a weekly print and online journal that covers a single contemporary topic in depth in each issue. This issue, titled "America's Border Fence," tackles the following questions: "Can a border fence stop illegal immigrants? Would blocking all illegal immigrants hurt or benefit the U.S. economy? Does the fence harm U.S. relations with Mexico?" To address these questions, Karaim looks at the history of "walls." As you read, note similarities between Karaim's historical examples and today's walls or border fences, and consider whether these examples clarify or complicate your understanding of the nature of borders.

Nations have been building walls or fences along their borders more or less since nations began.

Consider Hadrian's Wall, built in the second century AD along Roman Britain's frontier. The wall was made of turf and stone instead of steel and concrete, but its commonly accepted purpose sounds familiar: to keep the poorer "barbarians" of ancient Scotland from invading the civilized and more prosperous empire.

The Great Wall of China, built over several hundred years, was a similar, even more expansive effort. Much like the U.S. border fence, it wasn't one structure but a series of walls totaling about 4,000 miles along strategic stretches of the border, designed to keep out the Mongols and other nomadic tribes from Central Asia.

More recently, the Berlin Wall appears to have been built for the opposite reason: to keep residents inside communist East Berlin. However, as former University of Arizona political science professor Williams points out, East Germany claimed the wall was designed to protect East Berliners from the "alien influences of capitalism."

American history is replete with its own examples of walls, notes Williams, who edited an upcoming special issue of the university's *Journal of the Southwest* entitled "Fences."[1] The Jamestown settlers and the Pilgrims built palisades—fences of pointed wooden stakes—around their small communities to keep out the Native Americans and wild animals.

The view atop the Great Wall of China.
LIUSHENGFILM/Shutterstock

Through the centuries barriers have been erected along borders "to protect 'us' from 'them,'" Williams says. "The same things are always said about the people on the other side of the fence—they're barbarians or savages or an alien force."

The question is whether they work. After all, the Berlin Wall fell, the Romans eventually abandoned Hadrian's Wall, the Manchu finally conquered China, and even the massive fortifications of the French Maginot Line, built between the world wars, were rendered ineffectual when the Germans simply went around them—an approach critics of the U.S. border fence say illegal migrants already are taking.

But such unequivocal dismissal, popular with critics of the U.S. fence, ignores the long periods during which certain fortifications proved effective. In his book about the Roman Empire, historian Derek Williams says after Hadrian's Wall was built, "decades passed without emergency." The Berlin Wall fulfilled its function for more than 40 years, he adds, and the Great Wall of China for much longer.[2]

"It would be very comfortable for my liberal consciousness to say these things don't work," says Williams. "But that's not the case. They do work."

But even if walls and fences work, says Maribel Alvarez, a folklorist at 10 the University of Arizona's Southwest Center, the U.S. barriers still create a simplistic view of the border. "It's a view locked in an either/or perspective," she says. "The border is treated as an untamed badlands. It assumes that in this badlands someone with higher knowledge needs to impose an order that is lacking."

Some of the rhetoric from Washington concerning the Southwestern border certainly fits Alvarez's description. Rep. Tom Tancredo, R-Colo., a strong opponent of illegal immigration, summed up the view in an article for *Human Events* magazine, titled "Mexico's Lawless Border Poses Huge Test for Washington."[3]

But history may provide an unexpected lesson, says Mary Beard, a classics scholar at Cambridge University in England. The Romans' view of frontiers was more complex than those who cite Hadrian's Wall as a forerunner of the U.S. fence would have it. The Romans did not see borders as clear divisions, Beard wrote in *The Times of London*, but rather as "frontier zones" where the empire gradually disappeared into foreign territory.[4]

> "The Romans did not see borders as clear divisions, . . . but rather as 'frontier zones' where the empire gradually disappeared into foreign territory."

Contacted by e-mail, Beard notes that one connection between Hadrian's Wall and "Bush's wall" is that both are partly symbolic in intent. Critics of the U.S. fence have argued it is primarily a political gesture intended to appease anti-immigration sentiment. Similarly, Hadrian's Wall was clearly designed as much to impress the Romans behind it as those on the other side, notes historian Williams.[5]

But Beard's description of the fluid nature of Roman borders, which were largely unfortified, describes the U.S.-Mexican border for much of its history.

Notes

1. *Journal of the Southwest*, Vol. 50, No. 3, University of Arizona, autumn 2008.

2. Derek Williams, *The Reach of Rome: A History of the Roman Imperial Frontier, 1st–5th Centuries AD* (1996), p. 111.

3. Tom Tancredo, "Mexico's Lawless Border Poses Huge Test for Washington," *Human Events*, February 6, 2006.

4. Mary Beard, "Don't Blame Hadrian for Bush's Wall." *Times Literary Supplement*, April 30, 2007, http://timesonline.typepad.com/dons_life/2007/04/dont_blame hadr.html.

5. Williams, *op. cit.*, p. 108.

Understanding the Text

1. Why have nations built walls or fences? List all the different reasons that Karaim mentions in his article.

2. What question does Karaim ask about these walls? How does he answer that question?

3. How did the Romans understand borders? What does Roman history teach us about border walls and fences?

4. Although this short essay is a "background piece" on the history of border walls, it still contains a position or thesis. Identify that position and the clues that helped you identify it.

Reflection and Response

5. Karaim uses several outside sources, including Maribel Alvarez from the University of Arizona's Southwest Center. Alvarez asserts that even if physical barriers work, they "create a simplistic view of the border" (par. 10). What does she find troubling about this view? How does Karaim integrate and further develop Alvarez's ideas? What is your position in relation to Karaim's and Alvarez's arguments?

6. Mary Beard, another scholar Karaim cites, points to the symbolic aspect of borders, walls, and fences — specifically, the U.S. border fence. What does she mean by "symbolic"? Do you agree that this fence *is* in part symbolic? Explain your position.

Making Connections

7. Karaim wrote this piece in 2008. Research the current status of the U.S. border fence and the recent controversy surrounding it. What connections can you make between your findings and some of the points in Karaim's essay? Do the recent changes and ongoing debates about the U.S. border complicate the concept of borders that Karaim presents? If so, in what ways?

8. If you have not yet done so, read Stuart Elden's "Territory without Borders" (p. 24). What would Elden add to this piece on building walls? In other words, if Karaim, Elden, and, perhaps, Beard were at a coffeeshop talking about borders, fences, and walls, what do you think each might say? For example, what would Elden want the others to consider and why?

How the States Got Their Shapes

Mark Stein

Mark Stein is a writer and playwright living in Washington, D.C., who has also taught at Catholic University and American University. His books include *How the States Got Their Shapes* (2008), which resulted in the History Channel series of the same name; *How the States Got Their Shapes Too: The People behind the Borderlines* (2011); and *American Panic: A History of Who Scares Us and Why* (2014).

The following reading is a group of selections from *How the States Got Their Shapes*. As you read, think carefully about the political and cultural conditions that influenced the creation of America's external and internal borderlines.

To teach us the boundaries of the states, my seventh grade geography teacher would hold up cutouts and we would raise our hands, vying for the chance to identify which state had the corresponding shape. How we distinguished Wyoming from Colorado, both rectangles, eludes me these many years later. Maybe she just didn't include them. After all, how much value is there in knowing which rectangle is Wyoming and which is Colorado?

Later in life, I came to realize that there is value in learning about the borders of Colorado and Wyoming, but that value resides, not in knowing *what* their shape is, but in knowing *why* it is. Why, for instance, are the straight lines that define Wyoming located where they are and not, say, ten miles farther north or west? Far more knowledge results from exploring why a set of conditions exists than from simply accepting those conditions and committing them to memory. Asking why a state has the borders it does unlocks a history of human struggles—far more history than this book can contain, though this book does aspire to unearth the keys.

Consider for a moment the cluster of states composed of Maine, New Hampshire, and Vermont. Why don't those states extend to their natural boundaries, the St. Lawrence River and the Atlantic Ocean? How come Canada got that land?

Why does Delaware have a semicircle for its northern border? What's at its center and why was it encircled? Why does Texas have that square part poking up? And why does the square part just miss connecting with Kansas, leaving that little Oklahoma panhandle in between?

The more one looks at state borders, the more questions those borders 5 generate. Why do the Carolinas and Dakotas have a North state and a

South state? Couldn't they get along? Why is there a West Virginia but not an East Virginia? And why does Michigan have a chunk of land that's so obviously part of Wisconsin? It's not even connected to the rest of Michigan!

This book will provide those answers. State by state (along with the District of Columbia), the events

"The more one looks at state borders, the more questions those borders generate."

that resulted in the location of each state's present borders will be identified.

A state border is both an official entrance and a hidden entrance. The official entrance is the legal threshold to a state. But its hidden entrance beckons us to the past. Here at the state line we can come in contact with struggles long forgotten and now overgrown by signs saying things like "Welcome to Kansas—Please Drive Carefully."

Don't Skip This: You'll Just Have to Come Back Later

Many of our state borders are segments of borders that date from England's and, later, the United States' territorial acquisitions, and they can be identified by looking for lines that provide multistate borders.

The French and Indian War Border

The French and Indian War (1754–63) resulted in the oldest of these multistate boundaries. In this war, England and her American colonists began what became the dismantling of France's possessions in North America. With this victory, England added to her North American possessions all the land between the Ohio River and the Mississippi River. The boundaries of that war are still on the map today, for they provide borders for the states of Ohio, Indiana, Illinois, and Wisconsin.

The division of this land acquired in the French and Indian War influ- 10 enced virtually every state border that followed. After the Revolution, Congress had to decide how best to divide this region, known as the Northwest Territory, into states. Congress assigned Thomas Jefferson the task of studying this matter and in 1784 Jefferson issued a report to Congress in which he proposed that the region be divided into states having two degrees of height and four degrees of width, wherever possible.

As it turned out, Congress didn't employ these borders when it enacted the Northwest Ordinance in 1787, the law that included the boundary lines for the future states to be created from the Northwest Territory. Congress did, however, adopt its underlying principle: All states should be created equal.

The Louisiana Purchase Borders

Probably the most notable American boundary is the long straight line that defines so much of the nation's northern border with Canada. This line is the 49th parallel. It first surfaced on the American map following the 1803 Louisiana Purchase. The document conveying France's remaining North American land—a tract that included all or some of Louisiana, Arkansas, Oklahoma, Missouri, Kansas, Iowa, Nebraska, South Dakota, North Dakota, Wyoming, Minnesota, Montana, and Colorado—states that the French Republic cedes to the United States "the Colony or Province of Louisiana with the same extent that it now has." This wording seems refreshingly brief and to the point for a legal document, if a bit vague. The vagueness is also the reason very little evidence of the Louisiana Purchase can be found in our state lines. Other than the boundaries provided by the Gulf of Mexico and the Mississippi River, no one knew what its boundaries were! Jefferson believed that all the land comprising the watershed leading to the Missouri and Mississippi rivers constituted the Louisiana Purchase. But, as he soon discovered, the United States' neighbors did not. In reality, France's American territory extended to the west as far as a Frenchman could go without getting shot by a Spaniard, and likewise to the north without getting shot by an Englishman.

The ambiguous borders of the Louisiana Purchase led England and the United States to negotiate where France's former lands ended and where British North America (Canada) began. Under the Convention of 1818, the two nations agreed upon the 49th parallel from the westernmost longitude of Lake of the Woods to the crest of the Rocky Mountains.

But the choice of the 49th parallel begs the question, why not 50? It's such a nice round number. The reason for the one-degree difference is that England needed to maintain her access to the Great Lakes via the westernmost of those lakes, Lake Superior. Such access was vital to England's fur trade in general and, in specific, to a major fur trading post located at the confluence of the Assiniboine and Red rivers—a place now known as Winnipeg. Had the border been located at the 50th parallel, Winnipeg would have been in American territory, as would the waterways that flow east to Lake Superior.

The Louisiana Purchase also sparked concern in Spain, which claimed 15 much of the land west of the Rockies. This concern led to the Adams-Onís Treaty (1819). The entire eastern border of Texas—the straight line of what later became its panhandle, the eastward flowing Red River, the straight line southward at the lower corner of Texas, and the Sabine River arcing southward to the Gulf of Mexico—all dates back to this treaty. Also emanating from the Adams-Onís Treaty is the long, multistate line

The boundary from the Adams-Onís Treaty (1819).
Library of Congress

that runs along the 42nd parallel, which later became the northern border of California, Nevada, and northwest Utah. But, as with every man-made line, there is the question, why put the line *there*?

The Border Inherited from England and Spain

The 42nd parallel already existed as a boundary before the 1803 Louisiana Purchase. In 1790, England and Spain had concluded a treaty known as the Nootka Convention.

The Nootka Convention? Nootka Sound is a small inlet in Vancouver Island (off the west coast of what is now Canada). In the late 1700s, England and Spain nearly went to war over their conflicting ambitions along the west coast of North America. The British needed the rivers and inlets of Vancouver Island and northwestern Canada to carry on their fur trade. But the Spanish claimed the land was already theirs—as is reflected to this day by names along the west coast of Canada such as the Juan de Fuca Strait, Port San Juan, Estevan Point, Vargas Island, Valdes Island, and Gabriola.

All of England's interests west of the Rockies would have been at risk had Spain succeeded in ousting England from Vancouver Island. In the Nootka Convention, England sought to protect its access to all those rivers and their tributaries vital to carrying out the fur trade. Key among those rivers was the Columbia River. And virtually all of the tributaries to the Columbia River are north of the 42nd parallel.

Below the 42nd parallel, virtually all of the rivers wend their way to San Francisco Bay. Commerce along these waterways was reserved exclusively for Spain with the 42nd parallel as the border. For its era, it was a great parallel. And evidently it has remained an effective border, since it's still there, dividing five states: Oregon, Idaho, California, Nevada, and Utah.

Multistate Borders Resulting from Slavery

Not all of our multistate borders have resulted from large land acquisi- 20 tions. Some multistate lines are vestiges of America's internal affairs. The long line that defines (with a few deviations) the southern borders of Virginia, Kentucky, Missouri, and the Oklahoma panhandle tells a tale of the struggle to contain the conflict over slavery. Just above that line is another line, this one defining the northern border of the Oklahoma panhandle and the southern borders of Kansas, Colorado, and Utah. The story behind this second line reveals the failure of the struggle to compromise when the issue was slavery.

Multistate Borders That Do Not Connect

Some of the most revealing multistate borders in the United States are difficult to detect because *they do not connect!* Despite this seeming contradiction, they are indeed multistate borders. Moreover, once detected, they reveal most strikingly the commitment by Congress to the principle that all states should be created equal.

One of these sets of multistate borders consists of the northern and southern borders of Kansas, Nebraska, South Dakota, and North Dakota. Though the borders of each of these states was finalized at a separate time, Congress located each with the result that all four of these prairie states have three degrees of height.

Just to the west of this column of states, the Rocky Mountain states of Colorado, Wyoming, and Montana, the borders of which were also created at separate times, all share the fact that they have four degrees of height.

And the western states of Washington, Oregon, Colorado, Wyoming, North Dakota, and South Dakota, again created over a number of years, all have almost exactly seven degrees of width.

The principle that all states should be created equal was deeply and 25 consciously rooted in the foundations of the United States. In forming a new government, our founders inherited thirteen colonies, now states, in whose creation by the British crown equality had never been a factor.

Some of the colonies were huge, extending—if not to the Pacific Ocean, as originally claimed—as far as the Mississippi River. Others were small.

Rather than redraw borders that in some cases had been in place for as long as 150 years, the founders sought to equalize the inequality of the first thirteen states, in part, by creating a bicameral legislature. The House of Representatives, in which representation is apportioned by population, favored the larger states. But the Senate, in which all states have two votes, favored the smaller states.

This solution contained a great irony. In a sense, the founders were imitating the government they had just overthrown! England's Parliament is also bicameral, having the House of Commons and the House of Lords. But the House of Lords existed not to create equality but to preserve *inequality*—in the form of the traditional privileges of the nobility.

But before becoming too smug, we need to ask if, in fact, all states are created equal. What about Texas and California? Don't they contradict this principle? Or are they exceptions that prove the rule? To find out, we now need to visit the individual states.

California

If Congress followed a policy that all states should be created equal, why did it create California? Answer: It didn't. California created itself. The

Land acquired from the Mexican War (1848).
Library of Congress

land that became California came into the possession of the United States in 1848 with the end of the Mexican War. Before Congress could go through the process of dividing it into territories, a man named James 30 Marshall spotted something shiny by the sawmill of his employer, John Sutter. It was gold.

Having been an American possession for barely a year, California was suddenly filled with a population, an economy, and a very high crime rate. So urgent was the need for government that Californians created their own state constitution and declared their own borders, skipping the fuss and bother of territorial status. Territories, after all, can have their borders altered; states (without their consent) cannot. Still, to become a state, Congress had to approve.

Congress said yes, despite the size of California and its wealth of natural resources. Indeed, if California were a nation today, it would have the fifth largest Gross National Product in the world. Why did Congress do it?

Many members of Congress were opposed to the extensive boundaries proposed by California. Nevertheless, many of those concerned by California's size voted in favor of its statehood. An echo of their reasoning reverberates in that modern-day statistic just cited: *if it were a nation*. Today we look at the map of the contiguous forty-eight states and assume these states to be one nation, indivisible. In 1849, that assumption did not exist. Rather, there was considerable fear that the states might divide into separate nations. This was primarily a concern about the slave states. But bear in mind that our other oversized state, Texas, which had also only recently joined the Union, had previously been a nation for nearly ten years.

The same concern applied to California, as expressed aptly and emotionally on the floor of the Senate by William Seward (who, eighteen years later as Secretary of State, would purchase Alaska for the United States):

[California] is practically further removed from us than England. We cannot reach her by railroad, nor by unbroken steam navigation. We can send no armies over the prairie, the mountain, and the desert. . . . Let her only seize our domains within her borders, and our commerce in her ports, and she will have at once revenues and credits adequate to all her necessities. Besides, are we so moderate, and has the world become so just, that we have no rivals and no enemies to lend their sympathies and aid to compass the dismemberment of our empire?

California violated the policy of equality among states because it could. The United States needed California more than California needed the United States. The size of its boundaries preserves these elements of mid-nineteenth-century American life. The *location* of its boundaries preserves something more. Since they were dictated by California, they were located with the concerns of California in mind, not, as when Congress located borders, with the concerns of the region as a whole.

Why, for instance, did the state's founders include southern California? 35 In those years, it contained far more desert than it does today, with the irrigation that has since been developed. The valuable harbor at San Diego certainly influenced the decision to extend the borders so far south. The importance of access to the ocean is also revealed by California's southeast border, the Colorado River. At the time that California established this boundary, the lower end of the Colorado River was navigable to the Gulf of California. Access to the Colorado River meant access to the sea.

California's Eastern Border

All of California's remaining borders are straight lines, raising the question, why there? The most striking of these straight lines is the long eastern border of California, a line that heads due south, then angles southeasterly until it reaches the Colorado River. The official reasoning for this line was that it paralleled, in a general way, the western border of the state at a distance of about 215 miles. True enough, but why 215? The answer is it encloses California's treasure.

California's eastern border is one of the few items from the Gold Rush that is still on the ground. Its existence is evidence of how important it

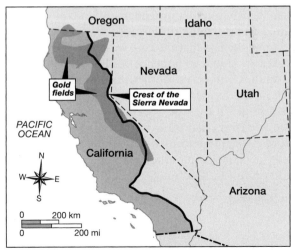

California's rejected eastern borders, which would have followed the crest of the Sierra Nevada.

Library of Congress

was to California to possess all of the gold-bearing mountains in the region. Had Congress created the border, it might well have followed the crest of the mountains, as many of the eastern states have borders along the crest of the Appalachians. Indeed, some years after California had been admitted to the Union, Congress broached the idea of locating the California/Nevada border along the crest of the Sierra Nevada. California told Congress to forget it.

California's Northern Border

California's northern border is simply a straight line, going east and west, along the 42nd parallel. It is a segment of a boundary that was already in place before California existed. Under the Nootka Convention (1790) Spain and England agreed upon the 42nd parallel as the boundary between their Pacific coast claims.

California's Southern Border

At California's opposite end, how come this expansive state stops so abruptly at a straight line just below San Diego? Logically, shouldn't it continue on down that peninsula? That land is even called Baja California—*Lower* California. And since California does stop there, why is the line slightly angled?

As it turns out, the United States *did* think California should extend 40 down that peninsula. In negotiating the treaty ending the Mexican War, President James Polk demanded Baja California. But the Mexicans wouldn't budge. In fact, Mexico wouldn't surrender any land south of the Gila River. Mexico insisted on preserving sufficient access for its army to reach Baja California, despite the fact that the land was of little commercial use. The Mexicans feared an American presence on their west, in addition to their north. As a result, California's southern border is a slightly angled line that cuts off Baja California from the rest of the state.

But why the angle? If the line went due west from the juncture of the Gila and Colorado rivers, San Diego would be a Mexican city located just below the border. The Americans were willing to relent on Baja California, provided they got the important port at San Diego, along with sufficient land to protect it. As a result, the slightly angled southern border was drawn.

Texas

Texas' Eastern Border

Texas first became a place of continual colonial settlement in 1691, when Spain grew alarmed at reports that Frenchmen had crossed the Sabine

River from Louisiana. The French, possibly testing the waters for colonial expansion, were befriending the local Indians, an alliance of tribes known by their native word for "allies," *tejas*. Spain dispatched an expedition to clear the area of the French and convert the Indians to Christianity. To ensure that the French stayed out and the Indians stayed Christian, Spain built missions throughout the region and established the province of Tejas. Its eastern border at the time was the Sabine River, which to this day is a segment of Texas' eastern border.

Spanish worries regarding French incursions into their North American domains came to an end in 1803, when the United States purchased the Louisiana Territory. Now Spanish worries regarded the Americans. In 1819, the United States and Spain concluded the Adams-Onís Treaty, defining the boundary between American and Spanish territory. A good deal of today's Texas border was established in this treaty. And a number of the border's segments also preserve elements in the history of Spanish Tejas.

The current border preserves not only the original eastern border of Tejas along the Sabine River but also the border to which the province later advanced, the Red River.

But why is this advance represented at the point where the Sabine crosses the 32nd parallel? Why not some other degree of latitude?° 45

In the negotiations between Secretary of State John Quincy Adams and Spanish envoy Lord Don Luis do Onís, the Red River was a particularly contentious element. It had become a boundary of Tejas when Spain advanced northward from the Sabine River to the Red River. For the United States, the Red River was an important avenue of commerce in Louisiana, flowing diagonally from its northwest corner across the territory to the Mississippi River.

By locating the border between the Sabine and the Red rivers by a vertical line heading north from the point at which the Sabine River crosses the 32nd parallel, the border that results gives the United States the entire diagonal segment of the Red River, along with a buffer west of the river which, at its narrowest point (in present-day Arkansas), is exactly 10 miles wide. In addition, the point at which this vertical line intersects the Red River gives Spain access to the rest of the Red River along its southern bank.

We can also see in today's eastern border of Texas another segment from the Adam-Onís Treaty, which specified that the U.S./Spanish boundary

---

latitude: any of the imaginary lines that circle the Earth and run parallel to the equator. A particular latitude is measured in degrees, totaling 90, by its distance north or south of the equator.

continued westward along the Red River to 100° W longitude, at which point it turned due north to the Arkansas River, Today, what remains of this line due north is the eastern edge of the Texas panhandle.

But why did they pick the 100th meridian° as the point at which the border would depart from the Red River and head north? Part of the reason is revealed in a letter Onís had written to Adams in February 1819:

I have to state to you that his majesty is unable to agree to [the boundary of] the Red River to its source, as proposed by you. This river rises within a few leagues of Santa Fe, the capital of [Spanish] New Mexico.

Ultimately, the two sides agreed upon a border farther north at the Arkansas River. For the point at which the boundary would jump from the Red River to the Arkansas River, they selected the midpoint between the headwaters of the Arkansas River and the point where it crosses into what was already the state of Louisiana. That midpoint is 100°.

Oklahoma would later dispute the Red River segment of the Texas 50 boundary, claiming that the north branch of the Red River, being the smaller branch, was not the legitimate boundary of Texas. In 1897, the Supreme Court agreed, shifting the Texas boundary to the south branch of the Red River.

Texas' Northern Border

Spain might have saved itself the effort of negotiating the Adams-Onís Treaty had it known that, only two years later, Mexico would win its independence. The worry of American incursion now belonged to the Mexicans, who continued the Spanish policy of prohibiting American settlements within their territory. But Moses Austin was able to get the Mexican government to grant him an exception, allowing him to establish a lead-smelting operation in the Mexican province of Texas. Austin's son, Stephen, took over the business, the success of which led Mexican authorities to permit other American ventures. By 1830, Americans outnumbered Mexicans in the province, and in 1836, Texas achieved independence under the leadership of Sam Houston.

The northern border of the Republic of Texas was strangely shaped but quite logical. It followed the boundaries set in the Adams-Onís Treaty. As things turned out, being its own country was a lot more expensive than Texas had anticipated. Deeply in debt, Texas joined the United States in 1846.

---

meridian: any of the imaginary lines that go from the North Pole to the South Pole.

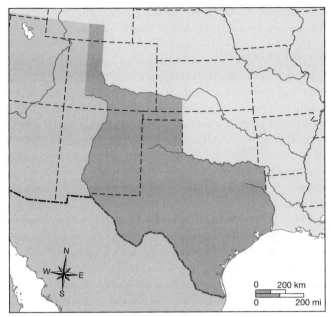

The Republic of Texas' borders (1836).
Library of Congress

Since, in the Republic of Texas, slavery was legal, the U.S. state of Texas had to comply with the Missouri Compromise if it wished to remain a slave state. This 1820 agreement prohibited slavery north of 36°30'. Texas therefore relinquished to the United States all of its land north of that latitude. This is why what would become the Texas panhandle is sliced off where it is, forming the northernmost border of Texas.

Texas' Southern Border

The 1836 treaty that ended the Texas War of Independence stipulated 55 that the Mexican army would withdraw south of the Rio Grande. The Rio Grande had never been the southern border of Texas in its days as a province of Mexico, but it was employed in the treaty to provide security. Texas anticipated that the river would become its officially recognized border. But Mexico never recognized the Republic of Texas. When Texas joined the Union in 1846, the United States stipulated that the southern border of the state of Texas would be the Rio Grande. Mexico, fearing that Texas might be the preamble to further American expansion, reasserted its claim to the entire region and backed that claim with its army. The United States did likewise, resulting in the Mexican War. In the 1848 treaty that followed Mexico's surrender, the Rio Grande became the officially recognized southern border of Texas.

Texas' Western Border

Texas continued to claim all its land south of 36°30', resulting in a state that so dwarfed every other state it undermined the principle that all states should be created equal. Congress passed a law stating that, if it desired, Texas could subdivide itself into as many as five states. Southerners in particular were attracted to this idea, desiring the additional slave states to help represent their cause in the U.S. Senate. But Texas wasn't wild about the idea.

Texas, however, remained burdened by crushing debts from its days as a republic. For this reason, under the Compromise of 1850, Texas sold the United States all of its land west of 103° and north of what was then the latitude of New Mexico's southern border. This sale resulted in the right-angled western border of Texas that we see today.

Even with the land Texas surrendered north of 36°30' and the land it later sold, Texas remains far larger than most other states. If Congress had been truly committed to the notion that all states should be created equal, how had this happened?

Congress did not create Texas. Texas created Texas. And when the opportunity presented itself to bring Texas into the United States, it was at a time when many Americans believed it to be the nation's destiny to possess all of North America. The opportunity to acquire Texas was too great to risk by imposing conditions regarding its division into smaller states. Congress did, however, require—and later persuade—Texas to release large sections of its land. These actions affirm, rather than refute, the notion that Congress sought to create states that were equal.

Understanding the Text

1. What argument does Stein present regarding the value of learning about state borders and their history? Why does he think this is important?

2. What was the underlying principle for enacting the Northwest Ordinance in 1787, and what is significant about this principle?

3. Explain how Congress followed the principle that "all states should be created equal" (par. 25). Make sure to consider both geographical and political concerns in your response.

4. What is the difference between a territory's borders and a state's borders?

5. In 1849, what fear existed regarding the "unity" of the nation? What was the primary cause of this fear?

6. What did California's boundaries protect? What influence did this have on its borders?

7. Explain the circumstances that allowed Texas to enter the Union as such a large state. How did Texas's size and borders change? Why did they change?

Reflection and Response

8. Stein peppers the first five paragraphs with questions about why states have the borders they do. Take a moment to look closely at a map of the United States. What questions come to mind about the lines that you see on the map? Which states or cluster of states do you find the most intriguing? Why?

9. Reflect on your own experience and knowledge of the United States' internal borders. How many of these state borders have you crossed? Did you see some kind of marker? How did you mark that crossing? What did you know about the history of the state borders before reading Stein's essay? After addressing some of these questions, write a response to Stein's assertion regarding the value of learning *why* a state is shaped the way it is. Do you think this knowledge is important or relevant to your own experiences? Why or why not?

Making Connections

10. Read "A Very Bordered World" by Alexander Diener and Joshua Hagen (p. 15). Then choose one of the territorial acquisitions that Stein presents in "Don't Skip This" and do more in-depth research into how those borders were negotiated, paying particular attention to what those negotiations reveal about issues of territoriality, jurisdiction, and sovereignty. Based on your research, what conclusions can you draw about the history of borders and the evolution of the concepts *territory*, *jurisdiction*, and *sovereignty*? How does what you learned relate to Diener and Hagen's points?

11. Choose a state other than Texas or California, research how it got its shape, and tell the story of its border as "both an official entrance and a hidden entrance" (par. 7), as Stein does in his essay.

danielvfung/Getty Images

2 Why Do Geographical Borders Matter?

E ven if we do not all live in a recognized *borderland*—a border community near an international border — each of us lives in a neighborhood, city, or town that borders another neighborhood, city, or town. Think about the boundaries that mark your neighborhood or city. What does it mean to live on one side or the other of that marker, even if that marker is invisible? How do you know when you have left your neighborhood or city? Can you discern a clear distinction between your neighborhood or city and the adjacent one? Picture the neighborhoods that form the "borders" between your city and the next or the streets that act as the boundaries of your neighborhood. Are those areas different from the more central parts of the city or neighborhood? The answers to these questions will help you understand the lived experiences of those inhabiting the borderlands, where distinct boundaries can split regions and deeply affect the people and cultures straddling the border.

Investigating the place of borders in our world involves looking at real borders — considering not merely the lines on our maps but the barriers and boundaries that traverse our landscapes. Once in place, these physical borders mark off territory, often separating groups of people from each other. Clearly, then, borders can affect both landscapes and individuals in significant ways.

This observation leads to larger and more complicated questions. For example, how do borders affect landscapes and people? If you push your inquiry further, however, you will soon identify even more questions: What are the political and social aspects of borders? How dynamic are borderlands? What are the history and politics of a specific region? What is the significance of the stories that people living in border spaces tell? How do various borders affect people and regions differently?

This chapter contains a diverse set of readings that explore why geographical borders matter. The first four readings deal with America's

photo: danielvfung/Getty Images

international borders. The first three selections, which focus on the U.S.-Mexico border, open with a poem by Gloria Anzaldúa. In "To Live in the Borderlands Means You," Anzaldúa represents a border identity, one "not knowing which side to turn to, run from" (p. 55). Next, Norma Cantú's "Living on the Border: A Wound That Will Not Heal" celebrates the blending of cultures while simultaneously reminding us of the border's power to push individuals into outside spaces, into the "in between." Both of these writers highlight the importance and difficulties of claiming an identity in the borderlands.

Writing as a travel writer and tourist, a perspective very different from either Anzaldúa's or Cantú's, Paul Theroux reveals the distinctiveness of and contradictions within U.S.-Mexico border communities. While describing his visit to Nogales, Mexico, he blends his own experiences with those of other tourists and the stories of local Nogalans, as well as those of the "lost souls" of El Comedor, a shelter in Nogales for individuals caught without papers on the U.S. side of the border.

Leslie Alm and Ross Burkhart, academics writing about Canada-U.S. border communities, stress the importance of stories in understanding the nature of the borderlands and the effects that borders have on individuals' perceptions of and experiences with borders and border crossings. The questions these two scholars raise about whether people view borders as bridges or barriers and their findings regarding shared values and issues of sameness push us to consider the strong influence that borders have on all of us. All four of these readings explore the effects of geographical borders on those who live so close to them. These writers raise critical questions regarding the personal, social, political, and cultural aspects of borders and borderlands.

Anzaldúa, Cantú, and Alm and Burkhart suggest that geographical borders put in place conceptual and cultural boundaries as well, and the article by Heewon Chang and Bill Moyers's interview with Sherman Alexie extend this idea. Both of these readings direct us to think more critically about how conceptual borders often parallel "real" ones. Specifically, Chang, in "Re-examining the Rhetoric of the 'Cultural Border,' " questions the effectiveness of retaining the territorial and geographical aspects embedded in the term *border* when examining cultural and multicultural identities. Whereas Chang warns us about using the phrase *cultural borders* uncritically, Alexie seems well aware of the term's implications and offers keen insights into a space outside such borders. As he describes the space of the "in between," he also talks about bordered spaces such as Indian reservations, as well as cultural borders. Throughout this interview, Alexie points to a key aspect of understanding the material consequences that borders have on our lives: namely, history.

The final three readings in this chapter are historical. Two directly address the Mason-Dixon Line, and one, the Missouri Compromise of 1820, does so indirectly. As both the article in the *Provincial Freeman*, "Mason and Dixon's Line," and Kate DeVan Filer's "Our Most Famous Border" make clear, eventually this boundary line determined whether a person was free or enslaved. In the Civil War era, the Mason-Dixon Line separated North from South, and its legacy remains.

As you consider each reading, ask yourself what conceptual and cultural borders you encounter, how they affect you, and how you negotiate these borders. Also keep in mind the governing question of this chapter: Why do geographical borders matter? These writers ask you to consider how recognizing the experiences of those living in the borderlands, of those challenging cultural borders, and of those inhabiting the "in between" allows us to explore how borders have defined, do define, and will define us individually and collectively as communities and as a country.

To Live in the Borderlands Means You

Gloria Anzaldúa

Gloria Anzaldúa (1942–2004), poet, writer, feminist, and cultural theorist, grew up on the Texas-Mexico border. She earned an M.A. in English and education from the University of Texas and did doctoral work at the University of California, Santa Cruz, which posthumously awarded her a Ph.D. Teaching formally as a writer-in-residence or visiting professor in colleges and informally as an organizer/facilitator of writing groups for women of color, Anzaldúa focused on the areas of feminism, creative writing, and Chicano/a studies. Among the many books she wrote are *This Bridge Called My Back: Writings by Radical Women of Color* (1981), coedited with Cherríe Moraga, which won the Before Columbus Foundation American Book Award and the American Studies Association Lifetime Achievement Award; and *Borderlands/ La Frontera: The New Mestiza* (1987), named one of the thirty-eight best books of 1987 by the *Library Journal*.

Borderlands/La Frontera, a foundational border studies work, opens critical conversations regarding the lived experiences of people — specifically women — inhabiting borderlands. Consisting of poetry and essays, the book blends the history of the border region with personal narrative and reveals how borders affect individuals and the consequences of these effects. "To Live in the Borderlands Means You," which appeared in *Borderlands/La Frontera*, speaks about crafting an identity in the contested site of the borderlands. As you read, pay close attention to how Anzaldúa situates the personal — the "you" in the poem — in relation to the history of the borderlands.

To live in the Borderlands means you
   are neither *hispana india negra española*°
   ni gabacha, eres mestiza, mulata° half-breed
   caught in the crossfire between camps
   while carrying all five races on your back   5
   not knowing which side to turn to, run from;

To live in the Borderlands means knowing
      that the *india* in you, betrayed for 500 years,
      is no longer speaking to you,

---

hispana india negra española: in Spanish, literally "Hispanic Indian black Spanish."
ni gabacha, eres mestiza, mulata: "nor a white woman, you are mixed-race, mulatto."

that *mexicanas* call you *rajetas,*°   10
that denying the Anglo inside you
is as bad as having denied the Indian or Black;

Cuando vives en la frontera°
    people walk through you, the wind steals your voice,
    you're a *burra, buey,*° scapegoat,   15
    forerunner of a new race,
    half and half—both woman and man, neither—
    a new gender;

To live in the Borderlands means to
    put *chile* in the borscht°   20
    eat whole wheat *tortillas,*
    speak Tex-Mex with a Brooklyn accent;
    be stopped by *la migra*° at the border checkpoints;

Living in the Borderlands means you fight hard to
    resist the gold elixir beckoning from the bottle,   25
    the pull of the gun barrel,
    the rope crushing the hollow of your throat;

In the Borderlands
    you are the battleground
    where enemies are kin to each other;   30
    you are at home, a stranger,
    the border disputes have been settled
    the volley of shots have shattered the truce
    you are wounded, lost in action
    dead, fighting back;   35

To live in the Borderlands means
    the mill with the razor white teeth wants to shred off
    your olive-red skin, crush out the kernel, your heart
    pound you pinch you roll you out
    smelling like white bread but dead;   40

---

rajetas: literally, "split," or having betrayed your word.
Cuando vives en la frontera: In Spanish, "When you live in the borderlands."
burra, buey: "donkey, ox."
borscht: a type of soup, often made with beetroots or tomatoes.
la migra: slang term for the immigration police or border patrol.

To survive the Borderlands
  you must live *sin fronteras*°
  be a crossroads.

sin fronteras: "without borders."

Understanding the Text

1. Mark the lines or stanzas in the poem that refer to the history of this border region. In your own words, explain this history.

2. Using specific evidence from the poem, explain the daily life of people living in the borderlands.

3. Anzaldúa frequently switches between English and Spanish in the poem. Underline any words you don't recognize and look up their definitions. What do you think her use of both English and Spanish adds to the poem?

4. Where and how does Anzaldúa bring the historical and personal together in the poem? Consider the places in the poem and poetic elements that personalize the historical. What does this blending achieve?

Reflection and Response

5. In the last stanza, Anzaldúa's speaker tells us what one must do to survive the borderlands. According to the speaker, on what does survival depend? How do you think the speaker arrived at this realization? Support your answer with evidence from the poem. If you live in or have lived in a border region, consider how your personal experiences might further support your answer.

6. How would you characterize the speaker of the poem? Why? What do you think Anzaldúa wishes to convey through this speaker and to whom? What elements in the poem support your answer?

Making Connections

7. Both Anzaldúa and Norma Cantú (p. 58) address border life. How would you describe life in the borderlands? Use both of these writers' descriptions to support your answer. In your response, also consider the following questions: How are Anzaldúa's poetic representations similar to and different from Cantú's descriptions? Where do the two writers' ideas intersect?

8. Anzaldúa's poem represents the violent aspects of the borderlands and emphasizes the physical and emotional effects of the violence experienced by those living and surviving in the region. Using specific examples from the poem and from Ann Marie Leimer's "Cruel Beauty, Precarious Breath: Visualizing the U.S.-Mexico Border" (p. 222), write an essay explaining the types of violence the readings depict and the effects of the violence on the people living in border regions.

Living on the Border: A Wound That Will Not Heal

Norma Cantú

In her fictionalized memoir, *Canícula: Snapshots of a Girlhood en la Frontera* (1995), Norma Cantú tells the story of growing up on the U.S.-Mexico border. Later as a professor, now emerita, at the University of Texas, San Antonio, Cantú taught border studies and Latina/o and Chicana/o literatures, and she is internationally known for her scholarship as a folklorist. Cantú's books include *Dancing across Borders: Danzas y Bailes Mexicanos* (2009), coedited with Olga Nájera-Ramírez and Brenda Romero, and *Chicana Traditions: Continuity and Change* (2002), coedited with Nájera-Ramírez. "Living on the Border: A Wound That Will Not Heal" is Cantú's contribution to the Smithsonian Institution Center for Folklife Programs and Cultural Studies' Borderlands Festival held in 1993.

In this piece, Cantú reveals the dynamism of the borderlands and the complex reality of "living on the border." As you read, keep in mind your own experiences with and knowledge about life in border regions, specifically noting the paradoxes that borders create and their effects on an individual's sense of self.

L iving in the geographical area where the United States and Mexico meet, the truth is always present. It gnaws at one's consciousness like a fear of rabid dogs and coyotes. Beneath every action lies the context of border life. And one must see that undergirding for what it is: the pain and sorrow of daily reminders that here disease runs rampant, here drug crimes take a daily toll. Here infant mortality rates [are] as high [as] or higher than those in third-world countries. Here one cannot drink the water, and here, this land that is our land—and has been our land for generations—is not really ours. But one must also see border life in the context of its joys, its continuous healing, and its celebration of a life and culture that survives against all odds. For to do otherwise condemns us to falling into the vortex of pessimism and anomie° where so many already dwell.

La frontera: the frontier, the edges, the limits, the boundaries, the borders, the cultures, the languages, the foods; but more than that, the unity, and disunity; es lo mismo y no lo es (it's the same and it isn't). Chicana novelist Gloria Anzaldúa speaks of this same terrain, this geography, but her words are hers: they are not mine, not ours, not those of

anomie: social instability caused by a breakdown of standards and values.

58

everyone living along the border. However similar experiences may be, they are not the same, for the frontera is as varied as the geography from Matamoros/Brownsville to Tijuana/San Ysidro, and the people that inhabit this wrinkle in space are as varied as the indigenous peoples that first crossed it centuries ago and the peoples who continue to traverse it today. The Aztec pantheon didn't really rule these northern lands, and the *norteño*° personality, customs, rites, and language are testament to that other native culture, now all but gone, which survives in vestiges sometimes as vague as an image in the sand, on the wall of a cave, or in the lexicon and intonation of a border native's speech.

These lands have always harbored transients, people moving sometimes north, sometimes south. Like birds making their annual trek, migrant workers board up their homes and pack things in their trucks, and off they go with the local priest's blessing. In Laredo, in Eagle Pass, and elsewhere, the matachines° celebrate on May 3, December 12, or another significant date, and as they congregate to dance in honor of the holy cross, the Virgin de Guadalupe, or other local devotions, they remember other times. Spanish and English languages both change along the border: Mariachis are flour tortilla tacos in Laredo and Nuevo Laredo and within a fifty-mile radius of the area; the "calo" (slang) of the "batos locos,"° lowriders, "cholos" or "pachucos"° maintains its literary quality in its excessive use of metaphor all along the stretch yet changes from community to community, just as the names for food and the foods themselves change. Differences have been there since the settlement of the borderlands in the seventeenth and eighteenth centuries, and the changes brought upon the border culture have occurred over the span of more than three hundred years; yet there are other changes as well, ongoing changes that will alter the very fabric of borderlands culture.

The collusion of a myriad of cultures, not just Mexican and U.S., makes the borderlands unique. It is a culture forever in transition, changing visibly from year to year. The population increases in number and in variety, as Koreans, Indians, and other peoples of non-European, non-indigenous, and non-Mestizo origin flow into the region. Because of such an influx, it also changes environmentally, economically, and even in style.

---

norteño: "northerner" in Spanish.
matachines: North American and South American Indian dancers who perform traditional ritual dances, often with swords.
"batos locos": literally "crazy dudes," or street gangs.
"cholos" or "pachucos": slang terms for men or boys of Mexican descent who typically belong to street gangs.

The names of the rivers may be different—Rio Bravo/Rio Grande—but 5 it's the same river whose life-giving waters flow down from Colorado, and whose life-taking waters spill out into the Gulf of Mexico. The same river is a political boundary between two nation-states, but people on both sides of the river retain the customs of the settlers from Spain and from central Mexico along with those from the original inhabitants, which they have inherited and adapted to their particular needs.

Newcomers integrate their ways into the existing culture, but the old ones remain. Intriguing syncretisms° occur. Weddings, for example, integrate traditional "Mexican" customs such as the Arabic arras (marriage coins) and the Native lazo (bonding cord) along with the German-style polka or conjunto music and the brindis (toast). An infant's baptism becomes an occasion for godparents to exchange prayers, an indigenous form encapsulated in a European logic. Conversely, a "quinceañera" (young woman's fifteenth birthday) becomes the modern-day puberty rite of a community. In local dance halls, dancers engage in weekly rites as culturally choreographed as those of the Catholic pilgrimages to santuarios from California to Texas: both customs embody forms and values that endure from times before European contact.

Gloria Anzaldúa says that "The U.S.–Mexican border *es una herida abierta* (is an open wound) where the third world grates against the first and bleeds" (Anzaldúa, 1987). And she continues the metaphor by adding that before the wound heals it "hemorrhages again, the lifeblood of two worlds merging to form a third country, a border culture." First shaped by the signing of the Treaty of Guadalupe Hidalgo that cut the area in two, the wound has continuously bled, as politics, economics, and most environmental pollution exacerbate the laceration. If some healing occurs and a scab forms, a new blow strikes, such was the economic blow struck by the 1982 Mexican devaluation.

Ours is a history of conflict and resolution, of growth and devastation, of battles won and lost in conflicts not always of our making. Often these contradictory outcomes issue from the same set of historical events, like the development of the *maquiladora* industry, which provides jobs even as it renders the river's waters "a veritable cesspool" (*The Laredo Morning Times*, 1993). The inhabitants of the borderlands live in the consequences of this history, in the bleeding that never stops. Those of us who inhabit this land must live with daily human rights violations, contrasting world views, two forms of currency, and different "ways of doing things" that in some cases make life easier but in others nearly intolerable.

syncretisms: the mergings of different forms of belief or practice.

Immigration and emigration have shaped the borderlands. The exodus of Texas border natives to the metropolitan areas of Houston, Dallas, and San Antonio or to California or the Midwest during the 1950s was due in large measure to the depressed local economy. But, as immigration to the north occurred, emigration from Mexico into the area continued. The unemployment rates often hovered around the teens and did not noticeably decrease, in spite of large numbers of families relocating elsewhere, settling out of the migrant labor stream in industrialized areas such as Chicago or going to work in other areas of Texas.

In the 1980s and 1990s, some of these people, now retiring from steel 10 mills in Illinois or factories in Detroit, returned as retirees and settled in the South Texas border communities they moved from forty years ago. For many, like my mother's cousins who moved away and worked for Bethlehem Steel, Christmas and summer vacation were times to visit relatives on the border; these days, it is their children who make the trip down south to visit them.

But in many cases the move was permanent. With little to come back to, families settled permanently in places like California, Wisconsin, and Nebraska. This was the experience of my father's cousin who lives in Omaha and who retired from the upholstering business she worked in for more than thirty years. She speaks of her life away and her reasons for leaving with great pain: There were no jobs to be had, political machines controlled the few jobs there were, the pay was below the national minimum wage, the schools were not good for their kids, and the streets

> "It is only the designation 'border' that is relatively new, and along with the term comes the life one lives in this 'in-between world' that makes us the 'other,' the marginalized."

weren't paved. At least up north, in spite of discrimination, language barriers, alien foods, and cold weather, there were jobs; one could dream of a better life. The border population is in transition once again as it has been for centuries. The healing occurs for but a short time when the newly formed scab is torn by a new element, and the process begins anew.

The border is not homogeneous [~~Some~~] in geography or in culture: there are many borders, resplendent in their heterogeneity. We who live in these realities celebrate our day-to-day life with family "carne asada"° gatherings: with civic events such as George Washington's birthday celebration

---

"**carne asada**": literally "grilled meat," or a form of Mexican cuisine with marinated beef.

with its numerous border icons like the *abrazo* (embracing) ceremony and the international parade; with high school graduations (currently attained by around fifty-five percent of students) and other markers of academic achievement; and with religious events, such as the matachines dance or the annual visit to the city by the image of the Virgen de San Juan de los Lagos in Mexico, venerated on both sides of the border.

The pain and joy of the borderlands—perhaps no greater or lesser than the emotions stirred by living anywhere contradictions abound, cultures clash and meld, and life is lived on an edge—come from a wound that will not heal and yet is forever healing these lands that have always been here: the river of people has flowed for centuries. It is only the designation "border" that is relatively new, and along with the term comes the life one lives in this "in-between world" that makes us the "other," the marginalized. But, from our perspective, the "other" is outside, away from, and alien to, the border. This is our reality, and we, especially we Chicanos and Chicanas, negotiate it in our daily lives, as we contend with being treated as aliens ourselves. This in essence is the greatest wound: the constant reminder of our otherness.

Works Cited

Anzaldúa, Gloria. *Borderlands/La Frontera: The New Mestiza*. San Francisco: Spinster/ Aunt Lute Press, 1987.

"Rio Grande Labeled 'Virtual Cesspool.'" *The Laredo Morning Times*, 21 April 1993.

Understanding the Text

1. The first paragraph provides a context for Cantú's argument and the rhetorical elements that she uses throughout the essay. What, according to Cantú's introduction, is the context of border life? How does the *conceptual* context relate to the rhetorical elements that she employs?

2. What evidence does Cantú provide to support her claim that border experiences "are not the same" (par. 2)? Which do you find the most effective? Why? Did you find any areas where you would have appreciated more details or explanation? Explain.

3. Explain Cantú's central argument in your own words. Specifically, where in the essay does she place her main argument? Why do you think she made this decision?

Reflection and Response

4. In the title and throughout the essay, Cantú evokes Gloria Anzaldúa's "open wound" metaphor, directly quoting Anzaldúa in paragraph 7. Note other places in the essay where Cantú uses this metaphor. Why do you think she does so? As you craft your response, consider how Cantú uses it — note when and in what context. Does she use it in the same way that Anzaldúa

does? Each time Cantú uses the metaphor, what point is she attempting to explain or clarify? Finally, explain how you respond to the metaphor.

5. If you live in, or have traveled to, a borderland, reflect upon your experiences. Your reflection can take the form of a critical dialogue with one or more of Cantú's points or a description of a specific event that represents border life to you. For example, what comes to mind when you think of a border region? Does this differ from Cantú's description? If so, how?

6. Cantú claims that the "collusion of a myriad of cultures, not just Mexican and U.S., makes the borderlands unique" (par. 4). How does this idea fit into the overall logic of her argument? What support does she offer for this claim?

Making Connections

7. What does Cantú's depiction of the borderlands as a space where many cultures collide suggest to you about the nature of borders and the experience of "living on the border," in a larger context beyond the scope of Cantú's essay? To answer this question, read Naomi Shihab Nye's beliefs about poetry's place in bordered spaces and its potential to traverse these spaces (p. 258). Then read Leslie Alm and Ross Burkhart's study on Canada-U.S. border communities (p. 73), noting what it adds to your understanding of the nature of borders and the experience of living in a border region.

8. Cantú ends her essay by linking "otherness" to "the designation 'border,'" arguing that "along with the term comes the life one lives in this 'in-between world' that makes us the 'other,' the marginalized" (par. 13). According to Cantú, what marks this otherness/marginalization for those living in this in-between world? In his interview with Bill Moyers, Sherman Alexie also talks about living "in the in between" and about marginalization (p. 104). Compare Alexie's experiences, perspectives, and assertions with Cantú's. In your comparison, explain the similarities and differences between the two writers. Both Cantú and Alexie refer to historical events and circumstances that created these borders/borderlands and that now affect their lives and the lives of those living on and within physical and cultural borders. To write a fully developed comparison of Cantú's and Alexie's views, do some further research into this historical context.

The Country Just over the Fence

Paul Theroux

Paul Theroux, an award-winning travel writer, novelist, short story writer, and journalist, is also a Fellow of the Royal Society of Literature and the Royal Geographic Society in Britain. His many awards include an American Academy and Institute of Arts and Letters Award for literature and the Thomas Cook Travel Book Award for his book *Riding the Iron Rooster* (1988). Among his many travel books, his best known is his first, *The Great Railway Bazaar* (1975), in which he writes about crossing the borders of Iran, Afghanistan, India, Burma, Vietnam, China, Japan, and the Soviet Union. Theroux has written about many other border crossings since 1975. His most recent travel book is *The Last Train to Zona Verde* (2013), and his latest short story collection is *Mr. Bones* (2014).

Theroux wrote "The Country Just over the Fence" for the travel section of the *New York Times* in 2012. As you read his description of his stay in Nogales, Mexico, think about Theroux's discoveries and the contradictory aspects of the city that emerge in this piece.

A simple painted sign on a wooden board—"To Mexico"—was propped near the door in the fence, but it was the fence itself that fascinated me. Some masterpieces are unintentional, the result of a freakish accident or an explosive act of sheer weirdness, and the fence that divides Nogales, Arizona, from Nogales, Mexico, is one of them.

In a lifetime of crossing borders I find this pitiless fence the oddest frontier I have ever seen—more formal than the Berlin Wall, more brutal than the Great Wall of China, yet in its way just as much an example of the same *folie de grandeur.*° Built just six months ago, this towering, seemingly endless row of vertical steel beams is so amazing in its conceit you either want to see more of it, or else run in the opposite direction—just the sort of conflicting emotions many people feel when confronted with a peculiar piece of art.

You can, of course, also go through it, which is what I wanted to do. And there was the entry way, just past J. C. Penney and Kory's clothing shop—a door in the wall at the end of hot, sunlit Morley Avenue.

After leaving my car at a secure parking lot ($4 a day), I showed my passport to the United States border guard, who asked about my plans. Business?

folie de grandeur: delusion of grandeur.

"Just curiosity," I said. When he made a disapproving squint, I added, 5
"Don't you go over now and then?"

"Never been there," he said.

"It's 10 feet away!"

"I'm staying here," he said, his squint now suggesting that I should be
doing the same.

I pushed the turnstile and stepped through the narrow door—no
line, no other formalities—into the state of Sonora, Mexico, where I was
instantly, unmistakably in a foreign land. The roads were bumpier, the
buildings vaguely distressed; I was breathing in the mingled aromas of
bakeries, taco stands and risen dust.

Glancing back a moment later, I could not see Arizona anymore, only 10
the foreground of Mexico—small children kicking a ball, men in sombreros conferring under a striped awning, steaming food carts.

I treasure border crossings, and the best of them are the ones where
I've had to walk from one country to another, savoring the equality of
being a pedestrian, stepping over the theoretical line that is shown on
maps, from Cambodia into Vietnam, from Pakistan into India, from Turkey into the Republic of Georgia. Usually a frontier is a river—the Me-
kong, the Rio Grande, the Zambezi; or a mountain range—the Pyrenees,
the Rwenzoris. It can also be a sudden alteration in topography, a bewil-
dering landscape transformation—hilly Vermont flattening into Que-
bec. But just as often a border is a political expedient—irrational yet un-
remarkable—creating a seamless no man's land, just a width of earth,
bounded by fences.

I am nattering on about this border fence, partly because it is a visual
marvel, something like a stockade,° and also because, as the guard demonstrated, it calls for a decision. Do you go through, or stay home? It
used to be a more casual proposition. Nogalans remember when it was a
modest enclosure known as *la linea*, the line, when the main street between the two towns was more or less contiguous.

"We had a parade every spring," Nicolas Demetrio Kyriakis told me.
Nicolas, from an entrepreneurial family of Greek immigrants to Mexico,
is a *regidor*, a Nogales town counselor and one of the advisors to Nogales's
mayor. "Floats went down the street and into Nogales, Arizona. A coro-
nation was held on a platform on *la linea*, and the Fiesta de Mayo Queen
was crowned. Both towns celebrated."

That was 30 years ago. Back then Nogales, Mexico, was still a destination for servicemen from big, busy Fort Huachuca, a United States Army
post about 25 miles as the crow flies to the northeast. Visitors from

---

stockade: a defensive barrier made of strong vertical wooden posts.

Tucson and beyond would pop over for a break from the routine, an opportunity to buy clay pots, sombreros, drink a world-class margarita, and visit a taqueria or sample local food. In the 1940s, cowboy films were made in the area. Hollywood actors crossed the border to eat and raise mild hell in La Caverna, a well-known club run by Nicolas's cousins.

Such was the bond of the two border towns that when the old elegant 15 Hotel Olivia on the Mexican side caught fire in the 1960s, and the situation became desperate, water hoses were tossed over the fence by the fire brigade in Arizona to help the local *bomberos* put it out, an act of neighborliness that is still fondly remembered by the Nogalans.

But everyone I spoke to agreed that conditions have changed. They said that when soldiers from Huachuca stopped visiting after 9/11 and guards started asking to see passports, the influx of visitors slowed to a trickle. And there was another theme: since the emphasis across America was on scrutinizing aliens, why would anyone wish to become an alien oneself? The repeated news stories of cartels taking over didn't help; cross the Mexican border and risk dying like a dog.

"After the bombing of the World Trade Center, things went down," Juan Cordero, the director of the Department of Economic Development in this part of Sonora, told me. "But it was massage parlors and bars on

Hundreds of cars wait to cross in the opposite direction, from Mexico into the United States, at the border crossing in Nogales, Arizona.
John Moore/Getty Images

Canal Street, and curio shops downtown, an old-fashioned business model. Sure, we still had lots of American factories in our industrial area—thousands of people are employed there—but we have just a few tourists."

And yet, here I was, a tourist, savoring the satisfaction of having eased myself into another country to enjoy the difference, with the tourist's presumption that I deserved a good time. And I had the instant gringo's assurance that my country, and my car, were just behind the tall fence at the *frontera*.

So what can you do with a couple of days in Nogales? Take advantage of its nearness, first of all. Buy cowboy boots, or pots, or folk art. I came away with a hand-carved set of dominoes, some silver coins and cleaner, whiter teeth.

On my first day I had a margarita at the Salon Regis. I asked the bar- 20 tender about events in town. He thought a moment, then said, "Super Bowl on Sunday."

Dinner at La Roca, which is just minutes from the fence, was pleasurable for my being in the hands of the sort of knowledgeable dark-suited old waiters that have disappeared from most of the world's restaurants. Many have worked at La Roca since it opened (its 40th anniversary was celebrated this year). These men were the stalwarts at the restaurant at my hotel too, the Hotel Fray Marcos. At La Roca I had tortilla soup and as an entrée a Mexican mélange of fresh shrimp from Guaymas on the Sonoran coast. Elsewhere in town, even the smaller places such as Leos or Zapatas offered plates of dried shredded beef known as *mochomos* and delicious tacos.

I found the Nogalans courtly and easy to meet, grateful to have a visitor to the point where one demonstration of neighborliness was an offer of a swig of *bacanora*, a drink made from agave and Sonora's gift to the world of drinkable rocket fuel—stronger than tequila.

It is obvious from the empty streets of downtown Nogales that very few visitors stay the night, but I found that overnighting simplified my experience of the place. The Hotel Fray Marcos has mixed reviews but I found it excellent (my suite went for around $80). It was also conveniently near the office of Dr. Jose Saturno, who on successive days worked on my teeth—the full *limpieza* ($54) *y blanquiamento*° ($250).

There have always been inexpensive dentists in Nogales, but the combination of rising health costs in the United States (and the fact that many retiree health plans don't include dental) along with the availability of cheap real estate in Nogales has created a dentistry boom here, which is expanding to include spa and other services as well.

***limpieza y blanquiamento*:** tooth cleaning and whitening.

At Laser Tech over on Obregon Street, Dr. Francisco Vazquez enlarged   25
his dental practice a year ago to include a dermatology unit, and his
wife (and mother of three), Martha Gonzales, opened a spa with treat-
ments that included not only massage and steam baths but also "ancient rituals" inspired by the Aztecs, and for good measure hired
Dr. Angel Minjares, whose specialties are theology and psychology, for
"assessments."

Their businesses are among the approximately 60 dental "wellness"
practices here, mainly concentrated in a three-block area all within easy
walking distance from the border gate. Most of the patients are American
retirees nipping over for the day from Tucson or nearby Green Valley.

Gerd Roehrig, an older Tucson resident originally from Germany, was
seeing Dr. Ernesto Quiroga about an implant. What would have cost him
$4,500 in his hometown of Tucson, he said, was about a third of that in
Nogales. Creating a further enticement, Dr. Quiroga recently invested
$150,000 in a 3-D scanning machine for CAT scans.

"I guess Canal Street could now be called Root Canal Street," I said to
Juan Cordero, after my treatment.

He sighed. "People are worried," he said. "They think Nogales is dangerous. You know the expression *poner salsa a los tacos?*"

Slather sauce on the tacos—exaggerate.   30

To try to get a handle on just how dangerous my visit was, I asked to
meet the Secretary for Public Safety in Sonora and was introduced to
Ernesto Munro Palacio, a 6-foot-3 businessman and former pitcher for
the Monterrey Sultans, who, since 2009, has been responsible for security in the state.

"Prior to [2009] there was very little investment in security," he said.
"But within the past two years Sonora had invested $100 million in heli-
copters, armored cars and surveillance planes, to find the landing strips
of organized crime and the marijuana farms."

Murders are a problem all over Mexico, and they have devastated
cities like Ciudad Juárez, which is a cartel battleground. But Secretary
Munro said that in Nogales the murder rate has declined from 210 in
2010 to 83 in 2011 and that they are almost exclusively drug related.

"Ask your people if they know the name of one American who's been
killed in Sonora," he said. "No tourist has ever been killed in Nogales."

The State Department said that in the two years from Jan. 1, 2010, to   35
Dec. 31, 2011, there were 21 reported homicides of American citizens in
Nogales and advises that visitors to Sonora travel on main roads and only
during daylight hours. Meanwhile, the Arizona governor, Jan Brewer,
who earlier this month said that she should be an "ambassador for Sonora," enthusiastically promotes tourism in the area. I heard even more

robust testimonials about Sonora, and Nogales in particular, from the Americans I met seeking dental care, who remarked on the hospitality of the city.

The Bianchis, a retired couple from Tucson I met in a waiting room, were content. "We come here all the time," Mr. Bianchi said. "I got bridgework. And, hey, people are nice."

Nogales is a border town trying to save itself, and I think succeeding. I was struck, walking the city, by the distinct air of foreignness mingled with a pleasing ordinariness—children at play on school playgrounds, shoppers, churchgoers—the pleasures and routines of Mexico. The visible absence of travelers gives the city a greater feel of difference, as do the brightly painted houses that dot hillsides, the result of a scheme by the Nogales mayor, José Ángel Hernández Barajas, who created an Urban Image Department, which provides free paint for any who wish to spruce up their home. He has also created schools and sports programs, as well as teams of street cleaners.

> "The fence, which I discovered is less than three miles long, had hidden all of this — the downtown, the factories, the restaurants, the residential subdivisions, the mall, the migrants, sad stories, happy stories."

The streets of Nogales are as tidy as any on the American side, and full of surprises. On my way to see the boomtown that lies beyond downtown and the dental clinics, I passed a two-story sculpture of a muscular naked youth spearing a winged reptilian figure sprawled at his feet. Officially known as *The Defeat of Ignorance* (*La Derrota de la Ignorancia*), the statue (designed by the Spanish sculptor Alfredo Just, in the late 1960s) is fondly referred to by Nogalans as *mono bichi*—"the naked guy" in a local phrase that is partly Yaqui. (Nogalans scatter their speech with Yaqui words that are incomprehensible elsewhere, like *buki* for child and *yori blanco* for white man.)

I was to discover that the neighborhoods just across the fence are not representative of the town at large, which is a lesson in how to know another country: stay longer, travel deeper, overcome timidity. Tourists usually stick close to the fence, which accounts for the density of curio shops, and now the density of dental practices. But that downtown of Nogales is misleading.

Driving a few miles south with Juan Cordero I saw how Nogales 40 sprawled, with newly built and modern subdivisions near more modest ones, all comprising Nuevo Nogales. "This is the main economic engine driving Nogales," Juan said. The majority of the 32,000 people employed in Nogales work in the Industrial Area in factories making cellphone components, semiconductors, air ducts for jumbo jets. Most of the names are familiar—Otis Elevator, Black & Decker, Chamberlain garage door openers, Rain Bird Sprinklers, General Electric, Watts Water Technologies, Flextronics, B/E Aerospace. Some companies like Kimberly-Clark and Motorola have been here since the late 1960s. The lives and working conditions of such employees are well described in William T. Vollmann's *Imperial*, an exhaustive account of an area that encompasses California and Mexico, which in its complexity and conflict resembles the Nogales border.

These are skilled workers. Those without education or manufacturing skills, the so-called *campesinos*, look elsewhere for work, and often cross the border to find it. Many who end up in the United States without papers are caught, jailed for a period, and bused to the border. This, too, is a revelation from the other side of the high fence.

Nogales is where they are dumped. Peg Bowden, a retired nurse, brought me to El Comedor, a shelter run by American Jesuits near the Mariposa gate just about a mile west of downtown Nogales. Ms. Bowden told me she was so shocked by the savage attack on Gabrielle Giffords in Tucson in January 2011 that she decided to do something humane: "I needed to connect with something positive." She joined a group of Samaritans—"a bunch of renegade senior citizens whose mission is to prevent deaths in the desert," and she volunteered at El Comedor, working a few days a week, crossing the border from Arizona.

As a trained nurse she is useful, treating bullet wounds and severe hypothermia and the effects of starvation and exposure—common among border crossers. "Last week we had a girl who'd been lost in the desert for three days. She was 14."

It was another day in Nogales, another revelation for me, and by far the most melancholy. In El Comedor, 160 lost souls, most of them adults, and four small children, were seated on benches, at communal tables, eating breakfast in an open-sided shelter at the side of the road.

Some had been longtime residents in the United States—Alejandro, a 45 restaurant worker in North Carolina for 13 years, Arnulfo a carpenter for 11.

"I spent 20 years in Napa picking strawberries," Maria, an older woman in a long black dress, told me. "My husband and children are there. I came to Mexico for my father's funeral." She was wearing her funeral dress. She couldn't return to the United States, nor did she have a home in Mexico anymore.

They were soft-spoken, humbled and hopeless. A woman in her 20s, Rosalba, had spent four days in the desert. She had blistered feet, a deep wound from a cactus thorn and a severe infection. Some had been caught making their first crossing. Others had been sent home after years in the United States.

The saddest case to me was a woman from Oaxaca. Abandoned, with no money, no prospects and no hope of making a living in Oaxaca, she left her three children in the care of her mother and crossed the border with four other women, in the hope of finding work. Somehow separated from the other women, she was found in the desert.

"It's like 'Sophie's Choice,'"° Peg Bowden said.

She accepted her fate, but I will never forget the sight of her alone at   50 the table, a plate of food before her, eyes tightly shut, hands together uplifted in prayer.

I was just a tourist. The fence, which I discovered is less than three miles long, had hidden all of this—the downtown, the factories, the restaurants, the residential subdivisions, the mall, the migrants, sad stories, happy stories.

It's there for anyone to discover, and so simple. It was as illuminating to me as any foreign travel I have taken anywhere in the world. In some ways, being so near home and taking less effort, it seemed odder, freighted with greater significance, this wider world at the end of Morley Avenue, just behind the fence.

"Sophie's Choice": a phrase referring to a difficult choice between two bad options, from the novel and film of the same name.

Understanding the Text

1. How does Theroux feel about the act of crossing borders, in general, and about this specific border between Nogales, Arizona, and Nogales, Mexico? Why is this perspective significant to his overall message?

2. Theroux provides a look back to "when the main street between the two towns was more or less contiguous" (par. 12). Explain how things at this border crossing changed. When and why did these changes occur? What is Theroux's purpose in including this backward glance?

3. What advice does Theroux give about how to know another country? Why do you think he includes this advice?

Reflection and Response

4. Theroux gives us insights into his assumptions about being a tourist (par. 18). Do a textual analysis of this passage by fully explaining his meaning. Look carefully at Theroux's word choice in this paragraph. Do certain words suggest something more in relation to this particular border and border town? If so, identify those words, and explain their connotative meanings.

5. As Theroux narrates his visit to Nogales, Mexico, he writes about the city "being full of surprises" but also "misleading" him and about his having "another revelation." What does he find surprising or misleading? What kinds of revelations does he describe? When you consider this aspect of Theroux's article, what sense of Nogales do you get? How would you characterize the town? Why?

6. Explain the connection between tourism and border crossings and how that connection might help us understand the experience of living in the borderlands. As you reflect on this issue, consider some of the following ideas and questions: Theroux writes that he has "a lifetime of crossing borders" (par. 2). When you think of "border crossers," what images come to mind? Does Theroux's position as a tourist complicate your understanding of the concept of a border crosser? Explain why or why not. If you have crossed a border and spent time as a tourist in a border town, use your own experiences to help you explain the connection between tourism and border crossings.

Making Connections

7. In "The Country Just over the Fence," Theroux is not merely describing his visit to Nogales, Mexico. Think about his larger purpose and what the article tells us about border regions, border crossings, and borders themselves. Then read Leslie Alm and Ross Burkhart's "Canada-U.S. Border Communities: What the People Have to Say" (p. 73). How do the two readings "speak" to each other? What passages could you use from Alm and Burkhart's article to provide a wider context for Theroux's ideas? How have these two readings influenced your understanding of individuals' experiences in border communities?

8. Both Theroux and Reed Karaim, in "Building Walls" (p. 32), discuss the U.S.-Mexico border fence. What connections do you see between these two readings? Explain your position regarding how the border fence *functions* and what it *symbolizes*. Use examples from Theroux's and Karaim's work to support your position. It may be helpful to use additional readings and research in your response.

9. If you have ever traveled to a border town, write a descriptive travel piece similar to Theroux's. If you have not done so, interview someone who has and describe his or her experiences. Before you write, revisit "The Country Just over the Fence," and note Theroux's use of specific details, personal narrative, historical context, and evidence. Consider the controlling ideas that he wishes to convey not only about Nogales but also about border towns in general. To write an effective piece, you may have to do some additional research on the border politics of the region as well as draw on your knowledge about the nature of borders and borderlands gleaned from other readings in this book.

Canada-U.S. Border Communities: What the People Have to Say

Leslie R. Alm and Ross E. Burkhart

Leslie Alm, a professor of political science, teaches in the Department of Public Policy and Administration at Boise State University. He researches environmental policy, specifically the science-policy linkage, the United States–Canada relationship, and borderland issues. Ross Burkhart, a political scientist at Boise State University, teaches in the Department of Political Science. He studies the explanatory factors of cross-national democratization patterns. Burkhart also researches environmental policy, political culture, and Canada-U.S. borderlands.

In "Canada-U.S. Border Communities: What the People Have to Say," which appeared in the *American Review of Canadian Studies* (2012), Alm and Burkhart explore what living in the borderlands means to the people inhabiting that space. As the title makes clear, the authors derive their analysis from the stories of men and women living in borderland communities. These two scholars ground their methodology in accepted social science practices of obtaining empirical evidence from discourse narratives. As you read, you will see that to understand borders, we need to listen to the stories of those who experience borders daily.

The search for understanding borderlands is often portrayed within the fabric of social and cultural discourses. As Prokkola submits, "borders are not located merely in the context of actual physical border-lines, but also in wider social and cultural processes and institutions" (2009, 22). In this regard, Brunet-Jailly (2005)—at the universal level—and Konrad and Nicol (2008, 2011)—at the Canada–United States boundary—have each made major inroads toward advancing and defining a broad-based borderlands model that includes a cross-border cultural component. Brunet-Jailly observes that local culture is an important analytical lens and that "although international borders divide stateless nations, borderland communities may remain unified by culture" (2005, 638). Konrad and Nicol (2008), based on an analysis of Brunet-Jailly's work, go so far as calling for a rearticulation of local culture into the discussion of a borderlands theory and, in fact, begin one of their latest research projects by stating that it is border culture "that ultimately sustains linkages, assures continuity and maintains prosperity between bounded states" (Konrad and Nicol, 2011, 70). They go on to expand on Brunet-Jailly's general theory of borders, emphasizing that within the Canada–United States borderlands, culture needs to be "re-imagined as a heterogeneous rather than a homogeneous concept," thereby incorporating diverse perspectives (Konrad and Nicol, 2011, 82).

More and more, social scientists are recognizing the cultural dimension of borderlands studies by using stories from "ordinary people" as a discourse technique for framing the study of particular borderlands regions (Megoran, 2006; Rumford, 2008). Simply put, "borders, and border subjects' experiences of them, are increasingly seen as sets of interlinked processes or formations through which traces are sedimented in border narratives and within a mental and physical landscape" (Schimanski and Wolfe, 2010, 42). It is within this context that Konrad and Everitt (2011) argue that a focus on socially constructed identities and cross-border culture is integral to establishing a general theory of borderlands. Broadly speaking, social scientists are increasingly basing their descriptive analysis upon empirical evidence culled from border narratives of people living in the selected regions. Hence, for our study we let the people talk, telling us how they view their lives in relation to the other side of the border. We use the cultural construct of discourse narratives as a method for evaluating the meaning of borders and borderlands, centering our analysis on the perceptions of people who make their homes in borderlands communities.

Specifically, we let the people of the Lake Superior borderlands region tell us how they feel about the border, about their relationship with their cross-border neighbors, and whether they believe there exists a special relationship that transcends the border. The Lake Superior borderlands region is defined by the two geographic corridors connecting Canada and the United States as bounded by Lake Superior: Sault Ste. Marie, Ontario/Sault Ste. Marie, Michigan (often referred to as the "Twin Saults") and Thunder Bay, Ontario/Duluth, Minnesota. We chose the Lake Superior region to study for one very simple reason: to date, it has received very little attention in the literature. While there is a rich and descriptive portrayal of many of the Canada-U.S. border regions (Border Policy Research Institute, 2010; Robertson, 2011), the regions bounded by Lake Superior have been largely ignored. In addition, these two border regions compare nicely with respect to the defining concept of distance, which is said by some to be irrelevant in today's globalizing world (Rumford, 2008). Two of the cross-border communities (Thunder Bay/Duluth) are separated by a great distance, while the other two (Twin Saults) are separated by a negligible distance. Yet, there is substantial evidence that the residents in both of these communities consider themselves to be living in a borderlands region.

It is our intention to use narrative interviews to analyze the Lake Superior borderlands region (as defined above) such that we can evaluate the usefulness of this discourse technique as it applies to borderlands theory-building. In addition, we use the perceptions of borderlands people to describe cross-border cultural, political, and social relationships. With this in mind, the next two sections delineate our framework of analysis and establish a description of the specific borderlands perspective that we use for exploring the Lake Superior region.

Stories: A Framework of Discourse Analysis

The move toward a general borderlands theory, as discussed above, is   5
cast in the idea that borderlands scholars must look beyond broader social processes by exploring the borders' contextual features. Used in such a manner, a narratives discourse serves as a way to maximize understanding of borderlands culture (Newman and Paasi, 1998; Paasi and Prokkola, 2008).

Prokkola (2009) recognizes, as Newman suggests, that it is not abstract sociological constructs that shed light on the notion of borderlands but the experiences of people as they go about their daily lives; that it is only through people's narratives that we can make sense of the border experience and develop a true understanding of borderlands. In short, "By listening to people's narratives it is possible to gain an understanding of the meaning of borders in the lives and identities of people" (Prokkola, 2009, 22). More importantly, Prokkola's work provides strong empirical evidence illustrating the power of narratives to explain borderland relationships. Other scholars continue to build on the theoretical constructs of stories and narratives. Such narratives provide structure to the critique of border relations and sit at the center of our exploration of the Lake Superior region.

A Borderlands Perspective

Before we touch on the narratives, however, it is essential to characterize the Canada–United States borderlands relationship as it appears today. Gibbins (2005)—who has conducted several extensive analyses of Canada-US borderlands—does just that. In essence, Gibbins makes the argument for two distinct beliefs about the Canada-U.S. borderlands (as described above). First, Canadian-American borderlands are neither culturally identifiable nor distinctive. Second, if one wants to make such a comparison, then only Canada can be described as a borderlands society; that American ideals "are so extensively woven into Canadian life that the national boundary all but evaporates. As a consequence, Canadian-American comparisons, slights both real and imagined, and undercurrents of anti-Americanism play prominent roles in the Canadian political culture and broader social fabric" (Gibbins, 2005, 153).

A contrasting way to look at Canada-U.S. borderlands is through the analytical description provided by Papademetriou and Meyers (2001). They argue that there is a remarkable degree of community-based cross-border cooperation between Canada and the United States on issues such as public health, access to education, environmental protection, joint regional planning, and law enforcement. Papademetriou and Meyers (2001) also speak of the uniqueness of border communities along the U.S.-Canada border, asserting that this uniqueness is a result of a variety of factors: history of the regions, economics of the border communities, degree of economic and social integration, and the size and composition of the local population—shaped by the physical/geographic settings, the nature of the border itself (land, water, mountain), whether the border crossings are publicly or privately owned, the types of people and goods crossing the border, and even the personalities of federal agents stationed at the border.

Both the Gibbins and the Papademetriou and Meyers perspectives on the Canada-U.S. borderlands relationship have merit as expressions of general ways that residents of borderlands view their counterparts on the other side of the border. Whether one tends to lean toward either one of these diverging views, the fact remains that the Canada–United States border, with its differing regional characteristics, offers a unique opportunity to explore cross-border community relationships. On the whole, as our investigative process plays out, readers will see that our findings suggest that a special relationship does indeed exist between the people who inhabit what we designate as the Lake Superior borderlands.

The Lake Superior Borderlands: Thunder Bay/Duluth and the Twin Saults

There is no shortage of descriptions setting out the characteristics of the 10 regions bounded by Lake Superior. The following two quotations were written specifically about Duluth, Minnesota:

For 10,000 years, people have been drawn to the Northland by its natural beauty and bounty. From the forests to the waters, from the large and small game to the rice, trees, fish and minerals, bounty has brought us up to this place, even as struggles for that wealth have at times divided us. . . . (Duluth News-Tribune, *2000, 1*)

[One] brags about [Duluth's] natural setting: its beauty, created by both man and God; and its stimulating climate. . . . It is located at the head of the largest body of fresh water in the world, Lake Superior. . . . It is one of the natural flyways of the hawk, bringing naturalists long distances to watch their annual migration. . . . And Lake Superior is always there at the foot of the hills. . . . Duluth is a city of seasons, and anyone who has been exposed to the four natural divisions of the year will always miss them if he moves to a more uniform climate. (Weygant, 1976, 3)

Yet, these descriptions easily apply to the entire region that surrounds Lake Superior, including the Duluth/Thunder Bay and the Twin Saults borderlands regions. Moreover, when people talk about the power and influence of geology and geography that defines place, including such things as immense and valuable forests and wilderness areas, the ideal location for shipping timber, grain, and iron ore, as well as the idea that people live here for the quality of life, they could be talking about any of the communities surrounding Lake Superior (Aubut and Norton, 2001; Axelson, 2011; Dickinson, 1981). And it all begins with the fact that Lake Superior contains 10 percent of the earth's surface fresh water and more than half of all the water in the Great Lakes combined, anchoring "a basin 89 percent forest covered and rich in [natural] resources" (Berg and LeMay, 2010). For all practical purposes, Lake Superior defines the borderlands region it encompasses and in one way or another, affects all that it touches.

While the economies of these borderlands regions are certainly tied to shipping, all four communities have morphed into their respective regional cultural centers as well as regional medical, educational and governmental centers (Berg and LeMay, 2010; Sandvik, 1983). Further, each of these communities represents some form of isolation, being geographically far from other urban centers and/or generally possessing the perception that they are ignored by their respective state or provincial, as well as national, governmental institutions (Mount, Abbott, and Mulloy, 1995).

Methods and Findings: The People and What They Have to Say

Now that we have a general overview of the Lake Superior borderlands region, it is time to hear what the people of the Lake Superior borderlands have to say about the border and their relationship to the people and communities just across the border. From December 2010 through December 2011, we conducted 262 interviews with people in all four communities (Duluth = 65; Thunder Bay = 60; Sault Ste. Marie, ON = 72; Sault Ste. Marie, M1 = 65). The vast majority of the interviews (91 percent) were conducted in person. All other interviews were conducted via phone and/or email.

The interviews consisted of asking open-ended questions, with the following questions serving as the focus of this particular study: (1) How many years have you had experience with and/or use of the border? When was the last time you crossed the border? Why did you cross? (2) Is there a special relationship between the two border communities? Why is it special? (3) Do you view the border as a bridge or a barrier? Explain why. (4) Did 9/11 change the border relationship? If so, how? (5) On a daily basis, do you follow what is happening on the other side of the border? and (6) Does what happens on the other side of the border affect your daily life?

Thunder Bay/Duluth Borderlands Region

Table 2.1 summarizes the interview results along the six broad interview   15
questions asked. Overall, a much higher percentage of Canadians (than Americans) have extensive experience crossing the border. On all other questions, Canadians and Americans had general agreement. A vast majority of both Canadians and Americans do not see a special relationship between Thunder Bay and Duluth, view the border more as a bridge than a barrier, comment on the substantial changes in crossing the border since 9/11, and do not follow or care what happens immediately across the border.

The tabulated results suggest that the interconnectedness between the cross-border communities of Duluth and Thunder Bay appears weak at best. And the content of the interviews themselves substantiates this view. First and foremost, if there is any type of flow between these two communities, it generally appears to move from Canada to the United States. Despite the fact that Duluth and Thunder Bay are officially declared Sister Cities (and many people on both sides of the border note this), the majority of those interviewed from Duluth and Thunder Bay see no special relationship between the communities.

But most view the closeness of the Duluth/Thunder Bay relationship with skepticism, as noted by the following observation.

I do not think there is a special relationship between Duluth and Thunder Bay. Even when Canadians come down here they tend to stay to themselves, at least when I see them. I can tell Canadians right away; not only the way they talk and dress but just that they are not from here. I think Thunder Bay is much more isolated and coming here is like coming to the big city for them. We certainly are different peoples. (Airport Employee, Duluth)

Table 2.1 **Percent Answering Questions as Listed**

		Thunder Bay	Duluth
Do you have extensive experience with the border?	Yes	93.3	44.6
	No	6.7	55.4
	(n)	(60)	(65)
Is the border relationship special?	Yes	32.1	21.5
	No	67.9	78.5
	(n)	(53)	(65)
Do you view the border as a bridge or barrier?	Bridge	81.1	73.3
	Barrier	18.9	26.7
	(n)	(53)	(60)
Do you see changes at the border since 9/11?	Yes	85.5	70.5
	No	15.5	29.5
	(n)	(55)	(61)
Do you follow what happens on the other side of the border?	Yes	16.9	13.8
	No	83.1	86.2
	(n)	(60)	(65)
Does what happens on the other side of the border affect your daily life?	Yes	5.0	12.3
	No	95.0	87.7
	(n)	(60)	(65)

Note: The data delineated in this table is solely the product of the authors' interviews.

This perception is also shared by many in Thunder Bay.

No, I do not see a connection between Thunder Bay and Duluth; not between governments, not between cities, not anything. Not universities either. I would say the two communities are pretty much separate. (Bookstore Clerk, Thunder Bay)

In general people from Duluth do not have much interest in Thunder Bay; nor do they regularly travel there. Minnesotans go north but stop somewhere along the North Shore of Lake Superior, never quite making it to the border.

I have not crossed the border since 1998 and I personally know very few people from Duluth that go to Thunder Bay or who have gone to Thunder Bay. And I do not follow anything that happens in Thunder Bay. I would guess that people from Thunder Bay follow what is happening in Duluth more than we follow them. Thunder Bay people come to Duluth based on the exchange rate and traditionally it is for shopping. Duluth is a bigger place. I think people from Canada, in general, keep track of what happens in the United States much more than the other way around and I would say that is true for Duluth and Thunder Bay too. (Employee, Duluth Public Library)

You see Ontario license plates all over the place in Duluth. People from Thunder Bay come to Duluth to shop. There is a one-way focus that way, Thunder Bay to Duluth. It does not go the other way. So many people from Duluth go to the North Shore but then they stop. They do not cross the border. We know Thunder Bay is there, that it is the closest Canadian city. But why go to Thunder Bay when everything you want is here in Duluth? (Administrator, University of Minnesota–Duluth)

The idea, as expressed by the people of Duluth, that the relationship 20 between Thunder Bay and Duluth is focused in one direction is also supported by those we interviewed in Thunder Bay. From their perspective, people from Thunder Bay regularly travel to Duluth, mostly for shopping but also for youth sporting events or simply to get away to a different locale.

The relationship between Thunder Bay and Duluth is pretty one-sided, if there is a sister relationship at all. Duluth benefits hugely because people from Thunder Bay spend so much money down there. But it is a one-way relationship. People from Thunder Bay spend lots of money in Duluth but people from Duluth never come to Thunder Bay, to spend money or for anything else. (Employee, Public Library, Thunder Bay)

People from Thunder Bay go to Duluth all the time but people from Duluth do not come up here. Thunder Bay is not a destination for them. In Duluth you see Canadians all the time. It is easy to observe. In Thunder Bay you'd never know if Americans were here or not. You don't notice it. It's just that obvious that you see Canadians in Duluth but you don't see people from Duluth here. In one city, Duluth, you notice. In the other city, Thunder Bay, you do not. You just do not see Duluth people here in Thunder Bay. (Accountant, Thunder Bay)

Even though the travel across the border, for the most part, flows in a southerly direction, the perception of the border as a bridge (rather than a barrier) is shared by both Canadians and Americans. Along this line of thought, for many in Thunder Bay and Duluth, crossing the border is considered easy, a routine matter.

The border is not a barrier for those of us who travel regularly. We have passports and it's no big deal to cross the border. But if you don't travel and don't have a passport, then it could be a barrier. Then you may want to cross but you don't have a passport so you can't go. (Member, Duluth Recreation Club)

There is no trouble crossing the border at all. In fact, for some of us, the border guards get to know who you are, and with a bus of young hockey players, they come on the bus but just wave us through. My Mom and Dad go across the border every week, to Portage to gamble, and they know the border guards and the border guards know them by name and It is "Hey, how you doing?" And they are on their way. They are actually on a first name basis. (Retired Accountant, Thunder Bay)

Despite the ease of crossing the border, the restrictions put in place following 9/11, especially the passport requirement, are viewed in a very negative light. In addition, many think the border guards (especially the American border guards) ask too many invasive and unnecessary questions. In these instances, people clearly view the border as a very unfriendly barrier to travel. And this is true for both Canadians and Americans.

It used to be so easy to cross the border before 9/11. Guards would ask, how you doing, and you would be on your way. Now, I don't know the words to describe the mess, but it is much stricter. You have to get out of the car, you are searched, and there is a bigger presence of security. It never used to be that way. It is much harder getting back into the US again, I don't have the words to describe my frustration. (Liquor Store Clerk, Duluth)

The border is definitely a barrier. I just don't go across. It is too much of a hassle. The border guards ask so many questions, ask people to pop the trunk. I am a middle-aged white lady. Are you kidding me, me a terrorist? It is a joke. Plus, American border guards are snarky; want the names of the restaurants you eat at, geez. (Public Administrator, Duluth)

It is more difficult than ever to cross the border. You have to have a passport and that is a lot more restrictive on its own. It is actually harder to get back into Canada. They don't like you spending money in the US instead of Canada and for some people there are quite strong feelings in that regard. A lot of people in Thunder Bay just bite the bullet and put up with it. There is some resentment in that people from Thunder Bay think they help pump up Duluth, put a lot of money into Duluth, build it up and don't get any credit for doing that. (Professor, Lakehead University, Thunder Bay)

People from Thunder Bay are much more apt to view having a passport as a routine matter. Simply put, Canadians stressed that getting (and having) a passport was no big deal.

The big change was the passport requirement. But Canadians get passports like there is nothing to it. It is part of our lives. Americans don't get passports like that. A lot of Americans don't even have passports. Americans are more interested in just themselves. (Accountant, Thunder Bay)

You need a passport and it is more rigorous now. There is much more security. But there should be. I don't see it as a burden. Just part of the world we live in now. Border guards are just doing their job. American border guards are very friendly. They ask questions when you cross but as long as you have your passport you are all right. One thing that did change is that you never used to have to open your trunk but now they ask you to pop the trunk. But that is OK. (Public Radio Employee, Thunder Bay)

People from Duluth, however, had a very different take on the passport requirement, viewing it as a burden and not worth the cost.

I have lived here six years, I graduated from UMD [University of Minnesota–Duluth] and stayed. I came from Minneapolis. I have never crossed the border. I have a passport but my friends do not. They think it is too much of a hassle to get a passport and the cost is over a hundred dollars and it is a bureaucratic nightmare, so people just don't do it. Not just to go across the border into Canada. I've been to Mexico, but not to Canada. (Bartender, Duluth)

I've lived here pretty much all my life, at least in the area. I have not crossed the border, ever. I have not been to Thunder Bay. I don't have a passport and have no desire to get one or go across the border. But even before the passport requirement I was happy to be where I am and really have no desire to go to Canada or cross the border. (Office Supply Business Clerk, Duluth)

The results portraying the perceptions of people crossing the border are quite interesting. But the real surprise, at least to us, was the almost complete lack of interest displayed by the people in each of these communities with the goings on in their Sister Community. While some people on each side of the border follow what is going on just across the border, most people in Duluth and Thunder Bay pay very little attention to what is happening on a daily basis in their Sister City. People from Thunder Bay do, however, follow what is happening in the United States at the national level, whereas people from Duluth do not, in general, follow what is happening at the national level in Canada. 25

I do not follow Thunder Bay at all. I grew up here and never left. I have never been to Thunder Bay and have no plans to go. (Resort Receptionist, Duluth)

I do not follow what is happening in Thunder Bay at all. We do get a lot of people from Thunder Bay coming to Duluth for shopping mostly. But we also get a lot of people from Minneapolis coming here too, lots. Duluth is a feeder for Thunder Bay and Minneapolis. We are a destination that way. But I don't follow Thunder Bay at all, not even a little bit. I couldn't tell you anything about it, not a thing. What happens in Thunder Bay does not affect me in any way and I really don't care what goes on there. (Restaurant Business Manager, Duluth)

I do not follow Canada and what goes on there, not at all; and I do not follow anything that is going on in Thunder Bay. I am not interested in Canada, and I have to simply say that it is the United States that dominates my news cycle. (Nurse Practitioner, Duluth)

I do not follow Duluth or what is happening there. I don't think anyone in Thunder Bay could tell you about Duluth, its politics, who the Mayor is or anything about it. I do not follow the newspapers, news, anything about Duluth. (City Employee, Thunder Bay)

The Twin Saults Borderlands Region

Compared to the Thunder Bay/Duluth region, the Twin Saults show a much higher degree of connectedness. Table 2.2 summarizes this finding. Both Americans and Canadians have a high degree of experience crossing the border and see major changes since 9/11. While a much higher percentage of people from the Twin Saults see a special relationship with their cross-border community (compared to Duluth and Thunder Bay), there is a substantial difference between the two sides, with a higher percentage of Americans (58.5 percent) viewing the relationship as special and just under a majority (48.6 percent) of Canadians feeling this way. And like their counterparts in the Thunder Bay/Duluth region (but to a lesser extent), the vast majority of Canadians and Americans do not follow or care what happens immediately across the border.

Just as was observed in the Duluth/Thunder Bay corridor, the flow of people for the most part appears to go substantially from Canada to the United States. However, in contrast to the weakness of the Duluth/Thunder Bay relationship, Ontario and Michigan communities that make up the Twin Saults appear to have a much stronger interconnectedness. A good many people on both sides of the border see a very special relationship. The proximity of the border and the daily interactions of the people in the Twin Saults provide a sense of sameness. This points to a distinct difference between the Duluth/Thunder Bay and Twin Saults corridors, with the Twin Saults (physically separated by only a river and bridge) showing a much higher level of integration than the geographically distant communities of Thunder Bay and Duluth.

Table 2.2 **Percent Answering Questions as Listed**

		Sault Ste. Marie, Ontario	Sault Ste. Marie, Michigan
Do you have extensive experience with the border?	Yes	97.2	80.0
	No	2.8	20.0
	(n)	(72)	(65)
Is the border relationship special?	Yes	48.6	58.5
	No	51.4	41.5
	(n)	(72)	(65)
Do you view the border as a bridge or barrier?	Bridge	62.0	45.3
	Barrier	38.0	54.7
	(n)	(71)	(64)
Do you see changes at the border since 9/11?	Yes	91.4	98.4
	No	8.6	1.6
	(n)	(70)	(63)
Do you follow what happens on the other side of the border?	Yes	38.9	26.2
	No	61.1	73.8
	(n)	(72)	(65)
Does what happens on the other side of the border affect your daily life?	Yes	25.0	27.7
	No	75.0	72.3
	(n)	(72)	(65)

Note: The data delineated in this table is solely the product of the authors' interviews.

Yes, in a way there is a special relationship between the two sides. It is not like crossing into a foreign country. We are the same kind of people, so I guess that is something we share. (Administrative Assistant, Algoma University, Ontario)

We have a very special relationship with the Michigan side. We are both community oriented. People don't leave or if they do, they come back. This is a very friendly community, very close knit. And across the border is just the same. We are a lot alike. (Grocery Store Employee, Ontario)

Yes, we are pretty much the same I'd say. There is not a lot of difference in the people on both sides. We cross the border so easily. It is really not that separate. The flow seems to be in both directions. The arts are big here. People from the other side bring their kids here for music, dance, theater, the arts. (Specialty Shop Owner, Ontario)

A lot of Michigan folks come here to the restaurants. I would describe the relations as amicable. It is very enjoyable going across the border. It is not like going to a foreign nation. Our relationship is excellent. However, I would also say that many more Canadians go across to the American side than Americans come here. (Public Library Employee, Ontario)

I think there is a special relationship between the two Saults; at least from my point of view. I really do not distinguish between Americans and Canadians. We are very closely tied, the same people. One difference is that on the United States side, Americans feel you should be proud of your country. Maybe we look a little more inward than Canadians. But I still think we are still much more alike than different. (Medical Doctor, Michigan)

However, there were also many of those interviewed, with Americans seemingly more adamant than Canadians, who do not see a special relationship.

There is no connection that makes the relationship special; no connection at all. It really is two separate places. I also think that a lot more Canadians cross to the other side than Americans come here; at least when you are talking about the two Saults communities. (Hairdresser, Ontario)

We are two completely different societies. You know they are Canadians and we are Americans. There is not a single community. There is no such thing as the "Twin Saults" as one big community. No, that is far from the truth. (Gift Shop Attendant, Michigan)

We are two foreign countries. They are Canada. We are America. And there is no in between. We are not the "Twin Saults"; that is not true. They just do that because we both have the same name. But we are not connected any other way. (Souvenir Shop Manager, Michigan)

The "Twin Saults" concept is not quite the way you would expect it to be. It has always been an emphasis of the city leaders but it is complicated by the changes from 9/11 and the bridge traffic. There are still lots of Canadians that come here. A lot more Canadians come here than Americans go over there. Lots of Americans cross but not the locals. It used to be so easy to cross. It was common. You would not even think about it. You would go to a movie. It was charming, we loved doing it. Now, it has changed drastically. (Professor, Lake Superior State University, Michigan)

Some in the Twin Saults cross the border regularly, almost as a routine part of their lives.

I cross the border relatively frequently. It is extremely close, a few minutes away. I just watch the web cam and when there is no traffic, I go. If I watch the web cam I can usually make it across in ten minutes or so. It is not a big deal to cross.

In fact, it is rather easy. I go across to golf as I belong to the club on the other side. But I also go to restaurants and shop on the other side too. The restaurants on this side are pretty limited other than a few good Italian ones. There are more options on the Michigan side. (Professor, Algoma University, Ontario)

I've been here all my life, 28 years. I cross all the time; at least once a week to shop, get gas, milk, drink beer. It is something that is part of my regular routine. (City Maintenance Worker, Ontario)

I cross frequently; both my wife and I. We cross to check out the art scene. My wife is involved in the local social network and is a volunteer for community events. We like to see what is new in the arts and you have to go over there to find out. It also has the best grocery store in the region with great choice. We also have a lot of friends on the other side. (Retired Professor, Lake Superior State University, Michigan)

Others in the Twin Saults—more so on the Michigan side, and especially 30 since 9/11 and the implementation of the passport requirement—find crossing the border to be difficult, unrewarding, and even humiliating.

It is humiliating crossing the border. When searches started, questioning became more personal. They have gone overboard. Many people think it is humiliating to answer these questions and go through all this. The emphasis is on security and it has definitely caused some people to say the heck with it; it is not worth it to go through. And it is typical of Americans to go overboard. (Administrator, Algoma University, Ontario)

I do have a lot of experience with crossing the border, and I can tell you there is not much I like about crossing. Because of my bad experiences I do not go across the border much anymore. You are very rigorously questioned, in detail; where do you live, what is your address. They certainly put you through the paces. That is crossing into the U.S. Coming back into Canada is a breeze. (Administrator, Sault College, Ontario)

No, I don't cross anymore. Well, maybe once every four months or so. I avoid crossing because of the inconvenience. It all changed with 9/11. I am very unhappy with the unpredictability of crossing, how long it will take. It is not too bad coming from the States' side to Canada but getting into the States is terrible. And Americans, they are less likely to leave home. They are isolating themselves. I used to travel to the States a lot but not very much anymore. It is just too inconvenient. (Professor, Algoma University, Ontario)

9/11 changed everything. We went from people going over every day, students, family members. Then the Canadians just followed the default position of the

United States. Thanks go to the Bush Administration. It's beginning to feel like the Berlin Wall. It has separated friends, families. It has shredded whatever relationships we had. (Administrator, Sault College, Ontario)

The bridge is a barrier because of the passport requirement and so much more. It is so difficult to cross the border and it should be. We are foreign and so are they, so there is a lot of caution, especially for the United States. We are a target and people do not think much of us anymore. We are not respected internationally. (Public Library Employee, Ontario)

While some people on each side of the border follow what is going on just across the line, most people in the Twin Saults pay very little attention to what is happening on a daily basis in the community just on the other side of the bridge. People from the Ontario side do, however, follow what is happening in the United States at the national level, whereas people from the Michigan side do not, in general, follow what is happening at the national level in Canada.

I don't follow the news from the other side, but keep up with some of the things that happen across the river because we get so many Canadians coming here to shop and I talk to them every day. They are a big part of our business and I hear things as I am ringing them up. (Department Store Checker, Michigan)

The other side really does not affect me. But I do think of the "Twin Saults" as a single community. Since I was born and raised here in the UP [Upper Peninsula], I consider the whole region to be a community, including the other side of the border. I've come to think of it as all one single place. I guess you get callous about it. You should make distinctions. But I don't. It is a regular routine and part of our lives that we see Canadians all the time. And I see a lot of Americans that cross the border and it is just not a big deal. And it is easy to cross if you have a passport. (Security Guard, Michigan)

I follow quite a bit what is happening based on Chamber of Commerce news. I'm always kind of aware of the Michigan side vis-à-vis gas prices and the exchange rate. I follow U.S. politics a lot. There is plenty of U.S. content on the television. I am affected by what happens on the Michigan side depending on the economy. For instance, if gas prices climb over here, then the bridge will be busier as Ontario goes to Michigan to gas up. (Chamber of Commerce Employee, Ontario)

It affects me very little. However, we do have joint emergency services agreements and several years ago, Sault Michigan had a major downtown fire that overwhelmed their fire department, so Sault Ontario responded. There is also a joint bridge authority that meets. (Employee, Mayor's Office, Ontario)

My wife and I don't really follow what happens in Sault Michigan. However, we are interested in American politics, as many Canadians are. So I suppose I am saying that while we don't pay much attention to what our immediate neighbors to the south are doing, we do look at what is happening in the nation as a whole. (Sault Star Newspaper Staff Member, Ontario)

Analysis and Conclusions

Our goals for this research project were twofold: (1) to highlight the Canada–United States cross-border relationship from the perspective of the people who actually live in borderlands regions; and (2) to evaluate the usefulness of narrative interviews as a contributing factor toward advancing the concept of a borderlands theory. Regarding our first goal, several things stand out. The border does appear to be more prominent in Canadian lives. Canadians in Thunder Bay and Sault Ste. Marie, Ontario, pay much closer attention to the border than do Americans in Duluth and Sault Ste. Marie, Michigan. This is evidenced by two things. First, the flow of border crossings clearly goes from Canada into the United States, especially in the Duluth/Thunder Bay corridor. Canadians are more likely to have passports, and to use them to cross into the United States. Americans not only are lacking possession of passports (compared to their Canadian counterparts), they are also less likely to cross into Canada. People from Duluth do not, as a matter of practice, travel to Thunder Bay, whereas there exists a very strong contingent of people from Thunder Bay who regularly travel to Duluth. In the Twin Saults the difference in flow across the border is not so prominent. What is prominent is that there are a good many people on the Michigan side who have never crossed the border or who have stopped crossing since the passport restrictions were implemented.

It is clear that Canadians, for the most part, follow what is happening in the United States. They are aware of United States politics at the national level and follow American media fairly closely. They know who the President is, when the elections are taking place, and who the Presidential candidates are. Americans, on the other hand, do not follow Canadian politics or media at the national level and are quite ignorant, in general, of what is happening in Canada. The disinterest in things Canadian came across very clear in the interviews. For the most part, people south of the border do not pay much attention to things happening either at the border or north of the border.

What is especially interesting to note is that the people of Thunder Bay and Sault Ste. Marie, Ontario, just like their counterparts in Duluth and Sault Ste. Marie, Michigan, generally do not follow what is happening just across the border. There is no specific knowledge of community issues, especially if that knowledge pertains to things on the governmental agenda or who is running the government. People know the price of gas and whether the casino is smoking or non-smoking, what the drinking age is, and the best time to cross the border. In general, however, the people of these communities do not follow the substantive issues occurring immediately across the border. Yet, there is something unique about this situation. Our interviews indicate that the border in and of itself is not important; that it is just a minor obstacle to be negotiated to get to the other side; that it is no big deal. It is accepted that there are two different, distinct countries, but not two different and distinct communities. In essence, there appears to be a substantial degree of sameness in these

> "It is accepted that there are two different, distinct countries, but not two different and distinct communities."

cross-border communities. Even though people that cross the border are aware they are in a foreign country, there is such a strong similarity between the communities and the people that the differences are just not that noticeable. This suggests a definitive sense of borderlands within both the Thunder Bay/Duluth and Twin Saults regions. The interviews of people living in these regions clearly demonstrate that in the geographical regions that surround Lake Superior, people on one side of the border share values, beliefs, feelings, and expectations with people on the other side of the border.

At the same time, there is a feeling among the Lake Superior borderlands people that the cross-border relationship between Canadians and Americans is not nearly as strong as it was several decades ago. Time after time, people in all four communities spoke of the "good old days" — a time when the universities and the communities had much closer ties: a time when both official and unofficial connections were much more common. Of course, this finding may simply purport to a generational gap, where older citizens are remembering the days when crossing the border used to be such an easy thing to do. Still, according to those interviewed, there are fewer formal or institutional connections today between governments, universities, and libraries across the border than there were in the past.

As noted above, the restrictions implemented since 9/11 — especially the passport requirement — have affected Americans in Duluth and Sault Ste. Marie, Michigan, much more than they have affected Canadians in Thunder Bay and Sault Ste. Marie, Ontario. For many, crossing the border is a hassle, especially when crossing into the United States. People who regularly crossed the border insisted that how easy it is to cross the border depends on which border guard you get. Furthermore, many who cross the border regularly describe the crossing as humiliating. Where once it was easy to cross in a timely manner, it has now become a much more difficult process, and many have decided it is not worth the effort. However, there still remains a vibrant crossing of the border in the Twin Saults region as well as a strong Canada to U.S. crossing of the border in the Duluth/Thunder Bay region. It is just that with the newly instituted barriers to freedom of movement, the sense that the two sides of the border represent a single community with shared values has been diminished. Crossing the border, for many, has turned into an anxiety-filled experience, at times even humiliating, and this experience accentuates the fact that people are crossing into a foreign country. Under these circumstances, building cross-border linkages becomes even more difficult.

There has definitely been a very negative backlash to the longer lines, the many more questions, and the general delay in crossing the border since 9/11. While most say that crossing continues to be fairly easy, most also say that the restrictions bring about bad feelings and mistrust. Canadians tend to emphasize the overzealousness of the American border guards and what they believe is an extreme emphasis on security, arguing that it is a bit much. Americans, as a whole, feel the same way. While there exists a general understanding that these safeguards are necessary, most still believe that it is too much of a hassle. Surprisingly, very few respondents on either side of the border mentioned terrorism when asked to describe the international border and its workings. When terrorists were mentioned, it was with respect to the fact that respondents felt like they were being treated like terrorists. When specifically questioned about terrorism, most responded that it is a concern, but it was not their primary concern regarding the border. The major concern of citizens crossing the border is the time and effort it takes getting through the checkpoints, not the possibility of terrorists using the border as an entry point (especially into the U.S.).

There are some important findings one can take away from the thoughts and ideas shared by the people living in these regions. In addition to what has already been described in this paper, there is a strong sense of shared values across these communities. They share very similar historical, geographical, economic and cultural settings. Founded on the abundance of natural resources (e.g., mining, timber, the great outdoors, the lake), as well as being situated at key points of transportation and shipping, each of these regions has also suffered the boom-and-bust periods of a natural resource-based economy and has developed a working-class culture and atmosphere. Because of these shared experiences and their inherent tie to the lake and land, the people who populate each of these regions, be they Canadian or American, pretty much look the same. Whether you are in Duluth or Thunder Bay or on either side of the St. Mary's River, other than the accents, it would be difficult to tell the people in these communities apart. When asked about what makes their communities special, time after time, the respondents named the same things. Moreover, to a person, respondents would say that despite the fact that there were differences between Americans and Canadians, they still shared the same basic values of family, hard work, and ties to the land and water. In other words, through their very own words, they portray a strong sense of living within a borderlands region.

References

Aubut, Sheldon, and Maryanne Norton. 2001. *Images of America: Duluth, Minnesota*. Chicago, IL: Arcadia.

Axelson, Gustave. 2011. "A Midwest Beer Tour to Cure Winter Blues." *New York Times*. February 4. http://travel.nytimes.com/2011/02/06/travel/06overnighter -beer (February 8).

Berg, Bob, and Konnie LeMay, eds. 2010. *Lake Superior: The Ultimate Guide to the Region*, 2nd ed. Duluth, MN: Lake Superior Port Cities, Inc.

Border Policy Research Institute. 2010. *Border Barometer*. Western Washington University and the University at Buffalo Regional Institute. February.

Brunet-Jailly, Emmanuel. 2005. Theorizing borders: An interdisciplinary perspective. *Geopolitics* 10: 633–649.

Dickinson, John. 1981. *To Build a Canal: Sault Ste. Marie, 1853–1854 and After*. Columbus, OH: Ohio State University.

Duluth News-Tribune. 2000. *Looking Back 2000: The Heroes and Villains, Victories and Disasters That Have Shaped the Northland*. Duluth, MN.

Gibbins, Roger. 2005. "Meaning and Significance of the Canadian-American Border." In *Borders and Border Politics in a Globalizing World*, ed. Paul Ganster and David E. Lorey, 152–165. Boulder, CO: SR Books.

Konrad, Victor, and John Everitt. 2011. Borders and belongers: Transnational identities, border security, and cross-border socio-economic integration in the United States borderlands with Canada and the British Virgin Islands. *Comparative American Studies* 9: 288–308.

Konrad, Victor, and Heather N. Nicol. 2008. *Beyond Walls: Re-inventing the Canada–United States Borderlands*. Burlington, VT: Ashgate Publishing Co.

Konrad, Victor, and Heather Nicol. 2011. Border culture, the boundary between Canada and the United States of America, and the advancement of borderlands theory. *Geopolitics* 16: 70–90.

Megoran, Nick. 2006. For ethnography in political geography: Experiencing and re-imagining Ferghana Valley boundary closures. *Political Geography* 25: 622–640.

Mount, Graeme, John Abbott, and Michael Mulloy. 1995. *The Border at Sault Ste. Marie*. Toronto: Dundurn Press.

Newman, David, and Anssi Paasi. 1998. Fences and neighbours in the postmodern world: Boundary narratives in political geography. *Progress in Human Geography* 22: 186–207.

Papademetriou, Demetrios, and Deborah Waller Meyers. 2001. *Caught in the Middle: Border Communities in an Era of Globalization*. Washington, DC: Carnegie Endowment for International Peace.

Paasi, Anssi, and Eeva-Kaisa Prokkola. 2008. Territorial dynamics, cross-border work and everyday life in the Finnish-Swedish border area. *Space and Polity* 1: 13–29.

Prokkola, Eeva-Kaisa. 2009. Unfixing borderland identity: Border performances and narratives in the construction of self. *Journal of Borderlands Studies* 24: 21–37.

Robertson, Colin. 2011. *Now for the Hard Part: A User's Guide to Reviewing the Canadian–American Partnership*. Ottawa. ON: Canadian Defence & Foreign Affairs Institute.

Rumford, Chris. 2008. *Cosmopolitan Spaces: Europe, Globalization, Theory*. New York: Routledge.

Sandvik, Glenn. 1983. *Duluth: An Illustrated History of the Zenith City*. Woodland Hills, CA: Windsor Publications.

Schimanski, Johan, and Stephen Wolfe. 2010. Cultural production and negotiation of borders: Introduction to the dossier. *Journal of Borderlands Studies* 25(1): 39–49.

Weygant, Noemi. 1976. "The City of Duluth." In *Duluth: Sketches of the Past*, ed. Ryck Lydecker and Lawrence Sommer, 3–16. Duluth: American Revolution Bicentennial Commission.

Understanding the Text

1. How do "narrative discourses," or the stories people tell, increase our understanding of borderlands culture?

2. In paragraphs 7–9, Alm and Burkhart "characterize the Canada–United States borderlands relationship." Summarize their key points. What do their findings indicate about borderland relationships in the region they study?

3. What significant conclusions do Alm and Burkhart reach in their analysis of the narratives of the people living in the Canada-U.S. border region? Describe their conclusions in your own words.

Reflection and Response

4. Among the many questions that Alm and Burkhart ask the participants in their study are the following: "Do you view the border as a bridge or a barrier? Explain why." And "Did 9/11 change the border relationship? If so, how?" Look at the participants' narrative responses and at Tables 2.1 and 2.2, which summarize responses to these questions. Explain both

the narrative responses to each question and the results. What do you find significant about them? What trends do you notice? Based on these questions, what do you conclude about how people living in border communities think about, define, and experience borders? (Alm and Burkhart offer their conclusions in paragraphs 32–38.)

5. Alm and Burkhart conclude by claiming that "there is a strong sense of shared values across these communities" (par. 38). Reread the various narrative responses in order to identify these values. Then, using examples from the various responses, write a fully developed explanation of the values that people living on both sides of the Canada-U.S. border share.

6. Consider the summary of the interview results (Tables 2.1 and 2.2). Which results surprised you? Which results did you expect? Why? If you were conducting this study, what would you want to know about people's experience in these border communities? What specific questions would you ask and why? Based on how individuals responded to Alm and Burkhart's questions, predict how they would respond to your questions.

Making Connections

7. Extend Alm and Burkhart's focus, and research another U.S.-Canada border community, such as one of the crossings in Washington, Montana, Minnesota, or Maine. Research the demographics of the area and each community's historical, political, and social relationship with the border. For example, you may be intrigued by the neighborly crossing between Hyder, Alaska, and Steward, British Columbia, or by the busyness of the Detroit, Michigan–Windsor, Ontario Tunnel (as well as the Ambassador Bridge controversy). What does your research reveal about the experiences of people in this borderland community and their attitudes toward the border? What larger conclusions can you draw about borderland experiences? Finally, how do your conclusions extend Alm and Burkhart's, or where do their ideas help you develop and explain your thoughts more fully?

8. Like Gloria Anzaldúa (p. 55 and p. 143), Norma Cantú (p. 58), and Ann Marie Leimer (p. 222), Alm and Burkhart address life in the borderlands. How are the various border regions these writers examine similar or different? How are these writers' ideas and claims about how borders shape the lives of those who inhabit borderlands similar or different? How do you account for these similarities and differences? Finally, blend your ideas with those of Alm and Burkhart, Anzaldúa, Cantú, and Leimer to explain why geographical borders matter.

Re-examining the Rhetoric of the "Cultural Border"

Heewon Chang

Heewon Chang received a Ph.D. in anthropology from the University of Oregon and is currently a professor of organizational leadership and education at Eastern University. Her research interests include educational justice and education, anthropology and education, autoethnography, and ethnography, the scientific study of the customs of individual peoples, groups, and cultures. Chang was the founding editor-in-chief of the *International Journal of Multicultural Education* and has published several books in the area of autoethnography.

In the following reading, which appeared in the *International Journal of Multicultural Education* in 1999, Chang challenges the idea that fixed boundaries define and constitute a culture. Her argument depends primarily on uncoupling the territorial aspect from the concept of borders. As you read, pay close attention to how Chang negotiates this uncoupling as she asks us to reconsider our understanding of cultural borders.

Constructing a topology of a multicultural society is never simple. Although cultural diversity is often defined by seemingly clear-cut categories such as ethnicity, race, class, religion, gender, sexual orientation, and exceptionality, sorting out "culture" intertwined with these multicultural categories is a complex process. I am not even sure whether anyone sees the value of taking on the challenge because different categories of people are considered synonymous with cultural differences. It is common to hear references to Asian-American culture, Black culture, Muslim culture, female culture, homosexual culture, and ADD culture as if they have clear boundaries and are distinguished entities. It is also assumed that if an Asian meets an African-American their presumed cultural differences are expected to form a cultural border. Or if a White teacher has a group of minority children in her classroom, the formation of a cultural border between them is considered inevitable. However, if the focus switches from a society (or group) to individuals, the power of the cultural border rhetoric seems to lose its potency. For example, the Korean and the African-American may share many cultural traits, so their racial and ethnic difference may not have such an enduring effect.

In this essay I attempt to probe into the assumptions of the cultural border rhetoric and assess the underpinning view of culture; here I identify it as the essentialist view° in the context of multiculturalism. Then I will introduce the constructivist view° of culture by switching our focus from societal culture to individual culture so that we may see the cultural differences as an embracing factor rather than as a divisive factor.

Cultural Border and Cultural Boundary

The terms "border" and "boundary" are physical in origin (Johnson and Michaelsen, 1997). The original imagery is not quite abandoned and is even intentionally played out when the terms are used in reference to culture. Cultural border and boundary often connote the border and boundary of a nation, a state, or a tribal community, which are clearly identifiable markers. The equation between a culture and a territory has dominated the discourse in anthropology (Erickson, 1997; Ewing, 1998; Goodenough, 1981; Lugo, 1997; Wax, 1993). The assumption is that as long as two distinct societies remain separate from each other, their boundaries exist and cultural distinctiveness is expected. It is further assumed that if two societies, identified with two distinct cultures, come in contact, a cultural border is expected to form between them. If an individual from Culture A is to voluntarily or involuntarily become part of Culture B, she/he is expected to literally leave his/her own society, cross the border, and enter a new society. This physical implication of the cultural border is fully entertained by scholars of Mexican immigrants, for whom crossing the border is a literal as well as a figurative experience (Delgado-Gaitan & Trueba, 1991; Johnson & Michaelsen, 1997).

To many scholars a border is not a neutral demarcation line. It is a symbol of power that imposes inclusion and exclusion. The more privileged dominant, hegemonious° side will actively control the border to keep border-crossers out. Erickson (1997) accentuated the political nature of a border by differentiating it from a boundary:

A cultural boundary refers to the presence of some kind of cultural difference. Cultural boundaries are characteristic of all human societies, traditional as well as modern. A border is a social construct that is political in origin. Across a border power is exercised, as in the political border between two nations. (p. 42)

essentialist view: a theory that regards cultural groups as homogeneous and group characteristics such as ethnicity and sexuality as fixed "essential" traits of members of each group.
constructivist view: a theory that regards cultural groups and societies as diverse, heterogeneous, and socially constructed.
hegemonious: ruling or dominant in a political or social context.

A cultural border connotes a barrier that a more powerful side con- 5 structs to guard its own political power, cultural knowledge, and privileges.

The cultural border rhetoric is grounded in the essentialist view of culture. This view makes several assumptions regarding culture: (1) a culture is viewed as a bounded system which is separate and distinguishable from others; (2) a culture is expected to be "homogeneous" (Lugo, 1997, p. 54); (3) a culture is expected to be shared by members of the society.

The first assumption is evident in the work of many anthropologists. The cultural boundary is viewed as coterminous with a nation, a state, a tribe, a community, or an organization that is clearly defined by an identifiable marker, often physical borders. Goodenough (1981) attributed this notion of culture to Franz Boas, a pioneer German-American anthropologist:

At the end of the nineteenth century, Franz Boas began to use "culture" to refer to the distinctive body of customs, beliefs, and social institutions that seemed to characterize each separate society. (Stocking, cited in Goodenough, p. 48)

The notion of one-distinct-culture-for-each-separate-society suggests that one culture represents a society and vice versa. This close match makes the conceptual interchange of culture and society acceptable. Henze and Vanett (1993) further explore this assumption of culture in the metaphor of "walking in two worlds" in their study of native Alaskan and Native American students.

The second assumption of cultural homogeneity suggests that a homogeneous, patterned prototype of a culture can be abstracted. It implies that a "pure" form of a culture exists. Any variation from the pure form is treated as an exception, peripheral to "the culture." This assumption ignores the dynamic nature of culture, in which people of a society change at different rates for different reasons. The diffusionist view° of culture argues against this notion of cultural homogeneity, for all cultures include elements borrowed from other cultures (Linton, 1937; Wax, 1993).

The third assumption of the cultural border is that a culture is "shared" 10 by members of a society. The extent of sharedness is debatable, yet sharedness is considered a trademark of culture. This assumption suggests that people within a cultural system share a set of traits unique to their group

---

diffusionist view: a theory that emphasizes the transmission of cultural characteristics or traits from earlier societies to all other cultures.

membership. Sharedness is considered a product of cultural transmission and acquisition which often take place through personal interactions among members of physical proximity. In other words, an Asian is expected to share with other Asians traits unique to Asian culture. When a group is small and specific, the extent of sharedness among members may be higher. However, if a group presents a large, cross-sectional or cross-national cultural identity, such as "female culture," "middle-class culture," and "Muslim culture," the sharedness of that particular culture is blurred by other cultural identities. Ewing (1998) examined how the cultural identity of Muslims shifts relative to national borders and the gender line.

This territory-oriented rhetoric of culture, cultural border, and boundary faces a great challenge in a multicultural society because intense contacts between various cultural carriers blur the clarity of demarcation lines.

Cultural Borderland

"Cultural borderland" is a notion created to accommodate a multicultural society. Foley (1995) explores the cultural borderland as a "space" created when two or more cultures and races occupy the same territory. He considers the space psychological and political: "[According to Rosaldo and Clifford, the borderland] generally refers to a psychological space at the conjuncture of two cultures. A cultural borderland is also a political space in which ethnic groups actively fuse and blend their culture with the mainstream culture" (p. 119).

The borderland is viewed as a psychological space in which border-crossers struggle with their bicultural or multicultural identities. In this borderland individuals decide how much they want to identify with their cultures of origin or of adoption. Too much of either can be the subject of ridicule. Saenz (1997) compared two distinguished Mexican-American writers who try to come to terms with their ethnic identities. He argued that Gloria Anzaldúa is "completely mortgaged to a nostalgia," a nostalgia to the Aztec origin of the Mexican culture (p. 87). Richard Rodriguez, on the other hand, "is completely mortgaged to an ideology that privileges the category of individual" (p. 87). In the eyes of Saenz, Rodriguez has taken too much of his adopted culture. In between lies Saenz's Mexican-American college student who refused to read "gringo" (White) poetry and Saenz himself, who insists on his identity as a Chicano writer.

The borderland is also highly political. The borderland is never on center stage. It is often viewed as a marginal space for cultural hybrids—those who have adopted "foreign," distinctly different, cultural traits—

who therefore do not fit the homogeneous prototypes of their original cultures. In Foley's Mesquaki Indian study the borderland is viewed as a threat to the integrity of the Indian culture. It was a space for Indian progressives (who proposed to modernize the Indian community and to collaborate with Whites), White "wannabes" (who tried to adopt the Indian culture), and "mixed-bloods" (biracial individuals of White and Indian parents).

The borderland rhetoric is still embedded in the essentialist view of cul- 15
ture. For example, Foley's notion of cultural borderlands creates an image of three separate zones: the "pure" Indian culture that is being guarded by "traditionalists" (let's call it Culture A); the "pure" White culture that is distinguished from the Indian (Culture B); and the borderland between them, a space for border-crossers. Chang (1997) questions this essentialist presumption of culture by wondering "just where the Indian culture ends and the White culture begins for border crossers" (p. 385).

How Real Is the Cultural Border?

The cultural border and boundary rhetoric focuses on a societal culture. If cultural diversity is viewed at the societal level, cultural borders seem authentic and real. Skin color, national origin, gender, religious affiliation, identification of disability, and group membership all serve as identifiable markers for subgroups. Since these categories are socially constructed and validated, cultural differences are assumed and expected. But when the cultures of individuals are under scrutiny, it becomes clear that cultural borders do not hold their dividing power. Cultural boundaries within individuals become blurred as components from diverse cultures become incorporated into their individual cultural identity, instead of remaining separate from each other.

Let us take a close look at four multicultural individuals who had a close connection with Korea but who live in the pluralistic U.S. society.

Jean Kohl, a 9-year-old daughter of a German father and a Korean mother, was born and raised in the United States. Her parents, fluent speakers of German and Korean respectively, adopted English as the primary language at home. "I am an American," proclaimed she, but she often ended her proclamation with an addendum that she was also German and Korean. For several summers she traveled to visit her maternal or paternal grandparents in Korea or Germany, during which she was exposed to her parents' native cultures and languages. The German, Korean, and U.S. heritage blended in her cultural repertoire. For Jean, where does the "American" cultural border end and other cultural borders begin?

Carrie Baumstein, a 20-year-old woman, was born in Korea and adopted by a Messianic Jewish-American couple when she was 2 years old. She has lived in the States ever since. She was not exposed to much Korean culture and language when she was growing up, but was instead surrounded by her parents' Jewish tradition. Despite her primary identity with the Jewish culture, she was often reminded by her relatives and neighbors of her Korean or Asian linkage. She was in an identity search for Asianness when she was attending a small Christian college on the East Coast. For Carrie, where do the cultural borders lie between the Korean and the American and between the Messianic Jew and the Christian?

> "If cultural diversity is viewed at the societal level, cultural borders seem authentic and real. . . . But when the cultures of individuals are under scrutiny, it becomes clear that cultural borders do not hold their dividing power."

Peter Lee, a 15-year-old, was born in the States to immigrant parents from Korea. His parents own and operate a dry cleaning shop in a suburb of Philadelphia. Their English is functional for the business but they prefer speaking Korean on all other occasions. Peter's family attends a Korean church regularly, which usually serves as a cultural community as much as a religious one. Peter's Korean is so limited that he usually speaks English, although his parents speak Korean to him. He is definitely an American in his mind and heart, perhaps a Korean-American occasionally. But his preference of Korean-American peers to others is a curious phenomenon. Where lies the cultural border that divides the Korean and the "American" for Peter?

Elaine Sook-Ja Cho, 50 years old, immigrated to the States 30 years ago to marry a Korean bachelor 10 years her senior. Her husband came to the States as a student and found employment upon completion of his study. Elaine was a housewife for 20 years before undertaking a small grocery business. She speaks "Konglish" (a mixture of Korean sentence structure and English words) but she seems to be at ease speaking English. She is Korean in her heart but "Americanized" in her own words and by her lifestyle. For Sook-Ja how far does the Korean cultural border stretch to meet the "American" culture?

I wonder how I would map the cultural topology (again a physical metaphor) of Jean Kohl, Carrie Baumstein, Peter Lee, and Elaine Sook-Ja Cho. How would I draw up the boundary of the Korean culture for each case? Would they cross cultural borders from the Korean to the German and so on daily? How cognizant would they be of crossing? Would it be possible for one to become culturally more Korean in the morning, German for lunch, "American" in the afternoon, and back to Korean in the evening? The early illustration of an individual leaving his/her society, crossing the border, and entering a new society may shed light on the problem with the cultural border rhetoric. Once you acquire cultural traits, whether in a certain territorial context or not, leaving the territory does not make an individual "lose" the culture. Sook-Ja is not any less Korean culturally now because she left her homeland 30 years ago. Carrie's minimal identity as a Korean is not surprising despite her origin. Peter and Jean, who were born and raised in the States, have acquired Korean cultural traits from their parents. In other words, the physical proximity or distance to Korea does not serve as an accurate gauge for their Koreanness in culture. It is also hardly imaginable that Jean's notion of the Korean culture is similar to that of Sook-Ja, although both claim to be Korean. What would Peter share about the Korean culture with others and to what extent? How would I compare these people's Korean culture with that of Koreans who have never left the country? With the essentialist image of culture in particular, the Korean culture seems to lose the clarity of its boundary as I probe into each individual's personal version of culture.

Conclusion

Everyone is cultural and multicultural (Erickson, 1997; Goodenough, 1976): "cultural" in that culture is not a property of an exotic people but "standards" that all human beings adopt for their daily operations; "multicultural" in the sense of being competent in multiple macro- or micro-cultural systems.

In a pluralistic society in which people from diverse cultures come in 25 constant contact, the cultural metamorphosis takes place noticeably in individual cultures. Thus the Boas-Benedict legacy of the "plural, separate, distinct, historically homogeneous" culture offers little help in understanding the multicultural society and its residents (Wax, 1993, p. 108). Rosaldo also critiqued the fallacy of cultural homogeneity, especially in the pluralistic setting:

[H]uman cultures are neither necessarily coherent nor always homogeneous. More often than we usually care to think, our everyday lives are crisscrossed by border zones, pockets and eruptions of all kinds. (Rosaldo, quoted in Logo, 1997, p. 51)

It also becomes clear that a culture is not bounded by a territory as earlier anthropologists believed. Rather, people are the carriers, movers, consumers, and inventors of a culture. When they move from one place to the other, they carry their cultures and their personal outlooks with them. Goodenough (1981) coined a term, "propriospect," to refer to the "private, subjective view of the world and of its content," which includes the various standards for perceiving, evaluating, believing, and doing that an individual attributes to other persons as a result of his or her experience of their actions and admonitions (p. 98). Wolcott (1991) elaborated on the meaning of the term "propriospect" to illustrate how individuals develop personal versions of a culture through personal contacts with others with different sets of standards. Through these contacts they acquire some of the new standards. As a result, they become increasingly multicultural.

This concept of culture sheds light on cultural differences. Since everyone has a unique cultural make-up, cultural differences are not really divisive and separable. Individual cultural differences are really different combinations of standards. Once different standards are embraced by individuals, the differences are incorporated into their individual cultures. In other words, the cultural differences are reframed into multiculturalism. It seems logical to me that we understand our individual multiculturalism as a pathway to understand our societal multiculturalism. The constructive view of individual cultures would be too useful and insightful to ignore.

References

Banks, J., and Banks, C. A. M. (1997). *Multicultural education: Issues and perspectives*. Boston, MA: Allyn and Bacon.

Chang, H. (1997). [Review of the book *The Heartland Chronicles*]. *Journal of Contemporary Ethnography, 26*(3), 382–385.

Delgado-Gaitan, C., and Trueba, H. (1991). *Crossing cultural borders*. New York, NY: The Falmer Press.

Erickson, F. (1997). Culture in society and in educational practice. In J. A. Banks and C. A. M. Banks (Eds.), *Multicultural education: Issues and perspectives* (pp. 32–60). Boston, MA: Allyn and Bacon.

Ewing, K. P. (1998). Crossing borders and transgressing boundaries: Metaphor for negotiating multiple identities. *Ethos, 26*(2), 262–267.

Foley, D. E. (1995). *The heartland chronicles*. Philadelphia, PA: University of Pennsylvania.

Goodenough, W. (1976). Multiculturalism as the normal human experience. *Anthropology and Education Quarterly, 7*(4), 4–6.

Goodenough, W. (1981). *Culture, language, and society*. Menlo Park, CA: The Benjamin/Cummings Publishing Company.

Henze, R. C., and Vanett, L. (1993). To walk in two worlds or more? Challenging a common metaphor of native education. *Anthropology and Education Quarterly, 24*(2), 116–134.

Johnson, D. E., and Michaelsen, S. (1997). Border secrets: An introduction. In D. E. Johnson and S. Michaelsen (Eds.), *Border theory* (pp. 1–39). Minneapolis, MN: University of Minnesota.

Linton, R. (1937). The one hundred percent American. *The American Mercury, 40,* 427–429. (reprint)

Lugo, A. (1997). Reflections on border theory, culture, and the nation. In D. E. Johnson and S. Michaelsen (Eds.), *Border theory* (pp. 43–67). Minneapolis, MN: University of Minnesota.

Saenz, B. A (1997). In the borderland of chicano identity, there are only fragments. In D. E. Johnson and S. Michaelsen (Eds.), *Border theory* (pp. 68–96). Minneapolis, MN: University of Minnesota.

Wax, M. L. (1993). How culture misdirects multiculturalism. *Anthropology and Education Quarterly,* 24(2), 99–115.

Wolcott, H. F. (1991). Propriospect and the acquisition of culture. *Anthropology and Education Quarterly, 22*(3), 251–273.

Understanding the Text

1. Identify and explain the assumptions of an essentialist view regarding culture. How does Chang respond to each assumption?

2. In your own words, explain the difference between "cultural border" and "cultural boundary." Why do you think Chang makes this distinction?

3. In paragraph 16, Chang writes: "But when the cultures of individuals are under scrutiny, it becomes clear that cultural borders do not hold their dividing power." Explain what Chang means and how she supports this claim.

Reflection and Response

4. Throughout "Re-examining the Rhetoric of the 'Cultural Border,'" Chang offers several examples and definitions of *culture* and *border*. Did she change your understanding of one or both of these concepts? If so, explain what she added to your understanding. If not, explain where your ideas about culture and borders intersect with and diverge from Chang's.

5. Do you agree with Chang's assertions in paragraph 27, specifically, her claim that "cultural differences are reframed into multiculturalism"? Why or why not? Provide evidence, reasons, and examples to support your position.

6. At the end of paragraphs 18, 19, 20, and 21, Chang poses a question regarding the cultural border in relation to each of the multicultural individuals she features in her article. Considering the evidence that Chang provides and your own knowledge and experience, how would you answer each question?

Making Connections

7. When Chang turns her focus to multicultural individuals, she provides some insights into how each must think about cultural differences and negotiate

cultural borders. Karla Scott, in "Communication Strategies across Cultural Borders: Dispelling Stereotypes, Performing Competence, and Redefining Black Womanhood" (p. 181), also looks at how individuals negotiate cultural differences. How do her analyses and arguments extend, support, or oppose Chang's?

8. Chang's insistence that we rethink the concept of cultural borders further complicates the idea of borders in general. Drawing on Chang's ideas, Sherman Alexie's insights regarding living outside cultural borders (p. 104), and Gloria Anzaldúa's claims about identity, language, and borders in "To Live in the Borderlands Means You" (p. 55) and "How to Tame a Wild Tongue" (p. 143), explain how "real" borders create and influence conceptual ones.

Sherman Alexie on Living outside Cultural Borders

Bill Moyers and Sherman Alexie

A political commentator and journalist, Bill Moyers has won more than thirty Emmys, nine Peabody Awards, and a Career Achievement Award from the International Documentary Association over the course of his career. He has worked in television news and served as White House press secretary for President Lyndon Johnson (1965–1967). Currently, Moyers hosts *Bill Moyers & Company*, a weekly series on public television and radio, featuring interviews with poets, writers, artists, journalists, scientists, philosophers, and scholars. The following reading is an excerpt from Moyers's interview with the poet, novelist, short story writer, and filmmaker Sherman Alexie.

A Spokane/Coeur d'Alene Native American, Alexie grew up on the Spokane Indian Reservation in Washington. Best known for his literary and film work, he also performs stand-up comedy. Alexie's 1998 film *Smoke Signals*, directed and produced by Chris Eyre, won the Audience Award and the Filmmaker's Trophy at the 1998 Sundance Film Festival. Alexie's novels and short story collections include *The Lone Ranger and Tonto Fistfight in Heaven* (1993), a PEN/Hemingway Citation Award winner; *Reservation Blues* (1995); *The Absolutely True Diary of a Part-Time Indian* (2007), a National Book Award winner; and *War Dances* (2010), a PEN/Faulkner Award winner.

Alexie, always provocative, challenges readers' expectations about Native American literature and their perspectives regarding Native Americans. His use of humor and inclusion of stereotypes causes some scholars to label him as a "cultural traitor" and others as a "moral satirist." Moyers raises the issue of stereotypes, and throughout the interview Alexie uses humor to make his points. Moyers and Alexie cover a wide range of topics; however, several key ones lie at the heart of the interview. As you read, find these main points and notice where Alexie might be speaking as a moral satirist from "outside cultural borders."

BILL MOYERS: Let's talk now with Sherman Alexie. He comes from a long line of people who have lived the consequences of inequality, Native Americans, the first Americans. They were the target of genocide, ethnic cleansing, which for years was the hidden history of America, kept in the closet by the authors and enforcers of white mythology.

How do you grapple with such a long denied history? If you are Sherman Alexie, you face it down with candor and even irreverence, writing poems, novels, and short stories, and even movies. Here's a clip from *Smoke Signals* that Alexie wrote and co-produced in 1998:

> VICTOR IN *SMOKE SIGNALS*: You got to look mean or people won't respect you. White people will run all over you if you don't look mean. You got to look like a warrior. You got to look like you just came back from killing a buffalo.
>
> THOMAS IN *SMOKE SIGNALS*: But our tribe never hunted buffalo, we were fishermen.
>
> VICTOR IN *SMOKE SIGNALS*: What? You want to look like you just came back from catching a fish? This ain't "Dances with Salmon," you know.

MOYERS: Alexie has published 22 books of poetry and fiction, including *The Lone Ranger and Tonto Fistfight in Heaven, War Dances*, and *The Absolutely True Diary of a Part-Time Indian*, a book for young adults and winner of the National Book Award. His latest work is a collection of short stories, old and new, with the title *Blasphemy*. I'll ask him why.

He now lives in Seattle, like many of his characters who left the reservation for the city, living in between, and traveling across boundaries both real and imagined. Sherman Alexie, welcome.

ALEXIE: Oh, thank you. It's good to be here.   5

MOYERS: Life for you is a lot of in between, isn't it?

ALEXIE: Well, as a native, as a colonized people you do live in the in between. The thing is I'm native. But necessarily because I'm a member of the country, I'm also a White American.

MOYERS: But you must feel at home in that in between now, because so many people are, as you say, living there.

ALEXIE: I was taught that it was not easy, that there was something destructive about it. I was taught by my elders, my parents that it was a bad, dangerous place to be. But I've come to realize it's actually, it's pretty magical. You know? I can be in a room full of Indians and non-Indians. And I can switch in the middle of sentences. So, and also because I'm ambiguously ethnic looking, you know, I come to New York and I can be anything. People generally think I'm half of whatever they are.

> "I was taught that it was not easy, that there was something destructive about [living in the in between]. . . . But I've come to realize it's actually, it's pretty magical."

So, I end up feeling like a spy in the house of ethnicity, you know? 10
Because people will talk around me as they would talk around the
people in their cultural group. So I get to hear all the secrets and jokes
and you know, I'm a part of every community because of the way I look.

MOYERS: Is that a big change from your parents' generation and your
generation?

ALEXIE: Oh, I mean, I grew up in a monoculture. We did a family tree in
sixth grade on the rez and everybody was related.

MOYERS: On the reservation?

ALEXIE: Yes, including the teacher. My mom and dad met when he
moved to the rez, when he was five and she was 14. And she helped
him get a drink at a water fountain. My mom was born in the house
where her mom was born. So we were as isolated in the sense of Native
Americans as anybody else. So, you know, I realized later on that
when I left the rez to go to the White high school on the border of the
rez I was a first-generation immigrant, you know? I'm an indigenous
immigrant.

MOYERS: What is it like to be an alien in the land of your birth? 15

ALEXIE: I mean, it's a destructive feeling. Because, you know, a lot of native culture has been destroyed. So you already feel lost inside your
culture. And then you add up feeling lost and insignificant inside the
larger culture. So you end up feeling lost squared. And to never be
recognized, to never have any power, you know, other minority communities actually have a lot of economic, cultural power. But we
don't, you know? Not at all.

I mean, you can still have the Washington Redskins, you know?
You can still have the Atlanta Braves and the Cleveland Indians,
which is by far the worst. And if you look at Chief Wahoo° on their
hats and put Sambo° next to him, it's the same thing. And, you know,
you could never have Sambo anymore.

Most, you know, at least half the country thinks the mascot issue is
insignificant. But I think it's indicative of the ways in which Indians
have no cultural power. We're still placed in the past. So we're either
in the past or we're only viewed through casinos.

MOYERS: Do you feel shoved back into that tight space, that closet, even
by the questions I ask about Indians, natives, reservation, all of that?

ALEXIE: Sometimes. But, I'm, you know, it's who I am. So I have no issue 20
talking about it. You know, I know a lot more about being White than

---

Chief Wahoo: the mascot of the Cleveland Indians, a professional U.S. baseball team.
Sambo: a stereotypical racial character that portrayed African American men as doc-
ile, simple-minded, irresponsible, or carefree.

you know about being Indian. I am extremely conscious of my tribalism. And when you talk about tribalism, you talk about living in a black and white world. I mean, Native American tribalism sovereignty, even the political fight for sovereignty° and cultural sovereignty is a very us versus them. And I think a lot of people in this country, especially European Americans and those descended from Europeans, don't see themselves as tribal, you know? I don't think, for instance, Republicans see themselves as tribal. I was speaking to a Republican here in New York, a friend of mine. And, you know, I asked him, "Do you think it's an accident that, what, 80 percent of Republicans are White males?" And he did. I mean, he—

MOYERS: Coincidence, huh?

ALEXIE: Yes. He couldn't even imagine that he's part of a tribe. So as a member of a tribe I think I have a more conscious relationship with black and white thinking. And I used to be quite a black and white thinker in public life and private life until 9/11, you know? And the end game of tribalism is flying planes into buildings. That's the end game. So since then, I have tried, and I fail often, but I have tried to live in the in between. To be conscious, what did Fitzgerald° say? The sign of a superior mind is the ability to hold two different ideas. Keats° called it negative capability. So I have tried to be in that and fail often, but I try.

MOYERS: That's what I get from your poems. You even see Yo Yo Ma's° cello differently from the rest of us. That's one of my favorites. Would you read it?

ALEXIE: Oh, yes—   25

MOYERS: Here it is.

ALEXIE: And this poem is called "Tribal Music."

> Watching PBS, it occurs
> To me that I want to be
> Yo Yo Ma's cello.
>
> Hello! Does this mean
> That I'm sexually attracted
> To Yo Yo Ma? Nah,

---

political fight for sovereignty: the belief that indigenous Native American tribes have an inherent right and authority to govern themselves within U.S. borders.
Fitzgerald: F. Scott Fitzgerald, American author most famous for *The Great Gatsby*.
Keats: John Keats, early-nineteenth-century English poet.
Yo Yo Ma: a famous Chinese American cellist who was born in France.

He's cute and thin
Looks great in a tux,
And makes the big bucks,

But I long to be simultaneously
As strong and fragile
As the cello. I want to be

The union of fingertip
And string. I want less
To be a timorous human

And desire more
To become a solid
Wooden thing, warm

To the touch but much
Colder when left
Alone in my case. I need

To flee the mystery
Of mortality and insanity
And become that space

Between the notes.
I no longer want to be the root
Cause of anybody's pain,

Especially my own.
O, Yo Yo Ma, I hem
And haw, but let's be clear:

I want to abandon
My sixteen-drum fear
And inhabit the pause

That happens between falling
In love and collapsing
Because of love. I want

To be sane. I want to be
Clean and visionary
Like a windowpane.

MOYERS: Where does that come from?

ALEXIE: Well, you know, number one, the cello looks like a woman to me. And, you know, the curves. And so I am in a way, and it's funny to admit this, I am sexually attracted to the cello, the curves really get me. So as I watched him play, you know, Yo Yo Ma is sort of making love to a beautiful woman.

And I want to be that beautiful. So I was thinking of that watching it. And then it occurred to me, you know, I'm a man. I don't want to be a woman. But I want to be the object of beauty. I want to be so clearly beautiful. And in a way it's a need for perfection, you know, the desire to be perfect, even though I can't be and even though if I really started thinking about it I don't want to be. But there's a state of nirvana or bliss especially when Yo Yo Ma's playing. I want to be that blissful. And it's so fleeting. And I'm just incapable of it.

MOYERS: Yearning for that moment of sanity or that place of sanity? 30

ALEXIE: Yes.

MOYERS: You say in there, "To be sane."

ALEXIE: Yes. Well, I'm bipolar.° So, you know, I myself veer between these extremes. And to be in the middle is a strong desire. And I mean, I'm working on this idea, I don't know where it's going to go, that being tribal, being colonized automatically makes you bipolar. I think the entire Native American world is bipolar.

MOYERS: But is this your imagination or are you clinically bipolar?

ALEXIE: I'm clinically— 35

MOYERS: You've been diagnosed— . . . Help me understand what the experience of bipolarity is, what happens to you?

ALEXIE: Well, you know, when you're depressed, you know, it's like the world has ended. Even getting out of bed takes the most massive amount of effort. But when you're manic, oh, it's so addicting. You know, I have finished novels in two weeks in manic stages.

Just staying up, you know, two days in a row writing and great stuff often. I mean, you're crazy. So you get these incredible images. You know, forget Yo Yo Ma's cello. I mean, it ends up being, you know, I'm,

---

bipolar: a mental illness characterized by extreme mood swings.

well, I'm hearkening back to somebody like Sylvia Plath,° you know, writing, "Colossus," you know, "Daddy," you know. "You do not do." You know, which directly comes out of mental illness. And depression and mania. I would venture that most of the world's great art has come out of manic periods in an artist's life.

MOYERS: But has it ever occurred to you that there's been more pre-occupation with Sylvia Plath's illness than with her poetry?

ALEXIE: Oh yeah. I mean, there's a new biography out about her. And it's 40 the same story. It's about her craziness.

MOYERS: Why is that?

ALEXIE: I think we're more interested in the biography.

MOYERS: The story.

ALEXIE. Yeah, and especially in this era, where there are no secrets any-more, where the audience in fact desires so much to know more about the artist. You know? You're supposed to now Twitter everything you're feeling, you know? You go to, you know, some artist's, writer's Twitters. And like everybody else, they're talking about what they had for din-ner, you know? All over writers' Twitter feeds and Facebook pages are pictures of what they had for dinner. And why anybody would care, you know, that I had a bowl of cereal in my hotel room this morning, I don't get it. And—

MOYERS: Sherry Turkle has written a book called *Alone Together* on just 45 this point. Talking about how the Internet has produced this serial isolation.

ALEXIE: Well, when I think the human is so complex, you know? And as we're relating here, we're relating on so many different levels that we don't consciously understand. I mean, we're actually smelling each other right now, but our, we, as we talk, don't know that, but our bod-ies know that, you know? My gestures, your gestures, the look in your eye. And the Internet takes all that away. There was, there is one level of communication on the Internet, which actually in a way is really insulting to the complexity of being human.

MOYERS: How so?

ALEXIE: It limits us to one sense.

MOYERS: One dimension.

ALEXIE: One dimension. And that's not who we are. The poetry, if you 50 will, of life is reduced to this sort of dry, scientific, you know, it's the

---

Sylvia Plath: a celebrated American poet and novelist who suffered from depression and eventually committed suicide.

worst sort of précis of who we are. And, you know, I don't have Facebook friends. I have friends. And a lot of my friends play basketball. And when we play basketball together, literally, we're touching each other.

And that can't be replicated in any form whatsoever with the Internet. And when people say they're really connecting with somebody, I think, it occurs to me that I don't know that they've ever really connected with anybody if they think the Internet is how you do it.

You know? It's postcard relationships. In order to know somebody through their words, I mean, it has to be an, it has to be a letter, you know? It has to be a long e-mail. It has to be a five-page handwritten letter, you know, it has to be overwhelming and messy and sloppy as humans are.

And Facebook and Twitter and these other social sites bring every, I mean, 140 characters. I mean, I'm on Twitter and I have fun. But I don't think anybody learns anything about me as a person.

You know, one of the things I've always tried to do as a public person is limit the gap between who I am on a daily basis and who I am on a stage. You know, I've tried to be as honest—

MOYERS: Consciously.   55

ALEXIE: Yes, I've tried to be as honest as possible.

MOYERS: How are you different?

ALEXIE: Well, I think I'm a more gentle person in private, maybe slightly more gentle. I mean, I'm a lot more confrontational in public, I mean, I'm a very angry person.

MOYERS: At what?

ALEXIE: Oppression.   60

MOYERS: Oppression?

ALEXIE: Racism, sexism, colonialism, the sins of capitalism, the sins of socialism, human weakness, human cruelty. You know, when we behave more like a lion pride than people with prehensile thumbs.

MOYERS: Is writing cathartic for you? Is it healing?

ALEXIE: No. I think it can be healing for readers. You know, I have been helped and healed by other people's words.

MOYERS: Same here.   65

ALEXIE: But I, my own words for myself, oh man, I don't think so.

MOYERS: Do you think of yourself as a poet first and foremost? Because that's how I first got introduced to you.

ALEXIE: I'm naturally a poet. I started as a poet. I think it's how I look at the world, you know?

MOYERS: What, how does it help you see the world?

ALEXIE: You know, I look at Yo Yo Ma's cello and want to be the cello. I 70
think a novelist would want to write about where the cello came from,
who built it. I don't care.

MOYERS: In this poem, "Tribal Music," whose tribal music are you writing about?

ALEXIE: Mine. A tribe of one. You know, one of the things about being
tribal, being a member of a tribe is the force that makes you, that
makes the tribe, for you to be like the tribe, to share similar values, to
be less of an individual and more a very conscious member of a community to share political beliefs, to share cultural beliefs.

And I've always resisted that. One of the misconceptions about Indians, you know, because liberals love Indians, you know? White liberals worship Indians. But actually, Indians are a conservative lot. I
mean, we by and large vote Democrat, but we live very Republican
lives, you know? Indian communities, there's no separation of church
and state, war is a virtue, guns are everywhere, by and large pro-life.
So, you know, once again, it's a very bipolar existence.

You know, this, you know, knowing that Democrats, by and large,
are going to support us more. But still behaving like Republicans. You
know, it occurs to me it's like big city Republicans, who live these incredibly liberal, secular lives in the city, while espousing small-town
religious politics.

MOYERS: You know that you've been described as both an explorer and 75
an exploder of Indian stereotype. And alcohol is surely one of the
most persistent stereotypes, correct?

ALEXIE: It's not a stereotype. It's a damp, damp reality. I mean, Native
Americans have an epidemic rate of alcoholism. I'm an alcoholic, recovering. My father was an alcoholic. My big brother's an alcoholic.
One of my little sister's an alcoholic. My mom's a recovering alcoholic.
Every single one of my cousins is a drinker. All of my aunts and uncles
were drinkers, some of them have quit, some of them never did. You
know, my classmates, you know, three have died in alcoholic-related
accidents. My brother has had five best friends die in alcohol-related
accidents. And we're not atypical.

MOYERS: What have you come to understand about that?

ALEXIE: It's medication. Trying to take away the pain. And in a way it has
substituted for cultural ways of dealing with the pain. So instead of
singing, we're drinking. And my father often said, "I drink because I'm
Indian," which, you know, is the saddest thing imaginable.

MOYERS: Why did you drink?

ALEXIE: Because I'm Indian. 80

MOYERS: How do you, how do you stay sober?

ALEXIE: Because I don't want to disappoint all those hungry sons out there, whose own fathers have failed them. Because whether or not I believe in visions or omens, the last time I drank, I completely destroyed my then girlfriend's birthday party with my alcoholic behavior. And woke up the next day, late in the afternoon feeling deeply ashamed and thinking once again, "I'm going to quit." You know, I tried eight or nine times. But I woke up, went and checked my mail, and the acceptance from "Hanging Loose" for my first poetry book was in the mail. And I thought, "Okay, this is a sign. Write poems, sober up."

MOYERS: And you did?

ALEXIE: And I did.

MOYERS: You live in Seattle now. You've lived there for how long?   85

ALEXIE: Twenty years.

MOYERS: But as a boy you lived on the Spokane—

ALEXIE: Indian Reservation.

MOYERS: —Reservation. How do you feel where you're in a place where your people were ethnically cleansed?

ALEXIE: We didn't make reservations. The military, the US military and   90 government made reservations. And it was a place where we're supposed to be concentrated and die and disappear. And I don't know, and I think it's only out of self-destructive impulses that Native Americans have turned reservations into sacred spaces.

MOYERS: You don't consider them sacred?

ALEXIE: No. Often the place where reservations are aren't where the sacred locations were for tribes. I think Spokane, because it's where Spokane Falls is, I think the city is actually far more sacred than the reservation.

MOYERS: Well, more Indians today live in the cities than live on reservations.

ALEXIE: It's almost 70 percent of natives live off the reservation. It's not easy to live in either place.

MOYERS: Can American Indians ever feel easy in a country that is   95 haunted by the memories of genocide, ethnic cleansing?

ALEXIE: I think for that process to begin, the United States would have to officially apologize. I mean, there's a Holocaust museum in the United States, which I think there should be.

MOYERS: Right in downtown Washington.

ALEXIE: But there should also be a Native American Holocaust Museum.

MOYERS: Why isn't there?

ALEXIE: This country's not good at admitting to its sins.   100

MOYERS: Have you ever heard an apology for what happened?

ALEXIE: From White liberals. But never from White conservatives.

MOYERS: These were, you were nearly exterminated. You—

ALEXIE: Oh, late nineteenth century, early twentieth, we almost blinked out. Ironically, the reservations also saved us, because they concentrated us.

MOYERS: How did that save you?

ALEXIE: Breeding. You know? It wasn't until much later when the U.S.   105 government realized that relocation, taking us out of, you know, highly-concentrated ethnic communities was the way to dissipate us. And that didn't work either, you know? There are blond Indians now, red-headed Indians. So it was cultural protection. It was sovereignty. The impulse to be together in a little group.

MOYERS: In this sense, possessed of a horrendous memory, do you sometimes think of yourself as Jewish?

ALEXIE: Constantly. I have a really strong identification with that. And, you know, it's funny, because my poetry editors are Jewish. And, you know, I have quite an international following. And one of my editors tells the story of, she and her husband were in Europe and these Italian scholars were really obsessed and questioning about, you know, "What is the relationship between Jewish people and Indians?" And using my work as sort of this universal idea. And they asked her, "What does the Native world think about," you know, "Jewish people and Native Americans?" And she said. "I think only Sherman talks about that." So I, it's a very personal vision.

The big thing is humor. Humor in the face of incredible epic pain. I mean, Jewish folks invented American comedy. When you're being funny in the United States, you're being Jewish. And despite all this incredible dislocation. And the thing, you know, even though it's pretty similar in population, the number of Jewish folks and the number of Native Americans, they've had this incredible success. They have this incredible cultural power.

And in a way, I wish that was us. In a way, that could have easily been us. You know? Indians with our storytelling and artistic ability could have created Hollywood. We could have created American comedy. So in some ways, we're the yin and yang of the American genocidal coin.

MOYERS: There's a poem that I have read several times in anticipation of 110 this meeting. And this one is troubling. "Another Proclamation."

ALEXIE: "Another Proclamation."

When
Lincoln
Delivered
The
Emancipation
Proclamation,
Who
Knew

that, one year earlier, in 1862, he'd signed and approved the order
for the largest public execution in United States history?° Who did
they execute? "Mulatto, mixed-bloods, and Indians." Why did they
execute them? "For uprising against the State and her citizens."
Where did they execute them? Mankato, Minnesota. How did
they execute them? Well, Abraham Lincoln thought it was good

And
Just
To
Hang
Thirty-eight
Sioux

simultaneously. Yes, in front of a large and cheering crowd, thirty-
eight Indians dropped to their deaths. Yes, thirty-eight necks
snapped. But before they died, thirty-eight Indians sang their
death songs. Can you imagine the cacophony of thirty-eight
different death songs? But wait, one Indian was pardoned at the
last minute, so only thirty-seven Indians had to sing their death
songs. But O, O, O, O, can you imagine the cacophony of that one
survivor's mourning song? If he taught you the words, do you
think you would sing along?

MOYERS: Talk about that.
ALEXIE: Well, essentially, they were executed for terrorism. The perception of being terrorists for defending themselves and their people
from colonial incursions.

---

largest public execution in United States history: On December 26, 1862, President
Abraham Lincoln ordered thirty-eight Dakota Indians to be hanged in Mankato,
Minnesota, for killing white settlers.

MOYERS: As the Whites had been pushing into Minnesota, pushing them further west. And promised them, as I understand it, food in exchange for land. And then the food didn't come. And the Indians reacted violently.

ALEXIE: And then all over the country massacres happening of people   115
they, you know, they would push these tribes and these people onto reservations and then send the soldiers in to wage war on them. I just learned, I don't know why I didn't know this, some sort of denial I guess. But they gave medals of honor to U.S. soldiers who participated at Wounded Knee,° absolute massacres of unarmed women, children, and elderly people.

They gave medals of honor. And, you know, this idea of Lincoln as this great savior. Which is true. But in deifying him, it completely, completely whitewashes the fact that he was also a complete part of the colonization of Indians, a complete part of the wholesale slaughter of Indians.

MOYERS: He lived in the in between like everyone. What I know of this incident is that 303 Indians were sentenced to death. President Lincoln commuted the sentences of 265 of them on the basis he himself said of not enough evidence, but allowed 38 of them to be hanged.

ALEXIE: So, the hypocrisy abounds. So once again, the way in which I watch *Lincoln* the movie is far different than most people watch *Lincoln*.

That movie in no way portrayed the complexity of human beings, and certainly does not portray the complexity of Lincoln, who for his genius was also, you know, an incredibly, as any politician, an incredibly conflicted and conflicting man, who was capable of ordering great evil. And who did, in fact, by ordering it, created a great evil, committed great evil, a sinful, sinful man that Lincoln.

MOYERS: Had you known about the story for a long time?   120

ALEXIE: You know, most Indians know a lot about the massacres. They're touchstones. They're a myth for us.

MOYERS: What saved you spiritually? What saved you inwardly?

ALEXIE: Storytelling.

MOYERS: How so?

ALEXIE: The age-old stories, you know, sort of an actual sacred nostalgia.   125
And keeping all the ghosts alive, keeping all the memories alive. If

---

Wounded Knee: an area in South Dakota and the site of the Battle of Wounded Knee or the Wounded Knee Massacre, in which more than two hundred Sioux men, women, and children were killed by U.S. troops on December 29, 1890.

you tell a story well enough, everybody in it is right there. So nobody ever dies.

MOYERS: Why did you call this book *Blasphemy*?

ALEXIE: Because I've been so often accused of it by Indians and non-Indians.

MOYERS: How so?

ALEXIE: Because I question everything. Because even though I do believe in the sacred, I believe just as strongly in questioning what people think is sacred. Because we're humans and we make mistakes. So, you know, I do my best to point out our weaknesses. And people don't like that. And the weaknesses of our institutions and the weaknesses of our politicians and the weaknesses of our religions.

Once again, 9/11 was the event for me. 9/11 turned all sorts of people into fundamentalists who weren't otherwise, on the left and the right, in the Christian worlds and in the Muslim worlds. And I refuse to participate.

MOYERS: So what do you mean by blasphemy? 130

ALEXIE: I don't believe in your God. And "your" means the royal "your."

MOYERS: Do you believe in your God?

ALEXIE: No.

MOYERS: What do you believe in?

ALEXIE: Stories. Stories are my God. 135

MOYERS: Would you read this for me?

ALEXIE: "Vilify."

> I've never been to Mount Rushmore. It's just too silly. Even now,
>   as I write this, I'm thinking
> About the T-shirt that has four presidential faces on the front and
>   four bare asses on the back.
> Who's on that damn T-shirt anyway? Is it both Roosevelts,
>   Jefferson, and Lincoln?
>
> Don't get me wrong, I love my country. But epic sculpture just
>   leaves me blinking
> With dry-eyed boredom (and don't get me started on blown glass
>   art. I really hate that crap).
> I've never been to Mount Rushmore. It's just too silly. Even now,
>   as I write this, I'm thinking
>
> That I'd much rather commemorate other presidents. Let's honor
>   JFK's whoring and drinking

Or the thirteen duels Andrew Jackson fought to defend his wife's
   honor. Why don't we sculpt that?
Who's on that damn Rushmore anyway? Is it McKinley, Arthur,
   Garfield, and Lincoln?

And, yes, I know, there's a rival sculpture of Crazy Horse,° but the
   sight of that one is ball-shrinking
Because Crazy Horse never allowed his image to be captured, so
   which sculptor do you think he'd now attack?
I've never been to Mount Rushmore. It's just too silly. Even now,
   as I write this I'm thinking

About George W's wartime lies, Clinton's cigars, and Nixon's
   microphones, and I'm cringing
Because I know every president, no matter how great on the
   surface, owned a heart chewed by rats.
Who's on that damn Rushmore anyway? Is it Buchanan, both
   Adamses, and Mr. Lincoln?

Answer me this: After the slaughterhouse goes out of business,
   how long will it go on stinking
Of red death and white desire? Should we just cover the presidents'
   faces with gas masks?
Who cares? I've never been to Rushmore. It's too silly. Even now,
   as I write this, I'm thinking:
"Who's on that damn mountain anyway? Is it Jefferson,
   Washington, Reagan, and Lincoln?"

MOYERS: Now go eight pages over to page 38 and read me your
   footnote.
ALEXIE: So it's footnote 13.
   Honestly, I've never been there. This is not a conceit for the poem. I've   140
truly never had any interest in visiting Mount Rushmore or the Crazy
Horse memorial. Once while driving in the region, I thought about
stopping by, but I didn't. I have no regrets. I've seen Alfred Hitchcock's
film *North by Northwest*, where Cary Grant's climactic battle with the
bad guys happens on the face of Mount Rushmore. It's exciting. But I
much prefer the ending where we watch Grant and Eva Marie Saint
start to make out in their train car, and then cut to the final shot of

Crazy Horse: Native American chief, tactician, and warrior in the Sioux resistance to
U.S. colonial expansion.

that awesomely phallic train penetrating a wonderfully vaginal mountain tunnel. I'm a lover, not a fighter.

MOYERS: And we're all glad for that. Sherman Alexie, I really enjoyed this time with you. And thank you very much for sharing it.

ALEXIE: Thank you, thank you.

Understanding the Text

1. What is the "in between" and Alexie's attitude toward it? How does tribalism relate to the in between? Who "lives" in this space and why?

2. Alexie talks about being "a first-generation immigrant" and "an indigenous immigrant" (par. 14). What does he mean? Moyers then asks Alexie to explain his experiences as "an alien in the land of [Alexie's] birth" (par. 15). Explain Alexie's answer and what it reveals about his status as an indigenous immigrant and, by extension, the status of most Native Americans.

3. Outline or list the major topics that Moyers and Alexie cover in this interview. How do you categorize these topics? What subtopics or points can you list under each major topic or category? Do you see a controlling theme, idea, or position emerging? If so, identify and explain it and support your explanation with examples from the interview. If not, explain what your outline and categories reveal about the major themes of the interview.

Reflection and Response

4. Consider the title of the reading. Do you think that the title accurately represents the content of the interview? Why or why not? To answer this question, identify the cultural borders outside of which Alexie lives, and explain his experience doing so.

5. Alexie and Moyers discuss Indian reservations, relocation, and genocide (pars. 88–121). What surprised you in this portion of the interview? Why? Does either man refer to historical events, people, or places of which you had no knowledge? If so, how did you process this information? If you had the opportunity to join the interview at this point, what questions would you ask and why?

6. Identify places in the interview where Alexie uses humor to convey a point. Describe the type of humor in each instance (for example, irony, satire, or put-down). Why do you think he chooses this approach? Do you think his use of humor is effective? Why or why not?

Making Connections

7. Look at paragraphs 88–121, where Alexie and Moyers discuss the history of Indian relocation, reservations, and genocide. Where do you see borders playing a critical role in these events? What specific aspects of borders seem the most relevant? Explain why. Write a short essay in which you take a position regarding what this portion of the interview reveals about how physical and cultural borders affect people. Support your position with evidence from this reading and several others from this book. For example,

Norma Cantú's "Living on the Border: A Wound That Will Not Heal" (p. 58) and Gloria Anzaldúa's "How to Tame a Wild Tongue" (p. 143) — both of which deal with issues of conflict, alienation, and identity — might prove helpful.

8. Research an Indian reservation and explain how its borders were determined. Look at Alexander Diener and Joshua Hagen's explanation of territoriality and sovereignty in "A Very Bordered World" (p. 15). How do these concepts relate to the establishment and maintenance of Indian reservations? Alexie also speaks about Indian reservations and Indian sovereignty (pars. 88–111). How do his insights extend your understanding of sovereignty?

Mason and Dixon's Line

The Provincial Freeman

This article appeared on April 14, 1855, in the *Provincial Freeman*, a weekly newspaper (1854–1957) published by free blacks in Toronto, Canada West (present-day Ontario). The paper's masthead read "Devoted to Anti-Slavery, Temperance, and General Literature." Although the paper identified Samuel B. Ward as the editor, Mary Ann (Shadd) Carey published and coedited it, writing many of the *Provincial Freeman's* articles. An activist and educator and the daughter of free blacks, Carey was the first African American woman publisher in North America.

The article begins with an important question regarding the original purpose of the 233-mile-long border between Maryland and Pennsylvania. The writer provides a brief history of the Mason-Dixon Line, ending by pointing out its significance in the lives of both white and black Americans. As you read "Mason and Dixon's Line," think about why Carey and Ward might have chosen to provide this history in their newspaper. Also keep in mind this article's prophetic closing line as you read Kate DeVan Filer's "Our Most Famous Border: The Mason-Dixon Line," which follows this reading.

What was the origin and purpose of it? We hear it frequently spoken of as connected with slavery, and as originally relating to that subject. Nothing can be further from the truth. At the time that line was established, slavery existed on both sides of it. A brief account of its origin may be of some interest just at this time.

As early as the year 1682, a dispute arose between William Penn and Lord Baltimore, respecting the construction of their respective grants, of what now form the States of Pennsylvania, Delaware, and Maryland. Lord Baltimore claimed to and including the 40th degree of north latitude; and William Penn mildly, yet firmly, resisted the claim. The debatable land was one degree of 69 English miles on the south of Pennsylvania, and extended west as far as the State itself. The matter was finally brought into the Court of Chancery, in England, and after tedious delays, on the 15th day of May, 1750, Lord Chancellor Hardwicke made a decree awarding costs against Lord Baltimore, and directing that commissioners should be appointed to mark the boundaries between the parties. The commissioners so appointed met at Newcastle on the 15th day of November, 1775, and, not being able to agree, separated. After a further litigation and delay, the whole matter was settled by mutual agreement between the surviving heirs of the original litigants.

In the year 1761, Mr. Charles Mason, of the Royal Observatory, was sent to Pennsylvania with all the needful astronomical instruments, to measure a degree of latitude. That duty he performed, and a report of his proceedings was made to the Royal Society of London, for the year 1767.

This Mr. Mason and Jeremiah Dixon were appointed to run the line in dispute, which appears to have been done in conformity with the Lord Chancellor's decree. This is the famous "Mason and Dixon's line," and the boundary between Pennsylvania on the south and Maryland on the north. Any one desirous of more detailed information will find it in Douglass's *History of America*, published in Boston, in 1751; Proud's *History of Pennsylvania*; the *Memoirs of the Historical Society of Pennsylvania*; and 1 Vesy's Reports, 352, Penn. Lord Baltimore.

> "Little did the actors in this matter think that in aftertimes, the line established with so much trouble and expense would ever be connected with a subject calculated to shake a great nation to its centre."

Little did the actors in this matter think that in aftertimes, the line 5
established with so much trouble and expense would ever be connected
with a subject calculated to shake a great nation to its centre.

Our Most Famous Border: The Mason-Dixon Line

Kate DeVan Filer

This history of the Mason-Dixon Line, written by Kate DeVan Filer, a communication major at Pennsylvania State University at the time, appears on the Pennsylvania Center for the Book's Web site. The Pennsylvania Center is one of the state centers affiliated with the Center for the Book at the Library of Congress. According to its Web site, the Center for the Book was "established by public law in 1977 to promote books, reading and libraries, as well as the scholarly study of books." Filer's piece, found on the Center's interactive map, is particularly relevant for Pennsylvanians; however, the story she tells reaches beyond the state's borders as well.

As you read, note the important stakeholders in establishing this line between Maryland and Pennsylvania and how the boundary took on a political and cultural significance that continues to resonate.

In the southwest corner of the state, near Mount Morris, there is a monument that reads: "MASON-DIXON LINE. Made famous as line between free and slave states before War Between the States. The survey establishing Maryland-Pennsylvania boundary began in 1763; halted by Indian wars 1767; continued to southwest corner in 1782; marked 1784." The text seems simple enough to understand. The marker stands to show where the North ends and the South starts. However, the story behind the boundary line is bitter, hostile, and, at times, violent; and the story dates back to the mid-seventeenth century.

In 1632, King Charles I gave Cecilius Calvert the land that has since been named Maryland. The boundaries for Calvert's land were: in the north, the state began at the 40 degree north latitude line; in the south by the Potomac River and the latitude through Watkins Point on the Eastern Shore; in the east, the Atlantic Ocean; and, in the west, by a meridian through the source of the Potomac River. Three of these borders were created by natural landmarks and were easy to determine exactly [where] Calvert's land began. However, the northern border would become a problem.

Nearly 50 years later in 1681, King Charles II gave William Penn the land that would be named Pennsylvania. Three of the boundaries for Penn's land were quite easy to measure: in the north, Penn's land ended at the 43 degree north latitude line; in the west, the land reached until a meridian five degrees west of the Delaware Bay; and in the east, the boundary was marked by the Delaware Bay. The southern boundary

123

extended eastward along the fortieth parallel of north latitude until it intersected an arc extending in a 12-mile radius from the courthouse in New Castle, which is now in Delaware. However, the 40 degree latitude line and the circle do not intersect anywhere—in fact, at the closest point, they were 13 miles away. This created what has now been dubbed "The Wedge," although that land is now considered to be part of Delaware.

> "The story behind the boundary line is bitter, hostile, and, at times, violent; and the story dates back to the mid-seventeenth century."

The dispute between the Penns and the Calverts began because they both claimed the land between the 39th and 40th parallels according to the charters granted to each colony. One of the reasons why this land dispute was so heated is that the historic city of Philadelphia falls within the disputed territory and both states wanted to claim the landmark as their own. However, land disputes were common in the seventeenth and eighteenth century because as American wilderness land was sold to English adventurers, the monarchs distributing the land did not have accurate maps, so new land proprietors only had a vague idea of what belonged to them.

For a while, Penn and Calvert each tried to convince the inhabitants of the disputed area that they were citizens of their state and should pay taxes appropriately. The residents did not necessarily care which state they lived in, but they did not want to pay taxes to both colonies. However, the battle between the Penn and the Calvert families continued for three generations without a truce. According to *The History of Maryland* by John Thomas Scharf, both William Penn II and Charles Calvert received a letter from the King of England in April 1681 requiring them "to make a true division and separation of the said provinces of Maryland and Pennsylvania, according to the bounds and degrees of our said Letters Patent and fixing certain Land Marks where they shall appear to border upon each other for the preventing and avoiding all doubts and controversies that may otherwise happen concerning the same." 5

Yet despite many meetings between the Penns and the Calverts in the coming years, no compromise was agreed upon and the tensions between the two families escalated even more. By the 1730s, the land dispute had grown increasingly violent. The hostilities launched Cresap's War, also known as the Conojocular War, which was series of skirmishes between the two colonies. The scuffle was named after Thomas Cresap, who had been raised in the colony of Maryland, but moved in 1730 to modern-day Wrightsville, in York County, Pennsylvania. Despite living in Pennsylvania, he remained incredibly loyal to Maryland. Since he was very vocal about his ties to Maryland, on several occasions, Pennsylvania mobs tried to murder him and although he was never injured, some of his attackers were wounded.

Aside from the colorful personality of Cresap, his actions only added fuel to the fire that was already raging between the two colonies. In 1736, the Maryland militia got involved and the Pennsylvania militia followed in 1737. Although the militias stopped fighting in 1738, after King George II enacted a cease-fire, it would take more than another decade to fully end the dispute. In 1750, King George II stepped in again to create a truce that granted the Penns the borderline land, but no one knew for sure where the boundary line was. So Charles Mason and Jeremiah Dixon, two of the most respected English surveyors, were commissioned to travel across the Atlantic Ocean in hopes of finalizing the agreement between the two colonies. In England, Mason was an astronomer who had worked at the Royal Observatory and Dixon was a well-known surveyor. The two had worked together on a previous assignment and were chosen in part for their prior success as a team. A finalized contract was signed in 1763 by the grandsons of William Penn and Cecilius Calvert and shortly after then, Mason and Dixon arrived in Philadelphia.

Beginning in November 1763, Mason and Dixon set about determining the exact location of Philadelphia, so they could then base all measurements off that point of reference. Based on the land charters, the Pennsylvania-Maryland border was to be laid 15 miles due south of Philadelphia; this would become known as the "Post mark'd West." Nearly six months after they arrived in the colonies, Mason and Dixon had established that "Post mark'd West" lay in the latitude of 39 degrees 43 minutes 18.2 seconds north. From this spot, the famous Mason-Dixon Line would extend due west and east. The rest of their journey seemed simple: all they needed to do was walk the line east and west putting down markers as they went. However, before they laid the north-south line, they needed to finalize Pennsylvania's eastern border between what would become Delaware. This boundary became known as the "Tangent Line" and ran more than 80 miles from the Delaware Middle Point, which had been established in 1751, to where it intersected a 12-mile circle surrounding New Castle, Delaware.

Finally, in early April 1765, Mason and Dixon were ready to begin surveying the Pennsylvania-Maryland border, which would become known as the Mason-Dixon Line. The first section of the West Line was easy enough to establish and by the end of May, they had traveled as far west as the Susquehanna River, which is the border of modern-day York and Lancaster counties. Once Mason and Dixon arrived there, they completed Lord Baltimore's eastern boundary from the Tangent Point due

MASON AND DIXON LAYING OUT THE
BOUNDARY LINE

A nineteenth-century illustration of Charles Mason and
Jeremiah Dixon drafting the boundary line.
© Bettmann/Corbis

north to the West Line. Continuing west from the Susquehanna River,
through modern-day York County, they had reached the foot of the
North Mountain, in modern-day Franklin County, by the end of October
1765. Beginning in the spring of 1766, Mason and Dixon made it from
the North Mountain to Savage Mountain, part of modern-day Somerset
County. Upon arriving at Savage Mountain, they had to stop again until
the Native American chiefs of the Six Nations agreed to allow the surveyors through the region.

Since their journey had been filled with delays due to weather and
Native American politics, Mason and Dixon used their free time to make
other scientific gains. For example, in early 1766, they were the first
people to measure the latitude in North America. Although ship captains
had used latitudes at sea to determine where to dock the ship, no surveyor had measured the latitude on colonial soil. This also proved impor-

10

tant in settling land disputes since frontiersmen had a more accurate way to mark their borders. The latitude measurement was primarily used by the Royal Society to add upon the work of the French Académie Royale des Sciences in defining the size and shape of the Earth.

Luckily for Mason and Dixon, by the end of 1766 they were on the move again and were able to extend the West Line eastward to the Delaware River. While they waited for the spring of 1767 to travel, they spent the winter making the first gravity observations in America. Mason and Dixon continued west again in July 1767 and made it to the Cheat River, which is part of the modern-day Fayette County. It had been nearly four years since they started their survey, but they had reached an impassable roadblock—hostile citizens. Mason and Dixon were unable to get any closer than about 36 miles away from the westernmost end of the line. The portion of the boundary line surveyed by Mason and Dixon was formally approved in early November 1768, which ended a battle between the Penns and the Calverts that had been ongoing for nearly 80 years. Ultimately, Mason and Dixon were not the ones to finish the project, although the boundary still bears their names in memorial. In 1774, David Rittenhouse, the city surveyor for Philadelphia, set the remaining borders between Pennsylvania and the surrounding colonies Maryland, New York, and Virginia, as well as what would later become the Northwest Territory. His boundary lines between Pennsylvania and Maryland extended Mason and Dixon's work the 36 miles needed to reach its western destination.

Although Maryland is not always considered to be a southern state, the Mason-Dixon Line has become known as the boundary between the North and the South. When Mason and Dixon surveyed the land in the late eighteenth century, the border was never about slavery, yet it took on that association on March 1, 1790, when the Pennsylvania Assembly passed legislation ending slavery in the state. They made the Mason-Dixon Line the boundary between slave territory and free land, since slavery was still allowed in Maryland. The border between Pennsylvania and Maryland became tied to the North and South divide, especially after the Missouri Compromise was passed in 1820, which prohibited slavery north of the Mason-Dixon Line. To the many slaves who used whatever means necessary to reach free land, the Mason-Dixon Line became important to their freedom. For the slaves located in Maryland, they only needed to get to the state line to secure their freedom, although many continued traveling north in an attempt to get as far away from their former masters as possible. Even today, the association of Pennsylvania's northern status lingers.

Even in popular culture references, it is clear to see the impact of Mason and Dixon's surveying. The 1953 Warner Brothers cartoon short "Southern Fried Rabbit," starring the typical Looney Tunes cast of characters, features the Mason-Dixon Line, as Bugs Bunny is trying to flee to the North and head to Alabama to escape a carrot famine. Throughout the movie, the North is depicted as being barren and empty, while the South is lush and green. More recently, the award-winning 2006 *Rocky Balboa* film, the final film in the Rocky series, features a character named Mason "The Line" Dixon, which is significant since the movie is set in Philadelphia. On the music charts, many country songs mention the south being defined as below the Mason-Dixon Line. Johnny Cash sings about the border in his 1954 song, "Hey Porter." In the lyrics, a railroad porter is asked how much longer until the train crosses the Mason-Dixon Line, because the singer is longing to be back in the South, even though Cash wrote this while being stationed at a military base in Germany. In the twenty-first century, Mark Knopfler and James Taylor wrote the song "Sailing to Philadelphia" about the construction of the Mason-Dixon Line. The songwriters cite Thomas Pynchon's book, *Mason & Dixon,* as the inspiration for their song. The 1997 novel brings the history of the surveyors and their work to life by suggesting what they may have experienced, based on their original journal entries.

More than 225 years since Mason and Dixon finished, the boundary still stands and it has become the "most famous border in America," according to Edwin Danson's book *Drawing the Line: How Mason and Dixon Surveyed the Most Famous Border in America.* When the Mason-Dixon Line was finished, it was marked by more than 200 12" square monuments at 1-mile intervals. Each stone marked had a P on the north side, representing Pennsylvania land, and on the south side, an M was engraved, marking Maryland. Also, there was a larger stone placed every five miles, which was engraved with the Penn coat of arms on the Pennsylvania side and the Calvert coat of arms on the Maryland side. However, not all of those stones remain in the twenty-first century. According to Bijal P. Trivedi's *National Geographic* article entitled "Saving the Mason-Dixon Line," for over a decade two current surveyors Todd Babcock and Dilwyn Knott have been working to locate and document every stone that Mason and Dixon laid in the late eighteenth century to mark the Pennsylvania-Maryland line. They do have the advantage of using modern Global Positioning System (GPS) tools that Mason and Dixon did not have. In the article, Babcock said: "We're losing (the stones) at an increasing rate so it's very important that we obtain the precise location of each stone so we can go back and repair damaged stones and replace lost ones." The

Mason-Dixon Line Preservation Partnership, of which Babcock is president, continues to work to preserve the history of the Mason-Dixon Line.

Sources

Bailey, Kenneth P. *Thomas Cresap: Maryland Frontiersman.* Boston: The Christopher House, 1944.

Bedini, Silvio A. "American National Biography Online: Rittenhouse, David." *American National Biography Online.* Feb. 2000. American Council of Learned Societies. 10 Sept. 2008 <http://www.anb.org/articles/13/13-01396.html>.

Danson, Edwin. "American National Biography Online: Mason, Charles and Jeremiah Dixon." *American National Biography Online.* Jan. 2002. American Council of Learned Societies. 10 Sept. 2008 <http://www.anb.org/articles/13/13-02640.html>.

Danson, Edwin. *Drawing the Line; How Mason and Dixon Surveyed the Most Famous Border in America.* New York: Wiley, 2000.

Ecenbarger, William. *Walkin' the Line: A Journey from Past to Present along the Mason-Dixon.* Boston: M. Evans & Company, Incorporated, 2001.

Lancaster County Historical Society. *Historical Papers and Addresses of the Lancaster County Historical Society,* 1909.

Mannix, Mary. "Biography of Thomas Cresap." *Maryland Online Encyclopedia.* 2005.

Mason, Charles, and Jeremiah Dixon. *The Journal of Charles Mason and Jeremiah Dixon.* Philadelphia, PA: American Philosophical Society, 1969.

Rosenberg, Matt. "The Mason-Dixon Line." *About.com.* 17 Aug. 2007. New York Times Company. 10 Sept. 2008 <http://geography.about.com/od/political geography/a/masondixon.htm>.

Scharf, John T. *History of Maryland: From the Earliest Period to the Present Day.* Hatboro, PA: Tradition Press, 1967.

"The Mason & Dixon Line Preservation Partnership." *Mason & Dixon Line Preservation Partnership.* Oct. 2007. Mason & Dixon Line Preservation Partnership. 3 Sept. 2008 <http://www.mdlpp.org/>.

Trivedi, Bijal P. "Saving the Mason-Dixon Line." *National Geographic Today.* 10 Apr. 2002. 10 Sept. 2008 <http://news.nationalgeographic.com/news/2002/04/0410_020410_TVmasondixon.html>.

Veech, James. *Mason and Dixon's Line: A History, Including an Outline of the Boundary Controversy Between Pennsylvania and Virginia.* Pittsburgh: W. S. Haven, 1857.

Understanding the Text

1. Both "Mason and Dixon's Line" (p. 121) and "Our Most Famous Border" open by drawing attention to the line's eventual association with slavery. Why do you think both writers chose to open this way? Consider the context of each piece — its original date of publication, purpose, and audience.

2. Explain when and how the Mason-Dixon Line became associated with slavery.

3. Filer tells us that "the story behind the boundary line is bitter, hostile, and, at times, violent" (par. 1). What violence erupted because of the dispute over the territory forming Maryland's northern border and Pennsylvania's southern one?

4. When Mason and Dixon began surveying this border, what difficulties did they encounter? Who was affected by this line?

Reflection and Response

5. What do these readings tell us about why and how we establish interior borders? What was (and often is) at stake and for whom? In your response, consider the difficulties that Mason and Dixon encountered and the length of time it took them to complete the project. What do these factors indicate about the nature of borders themselves?

6. Once the Mason-Dixon Line became associated with slavery, crossing that line became extremely significant in the lives of many individuals. Many of these border crossers claimed new names, and they were "re-labeled" because of a shift in their status. What was that shift, and what label accompanied it? Make a list of the various terms, labels, and names for those who cross borders (international and interior, past and present). Can you identify patterns or categories? What do these terms and categories reveal about the effect borders have on us both individually and collectively?

Making Connections

7. Filer writes, "[T]he Mason-Dixon Line became important to [many slaves'] freedom. For the slaves located in Maryland, they only needed to get to the state line to secure their freedom" (par. 12). What does this statement suggest for individuals who lived south of the Mason-Dixon Line? Do some research into the importance of this boundary line in African American history. What was the reality for slaves who crossed this boundary? Did doing so "secure" their freedom? When you consider these border crossers, what other critical issues arise related to how borders function? (Look at Alexander Diener and Joshua Hagen's "A Very Bordered World," p. 15.) Can you make connections between the promises of the Mason-Dixon Line and current issues regarding borders, border crossings, and border crossers?

8. Compare the "brief" account of the origins of the Mason-Dixon Line, published in the *Provincial Freeman* (p. 121), with Filer's fuller account and with one that you find on your own. (Filer's "Sources" is a good resource.) What do these three accounts reveal about the line's place in America's cultural, political, and social history? What conclusions do you draw regarding how we understand the physical borders, boundaries, or lines that demarcate land as well as the ones that create cultural divides? Are they the same? Why or why not?

9. Research why and how we draw boundary lines today (for example, electoral districts and school districts). Write an essay explaining and analyzing the process, and include a visual representation of the boundary. In your paper, explain who or what determines this district. Identify the key players involved in making the decisions as well as those affected by these boundary lines. What controversies or politics emerge in drawing these lines? What geographical or physical difficulties exist in establishing the boundaries? What issues regarding inclusion, exclusion, access, or power arise? How are these issues negotiated?

The Missouri Compromise (1820)

U.S. Congress

The Missouri Compromise of 1820 ended a rancorous congressional debate over new states' rights to choose slavery versus Congress's right to prohibit it as states entered the Union. The bill admitted Missouri as a slave state and Maine as a free one and, with the exception of Missouri, excluded slavery from the Louisiana Purchase lands north of latitude 36° 30'. This last provision created an invisible line — or boundary — across a vast expanse of land. Invisible or not, this boundary profoundly affected the lives of many people. As you read the document that established Missouri's statehood, consider the consequences of drawing these sorts of lines across territory.

*A*n Act to authorize the people of the Missouri territory to form a constitution and state government, and for the admission of such state into the Union on an equal footing with the original states, and to prohibit slavery in certain territories.

Be it enacted by the Senate and House of Representatives of the United States of America, in Congress assembled, That the inhabitants of that portion of the Missouri territory included within the boundaries herein after designated, be, and they are hereby, authorized to form for themselves a constitution and state government, and to assume such name as they shall deem proper; and the said state, when formed, shall be admitted into the Union, upon an equal footing with the original states, in all respects whatsoever.

SEC. 2. And be it further enacted, That the said state shall consist of all the territory included within the following boundaries, to wit: Beginning in the middle of the Mississippi river, on the parallel of thirty-six degrees of north latitude; thence west, along that parallel of latitude, to the St. Francois river; thence up, and following the course of that river, in the middle of the main channel thereof, to the parallel of latitude of thirty-six degrees and thirty minutes; thence west, along the same, to a point where the said parallel is intersected by a meridian line passing through the middle of the mouth of the Kansas river, where the same empties into the Missouri river, thence, from the point aforesaid north, along the said meridian line, to the intersection of the parallel of latitude which passes through the rapids of the river Des Moines, making the said line to correspond with the Indian boundary line; thence east, from the point of intersection last aforesaid, along the said parallel of latitude, to the middle of the channel of the main fork of the said river Des Moines;

thence down and along the middle of the main channel of the said river Des Moines, to the mouth of the same, where it empties into the Mississippi river; thence, due east, to the middle of the main channel of the Mississippi river; thence down, and following the course of the Mississippi river, in the middle of the main channel thereof, to the place of beginning: Provided, The said state shall ratify the boundaries aforesaid. And provided also, That the said state shall have concurrent° jurisdiction on the river Mississippi, and every other river bordering on the said state so far as the said rivers shall form a common boundary to the said state; and any other state or states, now or hereafter to be formed and bounded by the same, such rivers to be common to both; and that the river Mississippi, and the navigable rivers and waters leading into the same, shall be common highways, and for ever free, as well to the inhabitants of the said state as to other citizens of the United States, without any tax, duty imposed, or toll, therefor, imposed by the said state.

> "Be it enacted . . . That the inhabitants of that portion of the Missouri territory . . . be, and they are hereby, authorized to form for themselves a constitution and state government . . . upon an equal footing with the original states, in all respects whatsoever."

SEC. 3. And be it further enacted, That all free white male citizens of the United States, who shall have arrived at the age of twenty-one years, and have resided in said territory: three months previous to the day of election, and all other persons qualified to vote for representatives to the general assembly of the said territory, shall be qualified to be elected and they are hereby qualified and authorized to vote, and choose representatives to form a convention, who shall be apportioned amongst the several counties as follows: From the county of Howard, five representatives. From the county of Cooper, three representatives. From the county of Montgomery, two representatives. From the county of Pike, one representative. From the county of Lincoln, one representative. From the county of St. Charles, three representatives. From the county of Franklin, one representative. From the county of St. Louis, eight representatives. From the county of Jefferson, one representative. From the county of Washington, three representatives. From the county of St. Genevieve, four representatives. From the county of Madison, one representative. From the county of Cape Girardeau, five representatives. From the county of

concurrent: simultaneous or happening at the same time.

New Madrid, two representatives. From the county of Wayne, and that portion of the county of Lawrence which falls within the boundaries herein designated, one representative.

And the election for the representatives aforesaid shall be holden on 5 the first Monday, and two succeeding days of May next, throughout the several counties aforesaid in the said territory, and shall be, in every respect, held and conducted in the same manner, and under the same regulations as is prescribed by the laws of the said territory regulating elections therein for members of the general assembly, except that the returns of the election in that portion of Lawrence county included in the boundaries aforesaid, shall be made to the county of Wayne, as is provided in other cases under the laws of said territory.

SEC. 4. And be it further enacted, That the members of the convention thus duly elected, shall be, and they are hereby authorized to meet at the seat of government of said territory on the second Monday of the month of June next; and the said convention, when so assembled, shall have power and authority to adjourn to any other place in the said territory, which to them shall seem best for the convenient transaction of their business; and which convention, when so met, shall first determine by a majority of the whole number elected, whether it be, or be not, expedient at that time to form a constitution and state government for the people within the said territory, as included within the boundaries above designated; and if it be deemed expedient, the convention shall be, and hereby is, authorized to form a constitution and state government; or, if it be deemed more expedient, the said convention shall provide by ordinance for electing representatives to form a constitution or frame of government; which said representatives shall be chosen in such manner, and in such proportion as they shall designate; and shall meet at such time and place as shall be prescribed by the said ordinance; and shall then form for the people of said territory, within the boundaries aforesaid, a constitution and state government: Provided, That the same, whenever formed, shall be republican, and not repugnant to the constitution of the United States; and that the legislature of said state shall never interfere with the primary disposal of the soil by the United States, nor with any regulations Congress may find necessary for securing the title in such soil to the bona fide purchasers; and that no tax shall be imposed on lands the property of the United States, and in no case shall non-resident proprietors be taxed higher than residents.

SEC. 5. And be it further enacted, That until the next general census shall be taken, the said state shall be entitled to one representative in the House of Representatives of the United States.

SEC. 6. And be it further enacted, That the following propositions be, and the same are hereby, offered to the convention of the said territory of Missouri, when formed, for their free acceptance or rejection, which, if accepted by the convention, shall be obligatory upon the United States:

First. That section numbered sixteen in every township, and when such section has been sold, or otherwise disposed of, other lands equivalent thereto, and as contiguous° as may be, shall be granted to the state for the use of the inhabitants of such township, for the use of schools.

Second. That all salt springs, not exceeding twelve in number, with six sections of land adjoining to each, shall be granted to the said state for the use of said state, the same to be selected by the legislature of the said state, on or before the first day of January, in the year one thousand eight hundred and twenty-five; and the same, when so selected, to be used under such terms, conditions, and regulations, as the legislature of said state shall direct; Provided, That no salt spring, the right whereof now is, or hereafter shall be, confirmed or adjudged° to any individual or individuals, shall, by this section, be granted to the said state: And provided also, That the legislature shall never sell or lease the same, at any one time, for a longer period than ten years, without the consent of Congress.

Third. That five per cent of the net proceeds of the sale of lands lying within the said territory or state, and which shall be sold by Congress, from and after the first day of January next, after deducting all expenses incident to the same, shall be reserved for making public roads and canals, of which three fifths shall be applied to those objects within the state, under the direction of the legislature thereof; and the other two fifths in defraying, under the direction of Congress, the expenses to be incurred in making of a road or roads, canal or canals, leading to the said state.

Fourth. That four entire sections of land be, and the same are hereby, granted to the said state, for the purpose of fixing their seat of government thereon; which said sections shall, under the direction of the legislature of said state, be located, as near as may be, in one body, at any time, in such townships and ranges as the legislature aforesaid may select, on any of the public lands of the United States: Provided, That such locations shall be made prior to the public sale of the lands of the United States surrounding such location.

Fifth. That thirty-six sections, or one entire township, which shall be designated by the President of the United States, together with the other

10

---

contiguous: touching or nearly touching along a boundary; adjacent.
adjudged: decided or pronounced judicially.

lands heretofore reserved for that purpose, shall be reserved for the use of a seminary of learning, and vested in the legislature of said state, to be appropriated solely to the use of such seminary by the said legislature: Provided, That the five foregoing propositions herein offered, are on the condition that the convention of the said state shall provide, by an ordinance, irrevocable without the consent [of] the United States, that every and each tract of land sold by the United States, from and after the first day of January next, shall remain exempt from any tax laid by order or under the authority of the state, whether for state, county, or township, or any other purpose whatever, for the term of five years from and after the day of sale; And further, That the bounty lands granted, or hereafter to be granted, for military services during the late war, shall, while they continue to be held by the patentees, or their heirs remain exempt as aforesaid from taxation for the term of three year[s], from and after the date of the patents respectively.

SEC 7. And be it further enacted, That in case a constitution and state government shall be formed for the people of the said territory of Missouri, the said convention or representatives, as soon thereafter as may be, shall cause a true and attested copy of such constitution or frame of state government, as shall be formed or provided, to be transmitted to Congress.

SEC. 8. And be it further enacted, That in all that territory ceded by France to the United States, under the name of Louisiana, which lies north of thirty-six degrees and thirty minutes north latitude, not included within the limits of the state, contemplated by this act, slavery and involuntary servitude, otherwise than in the punishment of crimes, whereof the parties shall have been duly convicted, shall be, and is hereby, forever prohibited: Provided always, That any person escaping into the same, from whom labour or service is lawfully claimed, in any state or territory of the United States, such fugitive may be lawfully reclaimed and conveyed to the person claiming his or her labour or service as aforesaid. 15

APPROVED, March 6, 1820.

Understanding the Text

1. What is the stated purpose of the Missouri Compromise?
2. What is the specific function of each section? In other words, what does each section "enact"?
3. Throughout this document, its writers refer to Missouri as both a territory and a state. Track the use of these words. When do the framers use these

words interchangeably? Explain the significance of doing so. When they do not, explain how and in what context each term is used. Why are they used differently?

Reflection and Response

4. Section 8 in the Missouri Compromise designates Missouri as a slaveholding state, thus labeling it a southern state. If you look at a map of the United States, do you consider Missouri part of the American South? Why or why not? If not, in what region would you place it? What section or sections in the Missouri Compromise could help you explain your answer?

5. As you read this document, what struck you as most important or most surprising? Explain what you found surprising or why you found something important. For example, what seems most relevant to understanding the political, social, or cultural role of borders?

Making Connections

6. Compare the territory granted to Missouri in 1820, as described in section 2, with the state's present shape. Research and explain the difference. Pay particular attention to Missouri's western and northern borders. What does each border suggest about power, sovereignty, and territoriality? Alexander Diener and Joshua Hagen's "A Very Bordered World" (p. 15) may prove helpful. You might also read the "Don't Skip This: You'll Just Have to Come Back Later" section from Mark Stein's *How the States Got Their Shapes* (p. 37) and consider his explanation regarding Congress's commitment to the principle that all states should be created equal.

danielvfung/Getty Images

3

How Do Borders Influence the Ways We Write and Speak?

We all make daily decisions regarding language, and many of us write almost every day, whether it is an essay for class on our computers or text messages on our smartphones. As we write and shift among the "languages" of various digital spaces, we often cross linguistic borders and cultural boundaries. Shifting among spaces, screens, audiences, and devices requires continual language play, code-switching, and border crossing. Perhaps you have never thought of the writing you do on Snapchat, Twitter, or Facebook as having to do with borders. However, once we realize that issues related to language and borders touch all of our lives, we can investigate how this relationship affects who we are and how we negotiate our world, including how we speak and write.

To understand how borders influence the way we communicate, we need to think about the multiple ways we can cross language boundaries. Some of these crossings are creative and playful; others are painful and shameful. These crossings sometimes involve easy transitions between languages and, at other times, tortured or imprecise translations. While many crossings involve writing or speaking, they often involve other forms of language behaviors as well. Finally, and almost without exception, crossing and identifying linguistic borders involve examining one's own identity and culture.

Language, culture, and identity provide the threads that weave together the readings in this chapter. Each writer explores some aspect of these three elements as they relate to crossing linguistic borders, speaking a border language, or developing communication strategies across cultural borders.

As Gloria Anzaldúa proclaims in "How to Tame a Wild Tongue," identity, culture, and history merge in her border language: "Ethnic identity is twin skin to linguistic identity — I am my language" (p. 150). Manuel Muñoz addresses similar issues from a vantage point far different from that of

photo: danielvfung/Getty Images

Anzaldúa. Whereas she claims a position within a borderlands, he writes from a shifting position of "arrivals and departures" as he looks at the consequences of Anglicizing Mexican names and vilifying Spanish.

Marginalizing a language and its speakers points to the personal and cultural aspects involved in the ways we write and speak. Chinese American writer Amy Tan explores these notions as she contemplates all the "Englishes" that she grew up with — among them is her "mother tongue," the "language that . . . made sense of the world" (p. 165). Yet this mother tongue originated from Tan's immigrant mother's "broken" English, and her mother's literal border crossing had initiated this language. Tan, however, challenges the commonly accepted idea that her mother's English, and the English of many other immigrants, is "broken," adding the adjective *impeccable* before *broken*. Thus Tan playfully and willfully reminds us that languages at the edges can move to the center.

Although not explicitly addressing the languages at the margins of society, François Grosjean explores the experiences of those whom society often marginalizes: bilingual or multilingual individuals. In his blog posts included in this chapter, he questions the link between language and identity as he explores the effects on personality of switching languages. Interestingly, Grosjean believes that culture, rather than language itself, is the crucial influence.

Culture also plays a major role in "Living in Two Worlds, but with Just One Language." In this interview, Michele Norris and Steve Inskeep talk with Elysha O'Brien, who shares her experiences as a Mexican American who does not speak Spanish. Norris argues that the issue is "specifically about how the language and the culture are intertwined" (p. 177). O'Brien offers insights about her uneasiness straddling two cultures — white American and Mexican — and how language contributed to that uneasiness. In "Communication Strategies across Cultural Borders," Karla Scott examines how young black women straddle and cross cultural borders. She reveals the often performative aspects of linguistic border crossings, and she, like Anzaldúa, reminds us that much is at stake for those who reside in border regions, wherever their locations. In Scott's study, identity, language, history, and culture collide in the participants' experiences, thus reinforcing the significance of keeping these elements in mind when considering the importance of borders in our lives.

The communication strategies that these young black women develop in order to negotiate their cultural border crossings often involve a form of "code-switching," a topic that Kristen Hawley Turner addresses in "Digitalk: A New Literacy for a Digital Generation." This form of linguistic border crossing is fast and frequent, involving "patterns of language [that] cross technological boundaries," blurring the lines between written discourse and the spoken word (p. 201). Turner recognizes "digitalk" as a literacy similar to other home literacies such as African-American Vernacular English. In this way, she analyzes a form of literacy and communication that many of us practice every day, perhaps unaware that we are crossing cultural and linguistic boundaries.

In what follows, think carefully about the multiplicity of experiences that unfold as each writer articulates his or her experiences with, perspectives on, and arguments about language. As you read, consider the pain and possibilities of writing and speaking within and across the shadows of borders.

How to Tame a Wild Tongue

Gloria Anzaldúa

Gloria Anzaldúa (1942–2004), poet, writer, feminist, and cultural theorist, grew up on the Texas-Mexico border. She earned an M.A. in English and education from the University of Texas and did doctoral work at the University of California, Santa Cruz, which post-humously awarded her a Ph.D. Teaching formally as a writer-in-residence or visiting professor in colleges and informally as an organizer/facilitator of writing groups for women of color, Anzaldúa focused on the areas of feminism, creative writing, and Chicano/a studies. Among the many books she wrote are *This Bridge Called My Back: Writings by Radical Women of Color* (1981), coedited with Cherríe Moraga, and *Borderlands/La Frontera: The New Mestiza* (1987), named one of the thirty-eight best books of 1987 by the *Library Journal*.

Throughout *Borderlands/La Frontera*, Anzaldúa uses a blend of languages, switching between Spanish and English, often without translation. This mix of languages heightens readers' awareness of language's exclusionary power. For Anzaldúa, language is a border that one continually confronts and crosses. As you read "How to Tame a Wild Tongue," which first appeared in *Borderlands/La Frontera*, pay close attention to how you negotiate the Spanish passages. Anzaldúa also interweaves her own personal experiences with her "home tongues" and the historical and collective experiences of Chicanas/os straddling the borderlands. Consider this blending of the personal and historical as Anzaldúa reveals the link among borders, language, and identity.

"We're going to have to control your tongue," the dentist says, pulling out all the metal from my mouth. Silver bits plop and tinkle into the basin. My mouth is a motherlode.

The dentist is cleaning out my roots. I get a whiff of the stench when I gasp. "I can't cap that tooth yet, you're still draining," he says.

"We're going to have to do something about your tongue," I hear the anger rising in his voice. My tongue keeps pushing out the wads of cotton, pushing back the drills, the long thin needles. "I've never seen anything as strong or as stubborn," he says. And I think, how do you tame a wild tongue, train it to be quiet, how do you bridle and saddle it? How do you make it lie down?

A sign outside Geno's Steaks, a sandwich shop in Philadelphia, demands that customers speak English because "This Is America."
AP Photo/Matt Rourke

Who is to say that robbing a people of its language is less violent than war?

—RAY GWYN SMITH[1]

I remember being caught speaking Spanish at recess—that was good for three licks on the knuckles with a sharp ruler. I remember being sent to the corner of the classroom for "talking back" to the Anglo teacher when all I was trying to do was tell her how to pronounce my name. "If you want to be American, speak 'American.' If you don't like it, go back to Mexico where you belong."

"I want you to speak English. *Pa' hallar buen trabajo tienes que saber* 5 *hablar el inglés bien. Qué vale toda tu educación si todavía hablas inglés con un* 'accent,'"° my mother would say, mortified that I spoke English like a Mexican. At Pan American University, I and all Chicano students were required to take two speech classes. Their purpose: to get rid of our accents.

Pa' hallar buen trabajo tienes que saber hablar el inglés bien. Qué vale toda tu educación si todavía hablas inglés con un 'accent': "To find good work, you have to know how to speak English well. What's all of your education worth if you still speak English with an 'accent'?"

Attacks on one's form of expression with the intent to censor are a violation of the First Amendment.° *El Anglo con cara de inocente nos arrancó la lengua.* Wild tongues can't be tamed, they can only be cut out.

Overcoming the Tradition of Silence

Ahogadas, escupimos el oscuro.
Peleando con nuestra propia sombra
el silencio nos sepulta.°

En boca cerrada no entran moscas. "Flies don't enter a closed mouth" is a saying I kept hearing when I was a child. *Ser habladora* was to be a gossip and a liar, to talk too much. *Muchachitas bien criadas*, well-bred girls don't answer back. *Es una falta de respeto* to talk back to one's mother or father. I remember one of the sins I'd recite to the priest in the confession box the few times I went to confession: talking back to my mother, *hablar pa' 'tras, repelar. Hocicona, repelona, chismosa*, having a big mouth, questioning, carrying tales are all signs of being *mal criada*. In my culture they are all words that are derogatory if applied to women—I've never heard them applied to men.

The first time I heard two women, a Puerto Rican and a Cuban, say the word *"nosotras,"* I was shocked. I had not known the word existed. Chicanas use *nosotros* whether we're male or female. We are robbed of our female being by the masculine plural. Language is a male discourse.

And our tongues have become
dry   the wilderness has
dried out our tongues   and
we have forgotten speech.

—IRENA KLEPFISZ[2]

Even our own people, other Spanish speakers *nos quieren poner candados en la boca.*° They would hold us back with their bag of *reglas de academia.*

First Amendment: constitutional amendment that guarantees freedom of religion, expression, assembly, and the right to petition.
Ahogadas, escupimos el oscuro. / Peleando con nuestra propia sombra / el silencio nos sepulta: "Drowned, we spit the dark. / Fighting with our own shadow / the silence buries us."
nos quieren poner candados en la boca: "want to put padlocks on our mouth."

Oyé como ladra: el lenguaje de la frontera°

Quien tiene boca se equivoca.°

—MEXICAN SAYING

"*Pocho*, cultural traitor, you're speaking the oppressor's language by   10
speaking English, you're ruining the Spanish language," I have been accused by various Latinos and Latinas. Chicano Spanish is considered by
the purist and by most Latinos deficient, a mutilation of Spanish.

But Chicano Spanish is a border tongue which developed naturally.
Change, *evolución, enriquecimiento de palabras nuevas por invención o adop-
ción°* have created variants of Chicano Spanish, *un nuevo lenguaje. Un lenguaje que corresponde a un modo de vivir.* Chicano Spanish is not incorrect,
it is a living language.

For a people who are neither Spanish nor live in a country in which
Spanish is the first language; for a people who live in a country in which
English is the reigning tongue but who are not Anglo; for a people who
cannot entirely identify with either standard (formal, Castillian) Spanish
nor standard English, what recourse is left to them but to create their
own language? A language which they can connect their identity to, one
capable of communicating the realities and values true to themselves—a
language with terms that are neither *español ni inglés*, but both. We speak
a patois, a forked tongue, a variation of two languages.

Chicano Spanish sprang out of the Chicanos' need to identify ourselves
as a distinct people. We needed a language with which we could communicate with ourselves, a secret language. For some of us, language is a
homeland closer than the Southwest—for many Chicanos today live in
the Midwest and the East. And because we are a complex, heterogeneous
people, we speak many languages. Some of the languages we speak are:

1. Standard English

2. Working class and slang English

3. Standard Spanish

4. Standard Mexican Spanish

5. North Mexican Spanish dialect

Oyé como ladra: el lenguaje de la frontera: "It sounds like barks: the language of the
borderland."
Quien tiene boca se equivoca: "Whoever has a mouth makes mistakes."
Change, evolución, enriquecimiento de palabras nuevas por invención o adopción:
"Change, evolution, enrichment of new words by invention or adoption."

6. Chicano Spanish (Texas, New Mexico, Arizona, and California have regional variations)

7. Tex-Mex

8. *Pachuco* (called *caló*)

My "home" tongues are the languages I speak with my sister and brothers, with my friends. They are the last five listed, with 6 and 7 being closest to my heart. From school, the media, and job situations, I've picked up standard and working class English. From Mamagrande Locha and from reading Spanish and Mexican literature, I've picked up Standard Spanish and Standard Mexican Spanish. From *los recién llegados*, Mexican immigrants, and *braceros*,° I learned the North Mexican dialect. With Mexicans I'll try to speak either Standard Mexican Spanish or the North Mexican dialect. From my parents and Chicanos living in the Valley, I picked up Chicano Texas Spanish, and I speak it with my mom, younger brother (who married a Mexican and who rarely mixes Spanish with English), aunts, and older relatives.

With Chicanas from *Nuevo México* or *Arizona* I will speak Chicano 15 Spanish a little, but often they don't understand what I'm saying. With most California Chicanas I speak entirely in English (unless I forget). When I first moved to San Francisco, I'd rattle off something in Spanish, unintentionally embarrassing them. Often it is only with another Chicana *tejana* that I can talk freely.

Words distorted by English are known as anglicisms or *pochismos*. The *pocho* is an anglicized Mexican or American of Mexican origin who speaks Spanish with an accent characteristic of North Americans and who distorts and reconstructs the language according to the influence of English.[3] Tex-Mex, or Spanglish, comes most naturally to me. I may switch back and forth from English to Spanish in the same sentence or in the same word. With my sister and my brother Nune and with Chicano *tejano* contemporaries I speak in Tex-Mex.

From kids and people my own age I picked up *Pachuco*. *Pachuco* (the language of the zoot suiters) is a language of rebellion, both against Standard Spanish and Standard English. It is a secret language. Adults of the culture and outsiders cannot understand it. It is made up of slang words from both English and Spanish. *Ruca* means girl or woman, *vato* means guy or dude, *chale* means no, *simón* means yes, *churro* is sure, talk

---

braceros: manual laborers. Under the bracero program, millions of Mexican farmworkers were allowed to come to the United States to work on short-term contracts between 1942 and 1964.

is *periquiar; pigionear* means petting, *que gacho* means how nerdy, *ponte águila* means watch out, death is called *la pelona*. Through lack of practice and not having others who can speak it, I've lost most of the *Pachuco* tongue.

Chicano Spanish

Chicanos, after 250 years of Spanish/Anglo colonization, have developed significant differences in the Spanish we speak. We collapse two adjacent vowels into a single syllable and sometimes shift the stress in certain words such as *maíz/maiz, cohete/cuete*. We leave out certain consonants when they appear between vowels: *lado/lao, mojado/mojao*. Chicanos from South Texas pronounce *f* as *j* as in *jue (fue)*. Chicanos use "archaisms," words that are no longer in the Spanish language, words that have been evolved out. We say *semos, truje, haiga, ansina*, and *naiden*. We retain the "archaic" *j*, as in *jalar*, that derives from an earlier *h* (the French *halar* or the Germanic *halon* which was lost to standard Spanish in the sixteenth century), but which is still found in several regional dialects such as the one spoken in South Texas. (Due to geography, Chicanos from the Valley of South Texas were cut off linguistically from other Spanish speakers. We tend to use words that the Spaniards brought over from Medieval Spain. The majority of the Spanish colonizers in Mexico and the Southwest came from Extremadura—Hernán Cortés° was one of them—and Andalucía. Andalucians pronounce *ll* like a *y*, and their *d*'s tend to be absorbed by adjacent vowels: *tirado* becomes *tirao*. They brought *el lenguaje popular, dialectos y regionalismos*.°⁴)

Chicanos and other Spanish speakers also shift *ll* to *y* and *z* to *s*.[5] We leave out initial syllables, saying *tar* for *estar, toy* for *estoy, hora* for *ahora* (*cubanos* and *puertorriqueños* also leave out initial letters of some words). We also leave out the final syllable such as *pa* for *para*. The intervocalic *y*, the *ll* as in *tortilla, ella, botella*, gels replaced by *tortia* or *tortiya, ea, botea*. We add an additional syllable at the beginning of certain words: *atocar* for *tocar, agastar* for *gastar*. Sometimes we'll say *lavaste las vacijas*, other times *lavates* (substituting the *ates* verb endings for the *aste*).

We use anglicisms, words borrowed from English: *bola*, from ball, *car-* 20 *peta* from carpet, *máchina de lavar* (instead of *lavadora*) from washing machine. Tex-Mex argot, created by adding a Spanish sound at the be-

---

Hernán Cortés (ca. 1485–1547): Spanish conquistador and explorer who conquered the Aztecs, thus claiming Mexico for Spain.
el lenguaje popular, dialectos y regionalismos: "the popular language, dialects, and regionalisms."

ginning or end of an English word such as *cookiar* for cook, *watchar* for watch, *parkiar* for park, and *rapiar* for rape, is the result of the pressures on Spanish speakers to adapt to English.

We don't use the word *vosotros/as* or its accompanying verb form. We don't say *claro* (to mean yes), *imagínate*, or *me emociona*, unless we picked up Spanish from Latinas, out of a book, or in a classroom. Other Spanish-speaking groups are going through the same, or similar, development in their Spanish.

Linguistic Terrorism

> *Deslenguadas. Somos los del español deficiente.* We are your linguistic nightmare, your linguistic aberration, your linguistic *mestisaje*, the subject of your *burla*. Because we speak with tongues of fire we are culturally crucified. Racially, culturally, and linguistically *somos huérfanos*—we speak an orphan tongue.

Chicanas who grew up speaking Chicano Spanish have internalized the belief that we speak poor Spanish. It is illegitimate, a bastard language. And because we internalize how our language has been used against us by the dominant culture, we use our language differences against each other.

Chicana feminists often skirt around each other with suspicion and hesitation. For the longest time I couldn't figure it out. Then it dawned on me. To be close to another Chicana is like looking into the mirror. We are afraid of what we'll see there. *Pena.* Shame. Low estimation of self. In childhood we are told that our language is wrong. Repeated attacks on our native tongue diminish our sense of self. The attacks continue throughout our lives.

Chicanas feel uncomfortable talking in Spanish to Latinas, afraid of their censure. Their language was not outlawed in their countries. They had a whole lifetime of being immersed in their native tongue; generations, centuries in which Spanish was a first language, taught in school, heard on radio and TV, and read in the newspaper.

If a person, Chicana or Latina, has a low estimation of my native tongue, 25 she also has a low estimation of me. Often with *mexicanas y latinas* we'll speak English as a neutral language. Even among Chicanas we tend to speak English at parties or conferences. Yet, at the same time, we're afraid the other will think we're *agringadas°* because we don't speak Chicano

---

agringadas: derogatory slang term for people, often Latinos/as, who act like gringos or foreigners.

Spanish. We oppress each other trying to out-Chicano each other, vying to be the "real" Chicanas, to speak like Chicanos. There is no one Chicano language just as there is no one Chicano experience. A monolingual Chicana whose first language is English or Spanish is just as much a Chicana as one who speaks several variants of Spanish. A Chicana from Michigan or Chicago or Detroit is just as much a Chicana as one from the Southwest. Chicano Spanish is as diverse linguistically as it is regionally.

By the end of this century, Spanish speakers will comprise the biggest minority group in the U.S., a country where students in high schools and colleges are encouraged to take French classes because French is considered more "cultured." But for a language to remain alive it must be used.[6] By the end of this century English, and not Spanish, will be the mother tongue of most Chicanos and Latinos.

So, if you want to really hurt me, talk badly about my language. Ethnic identity is twin skin to linguistic identity—I am my language. Until I can take pride in my language, I cannot take pride in myself. Until I can accept as legitimate Chicano Texas Spanish, Tex-Mex, and all the other languages I speak, I cannot accept the legitimacy of myself. Until I am free to write bilingually and to switch codes without having always to translate, while I still have to speak English or Spanish when I would rather speak Spanglish, and as long as I have to accommodate the English speakers, rather than having them accommodate me, my tongue will be illegitimate.

> "Ethnic identity is twin skin to linguistic identity — I am my language."

I will no longer be made to feel ashamed of existing. I will have my voice: Indian, Spanish, white. I will have my serpent's tongue—my woman's voice, my sexual voice, my poet's voice. I will overcome the tradition of silence.

My fingers
move sly against your palm
Like women everywhere, we speak in code. . . .

—MELANIE KAYE/KANTROWITZ[7]

"Vistas," corridos, y comida:° My Native Tongue

In the 1960s, I read my first Chicano novel. It was *City of Night* by John Rechy, a gay Texan, son of a Scottish father and a Mexican mother. For days I walked around in stunned amazement that a Chicano could write

"Vistas," corridos, y comida: "'Views' [or movies], ballads, and food."

and could get published. When I read *I Am Joaquín,*[8] I was surprised to see a bilingual book by a Chicano in print. When I saw poetry written in Tex-Mex for the first time, a feeling of pure joy flashed through me. I felt like we really existed as a people. In 1971, when I started teaching High School English to Chicano students, I tried to supplement the required texts with works by Chicanos, only to be reprimanded and forbidden to do so by the principal. He claimed that I was supposed to teach "American" and English literature. At the risk of being fired, I swore my students to secrecy and slipped in Chicano short stories, poems, a play. In graduate school, while working toward a Ph.D., I had to "argue" with one advisor after the other, semester after semester, before I was allowed to make Chicano literature an area of focus.

Even before I read books by Chicanos or Mexicans, it was the Mexican 30 movies I saw at the drive-in—the Thursday night special of $1.00 a carload—that gave me a sense of belonging. *"Vámonos a las vistas,"* my mother would call out and we'd all—grandmother, brothers, sister, and cousins—squeeze into the car. We'd wolf down cheese and bologna white bread sandwiches while watching Pedro Infante in melodramatic tearjerkers like *Nosotros los pobres,* the first "real" Mexican movie (that was not an imitation of European movies). I remember seeing *Cuando los hijos se van* and surmising that all Mexican movies played up the love a mother has for her children and what ungrateful sons and daughters suffer when they are not devoted to their mothers. I remember the singing-type "westerns" of Jorge Nogrete and Miguel Aceves Mejía. When watching Mexican movies, I felt a sense of homecoming as well as alienation. People who were to amount to something didn't go to Mexican movies, or *bailes,* or tune their radios to *bolero, rancherita,* and *corrido* music.

The whole time I was growing up, there was *norteño* music, sometimes called North Mexican border music, or Tex-Mex music, or Chicano music, or *cantina* (bar) music. I grew up listening to *conjuntos,* three- or four-piece bands made up of folk musicians playing guitar, *bajo sexto,* drums, and button accordion, which Chicanos had borrowed from the German immigrants who had come to Central Texas and Mexico to farm and build breweries. In the Rio Grande Valley, Steve Jordan and Little Joe Hernández were popular, and Flaco Jiménez was the accordion king. The rhythms of Tex-Mex music are those of the polka, also adapted from the Germans, who in turn had borrowed the polka from the Czechs and Bohemians.

I remember the hot, sultry evenings when *corridos*—songs of love and death on the Texas-Mexican borderlands—reverberated out of cheap amplifiers from the local *cantinas* and wafted in through my bedroom window.

Corridos first became widely used along the South Texas/Mexican border during the early conflict between Chicanos and Anglos. The *corridos* are usually about Mexican heroes who do valiant deeds against the Anglo oppressors. Pancho Villa's° song, "*La cucaracha,*" is the most famous one. *Corridos* of John F. Kennedy and his death are still very popular in the Valley. Older Chicanos remember Lydia Mendoza, one of the great border *corrido* singers who was called *la Gloria de Tejas.* Her "*El tango negro,*" sung during the Great Depression, made her a singer of the people. The everpresent *corridos* narrated one hundred years of border history, bringing news of events as well as entertaining. These folk musicians and folk songs are our chief cultural mythmakers, and they made our hard lives seem bearable.

I grew up feeling ambivalent about our music. Country-western and rock-and-roll had more status. In the 50s and 60s, for the slightly educated and *agringado* Chicanos, there existed a sense of shame at being caught listening to our music. Yet I couldn't stop my feet from thumping to the music, could not stop humming the words, nor hide from myself the exhilaration I felt when I heard it.

There are more subtle ways that we internalize identification, especially in the forms of images and emotions. For me food and certain smells are tied to my identity, to my homeland. Woodsmoke curling up to an immense blue sky; woodsmoke perfuming my grandmother's clothes, her skin. The stench of cow manure and the yellow patches on the ground; the crack of a .22 rifle and the reek of cordite. Homemade white cheese sizzling in a pan, melting inside a folded *tortilla.* My sister Hilda's hot, spicy *menudo, chile colorado* making it deep red, pieces of *panza* and hominy floating on top. My brother Carito barbequing *fajitas* in the backyard. Even now and 3,000 miles away, I can see my mother spicing the ground beef, pork, and venison with *chile.* My mouth salivates at the thought of the hot steaming *tamales* I would be eating if I were home.

Si le preguntas a mi mamá, "¿Qué eres?"°

Identity is the essential core of who we are as individuals, the conscious experience of the self inside.

—GERSHEN KAUFMAN[9]

Pancho Villa (1878–1923): famous and popular Mexican revolutionary who fought in the Mexican Revolution against dictator Porfirio Díaz.
Si le preguntas a mi mamá, "¿Qué eres?": "If you ask my mom, 'What are you?'"

Nosotros los Chicanos straddle the borderlands. On one side of us, we are constantly exposed to the Spanish of the Mexicans, on the other side we hear the Anglos' incessant clamoring so that we forget our language. Among ourselves we don't say *nosotros los americanos, o nosotros los españoles, o nosotros los hispanos.* We say *nosotros los mexicanos*° (by *mexicanos* we do not mean citizens of Mexico; we do not mean a national identity, but a racial one). We distinguish between *mexicanos del otro lado* and *mexicanos de este lado.*° Deep in our hearts we believe that being Mexican has nothing to do with which country one lives in. Being Mexican is a state of soul—not one of mind, not one of citizenship. Neither eagle nor serpent, but both. And like the ocean, neither animal respects borders.

> *Dime con quien andas y te diré quien eres.*
> (Tell me who your friends are and I'll tell you who you are.)
> —MEXICAN SAYING

Si le preguntas a mi mamá, "¿Qué eres?" te dirá, "Soy mexicana." My brothers and sister say the same. I sometimes will answer *"soy mexicana"* and at others will say *"soy Chicana" o "soy tejana."* But I identified as *"Raza"* before I ever identified as *"mexicana"* or "Chicana."

As a culture, we call ourselves Spanish when referring to ourselves as a linguistic group and when copping out. It is then that we forget our predominant Indian genes. We are 70–80 percent Indian.[10] We call ourselves Hispanic[11] or Spanish-American or Latin American or Latin when linking ourselves to other Spanish-speaking peoples of the Western hemisphere and when copping out. We call ourselves Mexican-American[12] to signify we are neither Mexican nor American, but more the noun "American" than the adjective "Mexican" (and when copping out).

Chicanos and other people of color suffer economically for not acculturating. This voluntary (yet forced) alienation makes for psychological conflict, a kind of dual identity—we don't identify with the Anglo-American cultural values and we don't totally identify with the Mexican cultural values. We are a synergy of two cultures with various degrees of Mexicanness or Angloness. I have so internalized the borderland conflict that sometimes I feel like one cancels out the other and we are zero, nothing, no one. *A veces no soy nada ni nadie. Pero hasta cuando no lo soy, lo soy.*°

---

nosotros los mexicanos: "we the Mexicans."
mexicanos del otro lado and **mexicanos de este lado**: "Mexicans from the other side" and "Mexicans from this side."
A veces no soy nada ni nadie. Pero hasta cuando no lo soy, lo soy: "Sometimes I am nothing or nobody. But even when I am not, I am."

When not copping out, when we know we are more than nothing, we 40
call ourselves Mexican, referring to race and ancestry; *mestizo* when af-
firming both our Indian and Spanish (but we hardly ever own our Black
ancestry); Chicano when referring to a politically aware people born
and/or raised in the U.S.; *Raza* when referring to Chicanos; *tejanos* when
we are Chicanos from Texas.

Chicanos did not know we were a people until 1965 when Cesar
Chavez° and the farmworkers united° and *I Am Joaquín* was published and
la Raza Unida° party was formed in Texas. With that recognition, we became a distinct people. Something momentous happened to the Chicano
soul—we became aware of our reality and acquired a name and a language (Chicano Spanish) that reflected that reality. Now that we had a
name, some of the fragmented pieces began to fall together—who we
were, what we were, how we had evolved. We began to get glimpses of
what we might eventually become.

Yet the struggle of identities continues, the struggle of borders is our
reality still. One day the inner struggle will cease and a true integration
take place. In the meantime, *tenémos que hacer la lucha. ¿Quién está protegiendo los ranchos de mi gente? ¿Quién está tratando de cerrar la fisura entre la
india y el blanco en nuestra sangre? El Chicano, si, el Chicano que anda como
un ladrón en su propia casa.°*

Los Chicanos, how patient we seem, how very patient. There is the quiet
of the Indian about us.[13] We know how to survive. When other races have
given up their tongue, we've kept ours. We know what it is to live under
the hammer blow of the dominant *norte-americano* culture. But more
than we count the blows, we count the days the weeks the years the centuries the eons until the white laws and commerce and customs will rot

---

Cesar Chavez (1927–1993): activist, union leader, and labor organizer who spent
many years as a migrant farmworker. In 1962, he founded the National Farm Workers Association, which joined with other groups to strike against grape growers in
California.
the farmworkers united: Starting in 1962, a number of farmworkers joined the United
Farm Workers, a labor union founded by Cesar Chavez for agricultural workers.
la Raza Unida: National United Peoples Party or United Race Party, established in
1970 as a political party to promote Chicano nationalism and to work for social and
economic change for Chicanos and other minorities.
*[T]enémos que hacer la lucha. ¿Quién está protegiendo los ranchos de mi gente?
¿Quién está tratando de cerrar la fisura entre la india y el blanco en nuestro sangre?
El Chicano, si, el Chicano que anda como un ladrón en su propia casa:* "We have to
wage the struggle. Who is protecting my people's ranches? Who is trying to close the
rift between the Indian and the white in our blood? The Chicano, yes, the Chicano
who walks like a thief in his own home."

in the deserts they've created, lie bleached. *Humildes* yet proud, *quietos* yet wild, *nosotros los mexicanos-Chicanos* will walk by the crumbling ashes as we go about our business. Stubborn, persevering, impenetrable as stone, yet possessing a malleability that renders us unbreakable, we, the *mestizas* and *mestizos*, will remain.

Notes

1. Ray Gwyn Smith, *Moorland Is Cold Country*, unpublished book.

2. Irena Klepfisz, "*Di rayze aheym*/The Journey Home," in *The Tribe of Dina: A Jewish Women's Anthology*, Melanie Kaye/Kantrowitz and Irena Klepfisz, eds. (Montpelier, VT: Sinister Wisdom Books, 1986), 49.

3. R. C. Ortega, *Dialectología Del Barrio*, trans. Hortencia S. Alwan (Los Angeles, CA: R. C. Ortega Publisher & Bookseller, 1977), 132.

4. Eduardo Hernandéz-Chávez, Andrew D. Cohen, and Anthony F. Beltramo, *El Lenguaje de los Chicanos: Regional and Social Characteristics of Language Used by Mexican Americans* (Arlington, VA: Center for Applied Linguistics, 1975), 39.

5. Hernandéz-Chávez, xvii.

6. Irena Klepfisz, "Secular Jewish Identity: Yidishkayt in America," in *The Tribe of Dina*. Kaye/Kantrowitz and Klepfisz, eds., 43.

7. Melanie Kaye/Kantrowitz, "Sign," in *We Speak in Code: Poems and Other Writings* (Pittsburgh, PA: Motheroot Publications, Inc., 1980), 85.

8. Rodolfo Gonzales, *I Am Joaquín/Yo Soy Joaquín* (New York, NY: Bantam Books, 1972). It was first published in 1967.

9. Gershen Kaufman, *Shame: The Power of Caring* (Cambridge, MA: Schenkman Books, Inc., 1980), 68.

10. John R. Chávez, *The Lost Land: The Chicano Images of the Southwest* (Albuquerque, NM: University of New Mexico Press, 1984), 88–90.

11. "Hispanic" is derived from *Hispanis* (*España*, a name given to the Iberian Peninsula in ancient times when it was a part of the Roman Empire) and is a term designated by the U.S. government to make it easier to handle us on paper.

12. The Treaty of Guadalupe Hidalgo created the Mexican-American in 1848.

13. Anglos, in order to alleviate their guilt for dispossessing the Chicano, stressed the Spanish part of us and perpetrated the myth of the Spanish Southwest. We have accepted the fiction that we are Hispanic, that is Spanish, in order to accommodate ourselves to the dominant culture and its abhorrence of Indians. Chávez, 88–91.

Understanding the Text

1. Explain "the tradition of silence" (pars. 7–12). Who is silenced? By whom? Why?

2. In your own words, explain Chicano Spanish. Why is it important to Anzaldúa and to her main argument in this piece? Use textual evidence to support your answer.

3. When discussing cultural identification, Anzaldúa uses the term "copping out" three times in paragraph 38. Then, in paragraph 40, she shifts to "not copping out." What does she mean by "copping out" and "not copping out"? Who is copping out and of what? What arguments regarding language and cultural identity does she make in paragraphs 38–40?

Reflection and Response

4. Why does Anzaldúa think that Chicanos need a "secret language" (par. 13)? And what does she mean when she says that "language is a homeland closer than the Southwest" (par. 13)? Use textual evidence from the essay to support your answer.

5. Anzaldúa writes, "So, if you want to really hurt me, talk badly about my language. Ethnic identity is twin skin to linguistic identity — I am my language" (par. 27). Do you agree? Explain why or why not. Consider your own relationship with language as well as Anzaldúa's reasoning.

6. Look at several of the passages containing Spanish and English, and note where Anzaldúa explains the Spanish in English and where she does not. How do you react to these passages? Do they pose a barrier to understanding her meaning? Why do you think Anzaldúa leaves the Spanish untranslated?

Making Connections

7. In paragraph 14, Anzaldúa describes all her languages, including her " 'home' tongues." Amy Tan writes about her "mother tongue" (p. 163), and Kristen Hawley Turner refers to "home discourse" and "home literacy" (p. 199). Read Tan's and Turner's essays and explore this idea of a home language or home literacy by putting these writers in conversation with each other. In other words, explain where their ideas intersect with each other's and with Anzaldúa's. Where do all three writers diverge? What does each writer add to the concept of a home language that can help you explain it? Make sure to add your own ideas on home languages to theirs.

8. Anzaldúa writes, "Chicanos did not know we were a people until 1965 when Cesar Chavez and the farmworkers united and *I Am Joaquín* was published and *la Raza Unida* party was formed in Texas . . . — we became aware of our reality and acquired a name and a language" (par. 41). Research the history of the Chicano movement, focusing on the importance of borders, borderlands, and language in the creation of the movement. Using your research and examples from Anzaldúa's essay, explain the significance of those three aspects in the Chicano movement.

Leave Your Name at the Border

Manuel Muñoz

A novelist and short story writer, Manuel Muñoz currently teaches creative writing at the University of Arizona, Tucson. He has published a novel, *What You See in the Dark* (2011), and two short story collections, *The Faith Healer of Olive Avenue* (2007) and *Zigzagger* (2003). His work has appeared in the *New York Times*, *Glimmer Train*, *Epoch*, *Eleven Eleven*, and *Boston Review*.

In "Leave Your Name at the Border," which first appeared in the *New York Times* in 2007, Muñoz considers the personal and collective consequences of Anglicized pronunciations of Mexican names. Pay attention to how he places his personal experiences within a wider cultural context in order to emphasize the complexity of language's place in our lives.

At the Fresno airport, as I made my way to the gate, I heard a name over the intercom. The way the name was pronounced by the gate agent made me want to see what she looked like. That is, I wanted to see whether she was Mexican. Around Fresno, identity politics rarely deepen into exacting terms, so to say "Mexican" means, essentially, "not white." The slivered self-identifications Chicano, Hispanic, Mexican-American and Latino are not part of everyday life in the Valley. You're either Mexican or you're not. If someone wants to know if you were born in Mexico, they'll ask. Then you're From Over There—de allá. And leave it at that.

The gate agent, it turned out, was Mexican. Well-coiffed, in her 30s, she wore foundation that was several shades lighter than the rest of her skin. It was the kind of makeup job I've learned to silently identify at the mall when I'm with my mother, who will say nothing about it until we're back in the car. Then she'll stretch her neck like an ostrich and point to the darkness of her own skin, wondering aloud why women try to camouflage who they are.

I watched the Mexican gate agent busy herself at the counter, professional and studied. Once again, she picked up the microphone and, with authority, announced the name of the missing customer: "Eugenio Reyes, please come to the front desk."

You can probably guess how she said it. Her Anglicized pronunciation wouldn't be unusual in a place like California's Central Valley. I didn't have a Mexican name there either: I was an instruction guide.

When people ask me where I'm from, I say Fresno because I don't expect them to know little Dinuba. Fresno is a booming city of nearly 5

500,000 these days, with a diversity—white, Mexican, African-American, Armenian, Hmong and Middle Eastern people are all well represented— that shouldn't surprise anyone. It's in the small towns like Dinuba that surround Fresno that the awareness of cultural difference is stripped down to the interactions between the only two groups that tend to live there: whites and Mexicans. When you hear a Mexican name spoken in these towns, regardless of the speaker's background, it's no wonder that there's an "English way of pronouncing it."

I was born in 1972, part of a generation that learned both English and Spanish. Many of my cousins and siblings are bilingual, serving as translators for those in the family whose English is barely functional. Others have no way of following the Spanish banter at family gatherings. You can tell who falls into which group: Estella, Eric, Delia, Dubina, Melanie.

It's intriguing to watch "American" names begin to dominate among my nieces and nephews and second cousins, as well as with the children of my hometown friends. I am not surprised to meet 5-year-old Brandon or Kaitlyn. Hardly anyone questions the incongruity of matching these names with last names like Trujillo or Zepeda. The English-only way of life partly explains the quiet erasure of cultural difference that assimilation has attempted to accomplish. A name like Kaitlyn Zepeda doesn't completely obscure her ethnicity, but the half-step of her name, as a gesture, is almost understandable.

Spanish was and still is viewed with suspicion: always the language of the vilified illegal immigrant, it segregated schoolchildren into English-only and bilingual programs; it defined you, above all else, as part of a lower class. Learning English, though, brought its own complications with identity. It was simultaneously the language of the white population and a path toward the richer, expansive identity of "American." But it took getting out of the Valley for me to understand that "white" and "American" were two very different things.

Something as simple as saying our names "in English" was our unwittingly complicit gesture of trying to blend in. Pronouncing Mexican names correctly was never encouraged. Names like Daniel, Olivia and Marco slipped right into the mutability of the English language.

I remember a school ceremony at which the mathematics teacher, a white man, announced the names of Mexican students correctly and caused some confusion, if not embarrassment. Years later we recognized that he spoke in deference to our Spanish-speaking parents in the audience, caring teacher that he was. 10

These were difficult names for a non-Spanish speaker: Araceli, Nadira, Luis (a beautiful name when you glide the *u* and the *i* as you're supposed to). We had been accustomed to having our birth names altered for convenience. Concepción was Connie. Ramón was Raymond. My cousin Esperanza was Hope—but her name was pronounced "Hopie" because any Spanish speaker would automatically pronounce the *e* at the end.

Ours, then, were names that stood as barriers to a complete embrace of an American identity, simply because their pronunciations required a slip into Spanish, the otherness that assimilation was supposed to erase. What to do with names like Amado, Lucio or Élida? There are no English "equivalents," no answer when white teachers asked, "What does your name mean?" when what they really wanted to know was "What's the English one?" So what you heard was a name butchered beyond recognition, a pronunciation that pointed the finger at the Spanish language as the source of clunky sound and ugly rhythm.

My stepfather, from Ojos de Agua, Mexico, jokes when I ask him about the names of Mexicans born here. He deliberately stumbles over pronunciations, imitating our elders who have difficulty with Bradley and Madelyn. "Ashley Sánchez. ¿Tú crees?" He wonders aloud what has happened to the "nombres del rancho"—traditional Mexican names that are hardly given anymore to children born in the States: Heraclio, Madaleno, Otilia, Dominga.

My stepfather's experience with the Anglicization of his name— Antonio to Tony—ties into something bigger than learning English. For him, the erasure of his name was about deference and subservience. Becoming Tony gave him a measure of access as he struggled to learn English and get more fieldwork.

This isn't to say that my stepfather welcomed the change, only that he 15 could not put up much resistance. Not changing put him at risk of being passed over for work. English was a world of power and decisions, of smooth, uninterrupted negotiation. There was no time to search for the right word while a shop clerk waited for him to come up with the English name of the correct part needed out in the field. Clear communication meant you could go unsupervised, or that you were even able to read instructions directly off a piece of paper. Every gesture made toward convincing an employer that English was on its way to being mastered had the potential to make a season of fieldwork profitable.

It's curious that many of us growing up in Dinuba adhered to the same rules. Although as children of farm workers we worked in the fields at an early age, we'd also had the opportunity to stay in one town long enough to finish school. Most of us had learned English early and splintered off into a dual existence of English at school, Spanish at home. But instead of recognizing the need for fluency in both languages, we turned it into a peculiar kind of battle. English was for public display. Spanish was for privacy—and privacy quickly turned to shame.

The corrosive effect of assimilation is the displacement of one culture over another, the inability to sustain more than one way of being. It isn't a code word for racial and ethnic acculturation only. It applies to needing and wanting to belong, of seeing from the outside and wondering how to get in and then, once inside, realizing there are always those still on the fringe.

> "The corrosive effect of assimilation is the displacement of one culture over another, the inability to sustain more than one way of being."

When I went to college on the East Coast, I was confronted for the first time by people who said my name correctly without prompting; if they stumbled, there was a quick apology and an honest plea to help with the pronunciation. But introducing myself was painful: already shy, I avoided meeting people because I didn't want to say my name, felt burdened by my own history. I knew that my small-town upbringing and its limitations on Spanish would not have been tolerated by any of the students of color who had grown up in large cities, in places where the sheer force of their native languages made them dominant in their neighborhoods.

It didn't take long for me to assert the power of code-switching in public, the transferring of words from one language to another, regardless of who might be listening. I was learning that the English language composed new meanings when its constrictions were ignored, crossed over or crossed out. Language is all about manipulation, or not listening to the rules.

When I come back to Dinuba, I have a hard time hearing my name   20 said incorrectly, but I have an even harder time beginning a conversation with others about why the pronunciation of our names matters. Leaving a small town requires an embrace of a larger point of view, but a town like Dinuba remains forever embedded in an either/or way of life. My stepfather still answers to Tony and, as the United States–born children grow older, their Anglicized names begin to signify who does and who does not "belong"—who was born here and who is de allá.

My name is Manuel. To this day, most people cannot say it correctly, the way it was intended to be said. But I can live with that because I love the alliteration of my full name. It wasn't the name my mother, Esmeralda, was going to give me. At the last minute, my father named me after an uncle I would never meet. My name was to have been Ricardo. Growing up in Dinuba, I'm certain I would have become Ricky or even Richard, and the journey toward the discovery of the English language's extraordinary power in even the most ordinary of circumstances would probably have gone unlearned.

I count on a collective sense of cultural loss to once again swing the names back to our native language. The Mexican gate agent announced Eugenio Reyes, but I never got a chance to see who appeared. I pictured an older man, cowboy hat in hand, but I made the assumption on his name alone, the clash of privileges I imagined between someone de allá and a Mexican woman with a good job in the United States. Would she speak to him in Spanish? Or would she raise her voice to him as if he were hard of hearing?

But who was I to imagine this man being from anywhere, based on his name alone? At a place of arrivals and departures, it sank into me that the currency of our names is a stroke of luck: because mine was not an easy name, it forced me to consider how language would rule me if I allowed it. Yet I discovered that only by leaving. My stepfather must live in the Valley, a place that does not allow that choice, every day. And Eugenio Reyes—I do not know if he was coming or going.

Understanding the Text

1. Why, according to Muñoz, do many in California's Central Valley, "regardless of the speaker's background" (par. 5), Anglicize the pronunciation of Mexican names? In answering this question, consider his explanations regarding the demographics of the small towns in the region and the prevailing perceptions of Spanish.

2. Muñoz claims that the Anglicization of his stepfather's name "ties into something bigger than learning English" (par. 14). Explain that "something bigger." How does this relate to the arguments Muñoz develops in paragraphs 14–17?

3. What does Muñoz learn by leaving Dinuba? How do this knowledge and his experience outside Dinuba influence his return to, and understanding of, his hometown?

Reflection and Response

4. In paragraph 9, what does Muñoz realize about what it means to be "white" and "American"? Why is this realization significant?

5. In paragraph 8, Muñoz mentions the stigma associated with speaking Spanish, saying that "Spanish was and still is viewed with suspicion." Do you agree that there is a stigma with speaking Spanish in the United States? Why or why not?

6. In paragraph 21, Muñoz describes his experiences as a "journey toward the discovery of the English language's extraordinary power." At the end of his journey, what conclusion does Muñoz reach about the pronunciation of his

name and the power of English? What does he have to understand about borders, language, identity, American identity, and power, among other things, in order to arrive at this conclusion?

Making Connections

7. Both indirectly and directly, Muñoz addresses the issue of assimilation, particularly as it relates to language and identity. Using his ideas as a starting point, choose at least two other readings from this chapter and conduct your own research on this topic. Then write a short essay in which you explain and analyze the relationship among assimilation, language, and identity.

8. Both the location and the demographics of Dinuba are important elements in Muñoz's piece. He wrote this piece in 2007, and although the town's location, obviously, has not changed, its demographics and population may have. Locate Dinuba on a map to get a sense of its physical boundaries. Research its most recent demographics, information about the town itself, its cultural events, its governance, and the demographics of a few similar towns in "the Valley." What does your research suggest about the cultural diversity of Dinuba and the surrounding area? Has it expanded beyond "whites and Mexicans"? Using this research, support or challenge some of Muñoz's ideas and arguments.

Mother Tongue

Amy Tan

Born in Oakland, California, to Chinese immigrants, Amy Tan is a best-selling author and novelist. Though her parents and teachers encouraged her to pursue a career in mathematics or the sciences, she changed her major from pre-med to English in her first year at college. She earned bachelor's and master's degrees from San Jose State University but did not begin writing fiction until she was thirty-three years old. Her first book, *The Joy Luck Club* (1989), was adapted in 1993 into a film, which Tan both cowrote and coproduced. She has also written several children's books, one of which, *Sagwa, the Chinese Siamese Cat* (1994), became a PBS animated series. Tan's novels include *The Kitchen God's Wife* (1991), *The Hundred Secret Senses* (1995), *The Bonesetter's Daughter* (2001), *Saving Fish from Drowning* (2005), and *The Valley of Amazement* (2013).

In many of her best-known works, Tan brings the Chinese American experience to life, exploring how individuals craft complex identities while confronting the challenges and possibilities of traversing cultural borders. In Tan's fiction, this experience often involves understanding mother-daughter relationships and coming to terms with multiple varieties of Englishes, as the following reading addresses. As you read, think about your own experiences shifting between languages — or using various versions of English — in order to accommodate a specific need, situation, or audience.

I am not a scholar of English or literature. I cannot give you much more than personal opinions on the English language and its variations in this country or others.

I am a writer. And by that definition, I am someone who has always loved language. I am fascinated by language in daily life. I spend a great deal of my time thinking about the power of language—the way it can evoke an emotion, a visual image, a complex idea, or a simple truth. Language is the tool of my trade. And I use them all—all the Englishes I grew up with.

Recently, I was made keenly aware of the different Englishes I do use. I was giving a talk to a large group of

> "Language is the tool of my trade. And I use them all — all the Englishes I grew up with."

people, the same talk I had already given to half a dozen other groups. The nature of the talk was about my writing, my life, and my book, *The Joy Luck Club*. The talk was going along well enough, until I remembered one major difference that made the whole talk sound wrong. My mother was in the room. And it was perhaps the first time she had heard me give a lengthy speech, using the kind of English I have never used with her. I was saying things like, "The intersection of memory upon imagination" and "There is an aspect of my fiction that relates to thus-and-thus"—a speech filled with carefully wrought grammatical phrases, burdened, it suddenly seemed to me, with nominalized forms, past perfect tenses, conditional phrases, all the forms of standard English that I had learned in school and through books, the forms of English I did not use at home with my mother.

Just last week, I was walking down the street with my mother, and I again found myself conscious of the English I was using, the English I do use with her. We were talking about the price of new and used furniture and I heard myself saying this: "Not waste money that way." My husband was with us as well, and he didn't notice any switch in my English. And then I realized why. It's because over the twenty years we've been together I've often used that same kind of English with him, and sometimes he even uses it with me. It has become our language of intimacy, a different sort of English that relates to family talk, the language I grew up with.

So you'll have some idea of what this family talk I heard sounds like, 5 I'll quote what my mother said during a recent conversation which I videotaped and then transcribed. During this conversation, my mother was talking about a political gangster in Shanghai who had the same last name as her family's, Du, and how the gangster in his early years wanted to be adopted by her family, which was rich by comparison. Later, the gangster became more powerful, far richer than my mother's family, and one day showed up at my mother's wedding to pay his respects. Here's what she said in part: "Du Yusong having business like fruit stand. Like off the street kind. He is Du like Du Zong—but not Tsung-ming Island people. The local people call putong, the river east side, he belong to that side local people. That man want to ask Du Zong father take him in like become own family. Du Zong father wasn't look down on him, but didn't take seriously, until that man big like become a mafia. Now important person, very hard to inviting him. Chinese way, came only to show respect, don't stay for dinner. Respect for making big celebration, he shows up. Mean gives lots of respect. Chinese custom. Chinese social life that way. If too important won't have to stay too long. He come to my wedding. I didn't see, I heard it. I gone to boy's side, they have YMCA dinner. Chinese age I was nineteen."

You should know that my mother's expressive command of English belies how much she actually understands. She reads the *Forbes°* report,

---

Forbes: a leading business magazine, founded in 1917, containing articles on finance, industry, investing, and marketing.

listens to *Wall Street Week*,° converses daily with her stockbroker, reads all of Shirley MacLaine's books° with ease—all kinds of things I can't begin to understand. Yet some of my friends tell me they understand 50 percent of what my mother says. Some say they understand 80 to 90 percent. Some say they understand none of it, as if she were speaking pure Chinese. But to me, my mother's English is perfectly clear, perfectly natural. It's my mother tongue. Her language, as I hear it, is vivid, direct, full of observation and imagery. That was the language that helped shape the way I saw things, expressed things, made sense of the world.

Lately, I've been giving more thought to the kind of English my mother speaks. Like others, I have described it to people as "broken" or "fractured" English. But I wince when I say that. It has always bothered me that I can think of no way to describe it other than "broken," as if it were damaged and needed to be fixed, as if it lacked a certain wholeness and soundness. I've heard other terms used, "limited English," for example. But they seem just as bad, as if everything is limited, including people's perceptions of the limited English speaker.

I know this for a fact, because when I was growing up, my mother's "limited" English limited my perception of her. I was ashamed of her English. I believed that her English reflected the quality of what she had to say. That is, because she expressed them imperfectly her thoughts were imperfect. And I had plenty of empirical evidence to support me: the fact that people in department stores, at banks, and at restaurants did not take her seriously, did not give her good service, pretended not to understand her, or even acted as if they did not hear her.

My mother has long realized the limitations of her English as well. When I was fifteen, she used to have me call people on the phone to pretend I was she. In this guise, I was forced to ask for information or even to complain and yell at people who had been rude to her. One time it was a call to her stockbroker in New York. She had cashed out her small portfolio and it just so happened we were going to go to New York the next week, our very first trip outside California. I had to get on the phone and say in an adolescent voice that was not very convincing, "This is Mrs. Tan."

And my mother was standing in the back whispering loudly, "Why he 10 don't send me check, already two weeks late. So mad he lie to me, losing me money."

Wall Street Week: a financial television show about investing, Wall Street, and long-term wealth creation.
Shirley MacLaine's books: Shirley MacLaine is an actress, author, and activist. Her interest in meditation, metaphysics, and spirituality influences her writing, providing the topics or themes of several of her books.

And then I said in perfect English, "Yes, I'm getting rather concerned. You had agreed to send the check two weeks ago, but it hasn't arrived."

Then she began to talk more loudly. "What he want, I come to New York tell him front of his boss, you cheating me?" And I was trying to calm her down, make her be quiet, while telling the stockbroker, "I can't tolerate any more excuses. If I don't receive the check immediately, I am going to have to speak to your manager when I'm in New York next week." And sure enough, the following week there we were in front of this astonished stockbroker, and I was sitting there red-faced and quiet, and my mother, the real Mrs. Tan, was shouting at his boss in her impeccable broken English.

We used a similar routine just five days ago, for a situation that was far less humorous. My mother had gone to the hospital for an appointment, to find out about a benign brain tumor a CAT scan had revealed a month ago. She said she had spoken very good English, her best English, no mistakes. Still, she said, the hospital did not apologize when they said they had lost the CAT scan and she had come for nothing. She said they did not seem to have any sympathy when she told them she was anxious to know the exact diagnosis, since her husband and son had both died of brain tumors. She said they would not give her any more information until the next time and she would have to make another appointment for that. So she said she would not leave until the doctor called her daughter. She wouldn't budge. And when the doctor finally called her daughter, me, who spoke in perfect English—lo and behold—we had assurances the CAT scan would be found, promises that a conference call on Monday would be held, and apologies for any suffering my mother had gone through for a most regrettable mistake.

I think my mother's English almost had an effect on limiting my possibilities in life as well. Sociologists and linguists probably will tell you that a person's developing language skills are more influenced by peers. But I do think that the language spoken in the family, especially in immigrant families which are more insular, plays a large role in shaping the language of the child. And I believe that it affected my results on achievement tests, I.Q. tests, and the SAT. While my English skills were never judged as poor, compared to math, English could not be considered my strong suit. In grade school I did moderately well, getting perhaps B's, sometimes B-pluses, in English and scoring perhaps in the sixtieth or seventieth percentile on achievement tests. But those scores were not good enough to override the opinion that my true abilities lay in math and science, because in those areas I achieved A's and scored in the ninetieth percentile or higher.

This was understandable. Math is precise; there is only one correct answer. Whereas, for me at least, the answers on English tests were always a judgment call, a matter of opinion and personal experience. Those tests were constructed around items like fill-in-the-blank sentence completion, such as, "Even though Tom was _____, Mary thought he was _____." And the correct answer always seemed to be the most bland combinations of thoughts, for example, "Even though Tom was shy, Mary thought he was charming," with the grammatical structure "even though" limiting the correct answer to some sort of semantic opposites, so you wouldn't get answers like, "Even though Tom was foolish, Mary thought he was ridiculous." Well, according to my mother, there were very few limitations as to what Tom could have been and what Mary might have thought of him. So I never did well on tests like that.

The same was true with word analogies, pairs of words in which you were supposed to find some sort of logical, semantic relationship—for example, "*Sunset* is to *nightfall* as _____ is to _____." And here you would be presented with a list of four possible pairs, one of which showed the same kind of relationship: *red* is to *stoplight, bus* is to *arrival, chills* is to *fever, yawn* is to *boring*: Well, I could never think that way. I knew what the tests were asking, but I could not block out of my mind the images already created by the first pair, "*sunset* is to *nightfall*"—and I would see a burst of colors against a darkening sky, the moon rising, the lowering of a curtain of stars. And all the other pairs of words—*red, bus, stoplight, boring*—just threw up a mass of confusing images, making it impossible for me to sort out something as logical as saying: "A sunset precedes nightfall" is the same as "a chill precedes a fever." The only way I would have gotten that answer right would have been to imagine an associative situation, for example, my being disobedient and staying out past sunset, catching a chill at night, which turns into feverish pneumonia as punishment, which indeed did happen to me.

I have been thinking about all this lately, about my mother's English, about achievement tests. Because lately I've been asked, as a writer, why there are not more Asian Americans represented in American literature. Why are there few Asian Americans enrolled in creative writing programs? Why do so many Chinese students go into engineering? Well, these are broad sociological questions I can't begin to answer. But I have noticed in surveys—in fact, just last week—that Asian students, as a whole, always do significantly better on math achievement tests than in English. And this makes me think that there are other Asian American students whose English spoken in the home might also be described as "broken" or "limited." And perhaps they also have teachers who are steering them away from writing and into math and science, which is what happened to me.

Fortunately, I happen to be rebellious in nature and enjoy the challenge of disproving assumptions made about me. I became an English major my first year in college, after being enrolled as pre-med. I started writing nonfiction as a freelancer the week after I was told by my former boss that writing was my worst skill and I should hone my talents toward account management.

But it wasn't until 1985 that I finally began to write fiction. And at first I wrote using what I thought to be wittily crafted sentences, sentences that would finally prove I had mastery over the English language. Here's an example from the first draft of a story that later made its way into *The Joy Luck Club*, but without this line: "That was my mental quandary in its nascent state." A terrible line, which I can barely pronounce.

Fortunately, for reasons I won't get into today, I later decided I should 20 envision a reader for the stories I would write. And the reader I decided upon was my mother, because these were stories about mothers. So with this reader in mind—and in fact she did read my early drafts—I began to write stories using all the Englishes I grew up with: the English I spoke to my mother, which for lack of a better term might be described as "simple"; the English she used with me, which for lack of a better term might be described as "broken"; my translation of her Chinese, which could certainly be described as "watered down"; and what I imagined to be her translation of her Chinese if she could speak in perfect English, her internal language, and for that I sought to preserve the essence, but neither an English nor a Chinese structure. I wanted to capture what language ability tests can never reveal: her intent, her passion, her imagery, the rhythms of her speech and the nature of her thoughts.

Apart from what any critic had to say about my writing, I knew I had succeeded where it counted when my mother finished reading my book and gave me her verdict: "So easy to read."

Understanding the Text

1. Tan admits to unease with the terms used to describe the English her mother spoke, particularly "broken," "fractured," and "limited." Why is her mother's speech described as "broken" and "limited"? What does Tan find wrong with using these terms as descriptors?

2. Tan describes the various Englishes with which she grew up, and she demonstrates several in her essay. List, categorize, and define each one. It may be helpful to include an example of each type from the reading as well.

3. Identify the places in the essay where Tan uses different Englishes. How does Tan incorporate these different Englishes into her writing to develop

her ideas? What do her examples tell us about the intersections of language, culture, and identity? What do they reveal about what it means to knowingly cross linguistic borders?

Reflection and Response

4. Explain the title of Tan's essay. How does her essay play on this common phrase? As you develop your explanation, consider all its possible interpretations, based on what Tan tells us about both her mother's and her own relationship to language.

5. In paragraph 14, Tan states: "Sociologists and linguists probably will tell you that a person's developing language skills are more influenced by peers. But I do think that the language spoken in the family, especially in immigrant families which are more insular, plays a large role in shaping the language of the child." Look at how Tan uses her own experiences to support this statement. What points seem most significant to you? Explain why. What insights into the complexity of negotiating linguistic borders does Tan provide?

6. Do you have a "mother tongue," or do you cross linguistic borders — that is, do you use different Englishes? Before answering "No," consider Tan's point about "a different sort of English that relates to family talk" (par. 4) or about code-switching. Then write an essay describing *your* different Englishes, when you use each, why you use each, and how they are different.

Making Connections

7. In paragraphs 10–15, Tan describes acting as a translator for her mother. In "Leave Your Name at the Border," Manuel Muñoz also points out that bilingual children often serve as "translators for those in the family whose English is barely functional" (p. 158). Gloria Anzaldúa, in "How to Tame a Wild Tongue," both does and does not translate non-English for her readers. Finally, Marilyn Chin, in an excerpt from her novel, presents Chinese American twins who translate for their grandmother. Read Muñoz's (p. 157), Anzaldúa's (p. 143), and Chin's (p. 323) pieces, and then think about Tan's experiences translating for her mother. Explain how the act of translation may or may not involve crossing cultural borders. As you develop your explanation, consider the link between language and identity, and, perhaps, shame and power; to support your points, provide examples from the readings.

8. Compare Tan's description of her different Englishes with Gloria Anzaldúa's description of her border tongues and her relationship to language (p. 143). Identify and explain the similarities of their experiences, noting where their relationship to language might also be similar. What accounts for these similarities? Where do you see differences in their experiences or perspectives? Explain why you think these differences exist.

Change of Language, Change of Personality? (Parts I and II)

François Grosjean

François Grosjean, Ph.D., is emeritus professor of psycholinguistics at the University of Neuchâtel in Switzerland and the founder of the Language and Speech Processing Laboratory at the university. In his work on bilingualism, he explores code-switching and borrowing, bilingualism and the deaf, and the holistic view of bilingualism.
Grosjean has written four books on bilingualism: *Life with Two Languages* (1982), *Studying Bilinguals* (2008), *Bilingual: Life and Reality* (2010), and *The Psycholinguistics of Bilingualism* (2013), coauthored with Ping Li, a fellow professor of psycholinguistics at Penn State.

Grosjean also writes a blog, "Life as a Bilingual," for *Psychology Today*. The following two blog posts, which appeared in 2011, ask us to consider how switching between languages might alter one's personality and sense of self. Grosjean includes personal testimonies from multilingual speakers and academic studies in order to answer the question posed by his title. As you read, think about whether Grosjean's posts resonate with your experience regarding language and personality.

Part I

Bilingual 1: *"When I'm around Anglo-Americans, I find myself awkward and unable to choose my words quickly enough. . . . When I'm amongst Latinos/ Spanish-speakers, I don't feel shy at all. I'm witty, friendly, and . . . I become very outgoing."*

Bilingual 2: *"In English, my speech is very polite, with a relaxed tone, always saying 'please' and 'excuse me.' When I speak Greek, I start talking more rapidly, with a tone of anxiety and in a kind of rude way. . . ."*

Bilingual 3: *"I find when I'm speaking Russian I feel like a much more gentle, 'softer' person. In English, I feel more 'harsh,' 'businesslike.'"*

Could it be that bilinguals who speak two (or more) languages change their personality when they change language? After all, the Czech proverb does say, "Learn a new language and get a new soul."

Despite the fact that many bilinguals report being different in each of their languages, only a few researchers have attempted to get to the bottom of this question. Early in her career, Berkeley Emeritus Professor Susan Ervin-Tripp conducted a study in which she asked Japanese American women to complete sentences she gave them in both Japanese and English. She found that they proposed very different endings depending on the language used. Thus, for the sentence beginning, "When my wishes conflict with my family . . . ," one participant's Japanese ending was, ". . . it is a time of great unhappiness," whereas the English ending was, ". . . I do what I want."

More than forty years later, Baruch College Professor David Luna and his colleagues asked Hispanic American bilingual women students to interpret target advertisements picturing women, first in one language and, six months later, in the other. They found that in the Spanish sessions, the bilinguals perceived women in the ads as more self-sufficient as well as extroverted. In the English sessions, however, they expressed more traditional, other-dependent and family-oriented views of the women.

The spontaneous reports by individual bilinguals, and the results of studies such as those mentioned here, have intrigued me over the years. I noted first of all that monocultural bilinguals who make up the majority of bilinguals in the world are not really concerned by this phenomenon. Although bi- or multilingual, they are in fact members of just one culture. But what about bicultural bilinguals? I proposed in my first book on bilingualism, *Life with Two Languages*, that what is seen as a change in personality is most probably simply a shift in attitudes and behaviors that correspond to a shift in situation or context, independent of language. Basically, the bicultural bilinguals in these studies were behaving biculturally, that is, adapting to the context they were in.

As we saw in an earlier post, bilinguals use their languages for different purposes, in different domains of life, with different people. Different contexts and domains trigger different impressions, attitudes and behaviors. What is taken as a personality shift due to a change of language may have little, if anything, to do with language itself. 5

Imagine the way we speak to a best friend and the behavior that we adopt. Then, think of how all this changes when we are speaking the same language to a superior (e.g., a school head, religious authority or employer). We behave differently and sometimes change attitudes and feelings even though the language is the same.

The same is true for bilinguals except that here the language may be different. It is the environment, the culture, and the interlocutors that cause bicultural bilinguals to change attitudes, feelings and behaviors (along with language)—and not their language as such. In essence, there does not seem to be a direct causal relationship between language and personality.

A Swiss German-French-English trilingual gives us a concluding statement that is fitting: "When talking English, French or German to my sister, my personality does not change. However, depending on where we are, both our behaviors may adapt to certain situations we find ourselves in."

Part II

In a first post on this topic, I discussed whether bilinguals who speak two or more languages change their personality when they change language. I reproduced personal testimonies and cited two studies that seem to give a positive answer. I then argued that it is the environment, the culture and the interlocutors that cause bilinguals to change attitudes, feelings and behaviors (along with language)—and not their language as such. In essence, there does not seem to be a direct causal relationship between language and personality.

My post received many comments which I went through carefully. 10 On the question of personality change, my respondents, probably all bilingual, were undecided. About a third thought there was no change in personality, a second third thought there was, and the remaining third didn't actually mention this aspect. This mixed reaction is not a surprise as even among researchers it is difficult to find a consensus as to how to define personality.

One respondent who believed in a personality change addressed the issue of whether there may nevertheless sometimes be a direct causal relationship between change of language and change of personality (and not always an indirect relationship as proposed above). He raised the intriguing possibility that an "initially indirect causal relationship can develop into a direct one" and he cited Pavlov's well-known study° involving his dogs' reaction to the ringing of a bell. This might explain, in part, another respondent's remark. She found that a teacher was quite strict and a bit intimidating when speaking one language and more friendly in the other. She continued as follows: "If you were in a room with her and she was giving you a hard time, it was a good idea to manipulate the conversation over into the other language!"

Although divided on the personality issue, most respondents agreed with the fact that different contexts, domains of life and interlocutors—

Pavlov's well-known study: Ivan Pavlov (1849–1936) was a Russian psychologist who developed theories in classical conditioning. His most famous study involved conditioning dogs to salivate in response to a bell.

which in turn induce different languages—trigger different impressions, attitudes and behaviors. Thus, as bicultural bilinguals we adapt to the situation or the person we are talking to, and change our language when we need to, without actually changing our personality. One respondent put it very nicely: ". . . it is not a personality change but simply the expression of another part of our personality that is not shown as strongly in our other language(s)."

Future research will hopefully use both explicit and implicit tests of attitudes and self-concept as suggested by yet another respondent. This is all the more important as it could be that not everyone is equally apt at judging that they "feel different" when they change language. In a recent study, researcher Katarzyna Ożańska-Ponikwia examined why some people report feeling different while others do not. She asked some 100 bilinguals made up of people who had grown up speaking two languages, immigrants who acquired their second language later on in life, as well as students who had stayed in a foreign country for an extended period of time, to give answers to two personality questionnaires and to give scale values to statements such as, "I feel I'm someone else while speaking English," or "Friends say that I'm a different person when I speak English."

> "As bicultural bilinguals we adapt to the situation or the person we are talking to . . . without actually changing our personality."

What she found was that only people who are emotionally and socially skilled are able to notice feeling different. According to her, some people do not report changes in their behavior or in their perception or expression of emotions when changing language, not because they do not exist, but because they are unable to notice them. She speculates that it is people with above-average levels of social and emotional skills who can notice that they adapt aspects of their personality and behavior when using another language.

I personally look forward to reading more studies on this topic in the years to come. Not only will they allow me to update my own thinking on the subject but they may also help me understand my bilingual conduct in case I belong to the category of those who do not notice changes in their attitudes, feelings and behavior when changing language! 15

References

Ervin, S. (1964). An analysis of the interaction of language, topic, and listener. In J. Gumperz and D. Hymes (Eds.), *The Ethnography of Communication*, special issue of *American Anthropologist, 66*, Part 2, 86–102.

Grosjean, F. Personality, thinking and dreaming, and emotions in bilinguals. Chapter 11 of Grosjean, F. (2010). *Bilingual: Life and Reality.* Cambridge, MA: Harvard University Press.

Luna, D., Ringberg, T., & Peracchio, L. (2008). One individual, two identities: Frame switching among biculturals. *Journal of Consumer Research, 35*(2), 279–293.

Ożańska-Ponikwia, K. (2012). What has personality and emotional intelligence to do with "feeling different" while using a foreign language? *International Journal of Bilingual Education and Bilingualism, 15*(2), 217–234.

Understanding the Text

1. In the first post (Part I), Grosjean distinguishes between monocultural bilinguals and bicultural bilinguals (par. 4). How do these two groups differ?

2. Does Grosjean think that bilinguals change personalities when they speak in different languages? What conclusion does he reach in the first post? Identify the key reasons he offers to support his conclusion.

3. Summarize and explain the reactions Grosjean received to his first post. Did the responses alter his position? In your answer, explain how Grosjean used the responses to further develop his position and the discussion on the topic.

4. Consider the second post, "Part II." What new information does Grosjean include here? Why do you think he does so? What conclusions does he reach in this post?

Reflection and Response

5. In "Part II," Grosjean notes that researchers have a difficult time reaching consensus regarding how to define the term *personality* (par. 10). How do you define the term? How do you think Grosjean uses it? Support your answer with some evidence from his blog posts. How does your definition support, extend, or counter Grosjean's arguments?

6. Write a response that you would post in the comment section to Grosjean's first post, posing additional questions for Grosjean and other readers to consider. For example, if you are a bilingual or multilingual speaker, you might share your own personal experience with switching between languages. If you are a monolingual speaker, you might want to share your observations of an encounter with a multilingual speaker.

Making Connections

7. In "Part I" and "Part II," Grosjean refers to previous posts. Explore his "Life as a Bilingual" blog on the *Psychology Today* Web site (https://www .psychologytoday.com/blog/life-bilingual). Choose two additional posts on Grosjean's blog, and summarize and explain these posts. Do they further support his argument? What do they add to your understanding about how and why individuals cross linguistic borders?

8. Other writers in this chapter might disagree with some of Grosjean's conclusions regarding how changing language affects one's personality or
   sense of self. Choose another reading from this chapter. Then write an
   essay in which you compare and contrast this reading and Grosjean's blog
   posts. Finally, as you explain and synthesize both the reading you chose
   and Grosjean's ideas, add your own voice and ideas to the conversation.
   How does switching between languages affect one's sense of self or personality? What is at stake when one crosses linguistic borders?

Living in Two Worlds, but with Just One Language

Steve Inskeep and
Michele Norris

Journalist Steve Inskeep is the cohost of National Public Radio's (NPR) news radio program *Morning Edition* and the author of *Instant City: Life and Death in Karachi* (2011). In addition to his hosting duties, he has covered the Senate, the Pentagon, the wars in Afghanistan and Iraq, and George W. Bush's 2000 presidential campaign. Inskeep won an Alfred I. duPont–Columbia University Silver Baton for excellence for "The York Project," a conversation about race that he produced with Michele Norris.

Michele Norris is a journalist, a special correspondent, and a fellow host for NPR, for which she produces in-depth profiles and interview series. Before coming to NPR, she spent ten years as a reporter for ABC's Washington Bureau. In 2009, the National Association of Black Journalists named Norris Journalist of the Year, and in 2006 she won the Association's Salute to Excellence Award for her coverage of Hurricane Katrina. Norris also garnered both Emmy and Peabody awards for ABC's coverage of 9/11.

"The York Project," with Inskeep, influenced "The Race Card Project," which, according to the Web site, "encouraged people to condense their observations and experiences about race into one sentence with just six words." Norris created the project after writing her family memoir, *The Grace of Silence* (2010), and interviews people who have shared their experiences on the Web site, often featuring them on *Morning Edition*.

The following three-way conversation, which took place on *Morning Edition* in 2013, raises critical questions about perceptions and stereotypes based on ethnic identities tied to language.

RENEE MONTAGNE (host): Our own Steve Inskeep is headed today to the Middle East on assignment. Before he left, Steve sat down—as he often does—with NPR special correspondent Michele Norris, to talk about the Race Card Project. Michele has been asking people to submit six-word stories about race or cultural identity; stories like this one.

ELYSHA O'BRIEN: My name is Elysha O'Brien, and my six words are: Mexican white girl doesn't speak Spanish. I chose these six words because whites see me as Mexican; Mexicans see me as white because I don't speak Spanish. I find it interesting that we don't qualify other ethnic identities on the basis of language.

STEVE INSKEEP: OK. So Mexican white girl doesn't speak Spanish—those are the six words from Elysha O'Brien, who lives in Las Vegas, Nevada.

And to talk about the meaning behind those words, Michele Norris joins us once again. Hi, Michele.

MICHELE NORRIS: Hey, Steve.

INSKEEP: And I guess this is a moment to remember that when we say 5 Hispanic, that's not a racial identity. There are lots of races of people who are Hispanic; it's about the language.

NORRIS: Well, and it's about the culture. And in this case, it's specifically about how the language and the culture are intertwined. And this represents one of those themes within the Race Card Project. We have received a lot of submissions from people who are Latino but don't speak Spanish, even though their parents spoke Spanish. They come from households where their parents made a deliberate choice that their kids were going to become more American, whatever that means; that their ambitions were wrapped up in making them more American. And for them, that meant making sure that they spoke perfect English. And even though the parents spoke Spanish, they didn't pass that on to the kids.

INSKEEP: How did Elysha end up not speaking Spanish?

NORRIS: Well, she was raised by parents who hail from Mexico. They spoke Spanish but in her household, Spanish was almost like the secret language—the language that the parents spoke when they didn't want the kids to hear about a tragedy in the family, or where the birthday presents were hidden.

"Mexican white girl doesn't speak Spanish."

INSKEEP: *Entiendo.*°

NORRIS: Yeah. And they decided not to pass on their language skills— 10 and that's what she calls them now, language skills. They didn't pass on their language to the kids for those same reasons. They wanted to make sure that they did well in school, but they also did it in part because of their own memory. She explains that.

O'BRIEN: I have talked to my father about this, and I've talked to my aunts and uncles individually about this; and they all give me the same reason. They said that they were so prejudiced against—growing up in Fort Worth, Texas—for speaking Spanish in school that they didn't want their children to endure that. They didn't want their children to get slapped on the wrist; they didn't want their children to get shushed in the lunchroom. They wanted their children to assimilate into the culture.

Entiendo: understood.

NORRIS: They were rapped on the knuckles if they spoke Spanish in class?

O'BRIEN: Yeah. They were—ears were turned; rapped on the knuckles; just—a bit of humiliation would occur if they spoke Spanish. My father failed first grade because he didn't speak English. You'd never hear of that now. He only spoke Spanish, and so he wasn't able to proceed to second grade. He had to repeat first.

INSKEEP: Michele Norris, this is such a classic immigrant tale. People come; they bring other languages, they bring other cultures. They are determined—many of them—to fit into the new country, or to make sure their kids fit into the new country.

NORRIS: And often, fitting in means speaking the language of the new homeland. And here in America, that—of course—means English. And that's why Elysha O'Brien's parents didn't speak Spanish to her, in part because of those memories of days before you had English-as-a-second-language classes in school, where they were penalized for speaking Spanish; but also because they wanted to give her something. And so, as she explains, she lives in this position where she has sort of a foot in two worlds and doesn't necessarily feel fully accepted in either, particularly when she is challenged by other Latinos who say, well, you're not really Mexican, if you don't speak the language. And over time, she really started—particularly when she was young—to internalize that criticism and really question herself. 15

O'BRIEN: Spanish always sounded like a bird singing to me. It was—my mom would watch the Mexican soap operas, and the women always sounded like they were chirping. And it was so fast and so quick, I couldn't discern where one word ended and another word began. It just all had this very musical quality to it. I couldn't tell. But it was just something I didn't have. It was my parents' language; it wasn't my language.

I used to say to a friend—actually, when you're kind of rebellious and trying to find your identity, I used to say, well, I'm not Mexican; my parents are—because of the comment that my friend said to me—well, not really my friend; but the comment that he said—well, you're not Mexican 'cause you don't speak Spanish. I think in trying to figure that out, I started responding to people, well, I'm not Mexican; my parents are.

NORRIS: How does that strike your adult ear now?

O'BRIEN: I think it sounds very flip. It sounds very—like I'm trying to make amends for a really deep wound, just trying to put a Band-Aid on something instead of digging out the infection that's there.

INSKEEP: So this gift that her parents worked so hard to give her—the 20
gift of being sure that she knew English really, really well—does she
regret not having learned Spanish?

NORRIS: It sounds like the whole family has a little bit of regret around
this. Her parents regret it now because they recognize that their children might be more marketable if they actually were bilingual.

INSKEEP: Spanish is an asset in the globalized world.

NORRIS: Yes, particularly if you live in a place like Las Vegas. So there's
regret around economic opportunity. Elysha regrets it for two reasons.
One is academic, and one is a little bit emotional. And the academic
side—she's a college professor—she would love to be able to read
Gabriel García Márquez in his native language; she would love to be
able to dream in Spanish. She would love to be able to tackle a language and really learn how to master it, as an academic. On the emotional side, she says that there's a piece of her family, of her elders in
her family, that's not available to her because she doesn't speak their
native language. But when they speak their native language, that there's
something musical about them; that's something that comes out. And
she says that most clearly when she talks about her grandmother, who
passed away two years ago.

O'BRIEN: Whenever we would go to Texas, the only thing that she knew
how to say in English was "I love you, *mija*, I love you." And so she
would say this to me over and over again—"I love you, *mija*, I love
you." For, I think, the first seven years of my life, I thought my name
was *mija*. I didn't realize that *mija* was an individual word in Spanish.
I thought it was my nickname.

NORRIS: What does that mean? 25

O'BRIEN: It means "my daughter," in Spanish. It's actually a shortened,
condensed version of "*mi hija*." "*Mi hija*" means my daughter; "*mi hijo*"
means my son. And "*mija*" is just a shortened version of those two words.

NORRIS: What do you lose, when you lose your language?

O'BRIEN: I think you lose home. I think about my grandmother and
how I wasn't able to communicate with her, and that sense of relationship that I lost.

NORRIS: If you could speak Spanish with your grandmother, what is it
that you would say?

O'BRIEN: I love you, *mi amor, abuela*. 30

INSKEEP: I love you, grandma—the words that Elysha wishes she could
say in Spanish, if she could speak it. Now, Michele, we should mention
that Elysha has three boys of her own. Does she want them to learn
Spanish?

NORRIS: Elysha is married. Her husband is Irish and Italian; thus, the last name O'Brien. And she has three sons, and she is going to make sure that they all are bilingual. And if you go to the website, you'll learn more about that.

Understanding the Text

1. Both Norris and O'Brien discuss why O'Brien's parents did not pass on their language skills to their children. What were those reasons? Which ones seem the most significant? Explain your answer.

2. Norris claims that O'Brien began to "internalize that criticism and really question herself" (par. 15). What types of criticism did O'Brien face and from whom? What questioning process initiated this internalization? Where else in the interview do you find an example of internalization? What were its results?

Reflection and Response

3. Inskeep notes that Hispanic is "not a racial identity"; rather, he restricts the focus to language and to those who speak Spanish. Norris, however, replies, "[I]n this case, it's specifically about how the language and the culture are intertwined" (par. 6). What do O'Brien's responses tell us about the relationship between language and culture?

4. Explain O'Brien's perspectives toward Spanish and, by extension, her "Mexican self." How do her explanations and insights help us understand her six-word sentence?

5. In paragraph 27, Norris asks O'Brien, "What do you lose, when you lose your language?" What is O'Brien's reply? Explain her response. Why do you think she feels this way? How would *you* answer the question? Explain.

Making Connections

6. In this interview, Inskeep uses the term *Hispanic*, Norris uses the term *Latino*, and O'Brien refers to herself as *Mexican*. Manuel Muñoz, in "Leave Your Name at the Border" (p. 157), adds *Chicano* and *Mexican-American* to the list, and Gloria Anzaldúa, in "How to Tame a Wild Tongue" (p. 143), adds *Chicanas*, *Latinas*, and *Spanish-American*. By deriving their meaning from the context within each essay and by doing some research, explain the distinctions among these terms. Why are these distinctions important? Explain what you learn about the roles that language and cultural/geographical borders play in understanding each term.

7. O'Brien describes how her father, aunts, and uncles were disciplined "for speaking Spanish in school" (par. 11). Several other writers in this chapter, notably Anzaldúa (p. 143) and Muñoz (p. 157), also write about punishment and censure for speaking Spanish. Read their essays. What do their insights, along with O'Brien's interview, suggest about the risks and rewards of linguistic border crossings? In your response, include specific textual evidence from all three readings.

Communication Strategies across Cultural Borders

Karla Scott

An associate professor of communications, Karla Scott also serves as the dean for diversity and inclusion in the College of Arts and Sciences at Saint Louis University. She focuses her research in the following areas: identity and culture, language, race, and black women's communicative practices. This article originally appeared in the journal *Women's Studies in Communication* in 2013.

For her study, Scott initiated a conversation among thirty-three young black women at various stages in their academic careers — from undergraduate to doctorate level — about the challenges they faced as black women in predominantly white environments, thus having to routinely cross cultural borders. Scott asked these women to discuss where and when they encountered stereotypes of black women and "how they communicated in response to those stereotypes." She further asked them to consider "how such choices influenced their own identities as Black women" (par. 13). As you read, note how Scott expands the idea of communication beyond writing and speaking, and also consider what each woman's lived experience of crossing cultural borders reveals about the importance of identity in relation to communication practices and strategies.

For Black women born in the decades following the civil rights movement and second-wave women's movement,° opportunities to move into educational, professional, and social worlds have become reality. Taking advantage of those opportunities, however, often means encountering the same disenfranchisement° faced by their mothers and grandmothers—only such occurrences are now more implicit, hidden, and institutionalized (Collins, 2004). For young Black women who are the first generation born postsegregation in the United States, those "opportunities" often require they live and move in environments and institutions where they are marginalized and their lived experiences denied by those who are not Black and female.

---

second-wave women's movement: a political and social movement from 1960 to the 1990s. The movement focused on issues of sexuality, reproductive rights, and social equality while critiquing patriarchy, capitalism, and heterosexism.

disenfranchisement: the deprivation of a legal right or privilege, especially the right to vote.

Understanding the motivation for, and outcome of, young Black women's specific communicative strategies used to negotiate identity in everyday lived experiences in different worlds and cultural communities can be furthered with research that puts Black women's communicative practices at the center of analysis (Houston & Davis, 2002). Feminist theorist and cultural critic bell hooks offers compelling evidence for examining Black women's everyday lived experiences through this theoretical lens in her groundbreaking 1984 book *Feminist Theory: From Margin to Center* in which she explains that her choice of book title reflects her experiences in the hometown of her childhood: "Living as we did—on the edge—we developed a particular way of seeing reality. We looked from both the outside in and the inside out. We focused our attention on the center as well as the margin. We understood both" (hooks, 2000, p. xvi).

Gloria Anzaldúa's (1987) theory of the borderlands captures hooks's concept of understanding both margin and center in the lived experiences of those who move across those edges. Anzaldúa describes the borderlands as "present whenever two or more cultures edge each other, where people of different races occupy the same territory. . . . it's not a comfortable territory to live in, this place of contradictions" (p. iii). Constant movement across edges and borders results in the consciousness of the borderlands, where communicative strategies and language use are key components of identity negotiation in this border-crossing process.

The process of communication across cultural borders guides the current study designed to explore the lived experiences of young Black women in predominantly White environments and the communication strategies they employ to negotiate identity in those contexts. Examining the communicative strategies and choices of young Black women, who in everyday lived experiences move into and out of predominantly White environments, can further knowledge of how identity as a Black woman is negotiated across those borders constructing alternative definitions of what it means to be Black and female in the twenty-first century (Houston & Scott, 2006). As feminist communication scholar Brenda Allen (2002) notes, such research on Black women is emancipatory: "Our research strives to illuminate and to fight gendered racism. We hope to release Black women from stereotypical, pejorative notions about us, to liberate Black women from imposed meanings that members of society have set on us and our ways of communicating, and to free us from the chains of negative labels such as *marginalized* or *stigmatized*" (pp. 22–23).

This study extends the work of Black feminist scholars who have long 5 argued that Black women's lived experiences reflect intersecting identities situated in contexts with racial and gendered power inequities. What still remains largely unexamined, however, is *how* Black women respond to those inequities and *why* they choose specific communicative strategies to negotiate identity in those contexts. Co-cultural communication is a theory particularly useful for better understanding the *why* and *how* of this phenomenological process. Building on the theories of cultural border crossings, Black feminist thought, and co-cultural communication, this study gives voice to the lived experiences of young Black women who enact specific communication strategies to negotiate identity, empower themselves, and redefine what it means to be Black and female in the twenty-first century.

Literature Review

Black Women's Communicative Strategies

Previous research reveals that for many Black women their communication practices, language choice, and style are a result of participating in speech communities where various forms of Black vernacular English are spoken as cultural practice even though participants are competent in standard spoken English (Houston, 1983, 1985). The choice of language style is often strategic to mark solidarity with other Black women or to mark identity as a Black person in predominantly White environments, such as college classrooms, where the speaker perceives a need to speak with authority, from her own racial worldview and experiences as a Black person, especially when the topic concerns issues in Black communities (Foster, 1995; Nelson, 1990; Scott, 1995, 2002). This form of cultural border crossing (Anzaldúa, 1987) has also been used to explain the strategy of negotiating identity to mark solidarity with other Black women while distancing from non-Blacks in predominantly White environments (Scott, 1995, 2000, 2002).

> "The choice of language style is often strategic to mark solidarity with other Black women or to mark identity as a Black person in predominantly White environments."

Black women moving in worlds that require constant adjustments to racial and gender identity is the focus of the work of Charisse Jones and Kumea Shorter-Gooden in the African American Women's Voices Project culminating in the publication of *Shifting: The Double Lives of Black Women in America*. The authors define "shifting" as "a sort of subterfuge that African Americans have long practiced to ensure their survival in our

society. From one moment to the next, they change their outward behavior, attitude or tone, shifting 'White' then shifting 'Black' again"
(Jones & Shorter-Gooden, 2003, pp. 6–7). The extensive study involving
333 Black women examined the impact of this identity negotiation process in various contexts of their lives such as family life, romantic relationships, professional life, religious communities, and language use.

Forms of shifting include changing outward behavior, attitude, and
tone, and adopting an alternate pose or voice "as easily as they blink their
eyes or draw a breath—without thinking about the roles they play" (Jones
& Shorter-Gooden, 2003, p. 7). Findings also provide insight into statistics indicating that Black women have a disproportionately high risk for
depression as a result of the constant scrutiny in such intercultural contexts (Jones & Shorter-Gooden, 2003; Williams, 2008). This large study
based on the concept of shifting and the publication of *Shifting* are valuable contributions that provide compelling evidence on the process of
identity negotiation and establish the need for further study of the lived
experiences of young Black women in intercultural contexts. The study
and book further highlight the need for more research on Black women's
communicative experiences in its chapter titled "Finding a Voice," which
captures Black women's reflections on communication strategies.

For this first generation of Black women born postsegregation, cultural border crossings occur frequently in the contexts of everyday lived
experiences as they take advantage of opportunities gained by both the
civil rights and second-wave women's movements. Their lived experiences
create an opportunity to examine the specific communicative strategies
of a particular generation of Black women who often still encounter stigmatized perceptions of their identity even as they strive to redefine Black
womanhood. Within the field of communication, co-cultural theory provides a productive context to frame a phenomenological study on the
communicative strategies of young Black women and further understanding of the motivation and outcome of such choices.

Co-Cultural Theory

Grounded in muted group theory° (Kramarae, 1981) and standpoint   10
theory° (Smith, 1987), co-cultural theory explores the communicative
practices of those who are traditionally marginalized. Among the basic

muted group theory: a theory introduced by Edwin Ardener, a British anthropologist,
who argued that many ethnographers generalized their studies to the male population, leaving women's voices "muted" or unheard.
standpoint theory: a theory that posits that social position—as influenced by race,
class, and gender—shapes what we know. Therefore, under this theory, knowledge is
socially constructed.

assumptions of co-cultural theory is the premise that "to confront oppressive dominant structures and achieve any measure of 'success,' co-cultural group members strategically adopt certain communication behaviors when functioning within the confines of public communicative structures" (Orbe, 1998, p. 11).

Co-cultural theory explicates 25 specific strategies of co-cultural communication and identifies 6 interrelated factors that influence choices to enact specific strategies, as summarized in the following:

Situated within a particular field of experience *that governs their perceptions of the* costs and rewards *associated with, as well as their* ability *to engage in, various communicative practices, co-cultural group members will adopt certain communication orientations—based on their* preferred outcomes *and* communication approaches—*to fit the circumstances of a* specific situation. *(Orbe, 1998, p. 129; emphasis in original)*

The current study adds to the body of knowledge of co-cultural communication with the identification of specific communicative strategies enacted in young Black women's everyday lived experiences of cultural border crossings. It also provides understanding of why a specific strategy is selected in a communicative context where racial and gendered identities are perceived as "double" (Beale, 1970) or even "multiple" jeopardy (King, 1989).

Method

As with many other studies that give voice to the experiences of co-cultural members (Orbe, 2000), this study employs a phenomenological approach for examining communicative strategies in the lived experiences of young Black women in predominantly White environments. The goal of phenomenology, the study of the life-world, is to collect lived experiences that can provide a meaningful reflective look at particular experiences (van Manen, 1990) resulting in scholarship that emphasizes the "experiential rather than the experimental" (Houston, 1989, p. 190). As phenomenology elicits experiential descriptions of everyday life, it furthers the understanding of cultural practices and how they operate in a larger context (Orbe, 2000).

In this study the first step of the phenomenological process involved collecting descriptions of young Black women's communicative experiences through focus groups.[1] Focus group questions were designed to create a conversation among the women, asking them to discuss challenges facing young Black women in predominantly White environments, knowledge of stereotypes of Black women, specific instances in predominantly White environments where they encountered such stereotypes, how they communicated in response to those stereotypes, and how such choices influenced their own identities as Black women. All of the women also responded to a request to provide a critical incident (van Manen, 1990) asking them to recall a specific experience and context in which they employed communication strategies to negotiate identity.

Each focus group lasted about two hours and was audio recorded. Women who were unable to attend due to geographic constraints responded in writing to the same questions guiding the focus groups. The focus groups and written questions included open-ended questions designed to allow participants an opportunity to share their own experiences. In focus groups, additional questions were used as probes when needed.

Responses and narratives generated about lived experiences were collected in five focus groups. The first group consisted of 10 women, the second consisted of 7 women, the third had 6 participants, the fourth had 5, and one was held with only 2 women, for a total of 30 focus group participants. Another 3 women who could not attend focus groups responded to the questions in writing, bringing the total number of respondents to 33. Four focus groups were held on the campus of a private university in the Midwest, and one took place at the home of a graduate student in the Southeast.   15

Convenience sampling° was used to recruit participants. Participants all identified as either Black or African American women attending and/or graduates of predominantly White universities in the Midwest, Southeast, and Southwest. Twelve of the women were enrolled in either a master's- or doctoral-level graduate psychology program; one was pursuing a master of social work degree; one was completing a doctorate in English; three were pursuing master's degrees in communication; another was working toward a doctorate in communication; and one recent graduate with a bachelor of arts degree was playing sports with a European team. The remaining 15 participants were all undergraduates, ranging from second- to fifth-year students, majoring in business, communication, psychology, or allied health. Participant ages range from 19 to 25, with one identifying as late 30s and another as in her mid 40s.

The second phase of the phenomenological process involves transcription of the focus group audio recordings. The 54 pages of transcripts along with written responses and critical incidents were read and

---

convenience sampling: using anyone available and willing to participate in a study or survey.

reviewed multiple times with attention to similarities and differences in descriptions of the communicative experiences and the communicative strategies employed in specific contexts. This second phase of analysis involves identifying any response that reflects a specific strategy to negotiate identity through a communicative strategy, verbal or nonverbal, or through the use of language. Eliminating any incidental or redundant information in participant responses reduced themes.

The third phase of the phenomenological process—the interpretation of themes—reveals the central ideas that connect the themes to the larger lived experience or phenomenon (Merleau-Ponty, 1962). In this study the connection of themes throughout the responses gives voice to both the everyday lived experience of young Black women's cultural border crossings and the role of communication strategies in that phenomenon. In this phase the interpretation of the themes reveals these young Black women are aware of a need to negotiate an identity counter to historical stereotypes—situating "why" they enact specific communication strategies, which demonstrates the "how." This interpretation illuminates a particular phenomenon in Black women's everyday lived experiences: the need to negotiate an alternate identity of Black women in predominantly White environments while at the same time redefining Black womanhood. This phenomenon becomes clearer in the next section, where participants give voice to the role and goal of communication strategies in the lived experiences in cultural border crossings.

Findings

Analysis of the responses of the young Black women in this study reveal that a "preferred outcome" of their communication strategies is to construct an alternate identity of a Black woman and redefine Black womanhood. The responses also indicate that, as Black women who spend much of their everyday lives in predominantly White environments, they are conscious of the stereotypes of Black women driving their encounters in various contexts. Awareness of the "multiple jeopardy" (King, 1989) of intersectional identities of race and gender (Crenshaw, 1995) is captured in the following comment made by Mary, a graduate student in psychology:

We are the lowest on the totem pole, not only Black but also women. Now, Black folks are less intelligent, and women are certainly unintelligent, so we're just double stupid [lots of laughter from other women]. So when you walk into a class, the professor doesn't look at you when he's talking or call on you when you raise your hand.

Reflections such as this one from Mary capture a particular phenomenon in the lived experiences of many young Black women in predominantly White educational institutions, such as those participating in this study. Analysis of their responses reveals they enact the co-cultural practices of (1) dispelling stereotypes and (2) overcompensating to negotiate an identity of competence and success—and in that process they also redefine Black womanhood.

Dispelling stereotypes involves inconspicuously setting a positive example through actions and allowing dominant group members to observe the vast diversity within different cultural groups (Orbe, 1998, p. 65). Overcompensating is enacted to construct an identity as worthy of being a part of an organization and involves diligence to fit in as an "exemplary team player"; it is a part of the belief system: "in order to get half as far you have to work twice as hard" (p. 71). Each of those strategies is discussed in the following section. 20

Dispelling Stereotypes: "I'm Not Her, and I Will Let You Know That"

In the focus group discussions about stereotypes of Black women, all participants said they are well aware of stereotypes such as "overbearing, too outspoken, strong, angry, gold diggers, materialistic, oversexed, have lots of children, and unintelligent" as the predominant images of Black women. Common to all responses was some version of the overbearing, strong, angry Black woman stereotype—one that Patricia Hill Collins (2004) discusses as a controlling image of Black womanhood, one who is confrontational and acutely aggressive.

In the cultural border crossings of these young Black women, dispelling stereotypes involves language use that ranges from specific verbal and nonverbal strategies to speaking out on race-related topics. According to co-cultural theory, "[D]ispelling stereotypes is a behavior that is largely unconscious and natural. . . ." (Orbe, 1998, p. 64). Cathy describes this behavior in the following response:

Immediately [snaps fingers] when I step into a setting where I'm not—where I'm the only Black, I'm feeling like all eyes are upon me, for my entire race, especially Black women. My tone changes, the way I speak, I speak properly, following the rules of language arts [laughter from other women]—not that I don't do it anyway, but I'm more alert, making sure that I don't stumble over certain words.

Similar to Cathy's experiences, the majority of the women described language use and nonverbal behaviors such as body movements and even clothing choices as specific communication strategies.

I've been successful; I've learned how to shift effortlessly and how to hold my tongue and speak my mind in situations where it won't harm me professionally, academically, or socially. From a very early age I was in a gifted program, so I've been surrounded by White students my whole life. . . . I'm very good at making them forget at certain moments I'm different from them in a crucial way, because I can speak like them if I want to. (Marie)

I find myself talking properly—articulating, enunciating, expanding my vocabulary while in class. (Sandra)

These narratives reflect both an awareness of the historical perceptions of Black womanhood and how specific communication strategies can both counter those stereotypical notions and redefine what it means to be a Black woman. Years of moving in and out of predominantly White environments have helped these young women develop and refine specific verbal and nonverbal strategies to communicate an alternate identity of Black womanhood. From this field of experience they know how this can be done, and they do it.

The following comments reflect the experiences of several women 25 who shared that dispelling stereotypes can also be done by calling attention to an identity as Black and female when speaking in class on race-related issues. Their "mere presence" creates a context for representing a particular standpoint.

I'm always talking in class, especially if the topic hits home. I feel responsible for talking in classes. (Mary)

In my introductory class we were discussing various theories and were asked if we ever used divergence [a separation or distancing from others while communicating] intentionally. I responded by saying I purposely diverge from the White members in the class as a means of demonstrating the pride I have as a Black woman. For example, I would frequently provide examples that utilized race or culture as a variable. In this way I both establish my identity as a Black woman and established my difference and distancing from the non-Black participants. (Marie)

In classes, because I'm the only one, it makes me feel like I'm speaking for all Black women. That either makes me want to say something or not speak. In that situation, we have a lot of power, and you have to be careful. Because I feel like we will be challenged in class period, like we have to be validated. (Destiny)

As these responses reveal, the young women create not only alternative definitions of Black womanhood with their communicative choices but also "teachable moments" in classroom contexts. Such choices seem to further support movement across cultural borders where they can communicate about specific topics and subjects reflecting an identity as a Black woman. Part of this process is a perception of responsibility to offer insight and inform those in predominantly White environments.

In the next responses, several women discuss specific strategies enacted in response to the image of the "angry Black woman" and also note the tension that arises in highly emotional contexts where they work to resist enacting stereotypical behavior.

I try to show people who I am through my actions. Yeah, maybe a part of me is the angry Black woman, and when I'm angry you'll see that, but there are other parts of me that aren't that person. . . . I'm more than stereotypes. (Mia)

I know so many times in class if you state your opinion, you're automatically angry. . . . [Uses example of another Black woman in class] just because her opinion differs from the White guy doesn't mean she's angry. Why can't you express your opinion and be Black without being angry? I admit I feel weak as a Black woman if I get angry in class. I'm like, "How could you let them get to you?" But then when I don't say anything, I feel I'm weak. It's like a losing battle. (Mary)

Here Mia and Mary discuss the balance between anger and assertiveness: a fine line requiring constant mindfulness and navigation as revealed in other women's experiences. Contexts such as the predominantly White classroom or work setting can challenge the credibility of these young Black women. Although certain language choices motivated by anger could certainly be considered a legitimate response for such slights, with the controlling image of "angry Black woman" ever present they cannot just react emotionally. They are concerned their reactions would be interpreted solely as further proof of the angry Black woman stereotype. Destiny sums up the women's reaction to the lived experience of this stereotype: "There is a difference between being emotional and wanting to pick a fight."

These young Black women are acutely aware of the negative stereotypes of Black women and are also aware that they can resist enacting them and, more important, can dispel them, through communication strategies. Whether it is their "mere presence" (Orbe, 1998), specific language use, or a nonverbal tactic, they empower themselves in contexts where their racial and gendered identities have historically rendered them powerless (Allen, 2002; Collins, 2009; Houston & Scott, 2006; Orbe, 1998). And as they dispel stereotypes these young Black women also negotiate identity by performing competence in those same contexts where they still encounter perceptions of incompetence and inferiority.

Overcompensating: Performing Competence and Playing the Game

Co-cultural group members who frequently interact with those of the more dominant cultures often practice overcompensation in response to a pervasive fear of discrimination and have accepted the age-old belief that "in order to get half as far, you have to work twice as hard" to be the "exemplary team player" (Orbe, 1998, p. 71). As noted by Sandra and Jessica in the following comments, it is an ongoing effort to prove the competence needed for organizational membership.

I feel I constantly have to prove myself as worthy of attending this university. I also feel as if I can't be late, can't sleep in class, and I have to sit in the front of the room, because I am constantly being watched. I feel like others get more chances than Black women to mess up because it might be missed. . . . I believe this has positively affected me in many ways, because it has made me a stronger person and helped me to be conscious of my actions, which will give me an advantage in the future as a professional. (Sandra)

I always try to be on time and do well because they expect you to fail, so you have to do better than everyone else to prove you can do as well. (Jessica)

Sandra and Jessica both refer to an ongoing commitment to arrive to class on time in an effort to prove worthiness. While timeliness is an expectation for any classroom context, these two women understand that for them it requires constant monitoring to counter the perception of tardiness as a lack of competence or commitment due to race.

Another first-year psychology graduate student, Ana, reflected on her interest in other cultures as part of a strategy to counter stereotypes of being a "typical Black woman":

I tried to learn Spanish, and I'll bust out with that and they're like, "Ooh." I have a lot of Spanish friends, friends from Argentina, Ecuador, and White friends. So who I hang out with is not typical, and maybe in some way that's one of the reasons my best friends are from other cultures, so I can get away from being what White people expect me to be. (Ana)

Even though these young women identify as high-achieving stu- 30 dents, they believe the negative stereotypes of Black women (still) enter the classrooms with them, no matter how talented or successful they are. As Linda notes, strategies of overcompensation enacted to negotiate a different identity of Black womanhood can also be dismissed as a mere "exception."

Many times I try to do things that are the opposite of what people expect, such as not getting angry when people make ignorant comments. I feel that I am a strong person because of the work I must do to succeed, but still there are people who either think of me as the exception because I'm not like other Black women they know or do not think that I am completely "Black" in their eyes because I don't fit into the stereotypes. (Linda)

Interestingly, the status of "exceptional" is not necessarily a point of pride for these young women; they see it as the norm. They also see it as an identity that can be emulated by other young Black women — revealing again the notion of responsibility that comes with successful experiences moving across cultural borders.

Responses also indicate that overcompensating to "fit in as an exemplary team player" (Orbe, 1998) includes the skillful performance of competence expected in specific contexts. As India's comments that follow relate, performing this competence requires learning how to "play the game" to succeed in predominantly White environments:

I'm trying to learn how "they" [Whites] do it [succeed]. I can only win the battle if I know how to play the game their way. I can't play into the stereotypes of who they think I am. I have to learn how to play their game—play it, and excel in playing the game when I'm playing against them. (India)

Communication strategies of "playing the game" reflect a field of experience that has allowed the young women to develop and refine the performance of competence as a specific skill. Cassandra provides further insight into how the specifics of language choices in overcompensating can be skillfully "playing the game."

I think you can see it as the art of language, just like the Art of War *[book by Chinese military strategist and philosopher Sun-Tzu]. It says you learn to use the enemy strategies in order to be able to fight that way—not to say White people are enemy, but we're in a constant battle. So learn their language. And if you have to, use it with them or against them, to let them know: I know your strategy, I know how you do things, and I can do it as well. (Cassandra)*

As the young women spoke of overcompensation and the skillful ability to cross cultural borders into such predominantly White environments, several women also revealed an inherent tension between how much of their identity is compromised when they "shift" (Jones & Shorter-Gooden, 2003) in the name of "playing the game" for success. For Oni and India, this tension is frustrating:

I feel like I'm trying to perform for them, and that makes me feel bad as well because I feel like I don't know how to be true to myself and dispel a lot of the stereotypes they have about us. (Oni)

I want to get to the point where I don't care, but I feel in order to get what I want, I have to do certain things. There's nothing wrong with that. To get some things, I think you have to play people's games. (India)

The dialectical tensions inherent in oppressive organizations (Hopson & Orbe, 2007) must also be negotiated by co-cultural group members as revealed in the narratives in this study. Helen has found her own way to navigate that tension, one that strategically communicates an identity of *competence and Black woman* in her everyday lived experiences: "Yes, I choose to wear my hair in twists, and I have the intelligence to back me up. I think my legs look good, but I have the brains to go with it."

These young Black women overcompensate to perform competence and "play the game" to further their success. And as a strategy they also communicate an identity of Black womanhood that is counter to historical stereotypes. Enacting this particular communication strategy is an everyday lived experience that enables them to redefine who they are as Black women as they go through the world.

Discussion

The young Black women in this study are well aware of the prevailing stereotypes of Black women and employ specific communication strategies to dispel historical perceptions and controlling images when in predominantly White environments. Helen's comment captures this phenomenon: "As a Black woman, I'm concerned about how we represent Black women. I've proven myself, and I find myself in the middle of two worlds, trying to be true to myself and definitely representing the race here at this university."

One way to "represent" in both worlds is to employ strategic communicative choices that are viewed as critical for continued success in predominantly White environments where these young Black women believe they are seen as outsiders by virtue of both race and gender. Analysis of those choices reveals they are consistent with the six factors identified in co-cultural communication theory and furthers understanding of how Black women communicate strategically to negotiate identity in everyday lived experiences.

Their narratives about strategic communicative practices in specific situations include preferred outcomes of dispelling stereotypes as they negotiate identity in contexts where their educational or professional success is the ultimate goal. And their responses reveal an understanding that to be successful requires they assimilate into another, more dominant culture—one often experienced as they participated in programs for the academically gifted throughout much of their lived experiences. It is within this field of experience they developed an ability to use language and nonverbal strategies when needed in situational contexts of classrooms and workplaces. The selection of a communication approach, interpreted as more passive but still assertive, is strategic to dispel long-held stereotypes of Black women's behavior. They believe to reinforce stereotypes of Black women would be costly for both their own success and the representation of their race. The reward is not only their own personal success but also, as they resist enacting stereotypes, their construction of new definitions of Black womanhood.

This construction of a new identity of Black womanhood is consistent   40
with recent discussions of "post Blackness": "It does not mean we are leaving Blackness behind, it means we are leaving behind the vision of Blackness as something narrowly definable and we're embracing every conception of Blackness as legitimate" (Touré, 2011, p. 12). The young Black women in this study know that race still matters in predominantly White environments where they are skilled at dispelling stereotypes, performing competence, and presenting alternate identities of Black womanhood. They are also aware that their communicative strategies may lead to questions about their racial identity in their own Black communities. Yet they do not perceive their actions as rejecting Black identity but rather as expanding the definition of Black womanhood.

These young Black women perceive themselves as having some measure of control in dispelling myths about Black women through the use of specific communicative strategies that are immediately available and well developed from a field of experience. This phenomenological exploration of their everyday lived experiences in communicative contexts reveals the strategies of dispelling stereotypes and overcompensation involve specific language use and nonverbal behaviors, including dressing a certain way, getting to class early, overwriting papers, and studying long and hard. They perceive such strategies as necessary and normal as they communicate self as a competent, successful Black woman and negotiate an identity counter to historical perceptions of Black womanhood. Allen (1995) discusses these instances of Black women's empowerment in predominantly White environments as a function of being "twice blessed," not doubly oppressed.

Conclusion

This study makes an important contribution to understanding the lived experiences of Black women, as it identifies specific communication strategies enacted to negotiate identity in predominantly White environments. In addition to revealing how that is done with specific language and nonverbal strategies, it also provides better understanding of why the young Black women enact them—illuminating a phenomenon in their everyday lived experiences.

As the motives for their communication strategies reveal, these young Black women perceive these strategies as a necessary skill for their success in such contexts. This specificity adds richness to the narratives on "shifting" shared in the African American Women's Voices Project (Jones & Shorter-Gooden, 2003) and provides further understanding of how such strategies can be used to support success in predominantly White environments despite tensions of identity negotiation. This closer look at Black women's cultural border crossings explores the communication strategies enacted in such situations and how those options can be empowering in everyday lived experiences as they contribute to a new definition of Black womanhood.

Note

1. A university institutional review board approved the research protocol for this study mandating that issues of confidentiality be addressed. Though the nature and structure of focus groups prohibits anonymity, it was possible to address confidentiality with the following strategies: Audiotapes and transcripts of the responses and written critical incidents were accessible only to the researcher and stored in a secured desk in a locked office. All participants were asked to submit a pseudonym to protect identity in transcripts and publications.

References

Allen, B. J. (1995, November). *Twice blessed, doubly oppressed: Women of color in academe*. Paper presented at the 81st Annual Meeting of the Speech Communication Association, San Antonio, TX.

Allen, B. J. (2002). Goals for emancipatory research on Black women. In M. Houston & O. I. Davis (Eds.), *Centering ourselves: African American feminist and womanist studies in discourse* (pp. 21–34). Cresskill, NJ: Hampton Press.

Anzaldúa, G. (1987). *Borderlands/La Frontera: The new mestiza*. San Francisco, CA: Aunt Lute.

Beale, F. (1970). Double jeopardy: To be Black and female. In T. Cade Bambara (Ed.), *The Black woman: An anthology* (pp. 90–100). New York, NY: Signet.

Collins, P. (2004). *Black sexual politics: African Americans, gender, and the new racism.* New York, NY: Routledge.

Collins, P. (2009). *Black feminist thought: Knowledge, consciousness, and the politics of empowerment* (3rd ed.). New York, NY: Routledge.

Crenshaw, K. W. (1995). Mapping the margins: Intersectionality, identity politics, and violence against women of color. In D. Danielson & K. Engle (Eds.), *After identity: A reader in law and culture* (pp. 332–354). New York, NY: Random House.

Foster, M. (1995). Are you with me? Power and solidarity in the discourse of African American women. In K. Hall & M. Bucholz (Eds.), *Gender articulated: Language and the socially constructed self* (pp. 330–350). New York, NY: Routledge.

hooks, b. (2000). *Feminist theory: From margin to center* (2nd ed.). Cambridge, MA: South End Press.

Hopson, M., & Orbe, M. (2007). Playing the game: Recalling dialectical tensions for Black men in oppressive organizational structures. *Howard Journal of Communication, 18,* 69–86.

Houston, M. (1983). *Code switching in Black women's speech* (Doctoral dissertation). University of Massachusetts, Amherst, MA.

Houston, M. (1985). Language and Black women's place: Evidence from the Black middle class. In P. Treichler, C. Kramarae, & B. Stafford (Eds.), *For alma mater: Theory and practice in feminist scholarship* (pp. 177–196). Chicago: University of Illinois Press.

Houston, M. (1989). Feminist theory and Black women's talk. *Howard Journal of Communications, 1,* 187–194.

Houston, M., & Davis, O. (2002). *Centering ourselves: African American feminist and womanist studies of discourse.* Cresskill, NY: Hampton Press.

Houston, M., & Scott, K. D. (2006). Negotiating boundaries, crossing borders: The language of Black women's intercultural encounters. In B. Dow & J. Wood (Eds.), *The Sage handbook of gender and communication* (pp. 397–414). Thousand Oaks, CA: Sage.

Jones, C., & Shorter-Gooden, K. (2003). *Shifting: The double lives of Black women in America.* New York, NY: Harper Collins.

King, D. (1989). Multiple jeopardy, multiple consciousness: The context of Black feminist ideology. *Signs, 14,* 42–72.

Kramarae, C. (1981). *Women and men speaking.* Rowley, MA: Newbury House.

Merleau-Ponty, M. (1962). *The visible and the invisible* (Trans. C. Smith; Trans. rev. F. Williams). Boston, MA: Routledge. (Original work published 1948)

Nelson, L. W. (1990). Code switching in the oral life narratives of African American women: Challenges to linguistic hegemony. *Journal of Education, 173*(3), 142–155.

Orbe, M. (1998). *Constructing co-cultural theory: An explication of culture, power, and communication.* Thousand Oaks, CA: Sage.

Orbe, M. (2000). Centralizing diverse racial ethnic voices in scholarly research: The value of phenomenological inquiry. *International Journal of Intercultural Relations, 24,* 603–621.

Scott, K. D. (1995). *"When I'm with my girls": Identity and ideology in Black women's talk about language and cultural borders* (Doctoral dissertation). University of Illinois at Urbana-Champaign, Urbana, IL.

Scott, K. D. (2000). Crossing cultural borders: "Girl" and "look" as markers of identity in Black women's language use. *Discourse and Society, 11*(2), 237–248.

Scott, K. D. (2002). Conceiving the language of Black women's everyday talk. In M. Houston & O. I. Davis (Eds.), *Centering ourselves: African American feminist and womanist studies of discourse* (pp. 53–73). Cresskill, NJ: Hampton Press.

Smith, D. (1987). *The everyday world as problematic*. Boston, MA: Northeastern University Press.

Touré. (2011). *Who's afraid of post-Blackness? What it means to be Black now*. New York, NY: Free Press.

van Manen, M. (1990). *Researching lived experience: Human science for action sensitive pedagogy*. Ontario, Canada: State University of New York Press.

Williams, T. M. (2008). *Black pain: It just looks like we're not hurting: Real talk for when there's nowhere to go but up*. New York, NY: Scribner.

Understanding the Text

1. In paragraphs 6–9, Scott reviews existing research on black women's communicative strategies. List and summarize the key points of this research. What does Scott hope to add to these studies, and how will she do so?

2. Scott sees great benefit in using co-cultural theory and a phenomenological approach to frame her study. Explain both the theory and the approach. What benefits does Scott see by using them?

3. Scott identifies phase three of the phenomenological process that grounds her methodology as "the interpretation of themes" (par. 18). What do the interpretations reveal? Fully explain the results of Scott's study, specifically noting how black women dispel stereotypes and redefine black womanhood.

Reflection and Response

4. A key topic for the study participants is the issue of stereotypes. What are the stereotypes that these young black women mentioned or experienced? What were the specific communicative strategies that these women used to confront, challenge, or dispel these stereotypes?

5. Have you ever been conscious of being a stereotype or of having crossed a cultural border? If so, describe that experience and the strategies you used to negotiate that crossing.

6. How does Scott use the terms *borderlands*, *borders*, *cultural borders*, *margin*, and *center*? Explain your answers.

7. In paragraph 40, Scott writes about "post Blackness," the importance of race in "predominantly White environments," the fear of being misunderstood as "rejecting Black identity," and the expansion of defining black womanhood. Revisit this paragraph, and do a close reading of it. How do you respond to Scott's points here? How do they fit with her other findings?

Making Connections

8. Scott's study focuses on how young black women in predominantly white environments deal with stereotypes of black women. How are issues of language implicated both in these stereotypes and in the strategies the women used to challenge them? What larger conclusions can you draw about language, cultural border crossings, and stereotypes? To develop your response fully, consider Amy Tan's "Mother Tongue" (p. 163) and Steve Inskeep and Michele Norris's "Living in Two Worlds, but with Just One Language" (p. 176).

9. Scott does not use the term *code-switching* in her study; however, her study both implicitly and explicitly deals with the issue. In paragraphs 7 and 8, Scott discusses "shifting," and several of the participants describe incidents of code-switching as they negotiate cultural border crossings. Identify the places in the essay that seem to address code-switching. Then do some research on the term and define it. Find out what it means first within the field of linguistics and then within a broader cultural sense. How does Scott's study illustrate the broader use of the term?

Digitalk: A New Literacy for a Digital Generation

Kristen Hawley Turner

Kristen Hawley Turner, an associate professor of English education and contemporary literacies, teaches in the Division of Curriculum and Teaching at Fordham University, where she also directs the university's Digital Literacies Collaborative. Turner's interest in student writing involves all the contexts in which writing occurs, including the intersection between technology and literacy. Her scholarship in this area looks at the digital literacy practices of adolescents. Turner's publications in this area include "Digitalk: The What and the Why of Adolescent Digital Language" (2014); "No Longer a Luxury: Digital Literacy Can't Wait," with T. Hicks (2013); and "Digitalk as Community" (2012).

In this article, which originally appeared in the journal *Phi Delta Kappan* in 2010, Turner challenges traditional ideas regarding literacy and helps us rethink notions of code-switching and linguistic border crossing. As you read, consider Turner's insistence that adolescents are adept manipulators of language in digital spaces.

LILY: heyyyy heyyyy (:
MICHAEL: wasz gud B.I.G.?
LILY: nm, chillennn; whatchu up too?
MICHAEL: WatchIn da gam3
LILY: mm, y quien ta jugandoo?
MICHAEL: Yank33s nd naTi0naLs.
LILY: WHAAAATT A JOKEEEEE, dime como yankees lostt againstt them yesterdaii.
MICHAEL: i n0e, th3y suCk.
LILY: & the nationalsss won like only 16 games . . . one of the worst teams homieeegee.
MICHAEL: t31L m3 b0uT it, i b3T y0u flv3 d0lLaRs th3Y g00nA l0s3.
LILY: AHA, naw gee thats easy $ for youu ! =p
MICHAEL: lol i waS plAyInG w/ y0u. =D
LILY: lol imma talk to you later . . . i got pizzaa awaitinggg meeeee (;
MICHAEL: iight pe3cE

As I copy this text conversation between two adolescents into Microsoft Word, the screen lights up with red. Every line in this exchange is marked. Microsoft Word, it seems, does not "get" the language of these speakers and attacks the black-and-white text with its red pen. For Microsoft Word, these writers are wrong.

When I first encountered "computer-mediated language" (Crystal 2001: 238), I was as confused as my word-processing program is today. An English teacher and one of our school's "grammar gurus," I couldn't understand why students were substituting "2" for "too" or "u" for "you" in their school writing. I was completely stumped by the language they were using to talk to each other digitally. Today, when I look at the exchange between Lily and Michael, I am amazed by their ability to manipulate language and to communicate effectively across time and space. I have evolved from being a grammar guru who questioned this teen language as a degradation of Standard English° to one who sees adolescent *digitalk* as a complex and fascinating combination of written and conversational languages in a digital setting.

The Journey of a "Grammar Guru"

I first ventured beyond e-mail into other forms of digital communication a decade ago when my brother installed an instant-messaging program on my personal computer. He taught me how to "see" him online and to exchange messages. A few years later, I used a similar instant-messaging program to "chat" with group members as we completed a class project for graduate school. Our inability to find a time for five adults to meet in person led us to use this technology, and our success in working together in a virtual space made me consider the pedagogical applications of instant messaging in my high school classroom.

When I first assigned a book discussion to be conducted by instant message (IM), my high school students looked at me quizzically. They hadn't thought about using IM as a learning tool. For them, it was a social space *outside* of school. They humored me, however, happy to be doing something "fun" rather than writing a literary essay about the book. As with any initial assignment, I wasn't sure what I would get when these students submitted their work. What I received were pages of writing that impressed me with truly critical thought about the text—and that shocked me with language that was far from Standard English.

I worked hard to decipher those first chat transcripts. I mentally capitalized letters and added punctuation marks. I translated phonetic spellings. I asked my brother or the students themselves to explain unknown acronyms. When it was time to grade the assignment, I was faced with a   5

Standard English: the most widely accepted or recognized system of English spelling, grammar, and vocabulary.

difficult decision. As an English teacher, I needed to hold them accountable for their use of language, and I certainly wouldn't have accepted this kind of writing had they submitted a traditional literary essay. However, the discussions of the novel were rich, and I wanted to reward their thinking despite their seemingly substandard language.

Ultimately, I let the grammar slide that time and began discussions about the nature of language and the purposes of writing. Through those discussions in my classroom, I began to realize that, to my students, writing online was separate from school writing. They used different languages in each of those contexts. By asking them to complete school-related work (the discussion of a literary text) in a social space (their IM chat rooms), I blurred the line between home and school. What they produced was a rich blend of the two discourses.

Digitalk

Since my first encounter with nonstandard IM language, the terms used to describe digital writing have changed. The shift from "netspeak" to "textspeak" followed developments in technology that affected how and where adolescents produced digital writing. However, like much in the digital age, where change occurs fast and frequently, these terms are already obsolete. Today's teens use both the Internet and their personal cell phones to communicate with peers, and patterns of language cross technological boundaries.

The manipulation of standard spellings and conventions most often occurs when teens "talk" to each other by writing in texts, IMs, and social networking tools. There are nonstandard conventions that cross these digital spaces. Writing in these venues blends elements of written discourse with those of the spoken word, and what the terms net*speak* and text*speak* share conceptually is an attention to the oral nature of the language used in these spaces. Whether teens are sending text messages or IMs, they invariably think of the communication as "talking." Talk, then, is the driving force behind much of the digital writing of adolescents.

For these reasons, I call the language that adolescents use in digital spaces *digitalk*. The term captures the nature of the writing, which in most cases replaces verbal communication, and it encompasses the wide variety of digital technologies (phone, Internet, computer, PDA) that allow for this exchange. Manipulating language so that it efficiently conveys an intended message and effectively represents the voice of the speaker requires both creativity and mastery of language for communicative purposes. Becoming an adept user takes practice and knowledge of the conventions of a community. For an outsider, it is difficult to decipher and even harder to produce in an authentic way. Digitalk, then, is a new literacy of the digital generation.

A recent study by the Pew Internet and American Life Project indi- 10 cates that teens are writing more than ever and that much of this writing is done in digital spaces. Interestingly, 60% of teens do not see the writing that they do electronically as *"real* writing" (Lenhart et al. 2008: 4).

Perhaps their view is shaped by the idea that they are talking to friends through IM, rather than writing to them. However, their dismissal of digital writing also might be a product of the societal bias against the informal language they use in digital spaces.

> "Today's teens use both the Internet and their personal cell phones to communicate with peers, and patterns of language cross technological boundaries."

The Pew study documents that "a considerable number of educators and children's advocates . . . are concerned that the quality of writing by young Americans is being degraded by their electronic communication, with its carefree spelling, lax punctuation and grammar, and its acronym shortcuts" (Lenhart et al. 2008: 3). I also hear these concerns from parents in my community. I'm alarmed by the prejudice that lies behind these statements.

Many adults fail to realize that today's teens are highly adept at using language and that their mastery of the digitally written word far surpasses that of many adults. Teens like Lily and Michael have learned to manipulate written language for social communication. They merge multiple language systems, break rules systematically, create and manipulate language and usage, and effectively communicate ideas with an intended audience. In the process, they create their own rules and rituals that are accepted by members of their language community. Their digitalk is intricate and complex. But in school and among adults, it is seen as deficient. In school, students are expected to use academic language, a discourse that may or may not resemble the primary discourse of their out-of-school language practices.

Lily and Michael, the two writers whose conversation opened this article, are *digital natives* (Prensky 2001), high school students who have grown up in a world saturated with communication technologies. They have access to computers in their homes and even in their bedrooms, and they carry cell phones wherever they go. Though they talk to their friends on the phone, they are just as likely, perhaps more likely, to communicate by text. Lily and Michael are immersed in a world outside of school where the written discourse differs from Standard English.

In discussing the language of urban students who speak African-American Vernacular English° (AAVE), Rebecca Wheeler and Rachel Swords (2006) explain that students must be taught to make choices about language, dialect, and register. They argue that teaching code-switching allows both home and academic discourse to have a place in the classroom. By valuing the language that students use outside of school, teachers can make school language more accessible. In short, out-of-school discourses are different, not deficient. Teachers should build on students' home literacy as they help them to acquire academic language.

Privileging Digitalk

Wheeler and Swords studied the patterns of error in the writing of students who speak AAVE and found that they were directly related to the grammatical structure of AAVE. They contend that these writers "are not making mistakes in Standard English. Instead, they are following the grammar patterns of their everyday language" (2006: 9). As students translate thought to writing, they unconsciously conflate the two languages.

Similarly, teens write—and perhaps even think—in digitalk. It's not surprising, then, that they require practice to switch to a more formal language in school and that many teens admit that elements of digitalk do filter into their school work. Some researchers suggest that the prevalence of these errors is not what popular opinion believes. Anecdotal evidence from teachers, however, suggests that not all students are adept at making the switch. Thus, teachers need to ask two important questions:

1. If students have trouble switching from digital language to Standard English, thus making frequent errors of standard usage in their school writing, how can teachers help them consciously switch to the appropriate language?

2. If students use digital language outside of school in creative and analytic ways to discuss real issues with their peers, how can teachers harness its power to help students learn content?

Giving digitalk a place in the classroom helps answer these questions. For example, one way to make students aware of the different contexts for language is to have them write, "Hello, how are you?" in four distinct

African-American Vernacular English: AAVE, often known as Ebonics, is a dialect of English characteristically spoken by African Americans in the United States. No one standard form of AAVE exists today; rather, it includes a range of dialects and grammatical patterns.

settings: classroom with teacher, text conversation with friend, lunchroom with friend, at home with parent. As the class analyzes the language of the settings, students can begin to look critically at the way they write in different situations. (See Turner et al. 2009 for lesson ideas.)

Conversations about language begin to ignite conscious choices for student writers. Following these conversations with an analysis of the writing they do in digital spaces will help them understand the choices they make in their digitalk. Some common patterns that emerge from the digital writing of adolescents include: 1) nonstandard capitalization, 2) nonstandard end punctuation, 3) use of multiple consonants or vowels within a word, 4) nonstandard use of ellipses, 5) lack of apostrophes, 6) use of phonetic spellings, 7) abbreviations, and 8) compound constructions to form new words (Turner et al. 2009). Instances of each of these patterns can be seen in the exchange between Lily and Michael. The writers choose the convention that best expresses purpose and voice, and they rely on the recipient's understanding of the convention to properly interpret the message. As with the conventions in Standard English that a writer might use unconsciously, teens who write daily in digitalk may not recognize the conventions they use. If teachers help students identify these patterns, they can contrast digitalk choices with the conventions of Standard English. Teachers can help writers create checklists for editing that focus on these common translation errors.

Making students conscious of the conventions of digitalk can help those who struggle to make the switch from the informal language of digital writing to the formal language of academia. In addition, allowing students to write some assignments using digitalk may allow teachers to harness the power of students' out-of-school literacy. Proponents of writing-to-learn strategies have argued that writing is closely related to thinking and that writing can help students develop and retain content knowledge. In order to achieve these goals, students are often encouraged to write freely without attention to editing. Content counts more than form when writing to learn.

Rhoda Maxwell (1996) identifies three levels of writing that are useful 20 in thinking about writing-to-learn activities. Level 1 writing allows students to develop their ideas or to reflect metacognitively on what they know about content. It does not focus on the presentation of those ideas to others. Level 2 writing, which may have a limited audience, attends somewhat more to form, but the purpose of the activity is to help students understand and develop content knowledge. Level 3 writing, on the other hand, attends to issues of grammar and mechanics. It is often published for a larger audience or to formally demonstrate a student's learning.

If language is less of an issue than content in some assignments (Level 1 and Level 2), then teachers might encourage students to use digitalk. Permitting students to take notes, write drafts, or complete other low-stakes writing assignments in whatever form of language is most comfortable places the emphasis on the content of the writing, rather than the mechanics. It also informs students that the writing they do outside of school is valuable. By giving digitalk a place in the classroom, students are able to bring their home literacy into the academic arena.

A Shift in Thinking

My argument is bound to be attacked by adults who are concerned with standards and rigor, with state tests and federal mandates. Digitalk is, after all, an easy target. Virtually any administrator, teacher, or parent is capable of marking as deficient a text riddled with digitalk. As Microsoft Word demonstrates, red pens can attack the language easily.

We should consider a shift in thinking about digitalk. Rather than seeing it as a deficiency, a lazy representation of Standard English, we should recognize its power in the digital, adolescent community. Teens today are writing a lot, but they aren't necessarily writing in Standard English. Switching from their digital writing to the requirements of academic writing can pose problems for some students. However, by valuing the language that adolescents use outside of school and engaging students in writing about content in less formal ways, teachers can focus writing on content and critical thinking, and they can give value to the literacy that students bring to class. And by teaching code-switching practices, teachers can help young writers become conscious of the language choices they make.

There is no question that students must learn academic English. All students should be held accountable to societal standards in their learning. However, the method by which we achieve these goals can build on students' existing knowledge, using their out-of-school skills to enhance their learning.

References

Crystal, David. *Language and the Internet*. New York: Cambridge University Press, 2001.

Lenhart, Amanda, Sousan Arafeh, Aaron Smith, and Alexandra Macgill. *Writing, Technology, and Teens*. Washington, D.C.: Pew Internet and American Life Project, 2008. www.pewintemet.org/PPF/r/247/report_display.asp.

Maxwell, Rhoda J. *Writing Across the Curriculum in Middle and High Schools*. Boston: Allyn and Bacon, 1996.

Prensky, Marc. "Digital Natives, Digital Immigrants." *On the Horizon* 9, no. 5 (October 2001): 1–6.

Turner, Kristen H., Jeta Donovan, Eytan Apter, and Elvira Katic. "Online and in Step: Community, Convention, and Self-Expression in Text Speak." Paper presented at the annual meeting of the National Council of Teachers of English, Philadelphia, Pa., 2009.

Wheeler, Rebecca S., and Rachel Swords. *Code-Switching: Teaching Standard English in Urban Classrooms*. Urbana, Ill.: National Council of Teachers of English, 2006.

Understanding the Text

1. Consider Turner's use of the term *digitalk*. What does this term mean? How does Turner use the term in her article?

2. What does Turner argue regarding teens' language abilities and writing skills? How does she support her argument? In your response, cite examples of evidence from the article.

3. Why, according to Turner, should teachers value digitalk and incorporate it in the classroom? What evidence or reasons do you find the most compelling or effective? Why?

Reflection and Response

4. Turner uses Rebecca Wheeler and Rachel Swords's arguments regarding African-American Vernacular English (AAVE) to support her call for using digitalk in the classroom (pars. 14–15). Explain Wheeler and Swords's arguments. How does Turner apply them to develop and support her own argument? Do you think she does so effectively? Explain why or why not.

5. In paragraph 13, Turner defines *digital native*. Do you consider yourself a digital native, fluent in digitalk? Why or why not? Be sure to define *digital native* and *digitalk* in your response.

6. What is *home literacy*, a term Turner uses in her article? What does this idea of home literacy suggest about language, borders, and linguistic border crossings for teens? How does it relate to their ability to code-switch and "merge multiple language systems" (par. 12)?

Making Connections

7. Turner does not address the effects of adolescents' code-switching on their sense of self or on their personality. Yet she does suggest that their mastery of digitalk is a type of bilingualism, a fluency in another "language." Read François Grosjean's "Change of Language, Change of Personality?" (p. 170). Using some of the information from Grosjean's blog posts, "Digitalk," and your own research, explore and analyze the link between personality and digitalk.

8. Do you think that speaking in digitalk involves crossing cultural borders? As you develop your response, carefully consider how Turner supports her position and the examples she provides. Also consider the various ways you might interpret "code-switching" and the multiple contexts in which one might code-switch. Other readings in this chapter or additional research into how linguists define *code-switching* and into its broader cultural meaning may also help you develop your ideas.

danielvfung/Getty Images

4 | Does Creativity Transcend Borders?

The question of whether creativity transcends borders may seem straightforward, and at first glance, the answer may seem obvious. The idea that barriers or boundaries can stop the flow of creative ideas and projects may seem difficult to believe. However, when we reflect more closely, we find that some complex ideas are at play. For starters, what is involved in going beyond a border's limits? How can we tell if a border has been crossed? What types of borders are involved? Are they physical, geographical, cultural, metaphorical? What do we mean by *creativity*? Is it imagination, originality, artistic creation? As you can see, this "straightforward" question — does creativity transcend borders? — leads to many other difficult questions and concepts.

The idea of transcending borders through creativity, in the forms of art, music, literature, film, and dance, draws on theories that view borders as dynamic, border crossings as fraught with peril and full of promise, and border crossers as individuals whose stories and experiences matter. The belief that creativity can cross geographical, cultural, and conceptual borders comes from those who view art and its production, circulation, and consumption (what some call "cultural production") as crucial elements in helping us understand the human condition, or the circumstances of our shared existence. Finally, exploring this topic means questioning the nature of borders themselves as well as examining how both geographical and invisible divides can often create uneasy relationships between individuals and between groups.

This chapter contains readings by a diverse group of writers — poets, scholars, artists, and musicians — all of whom address various aspects of the chapter's framing question. In "The Map," poet Elizabeth Bishop uses metaphor and imagery to question the lines on a map, ultimately blurring the mapmakers' markings. She reminds us that borders themselves may not be natural, so we too can blend colors and smudge borderlines. Indeed, in "Can Music Bridge Cultures and Promote Peace?" pianist Omar

photo: danielvfung/Getty Images

Akram writes about how he has learned to blend different cultures in his music, to worldwide acclaim. His assertion that his music can speak across international borders resonates with John Eger, who argues that art, and perhaps only art, can function as a universal language. Eger sees our world as "inextricably interconnected" because of the World Wide Web, and in "Art as a Universal Language" he proposes building virtual bridges as a powerful means of promoting cultural exchange and understanding.

This cultural exchange also concerns the authors of the next three readings. In "Cruel Beauty, Precarious Breath: Visualizing the U.S.-Mexico Border," Ann Marie Leimer focuses on the border art of four Chicano/a artists, spanning almost three decades, which she analyzes within a framework provided by the Chicana feminist Gloria Anzaldúa. Leimer highlights the role of art and the artist in making visible the diverse experiences of border culture and border crossings. Like Leimer, Gabriela Valdivia, Joseph Palis, and Matthew Reilly focus on the experiences of U.S.-Mexico border crossers. Valdivia, Palis, and Reilly expand the concept of border art and border communities by examining the work of Mexican artist Cornelio Campos, who lives in North Carolina and whose artwork represents migrant experiences. They suggest that artists like Campos may shape how non-Latinos/as understand Latino/a communities in the United States because these artists have "moved" the U.S.-Mexico border into nonborder communities.

Finally, in "Poetry Peddler" poet Naomi Shihab Nye extends this notion of wandering borders with her trope of a traveler crisscrossing borders with her poetry. For Nye, poetry provides a place for differences and contrasts to "abide," as sharing and writing poetry with others involve exposing one's uncertainties and talking about them "across borders, cultures, religions, ages" (p. 262). This creative process fosters connection, revealing the fluidity of borders and the possibilities of discovering shared experiences.

These writers do not answer all the questions about how creativity transcends borders, if, indeed, it can do so. However, as each writer confronts the place of art and creativity in relation to borders, all of them see borders as generating creative possibilities. Perhaps the photograph of David Avalos's art installation *Border Fence as Möbius Strip*, which follows Valdivia, Palis, and Reilly's essay, most vividly portrays this possibility as he upends our traditional expectations of both fences and borders. In different ways, these authors and artists reveal the complex dynamics among art, artist, and borders as they each try to push beyond borders' limits in order to figure out what it means to be human.

The Map

Elizabeth Bishop

A respected and influential American poet, Elizabeth Bishop (1911–1979) was born in Worcester, Massachusetts, and grew up in both Worcester and Nova Scotia, Canada. After graduating from Vassar College, she traveled throughout Europe and for fifteen years lived in Brazil. Many of her poems reflect her experiences as a traveler, often dealing with landscapes and geography.

Although she did not publish a great number of poems, many critics regard Bishop as one of the twentieth century's most important poets because of her keen sense of observation, attention to detail, and poetic precision. In addition to being awarded two Guggenheim Fellowships and serving as the Poet Laureate of the United States from 1949 to 1950, Bishop was the first American and the first woman to win the Book Abroad/Neustadt International Prize for Literature, in 1976.

As the titles of her books indicate, places, spaces, and our relationship to them intrigued Bishop. Her books include *North and South* (1946); *North and South — A Cold Spring* (1955), which won a Pulitzer Prize; *Questions of Travel* (1965); *The Complete Poems* (1969); and *Geography III* (1976), which garnered the Book Critics' Choice Award in 1977.

In "The Map," which first appeared in *North and South*, Bishop asks us to reexamine and reimagine both the features of maps and the process of mapmaking. As you read, note the metaphors she uses to represent the lines and colors on a map as elements of wonder and significance.

L and lies in water; it is shadowed green.
Shadows, or are they shallows, at its edges
showing the line of long sea-weeded ledges
where weeds hang to the simple blue from green.
Or does the land lean down to lift the sea from under,   5
drawing it unperturbed around itself?
Along the fine tan sandy shelf
is the land tugging at the sea from under?

The shadow of Newfoundland lies flat and still.
Labrador's yellow, where the moony Eskimo   10
has oiled it. We can stroke these lovely bays,
under a glass as if they were expected to blossom,
or as if to provide a clean cage for invisible fish.
The names of seashore towns run out to sea,

the names of cities cross the neighboring mountains   15
—the printer here experiencing the same excitement
as when emotion too far exceeds its cause.
These peninsulas take the water between thumb and finger
like women feeling for the smoothness of yard-goods.

Mapped waters are more quiet than the land is,   20
lending the land their waves' own conformation:
and Norway's hare runs south in agitation,
profiles investigate the sea, where land is.
Are they assigned, or can the countries pick their colors?
—What suits the character or the native waters best.   25
Topography displays no favorites; North's as near as West.
More delicate than the historians' are the map-makers' colors.

Understanding the Text

1. What questions does the poem's speaker ask? Can you identify one over-
   arching question that seems to concern the speaker?

2. What is the dominant impression or image of each stanza? How does
   Bishop use these elements to unify the poem?

3. What statements does the speaker make throughout the poem? How do
   the poem's statements, questions, and images relate to its overall theme?

Reflection and Response

4. Look at the geographical markers that Bishop mentions in her poem. What
   map do you see from these places and descriptions? What borders do you
   see? Could you draw a map based on the descriptions and images in the
   poem? Why or why not?

5. Which image, metaphor, or lines seem to most directly address this chapter's question: Does creativity transcend borders? Fully explain your
   answer.

Making Connections

6. Bishop's poem imbues cartography, or mapmaking, with a creative and
   artistic quality. Do you consider cartography an art? Research both past
   and current cartography methods and maps, and write an essay exploring
   the possibility that mapmaking is an artistic process or that maps are
   cultural productions. What conclusions can you draw about the cultural
   significance of maps and the borders they present?

Can Music Bridge Cultures and Promote Peace?

Omar Akram

Omar Akram is a pianist and recording artist. Akram considers himself a cultural diplomat by virtue of his upbringing, experiences, and music. As the son of a United Nations diplomat, he has crossed many international borders, living in France, the Czech Republic, Cuba, and Afghanistan. He has written for or has been featured in *Origin Magazine, Los Angeles Magazine, The Huffington Post*, and the BBC and won a Grammy for his album *Echoes of Love* (2012), making him the first Afghan American to win the award.

Akram wrote this essay as an op-ed for *The Huffington Post* in 2013. As you read, think about your own experiences listening to or playing music and which cultural borders, if any, you crossed while doing so.

I met Fidel Castro° when I was 14 years old. I was at one of my father's diplomatic functions, and I had the opportunity to strike up a conversation with Castro about music. He knew I played the piano and asked me if I'd been to any of the local African jazz clubs. I was too young to enter the clubs at the time, but to my surprise the dictator wielded his power to get me in. I entered some of Cuba's best jazz clubs by simply using his name, and no one questioned it. I would go on stage and play the piano between sets, and the musicians would improvise with me and encourage me to play. This is one of the most powerful ways I was able to absorb the culture, and bring it with me in my own art.

After I was thrust into the international spotlight as the first Afghan American to win a Grammy award this year, I learned some important lessons about the power of music. I was born in New York as the son of a UN diplomat. I've lived all around the world, from the U.S. to the Czech Republic, Cuba, Switzerland and Afghanistan. Although my parents are from Afghanistan, I've never felt confined by the borders of just one culture, and I've learned to weave these many cultures into my compositions. One reason why I think my music in particular has been able to easily flow between international borders is because there is no singing or language. I receive letters from amazing fans all around the world who are able to create their own images and impressions about what my music means because they are not being directed by words or a certain language. It is the reason I started playing instrumental music.

Fidel Castro: Cuban revolutionary leader who served as president of Cuba (1976–2008).

The Grammy win brought me a lot of attention, both from the Afghan media and the people of Afghanistan. Afghanistan is a very divided country that is made up of many different ethnicities and social groups. After being on the radio and television I heard from everyone. The people there can hardly ever unite behind anything, and after I won the Grammy award there was a shared sense of accomplishment. It was a kind of unity I've never seen that I was very happy to be a part of.

I've received very touching letters and emails from people all around the world. I once received a letter from a man in Iraq who had just lost his family and his job. He was on the brink of committing suicide and someone gave him my CD. He told me that the music gave him the hope to move on. A woman in Australia wrote to me about her father who had terminal cancer. She said that after playing my music for him his whole demeanor changed, and now he leaves it playing in the background 24/7. I've received letters ranging from an overworked father in the U.S. who is soothed by my music during his grueling commute to work, to an electricity deprived family in Afghanistan who were mystified after hearing music unlike anything they are used to through the radio. I guess you could say music at its best could provide a sort of positive culture shock.

> "One reason why I think my music in particular has been able to easily flow between international borders is because there is no singing or language."

Music can positively affect people on many different levels. It can be a tool to communicate culture and a remedy for suffering just as much as it is a form of entertainment. I've learned to meld cultures and bring in instruments from around the world without hesitation. Embrace the culture you are from. It's who you are and it is a part of what makes you unique. In some ways, you can promote diplomacy through music, but it's important to understand that diplomacy does not always have to be political. Don't be afraid of who you are and where you are from. When you keep an open mind and an open heart to the many cultures of the world, you can turn your musical instrument into an instrument of peace. 5

Understanding the Text

1. How did Akram's experiences as a diplomat's son and the first Afghan American Grammy winner influence his understanding of music's power to bridge cultural divides? Explain your answer in your own words.

2. Why does Akram think his music can "flow between international borders"? What conclusions does he draw about the relationship between language and culture?

3. How does Akram answer the question he poses in the title? How does he support his answer?

Reflection and Response

4. What aspects of Akram's argument do you find most effective or compelling? Do you agree that music has the power to "bridge cultures and promote peace"? Explain your answer.

5. In paragraph 5, Akram writes, "In some ways, you can promote diplomacy through music, but it's important to understand that diplomacy does not always have to be political." Respond to his ideas and explain what you think he means, whether you agree or not, and identify other places in the reading that seem to support this notion.

6. Describe a time when music was a "positive culture shock" for you as either a listener or a musician. In your description, consider whether this experience involved crossing cultural borders. If it did, identify the cultures involved and the ways in which music crossed cultural barriers.

Making Connections

7. Read Norma Cantú's "Living on the Border: A Wound That Will Not Heal" (p. 58), paying close attention to her descriptions of the mix of people and cultures in the borderlands. Consider how her examples intersect with Akram's arguments. Using both of these readings and your own research, stake out your own position regarding the role that music can play in bridging cultural divides.

8. Akram's belief in his music's power to cross cultural borders links to his ideas about its relationship to language and culture. Naomi Shihab Nye might or might not agree with Akram on this issue of language. Read Nye's "Poetry Peddler" (p. 258) and John Eger's "Art as a Universal Language" (p. 218), and construct a conversation among the musician, the poet, and the scholar about this issue. Ground the dialogue in their respective readings, adding your own perspective to the conversation.

Art as a Universal Language

John Eger

John Eger teaches in the School of Journalism and Media Studies at San Diego State University (SDSU), where he is the Lionel Van Deerlin Endowed Chair of Communication and Public Policy and the director of the Creative Economy Initiative. His research focuses on education and economic development, creativity, and innovation, and he has written two books on the subjects: *The Creative Community: Linking Art, Culture, Commerce, and Community* (2013) and *Arts Education and the Innovation Economy* (2011).

Eger originally wrote "Art as a Universal Language" for SDSU's NewsCenter in 2011. In it he points to our ability to use art and new technologies to "build virtual bridges into unknown cultural territory." However, in this essay, Eger does not define what art is. As you read, consider your own understanding of art and its place in society.

There can be no more distilled expression of a culture than its works of art.

In the coming decade, the challenge for humanity will be whether we can come to grips with the idea of a world community, shared governance and the notion that the differences between us—the art and culture and wonder and beauty of those differences—must be something we can respect, honor, grow to appreciate and welcome.

In creating art, consciously or not, artists are attempting to communicate at a powerful emotional level to those within their own culture. The best work transcends its cultural matrix and speaks directly to our common humanity.

Already, the world is so inextricably interconnected that cultural and economic isolationism is unthinkable, even if it were desirable. But more needs to be done, and perhaps the most effective thing that can be done is to aggressively promote multicultural understanding. By doing so, perhaps, we can create the world community reflective of the world economy in the making.

Given the ubiquitous nature of the World Wide Web, we can use the new technologies—with their powerful capacity for shaping and delivering human interchange—as virtual bridges across the vast distances separating cultures. 5

Over the last few decades we were witness to a basic change in our modern-day world: globalization, the rise and rebirth of the region state, and the resurgence of age-old hostilities—racial, tribal and religious strife—that lay just beneath the surface for the last 100 years.

Globalization—something still not understood but feared—has forced us to think about the rest of the world, not just ourselves. For globalization to work, as former President Bill Clinton has observed, we need to be sensitive to the social and political values nation to nation as well as the economic opportunities.

As Thomas Friedman observed in his book of the same name, suddenly The World Is Flat.

By the turn of the century and the onset of a new millennium, the Internet changed the way the world communicated with one another around the world, as it changed the structure of the world economy. The World Wide Web wasn't invented until the late 1990s, but by the year 2000, the Net seemed to be growing at 15 percent per month worldwide.

Everybody is now communicating with everyone else; every person, every community is competing with every other . . . and in the process, the question is being raised about the future of the world, and of the current geopolitical order. 10

Friedman calls it Globalization 3.0.°

While there are countless disciplines, which might reasonably serve as a means to understanding culture, such as history, sociology, mathematics and science, only art lends itself to the full range of experiential capabilities offered by the new technologies.

This is why art serves so superbly as a universal language—as a means toward understanding the history, culture and values of other peoples. As human beings build virtual bridges into unknown cultural territory—and there learn,

> "As human beings build virtual bridges into unknown cultural territory — and there learn, share dreams and creatively work together — mankind will know itself as citizens of a rich and truly global society."

share dreams and creatively work together—mankind will know itself as citizens of a rich and truly global society. And if citizens of a global society are to live in peace, goods, services and technical information are exchanged, but values and visions, as well.

It is this new technological marvel that has made the world smaller that compels worldwide debate and discussion, and provides the threshold for

---

Globalization 3.0: Thomas Friedman's third and final phase of globalization, in which the world has "shrunk" significantly through the globalization of individuals.

A man looks on as artists from the Face2Face project put up photos of a Palestinian Muslim cleric, an Arab Christian priest, and an Israeli Jewish rabbi on the Israel-Palestine wall. The French artists hope the posters will promote a shared understanding between the cultures.

David Silverman/Staff/Getty Images

the world's greatest assets of art and culture to become the glue for discussion about a New World community. Everybody it seems has an app for almost every human endeavor. Maybe, America—in partnership with other governments and institutions around the world—should create the cultural databases that truly bring people together.

Maybe it is naive to say art is the universal language, and that we can 15 open windows for all to see that we are just folks, and that we are one community. Yet, if art can't, nothing can.

Understanding the Text

1. What are Eger's stated and unstated assumptions about art? What does he think artists are trying to accomplish through art? What specific passages support your answers?

2. Eger offers several claims about art and its role in society. Identify his major argument and explain how he supports it.

3. Explain what Eger means by a "world community." Is it the same as the "global society" to which he refers in paragraph 13? If so, explain the similarities; if not, describe the differences.

Reflection and Response

4. Eger does not specify what comprises art, yet he identifies art as a universal language. What do you consider art? What is Eger's theory of art? Does his theory agree with your ideas about art? Why or why not?

5. Why does Eger view the World Wide Web as such a valuable resource for the coming decade? Do you think his perspective is accurate? As you explain your position, remember that we are already well into Eger's "coming decade."

6. Reread paragraph 13. Observe the details in the passage — the specific words, their order, their connotations and dictionary meanings, as well as the tone of the passage — and interpret your observations. As you analyze this passage, also identify and explain Eger's stated and unstated assumptions.

Making Connections

7. Revisit Eger's major argument. Write an essay clearly articulating his position and reasoning, and then either challenge or extend his ideas. As you develop your own position, consider other readings from this chapter and do some independent research on the efficacy of art and technology in transcending borders.

8. Read Ann Marie Leimer's "Cruel Beauty, Precarious Breath: Visualizing the U.S.-Mexico Border" (p. 222) and Gabriela Valdivia, Joseph Palis, and Matthew Reilly's "Borders, Border-Crossing, and Political Art in North Carolina" (p. 234). Explain how the artists' work discussed in these readings might exemplify Eger's ideas about art's ability to serve as a universal language and to convey cultural values and visions.

9. Write an essay addressing the implications of Eger's arguments regarding a borderless world. Do you think his ideas about art as a universal language and the necessity of building virtual bridges suggest a world without borders? To develop your ideas, investigate Eger's reference to Thomas Friedman's book *The World Is Flat* and his theory of Globalization 3.0, and read Gabriel Popescu's "Borders in the Era of Globalization" (p. 273). Use your research and passages from these readings to support your position.

Cruel Beauty, Precarious Breath: Visualizing the U.S.-Mexico Border

Ann Marie Leimer

Ann Marie Leimer is an associate professor of art history at the Juanita and Ralph Harvey School of Visual Arts at Midwestern State University, where she researches issues of spirituality, space, place, and identity construction in contemporary Chicano/a art, Latin American art, and the Indigenous Americas. "Cruel Beauty, Precarious Breath: Visualizing the U.S.-Mexico Border" first appeared as a chapter in *New Frontiers in Latin American Borderlands* (2012), a collection of essays addressing political borders as well as those constructed by social policy, art, and the human body. As you read Leimer's interpretations of the specific works of art, consider the various borders that the artists depict, challenge, cross, and, perhaps, celebrate.

Introducción[1]

Since the mid-nineteenth century, the border between the United States and Mexico has been celebrated for its complex mix of cultures, contested for its daily flow of migratory workers, both documented and those without papers, and condemned for its ruthless violence and drug trafficking. Artists, living in the border regions and beyond its confines, have produced comprehensive bodies of work that record the economic, political, social, and spiritual ramifications of this serpentine stretch of nearly 2000 miles, as well as the toll it exacts on inhabitants and on the earth.[2] This chapter uses Chicana lesbian feminist Gloria Anzaldúa's (1987) notion of *una herida abierta* or an open wound to analyze portrayals of the border produced by Chicana and Chicano artists. After a brief introduction to Anzaldúa's ideas, I analyze depictions by artists Malaquias Montoya, Jacalyn López García, Delilah Montoya, and Consuelo Jiménez Underwood, and argue that they visualize the border as a place of continual transition, of dangerous beauty, of profound ugliness, of corporate and international greed, and of cruel realities.

Gloria Anzaldúa presented her theories of *la conciencia de la mestiza* or Mestiza consciousness and the *Coatlicue* state in *Borderlands/La Frontera*, first published in 1987. Considered a milestone in Chicana feminist theory, Anzaldúa continued to develop these concepts throughout the remainder of her life, and scholars have productively applied these theories in a range of disciplines over the past twenty-four years.[3] Anzaldúa's Coatlicue state takes its name from the divine mother of Central Mexico's indigenous pantheon.[4] Anzaldúa used this reference to the female earth goddess to articulate the Coatlicue state as an inner process of reclamation where Chicanas can confront multiple and conflicting identities and can find a place of wholeness and integration. She viewed the Coatlicue state as a necessary first step toward a state of being she termed Mestiza consciousness. Anzaldúa understood Mestiza consciousness as a consciousness of the borderlands, one that describes an individually constructed feminist political subject position and a worldview that involves active commitment to social change (Anzaldúa 1999, 99).

Anzaldúa (1999, 24–25) began *Borderlands/La Frontera* with a poem:

> I press my hand to the steel curtain—
> chainlink fence crowned with rolled barbed wire—
> rippling from the sea where Tijuana touches San Diego
> unrolling over mountains
> and plains
> and deserts,
> this "Tortilla Curtain" turning into *el río Grande*
> flowing down to the flatlands
> of the Magic Valley of South Texas
> its mouth emptying into the Gulf.
>
> 1,950 mile-long open wound
> dividing a *pueblo*, a culture,
> running down the length of my body,
> staking fence rods in my flesh,
> splits me   splits me
> *me raja   me raja*
> This is my home
> this thin edge of
> barbwire.[5]

The author places the division of earth in her body, she feels fence posts pierce her flesh and rend her with an injury that has little hope of healing. Yet, she dwells in this precarious and painful margin and claims the borderlands as her home. If Anzaldúa, as a Chicana writer, equates the border with something as intimate as her flesh, how do Chicana and Chicano artists visually engage this complex issue?

Sin Papeles

In 1981, Northern California master printmaker Malaquias Montoya produced a serigraph° titled *Undocumented,* where he depicted a sole human figure literally and figuratively caught "between" repeated strands of barbed wire while in the process of border crossing (Figure 4.1).[6] The figure falls forward and downward, as if struck from behind. Its torso collapses over the tightly ensnared lower body, with the weight of the figure suspended at various points among the multiple lengths of wire. The upper garment splays sharply backward on each side of the human form, suggesting a sudden cessation of movement. This abruptly arrested pose reveals the often-harsh reality of increasingly militarized border re-

Figure 4.1 *Undocumented* (1981)

Undocumented, silkscreen, 1981, by Malaquias Montoya

serigraph: a print made by a silkscreen process.

gions. The artist's depiction also visually echoes Anzaldúa's notion of a "1,950 mile-long open wound . . . running down the length of my body," with spatters of red pigment that flow over the entire form. While Montoya may have spontaneously executed the rivulets of what reads as blood during the printmaking process, four clearly defined areas suggest bullet wounds. One wound lies at the top of the composition just behind the head, and two others bracket the neck and upper chest, while the fourth appears on the figure's left lower leg. The artist places the figure in a pose that resembles the crucified Christ to not only suggest suffering and death, but also to emphasize the victimization border crossers typically experience as they often find themselves caught in intermingled webs of exploitation.

Anzaldúa (1999, 25–26) expands her initial description and reiterates 5 the border as a wounded and wounding place when she states:

The U.S.-Mexico border es una herida abierta where the Third World grates against the first and bleeds. And before a scab forms it hemorrhages again, the lifeblood of two worlds merging to form a third country—a border culture. Borders are set up to define the places that are safe and unsafe, to distinguish us from them. . . . Tension grips the inhabitants of the borderlands like a virus. Ambivalence and unrest reside there and death is no stranger.

In this serigraph, Montoya plays with positionality and wields a purposeful ambivalence. The artist renders the figure's gender, ethnicity, nationality, and age unreadable, due to an obscured face and an indeterminate form. The exact location of the event remains undefined and he deliberately leaves the source of the figure's demise unclear. However, using a limited palette that sharply juxtaposes primary colors against earth tones, he likely placed red and blue hues against the white of the print's paper to intentionally suggest the colors of the North American flag. The oblique placement of the red text "UNDOCUMENTED" in the lower third of the composition not only physically parallels the shallow diagonals of the barbed wire along the print's lower register, but the bold graphic also leaves no question as to the figure's political position within Anzaldúa's "border culture." These formal choices expand how we might interpret this work because they create an inclusive depiction of those who cross borders and indict all borders whether local, regional, national, or transnational. Lastly, Montoya's portrayal implicates the viewer as participant in a system that creates and maintains inequity and injustice and further reminds us of Anzaldúa's statement "death is no stranger" in the borderlands.

Los Sueños de Califas

In a sepia-toned and hand-tinted silver gelatin print from 1997 titled *California Dreaming*, Southern California photographer and multi-media artist Jacalyn López García deeply engages Anzaldúa's idea of the border as place of ambivalence. She visually echoes Malaquias Montoya's use of barbed wire and expands his treatment of the border to include the "chainlink fence" topped with barbed wire mentioned by Anzaldúa (Figure 4.2). The artist divides the photograph in half horizontally, perhaps to contrast the space of exclusion that constitutes the bottom half against the space of dreams in the upper half of the image. In the lower section of the work, the forearms and hands of two hidden figures reach over the chainlink limits and through a double strand of horizontal wire. While their unseen bodies remain solidly on one side of the fence, their arms penetrate

Figure 4.2   *California Dreaming* **(1997)**
Jacalyn López García, © 1997

the top half of the composition where possible economic improvement remains agonizingly just beyond their grasp. The artist pictures this greater financial potential with paper currency from the United States that floats mere inches above eagerly outstretched hands. Ironically, the depicted money consists of very small bills that total only twenty-seven dollars, the price of an inexpensive pair of shoes or a small bag of groceries. The photograph's upward motion stands in direct opposition to the downward directionality of Montoya's serigraph. And unlike Montoya's depiction, López García's figures remain vibrantly alive, while still caught in the often-false promise of the so-called American dream.

López García visually refers to the sense of liminality or the state of being in-between that border crossers often experience, when they physically dwell on one side of the border while living in their imagination on *el otro lado*. The artist's choice of "California Dreaming" for the photograph's title gives a profoundly ironic twist to The Mamas & The Papas' song of similar name (Phillips and Phillips 1965):

All the leaves are brown and the sky is gray
I've been for a walk on a winter's day
I'd be safe and warm if I was in L.A.
California dreamin' on such a winter's day.

The lyrics from the song locate Los Angeles as a place of warmth and safety in the midst of a dying winter season and overcast skies, and, in this context, position "el A" as a desired destination for many crossers coming from the south. These words emphasize the longing for a better life and situate North America as a source of increased opportunity. The artist's portrayal poignantly depicts the allure that the United States holds for many migrants, immigrants, and border crossers. She also implicates corporate greed and transnational industry in this representation because *maquiladores*, factories owned and operated by multi-national corporations, densely populate Mexican cities that lie immediately across the U.S. border. These factories frequently mislead workers with pledges of positive working conditions and good wages, while low pay and 60-hour workweeks are often their harsh reality. Therefore, López García indicts the deep economic disparity between Mexico and the United States and presents the border as a place of danger and delusional dreams.

Yo Tengo Sed

In 2004, Chicana photographer Delilah Montoya created a photographic installation and documentary series titled *Sed: The Trail of Thirst*, conceived and executed in collaboration with Orlando Lara.[7] One year earlier, Montoya and Lara traveled to the Arizona-Mexico border and photographed routes taken by workers and other migrants passing through the Sonoran Desert into the United States. In this work, the artist powerfully visualizes Anzaldúa's understanding of imposed borders that delineate areas of safety and peril. Montoya captured the trails that crisscross the terrain, cast-off objects found along these paths, and the impact of the migrant's journey on the desert landscape. The artist debuted the project at *Talento Bilingüe de Houston*, Houston's local Latino art and cultural center, as part of the city's widely acclaimed FotoFest.

> "Visual representations of this third space by Chicana and Chicano artists show us the border's inherent dangers, as well as its potent possibilities."

In its initial showing, the work consisted of a wall-sized photomural, a video that recorded the process of walking along the migrant trail, and an altar comprised of objects left behind during migration. Montoya composed the photomural with numerous small-scale images, visually "stitched" them together using computer software, and produced them as a single piece displayed full-length on the gallery wall. In 2008, the series opened at the Patricia Correia Gallery in Los Angeles simply titled *The Trail of Thirst*. In this most recent version, the artist enclosed the viewing public with highly saturated large-scale panoramic color photographs displayed on all four sides of the exhibition space.

Some of the trails captured by Montoya run through lands of the Tohono O'odham Nation in Arizona's Pima County near the Ironwood National Forest. Individual tribal members had placed plastic containers of water along the trail as acts of mercy and in an attempt to reduce deaths along these dangerous corridors. In *Water Trail, O'odham Reservation, AZ*, the translucent water jugs glow eerily against the textures of tree, cacti, and rock. The jugs' placement orders the path and indicates the next step in the migrant's passage. Montoya's lens records the stark and desolate beauty of the desert landscape now embedded with historical narratives of border crossers and those who compassionately assist them. In contrast to representations by Malaquias Montoya and López García, the absence of the human figure intensifies the viewer's experience and heightens our understanding of the fear and uncertainty of those who take this journey.

La Zona de la Muerte: Las Flores Sobre la Línea

Artists increasingly reveal the environmental expense exacted by the border. Along with Delilah Montoya's recent work *Sed*, Consuelo Jiménez 10

Figure 4.3 **Undocumented Border Flowers (2009)**
© Consuelo Jiménez Underwood, *Undocumented Border Flowers, 2009*;
Photo by José Estrada.

Underwood established new frontiers in the portrayal of border realities in her recent tour-de-force, *Undocumented Border Flowers* (Figure 4.3). The Triton Museum of Art in Santa Clara, California, exhibited this mixed media installation in the spring of 2010 as part of a group show titled *Xicana: Spiritual Reflections/Reflexíones Espiritúales*. María Ester Fernández curated the show as the inaugural exhibition in a series titled *Bay Area Chicana*. In *Undocumented Border Flowers*, the artist used a mural format installed with fabric flowers to visually describe a "dead zone," a five-mile area framing each side of the border between Mexico and the United States that has become, in Jiménez Underwood's words, a "desert wasteland."

To create the work, Consuelo Jiménez Underwood, Betty A. Davis, and their assistants, Erica Diazoni and José Estrada, painted a representation of the physical areas that form the border between Mexico and the United States on the museum wall. Ten fabric flowers of various sizes, shapes, and colors surround the geographic reference to this dead zone, and a series of nails intertwined with a mix of wire create the line between the two countries. The fabric flowers correspond with ten groups of sister cities that lie next to each other and yet on opposite sides of the border, such as El Paso, Texas, and Ciudad Juárez, Chihuahua, Mexico; and Calexico, California, and Mexicali, Baja California, Mexico. The artist created place markers that name the pairs of sister cities and located three of these pairings on the right of the central image and the seven remaining pairs on the left side. Each of the ten place markers consists of simple metal wire wrapped with colored wire and fibers of varying thicknesses. Jiménez Underwood also wrapped lengths of cord that hold not only the individual letters identifying each paired location, but also a variety of objects such as shells, bottle caps, bits of dried flowers, beads, feathers, and small pieces of cloth printed with the ubiquitous "Caution" sign. In the late 1980s, the San Diego California Department of Transportation (CADOT) asked graphic artist John Hood to produce a traffic sign in response to rising numbers of deaths along border freeways. CADOT installed Hood's image at popular border crossings to warn drivers that people might run among vehicular traffic in an attempt to cross the border. The now-iconic representation, rendered with a yellow background and black text announcing "CAUTION," prominently depicts a three-member family in flight.

Jiménez Underwood's treatment of the line that represents the border, while beautiful, also evokes pain when she inserts nails at specific sites to represent the border sister cities and to suspend the wire away from the museum wall. The artist references Anzaldúa's idea of an open wound when she depicts the border three-dimensionally with wire, nails, and assorted fibers, but she complicates Anzaldúa's concept when she leaves a small unpainted strip underneath the wire representing the border fence. This untreated section of the wall represents the dead zone in all its ugliness. Its stark whiteness stands in sharp contrast to the rich blues of the surrounding land mass, and symbolizes death along with the irreparable injury to nature's mutually interdependent web of life. The artist understands this area as a desert wasteland where flowers refuse to grow and animals no longer thrive, a zone that has formed alongside the fence separating the two countries during the past several years. While Jiménez Underwood cares deeply about the impact of the border on humanity, this piece emphasizes the cost in terms of the imbalance of nature and the disruption of harmonious relationships in multiple micro-environments of border regions. The artist wanted to express her anger in the work, but most importantly she wanted us to see the joy, beauty, and perseverance of border dwellers and crossers, be they human, animal, or plant.

El Fin

In this [article], I have used Gloria Anzaldúa's notion of the border between Mexico and the United States as an open wound to visually interrogate the physical, mental, and spiritual disjunctures caused by the border as depicted by four contemporary artists. The works I have examined include a diverse range of media from printmaking to photography to mixed media installation. Their time frame spans nearly three decades, indicating the continuing power of these regions as lived reality, but also as a persistent presence in social, political, and cultural imaginaries. Anzaldúa believed a third country formed from the painful and productive interaction between border inhabitants and crossers, a country she termed "a border culture." Visual representations of this third space by Chicana and Chicano artists show us the border's inherent dangers, as well as its potent possibilities. Malaquias Montoya, Jacalyn López García, Delilah Montoya, and Consuelo Jiménez Underwood each question societal factors that produce and naturalize the polarizing notion of *us* and *them* and deeply critique the border's toll on sentient° life. These artists imagine the fragility and the tenacity of life along the borderlands. They honor the precarious breath of its most vulnerable creatures and recognize its profound beauty, a beauty at once cruel and compelling.

Notes

1. Anzaldúa (1999, 75–86) often wrote about the tactic of "linguistic terrorism," and moved fluidly in her writing between Spanish and English, without providing translations for either language. Following Anzaldúa, I use headings in Spanish without translation to demarcate sections of the essay. For her work on linguistic terrorism, see "How to Tame a Wild Tongue."

2. For border art exhibitions and texts that critically assess some of these bodies of work, see Malagamba-Ansótegui (2006), Fox (1999), Chávez and Grynsztejn (1993), and Border Art Workshop/Tallér de Arte Fronterízo (1988).

3. Readers interested in the development of Anzaldúan thought and scholarship, please see Norma E. Cantú et al. (2010). The Society for the Study of Gloria Anzaldúa (SSGA) will hold its third international conference in May 2012.

4. The peoples of Central Mexico at the time of the Spanish conquest (1521) consisted of the Mexica, Acolhua, Chalca, Tepaneca, Tlahuica, Tlaxcalteca, and the Xochimilca, and these groups spoke regional variants of the indigenous language Nahuatl. In common parlance, these indigenous peoples are generally termed Aztec, a word coined by German explorer and naturalist Alexander von Humboldt and later normalized by William H. Prescott (1843).

5. Anzaldúa visually reinforces the reader's understanding of how the fence moves along the border, "rippling from the sea" and "flowing down to the flatlands," with her phrase formatting and her arrangement of words on the page.

6. For a monographic treatment of Malaquias Montoya, see Terezita Romo (2011).

7. For more information on this series by Montoya, see Ann Marie Leimer (2008).

sentient: characterized by sensations and consciousness.

References

Anzaldúa, Gloria. 1987. *Borderlands/La Frontera: The New Mestiza.* San Francisco: Aunt Lute Books.

———. 1999. *Borderlands/La Frontera: The New Mestiza.* 2nd ed. San Francisco: Aunt Lute Books.

Border Art Workshop/Tallér de Arte Fronterízo. 1988. *The Border Art Workshop (BAW/TAF) 1984–1989: A Documentation of Five Years of Interdisciplinary Art Projects Dealing with U.S.-Mexico Border Issues.* San Diego: Border Art Workshop/Tallér de Arte Fronterízo.

Cantú, Norma E., Christina L. Gutiérrez, Norma Alarcón, and Rita E. Urquijo-Ruiz, eds. 2010. *El Mundo Zurdo: Selected Works from the Meetings of the Society for the Study of Gloria Anzaldúa, 2007 & 2009.* San Francisco: Aunt Lute Books.

Chávez, Patricio, and Madeleine Grynsztejn. 1993. *La Frontera/The Border: Art About the Mexico/United States Border Experience.* San Diego: Centro Cultural de la Raza and the Museum of Contemporary Art, San Diego.

Fox, Claire. 1999. "Establishing Shots of the Border: The Fence and the River." Chapter 2. In *The Fence and the River: Culture and Politics at the U.S.-Mexico Border*, 41–67. Minneapolis: University of Minnesota.

Leimer, Ann Marie. 2008. "Chicana Photography: The Power of Place." *Poesía, Baile y Canción: The Politics, Implications, and Future of Chicana/os' Cultural Production.* http://scholarworks.sjsu.edu/naccs/2008/Proceedings/13.

Malagamba-Ansótegui, Amelia. 2006. *Caras vemos, corazones no sabemos = Faces Seen, Hearts Unknown: The Human Landscape of Mexican Migration.* Notre Dame: Snite Museum, University of Notre Dame.

Phillips, John, and Michelle Phillips. 1965. California Dreamin'. On *You Can Believe Your Eyes and Ears.* Dunhill Records.

Prescott, William Hickling. 1843. *History of the Conquest of Mexico, with a Preliminary View of the Ancient Mexican Civilization, and the Life of the Conqueror, Hernando Cortés.* New York: Harper and Brothers.

Romo, Terezita. 2011. *Malaquías Montoya.* Vol. 6, A Ver. Los Angeles: UCLA Chicano Studies Research Center Press.

Understanding the Text

1. Leimer uses Gloria Anzaldúa's concept of an open wound to frame her analyses and arguments. Identify Leimer's main argument and explain Anzaldúa's ideas.

2. Summarize Leimer's analysis of each of the four artists' work: Malaquias Montoya's *Undocumented*, Jacalyn López García's *California Dreaming*, Delilah Montoya's *Sed: Trail of Thirst*, and Consuelo Jiménez Underwood's *Undocumented Border Flowers*.

Reflection and Response

3. Choose one of the images included with this reading, and reread Leimer's analysis of it. Why did you choose this artwork? What questions does the

artwork raise for you? What might you add to Leimer's analysis and arguments? Do you interpret this work differently than Leimer does? Why? Explain your process of interpretation.

4. Reread the first three paragraphs and locate Leimer's main argument. Do you think she fulfills the promise of her argument? As you explain your answer, include passages that you find effective and identify places in the reading where you would like more information or more fully developed ideas.

5. Consider the title of this essay. Write a response explaining those specific words and how they relate to Leimer's argument, using evidence from the text to illustrate and support your explanation. Leimer's closing remarks (par. 13) might prove helpful.

Making Connections

6. Both Leimer and Valdivia, Palis, and Reilly, in "Borders, Border-Crossing, and Political Art in North Carolina" (p. 234), focus on art and its relationship to border politics and "social, political, and cultural imaginaries." What do these authors suggest about art's role in this relationship? Compare and contrast Leimer's ideas with yours and with those of Valdivia, Palis, and Reilly.

7. Evoking Gloria Anzaldúa's notion of border culture as a "third country," Leimer concludes that "[v]isual representations of this third space by Chicana and Chicano artists show us the border's inherent dangers, as well as its potent possibilities" (par. 13). Using this statement as a starting point, explore this idea — border regions as a third space both painful and promising — and how artists visualize this space and its paradoxes. To develop your exploration, you may want to read Gabriela Valdivia, Joseph Palis, and Matthew Reilly's "Borders, Border-Crossing, and Political Art in North Carolina" (p. 234), Anzaldúa's "To Live in the Borderlands Means You" (p. 55), and Norma Cantú's "Living on the Border: A Wound That Will Not Heal" (p. 58).

Borders, Border-Crossing, and Political Art in North Carolina

Gabriela Valdivia, Joseph Palis, and Matthew Reilly

Gabriela Valdivia is an assistant professor in geography at the University of North Carolina, Chapel Hill (UNC). She leads the Social Cartographies of the Americas, a working group that traces many different types of border crossings. Her research interests include Latin American environment, identity and government, critical resource geography, and political ecology, and she also investigates how political art and activism may initiate conversations about border crossings and border crossers.

Joseph Palis is an assistant professor of interdisciplinary studies at North Carolina State University. His research focuses on emergent geographies, including nightscapes, archipelagic studies, and cinematic cartographies. Matthew Reilly studies urban geography, focusing on public spaces, in Havana, Cuba. He was a lecturer in the geography department at UNC when "Borders, Border-Crossing, and Political Art in North Carolina" was published in 2011.

In the following essay, the authors pose critical questions regarding art's potential to shape our thinking about borders and border crossers. As you read this piece, consider what the authors suggest about art's potential to help us understand ever-shifting borders.

More so than any other region in the United States, the South now accounts for the greatest share of growth in Latina/o populations (Kochar et al. 2005; Frey 2008). In North Carolina, since 1990, the foreign-born Latina/o population has grown by 1,050 percent (Winders 2005). This population is predominantly of Mexican descent and represents 75 percent of the total Latina/o population in the state (Cravey 2003). This Latinization of North Carolina is increasingly evident in its everyday spaces of existence. In the area of Raleigh, Durham, and Chapel Hill, for example, there is a proliferation of restaurants, dance halls, markets, and stores that cater to Latin American palates and entertainment needs, two well established Spanish language newspapers (*Qué Pasa* and *La Conexión*), and yearly public events that celebrate Latina/o diversity and provide local spaces for community-building and cultural exchange.[1] *La Fiesta del Pueblo*, for example, a 2-day event held annually at the North Carolina State Fairgrounds in Raleigh, showcases music, art exhibits, and crafts along with cuisine and sports for approximately 20,000 visitors from all over North Carolina.

In 2009, more than 30 artists (music, dance, and performance) participated in *La Fiesta* to make connections with the broader community and circulate culturally affirmative references about homeland and migration. Through music, storytelling, visual representations, and/or social commentary, these artists tell their version of Latina/o diaspora° and communicate their messages to Latina/o and non-Latina/o audiences. Our paper focuses on how such artistic work shapes perceptions of Latinization among non-Latina/o residents in North Carolina.[2] We focus on the work of one Mexican artist residing in North Carolina, Cornelio Campos, whose work represents journeys of Mexico-U.S. migration and imaginaries of political, cultural, and physical boundaries. According to our research, no other artist in the area has exhibited as extensively on issues of Latina/o migration and diaspora as Campos. While not formally trained in the arts, Campos has exhibited widely and frequently in the Triangle Area,[3] which attests to the growing significance of his work. Reviews of Campos' artwork have appeared in several newspapers, including the *Durham News and Observer* and the *Chapel Hill News*. He has been invited to speak in radio shows (e.g., Radio Pa'lante, a show run by Latino teens from Chapel Hill and Carrboro that includes music, radio documentaries, a community calendar and interviews with artists) and has exhibited in a variety of cities, from Greenville, to Wake Forest, to Raleigh, and venues, including small galleries, churches, middle schools, community colleges and universities, Latina/o heritage celebration events, and *La Fiesta*. Finally, both the University of North Carolina at Chapel Hill and Duke University, two of the main institutions for higher education in the area, have purchased and currently exhibit Campos' work on their campuses.

The work of artists such as Cornelio Campos can have societal effects, such as enhancing civic engagement and activism as well as building community capacity (Hernandez-Leon and Zuniga 2000; Wali et al. 2002; Moriarty 2004; Garcia 2005; Stern et al. 2008). A study on networking among migrant groups conducted in Chicago, for example, found that arts and cultural production created transnational cultural connections between Mexican migrants and their home communities that fostered community building, reduced social isolation, and created cultural affirmation (Wali et al. 2007). Aside from Chicago, studies conducted in Silicon Valley° and Philadelphia all reported that immigrant artists not only aided

---

diaspora: a group migration or flight from a country, region, or homeland.
Silicon Valley: the hub of America's high-tech industries, located in the southern part of the San Francisco Bay Area in California.

in the building of community capacity, but also helped link immigrant groups within the same area as well as in other places (Wali et al. 2002; Moriarty 2004; Wali et al. 2007; Stern et al. 2008). However, the activism of artists does not always guarantee that the intended message of their artwork will be received unchanged by the audience. Their contributions to society depend on the institutions that support and mediate their work and the audiences that receive and interpret it. Moreover, audiences of different ethnic, class, and political backgrounds will interpret and give meaning to the artwork differently, thus producing different ways of knowing Latina/o diaspora through their engagement with the artwork (Eco 1979; Nightingale 1996; Hall 1997).

Notwithstanding these mediating factors, our goal is to examine how Campos' artwork shapes geographic imaginations of Latinization among non-Latina/o audiences in North Carolina. We do so by, first, situating Campos' artistic imagination within the specific places he has lived in the U.S. We conceptualize his artwork as a situated process of storytelling about the Latina/o diaspora. To contextualize Campos' artistic production, we draw on a variety of sources: (1) Three thirty-minute interviews with Campos conducted in venues where his work was being exhibited: at East Carolina University (ECU) during a one-day AMEXCAN (*Asociación de Mexicanos en Carolina del Norte*) convention in June 2009, *La Fiesta* in August 2009, and at McDougle Middle School during a temporary exhibit in February 2010; (2) Participant observation at the ECU and McDougle exhibits, which lasted approximately two hours and was conducted by three individuals, and at *La Fiesta*, which included approximately one-hour-long observation periods of the art booths, by three different people, during the same day and conducted independently; (3) Four additional one-hour-long, in-depth interviews with Campos set up specifically for this project in 2009 and 2010 (audio-recorded and conducted in Spanish). All interviews with Campos were transcribed and translated by the Spanish-speaking authors; and (4) Two thirty-minute interviews with individuals that helped set up exhibit venues for Campos in the Triangle area.

The second part of the paper examines reception to Campos' work 5 by a largely non-Latina/o subgroup of the North Carolina population: undergraduate university students of UNC–Chapel Hill.[4] We asked forty-six students from the undergraduate geography course on Latin America taught at UNC in 2010 to view and analyze a selection of Campos' paintings as part of a class fieldwork project. Students included 36 seniors, 3 juniors, and 7 sophomores. Most came from North Carolina (e.g., Guilford, Wake, Mecklenburg, Henderson counties) but also from other states, including New York, Florida, and California. Permission from students to include their responses was sought after the fieldwork exercise took place and after the course was over. The anonymous inclusion of responses in this paper did not affect their grade in the course. The project had ten questions that explored content and audience of Campos' art. Students visited, on their own, three different sites to observe Campos' art: an online archive, an on-going exhibit, and a permanent exhibit. Answers averaged 400 words per question. Student answers were initially coded according to themes that they identified in each painting (e.g., specific things and people, relationships, or stories that caught their attention). A second focused coding process looked at how students interpreted these themes (e.g., what sorts of reflections, feelings, and thoughts students associated with the themes they identified). The analysis is based on the focused coding (the themes most frequently mentioned by students and their related interpretations) and linked to theoretical codes, codes derived from the data and based on existing theory in the social sciences and humanities, to provide a structured discussion of audience reception.

Situating the Artist and the Artwork

From Agricultural to Cultural Worker

Coming from the town of Cherán in the state of Michoacán, Mexico, Campos has lived in California, Georgia, Missouri, and North Carolina. He came to the U.S. for the first time in 1989 to visit family members in California and started to work in the agricultural sector. In 1990, encouraged by a family member who worked regularly in North Carolina, he came to pick tobacco leaves in Henderson during the warm months of the year. Not having traditionally worked in agriculture, he found the experience less than ideal: housing infrastructure consisted of mobile homes that were not adequate for human living and the work performed was hard and at times hazardous. According to Campos, this was the beginning of his recognition of "seeing difference" and the "contradictions of the experience of migration" for the undocumented migrant; the American Dream and the realities of working in the U.S. were two very distinct things, a theme that recurs in much of his work (Campos, May 30, 2009).

According to Campos, in the early 1990s, North Carolina was "a virgin state for migrants": work was largely available and to him it seemed that few employers were concerned with the repercussions of hiring undocumented labor. He continued to travel between California, Florida, and North Carolina, joining a network of mostly male agricultural migrants that crisscrossed the nation to follow the seasonal agricultural labor market. In 1993, due to lack of funds at the end of the tobacco season and unable to travel back to his family in California, Campos decided to stay and moved to Durham with a distant relative to spend the winter months in North Carolina. In Durham, he worked in landscaping and found this to be much less arduous than the tobacco fields. By the time the tobacco season started again, Campos had made up his mind: he would remain in Durham. He started taking English classes and married his first wife, a U.S. citizen.

Throughout his agricultural employment, Campos hardly painted, despite having developed a keen interest in the arts since the age of nine. In Durham, however, his life changed drastically. He remembers this as a period of turbulence. Living in one of the poorest neighborhoods in northern Durham, Campos found out that the few Hispanic families in town were constant victims of racial harassment and petty crimes. He sought help from the recently established Centro Hispano, a grassroots community-based organization dedicated to strengthening the Latino community and improving the quality of life for Latina/o residents in Durham. As he describes, this experience helped him develop an understanding of the need for political activism. He learned about the right to seek police protection in case of violence, or the steps required to report assaults and confront violence. He also reacquainted himself with painting, seeing it as a way of reflecting upon the problems he encountered and heard about. Using connections forged throughout his community, his work has been slowly but steadily recognized among grassroots organizations and community organizers.

Campos uses the canvas to convey the migration experience and the 10 experience of Latina/o diaspora in the U.S., his own along with that of those he has met while in the U.S. This is not surprising. When individuals migrate, they bring with them various identities and imaginaries that are challenged and changed as they encounter new material, political, social, and cultural domains. Schmidt Camacho (2008) uses the term "migrant imaginaries" to describe the complex aspirations, hopes, dreams, and knowledge of increasingly mobile Mexican border crossers that compose one part of the transnational migratory circuit (p. 5). Campos' work exhibits these "migrant imaginaries" strongly. Whether depicting people, things, or money crossing physical, cultural, and imaginary boundaries between Mexico and the U.S., his work represents a growing social consciousness and community formation within the rapidly growing Latina/o community in North Carolina. In an interview conducted in 2010, he elaborated on the reasons why he uses art as a way of expressing the experience of migration: "When we talk about the border, or migration, we talk about it as a political problem. But we hardly ever talk about the human feeling, or the people that cross the border. We hear about people being legal or illegal. I [use my work] to imagine and remember the humanity of people, what they encounter and what they leave behind. They focus on the political and forget about the sacrifice, suffering, and losses that people experience when they chose to cross that border illegally" (Campos, February 28, 2010).

Art as Activism

Drawing on his "migrant imaginaries," Campos produces two main types of canvas representations. First, what he terms "political art": art to educate about and disrupt established notions about the process of Mexican migration. This art typically involves a muralist and mosaic style that depicts migration stories and the movement of people, goods, and ideas across geopolitical boundaries and other real and imagined borderlines. He often juxtaposes these with pre-Columbian° motifs that point to the crossing of temporal boundaries. His subjects are migrants and their families, communities, and larger society in Mexico. Campos' highly politicized aesthetic addresses issues of immigration, the border, U.S./Mexican relations, identity and cultural integrity, and challenges notions of alienness, (il)legality, and citizenship. As Herrera-Sobek (2006) would say, Campos' use of modern and pre-Columbian symbology and the ways in which he depicts stories of difference are forms of aesthetic activism that promote social questioning. In this light, Campos' work can be seen as the legacy of both the Mexican Muralist movement of the early and mid-twentieth century and the subsequent Chicano arts movement in the United States during the latter part of the twentieth century.[5] Second, Campos has developed an original "folkloric" art style that builds on Mexican folkloric traditions and his own memories of events observed and lived. For Campos, this folkloric art is not only a public action but also a personal one. Produced on canvases of a smaller scale, these paintings represent everyday scenes of men, women, and children performing mundane tasks (like selling flowers or plowing fields) or religious celebrations. Both of these artistic representations, the political and the folkloric, are intended to shape geographic imaginations about Mexican and Latina/o national and transnational spaces and have the potential to disrupt established perspectives and relationships among distinct collectives in North Carolina.

pre-Columbian: refers to indigenous American Indian cultures in parts of Mexico, Central America, and western South America before the Spanish conquest in the sixteenth century.

Campos describes himself as an educator, historian, and activist, and as such, his choice of venue is significant to his work. His political art tends to be exhibited in public venues (community colleges, middle school libraries, and churches) to raise awareness among a broad audience about immigration issues. His position regarding the appropriate venues to display his political art parallel those of the Mexican Muralists who saw their art as aimed at a different audience, not the traditional collectors and museums, but the public (Davies et al. 2001). His folkloric art, on the other hand, tends to be more broadly placed. Ranging from art galleries to restaurants and public institutions, these artworks aim to increase awareness of the rich heritage of Mexican identity. As Campos describes, they tend to be seen as "apolitical" because they do not tackle issues of immigration directly. Instead, they depict a politics of the everyday life in rural Mexico that doesn't seem to be as "intimidating" as his political art.

In the next sections, we review three examples of Campos' cultural work and then address the question of how audiences receive this work. We focus specifically on his political art, where he draws on geographic imagination of border-crossing and people being crossed by borders to represent the experience of migration.

Campos' Art: Border Stories

Campos' "political art" uses the themes of borders (physical, geopolitical, economic, emotional and so on) and border-crossings to explore the relationship between the U.S. and Mexico. He frequently partitions canvas space whereby each section tells a different yet interrelated story. This artistic device emphasizes a dialectic tension between representations of either the U.S. or Mexico, which invariably becomes the imaginary and material border that divides the two nations. This juxtaposition of visual representations creates a series of binary oppositions: between a modern/bountiful/democratic/male/white "Self" (the United States) and a pre-modern/barren/backward/feminine/colored "Other" (Mexico). Color also highlights this tension with the colors representing Mexico usually dark and earthy as brown, arid, and barren while the U.S. is in bright colors as green, verdant, and full of life. Below, we expand on three paintings that exemplify Campos' political art and were most frequently discussed by students in their field projects.

Libre Comercio (2004) explores the emotional trauma of migration and the contradiction of how the free flow of trade and money that circulates the hemisphere and the globe does not also include the free flow of people. The painting is typically exhibited at Latina/o heritage or empowering events such as those sponsored by AMEXCAN, which aims 15 to promote the understanding of Mexican culture in North Carolina. Campos tells interlocking stories of loss, surveillance, money, and border-crossing by dividing the painting into sections. In the middle is a vigilant eagle with binoculars as its legs who watches over the world of commerce and trade while simultaneously guarding the border. Below the eagle are row upon row of crosses representing the unknown migrants who perished on their journey across the border. There is also a representation of the Rio Grande in the shape of the Americas, with a skeleton head resting atop South America and barbed wire running the length of the spine of the continents. One hundred dollar bills circulate over the map, out of reach of the figures on the ground, representing the unidirectional free flow of money that comes with free trade. At the bottom on the U.S. side is a figure from the film *The Terminator* that enforces border security. Above are the verdant agricultural fields worked by the silhouettes of distant workers and the skyline of Raleigh, NC. At the top is the distorted face of a politician (reputedly Bill Clinton) with the U.S. flag waving behind him. On the bottom side that represents Mexico is a family that mourns next to a coffin draped in the Mexican flag at the airport. There is also a sign of a Wal-Mart store, next to a pyramid. At the top are the blacked-out faces of Mexican politicians. When describing the Wal-Mart sign, Campos says: "Money is power. . . . Here is an archeological site and they put a Wal-Mart next to it. There is a law that says you can't do that, that you can't do business at a certain distance [from an archeological site]. But Wal-Mart did it because there is money to be made. The [Mexican] politicians are involved in accepting Wal-Mart" (Campos, May 30, 2009).

According to Campos, this painting is about NAFTA° and personal suffering: "some friends told us about how when crossing [the border], they would find the skeletons of people with handkerchiefs on the leg or hand, I imagine that means they were bitten by a snake . . . but sometimes people minimize the trauma. That is why I see my work as educational. . . . My own experience is not as relevant as the things I paint. When I crossed twenty years ago, it wasn't like this. But for my nephew, who crossed three years ago, it was very different. He saw a man that had baby bottles with him. He had been looking for his wife and child for a day and a half. He was asking around to see if anybody had seen them. . . . The borders are like cemeteries because people die crossing. . . . I imagine that these people, in their last few minutes of crossing the desert, prefer to die and stop the suffering. So I see [skeletons] as an aid. . . .

NAFTA: North American Free Trade Agreement, enacted in 1994, which removed tariffs among the United States, Mexico, and Canada.

You don't need to be the person that had the experience but to understand the pain of others. In another occasion, a man of about sixty told me about his daughter's husband, a young man that drowned in the river and nobody could find his body. The Río Bravo is not easy to cross. . . . That is the trauma that the paintings express. When people tell me stories like this, it is not my personal trauma. It is a collective trauma" (Campos, June 5, 2009).

Realidad Norteña (2003) is located in the building of the Campus Y at UNC–Chapel Hill, which houses student organizations on campus that focus on social justice issues. It was purchased by the board of the Campus Y in 2008. It conveys a different aspect of the migration experience, focusing on the realities of adapting and growing in the U.S. for those coming from Mexico. The central theme is the merging of two potent symbols of each country: the Statue of Liberty and the Virgin of Guadalupe. The Virgin of Guadalupe, a repeated symbol in many of Campos' pieces, represents a source of faith and hope. She protects immigrants on their journey across the border and in their new lives in the U.S. The Statue of Liberty also has long been a symbol of freedom, liberty, and hope for migrants, and Campos' merging of the images points to this similarity. The line that divides the two halves of the painting is also the line that divides the two halves of the Virgin of Guadalupe and the Statue of Liberty, which are at the forefront of the painting, along with a monarch butterfly, and a flower that is half a bird of paradise (representing Mexico) and half a dogwood flower (the state flower of North Carolina).

For Campos, this painting represents stories of intimacy that cross the geopolitical border. On the Mexican side the landscape is brown and arid and devoid of life, with the figure of an indigenous mother and child waiting while their husbands, fathers, and brothers, across the border, send remittances back home. The U.S. side is filled with bright green tobacco fields, worked by the same male migrant labor while the woman and child await. At the bottom, on the United States side, are crosses in a bleak inhospitable landscape and twisted Daliesque suffering figures.

Campos says this painting is about a "personal vision connected to the suffering of people. . . . I painted this after a long hiatus of painting, about ten years. It is the story of being in the U.S. up to that point. I wanted to express the personal. It has Aztec symbology. It has the Statue of Liberty, which means hope. The same as the Virgin of Guadalupe. . . . The tobacco fields is me working in agriculture. In construction there are also very young people. They stop working the fields in Mexico, leave their mothers, wives, and kids. But at the same time they have a solid base from our ancestors. And this is what we see. . . . I also have the monarch butterfly that migrates from Michoacán. It means there are no borders. The self-sacrifice is in the desert. The mother of my child is American, my son is in the middle. The new generations are about people united. Maybe they will see a different world. The Mexican American. That is what the bird of paradise and dogwood represent. . . . The fact that UNC chose to purchase this painting was very surprising and important to me. I feel like I have reached a point in my life where I see this personal expression of the mixing for me, it is as if people are coming to accept my personal idea of how I see things" (Campos, May 30, 2009).

Anzaldúa (1993) describes the immigrant artist as living in a state of "*nepantla*," a Nahuatl word meaning being in a state of in-betweenness when moving or crossing from one identity to another (p. 110). This is a fitting term to describe the reflections that Campos shares. The border is a powerful historical and metaphorical site within immigrant imaginaries—it is a site of dislocation, trauma, stretching, becoming, or radical possibility (Hooks 1990, p. 341). For Campos, the border is not only about physical characteristics but also subjective associations. It is "a metaphorical trope, a material geographical reality, a set of relations between and among people" (Berelowitz 1997, p. 71).

In *Antorcha Guadalupana* (2007), Campos examines the relationship between immigration to the U.S. and the American Dream. Campos typically displays this painting at the Immaculate Conception Catholic Church in Durham, during the annual event of *La Antorcha Guadalupana*, a 3,800 mile relay run from Mexico City to New York that brings together thousands of families divided by the Mexico-U.S. border. Departing from the Basilica of Our Lady of Guadalupe in Mexico City, the torch passes through every state where families of immigrants reside, including North Carolina. In this run, family members of Mexican immigrants carry a torch in Mexico which will be touched later on by their relatives who live in the New York City area. One of the reasons this painting is exhibited during the time of the *Antorcha* event is that there is a figure of a runner carrying the torch from Mexico to the U.S, carrying the migrant's message.

In this piece, a Statue of Liberty towers over the Washington, D.C. Capitol Building in the center of the painting over neat rows of agricultural farmland. Campos says that while many immigrants set out from their home countries seeking the American Dream, "they do this by being misinformed. They know they need to be successful. Once you cross the border you think you will be successful in everything. But across the border is where the problems begin" (Campos, June 5, 2009). The left side of the painting is the Virgin of Guadalupe, along with a pre-Columbian pyramid and a colonial Catholic church, while the right side is dominated by skyscrapers and construction equipment, images of the supposed modernity, progress, and industry of the United States. On the bottom half are Aztec and Mayan images, skeleton heads, and archeological artifacts juxtaposed amongst twisted steel girders and rotting wooden planks and hi-tech futuristic surveillance cameras. In the skies above both Mexico and the U.S. are UFOs flying over the landscape while a Homeland Security officer leads away an extraterrestrial alien in handcuffs. In an interview for the documentary *The Virgin Appears in the Maldita Vecindad* (2009), created by Altha Cravey, Elva Bishop, and Javier García Mendez, Campos explains the use of the extraterrestrial motif in this painting: "I am from Mexico and every day we hear on the radio, on TV, in the newspapers they focus on us as 'illegal aliens'. . . . For me, 'aliens' can mean many things. It implies to me something out-of-place, something that does not belong. They use it as a term to exclude us. It makes it sound as if we are creatures from another planet. . . . When I hear 'aliens,' I immediately think of extraterrestrials."

When asked what his contribution to contemporary art in the U.S. was, well-known Chicano mural artist Leo Tanguma said: "I bring into the mainstream a consciousness and an imagery that is humanizing to the whole society, as well as images that have been suppressed and repressed in America" (Lettieri 2001, p. 142). In much the same way, Campos uses his work to "help people in the U.S. see what is behind us, immigrants," and present his culture and people and their traditions along with what he sees as a collective trauma resulting from the intersection of economic policies and desires on both sides of the U.S.-Mexico geopolitical border.

While Campos' intentions and moral commitments are significant for understanding his art as activism, the significance of his artistic products also depends on how audiences engage with them to represent themselves. It is to these engagements that we now turn.

Audience and Campos' Artwork

Audience reading and interpretation of Campos' art provides insights into how spectators engage the artwork (see Katz et al. 1974; Hebdige 1979; Eco 1979; Nightingale 1996). We focus specifically on how one segment of Campos' audience thinks about his artistic work: undergraduate students from UNC–Chapel Hill. Campos has expressed interest in communicating with student audiences, hoping that his work will "make a difference: that is why I continue to paint. It is not to solve the problems of the world, but to express what is within me about this [the migration experience], to bring attention and make people conscious of these issues, for example, students" (Campos, May 30, 2009). To examine responses to Campos' artwork, we asked undergraduate students of a Latin America geography course to visit three sites where his art is exhibited: an online archive of Campos' paintings created specifically for the students, a short-term exhibit at the Carrboro Public Library located at McDougle Middle School, and the UNC–Campus Y building. Students were asked to view the art and interpret the stories gleaned from the images. Specifically, the students were asked about: (1) Content: To consider the stories told by the artist and what they found compelling/most interesting about the paintings. (2) Audience/spectatorship: To consider who is the intended audience, the place chosen for the exhibit, and how different audiences would react to the artwork.

How Students Analyze Migration Stories

Students broadly identified three interlocking themes in Campos' art. First, what we call *geopolitical imaginaries*, the representation of borders, border-crossing, and the physical differences between U.S. and Mexico territories. Students mostly identified and reflected upon the physical, concrete borders (fences, walls) as well as the instruments that make borders a lived experience (passports, deportations, visas, ICE agents) in Campos' art. Students also recognized Campos' particular narrative of geopolitical knowledge, specifically, his interrogation of the migration experience, the politics and practice of security, and the focus on the "embodied scale" of geopolitics (cf. Hyndman 2004), for example, in his depictions of the emotional and traumatic experiences of people who live on and across borders. One student, for example, reflected on how the formal representations of geopolitical boundaries—flags and visas—are intertwined with life and death in *Libre Comercio*: "This painting tells the story of an immigrant adjusting to life and death in the U.S. . . . the coffin with a Mexican flag, as if the workers are repatriating the remains of a friend to Mexico, acknowledging that the end and the beginning are the same. Another couple gazing off into the distance, where H2A-H2B is written above the horizon. The skyline of Raleigh and the NC flag show up above the workers."

From depictions of foreign relations, a watchful eagle, to homeland public policy, students also discussed Campos' art as a sort of "geograph" (Dalby 1990) or spatialized discourse about the relationship between the U.S. and Mexico, here and there, one that scrutinizes details about how things work and articulates them with the activities, lives, and emotions of individuals involved in them. In particular, students focused on how depictions of the eagle, barbed wire, and fences represent the spatial exclusion, competing territories, and forms of (in)security that shape the border-crossing experience. When describing the themes observed in *Libre Comercio*, students focused on the prominent role of the eagle. One student observed: "The entire process is monitored and strictly governed by the watchful, all-seeing eyes of the bald eagle, representing the evident as well as the inconspicuous forms of cataloguing, scrutiny, and discrimination that take place within the U.S. and its government." The focus on the eagle's role in the context of NAFTA, borders, and labor markets is echoed by another student, who interprets the situation as a predatory one: "An icon of the United States that is also a predatory bird looking down, perhaps in search of prey, would be an appropriate image for the NAFTA agreement given the political backing by the U.S. and the negative effects NAFTA had on many Mexican laborers." Another student commented on how the spatial organization of the canvas communicated uneven geopolitical power relations: "Spatial orientation is [also] used in *Libre Comercio* as a means to engage the power dynamic between the various actors involved in NAFTA: U.S., Mexican governments, Mexican population, and multinational corporations."

A second theme students identified is the *political economy of migration*. Campos' art narrates both the hegemonic understanding of development and progress in relation to immigration processes and complicates it by relating the varied social and cultural effects these constructs have on the U.S. and Mexican societies and economies (for example, his depiction of Wal-Mart). When students discussed *Libre Comercio*, they linked the representations of state governments, politicians, and the desire for the accumulation of wealth with the flows of people, goods, and capital. As one student pointed out, "A point Campos makes is that free trade only applies to goods, not people, from Mexico to the U.S. To me, the depiction represents America extracting all the cheap goods they can get out of Mexico but not allow[ing] the Mexican people to migrate into the U.S. and benefit from our society." Another student shares a different interpretation of the events depicted: "The painting shows the results of the [NAFTA] treaty, in which many people try to cross the border for supposed free trade and free flow of people, but many die trying as they do it illegally . . . the free flow of people is prevented by the eagle . . . it shows the transnational story of free trade . . . what I find most interesting is the expectations that Mexicans and Campos alike had about NAFTA. They thought it would tear down boundaries and allow for totally free movement, like the EU,° but they were ignorant and wrong."

EU: European Union, consisting of twenty-eight countries participating as one economic unit, with the euro as its official currency.

Students also engaged the theme of "progress" in relation to *Libre Comercio* and *Realidad Norteña*, and reflected upon its relation to the improvement of the life of the individual and the individual's "natural right" to such improvement. As students pointed out, the search for progress is depicted through the mobility, movement, and migration of individuals across physical and discursive borders and in relation to better economic opportunities "on the other side." For example, one student sums up the pathos of the story of progress in *Realidad Norteña*: "the story in the desert portion of the U.S. side . . . seems to be a sad story of lives lost on the journey towards 'a better life.'" Another student reflects on the juxtaposition of U.S. and Mexican landscapes in Campos' art: "The story that stands out to me is the juxtaposition between the migration section and the U.S. section. It is easy for me to visualize the opportunities that exist in the U.S. because I have lived here all my life. It is difficult for me to visualize how hard it is to make the journey to get to the U.S. Campos' representation made me think about how hard the choice to migrate would be, and whether the initial suffering is worth the possibility of prosperity. This [scenario] helped me respect the journey that immigrants from Latin America are forced to undertake." Another student draws on the artwork to characterize a feeling of border-crossing for Latina/os: "The mosaic that stands out to me is the bottom section with the desert and the American flag. What seem to be border-crossers lay stranded in the desert, moving against the wind toward the tattered American flag, struggling against great odds to reach the green agricultural fields. This sums up the struggles, mental and physical, that border-crossers undergo in their attempt to relocate to the U.S. for a better life." *Antorcha Guadalupana* elicited similar comments: "This is a story of immigration. He [the migrant] looks up to the U.S. and sees opportunities. But he still faces alienation and persecution. Luckily, he has the faith necessary to keep his head up and working towards a better life. The Virgin is always looking over him, reminding him of his humble background and upbringings, reminding him that the meek will be rewarded in the end." Other students interpreted the representations of migrant stories differently, showing a more ambivalent position in relation to the stories related by Campos and questioning the message of the artwork. For example, in reference to *Realidad Norteña*, a student commented that: "The story that sticks out to me is the one about the desert and the skeleton in the sand with the shredded American flag. It makes me think about the harsh conditions that illegals take to get into this nation illegally and the emotion the creator is trying to evoke. However, he fails to evoke emotion because illegal immigration is illegal and their deaths were a result of their poor individual choices. If they did it legally and went through the proper channels then these deaths would not occur."

The third theme explored is *cultural juxtapositions and Orientalisms.* 30 Students identified the representation of other cultures, societies, histories in relation to those of the U.S. as a central theme of Campos' work. For example, students commented on how "The juxtaposition between the old and the new suggests the dominant perception in the U.S. of Mexico as 'behind' the U.S., not as advanced as we are." Said's concept of Orientalism is useful for framing this engagement between students and Campos' work. Orientalism highlights the production of multiple lines of separation and/or difference between West and East (in this case, U.S. and Mexico), what Said terms an "imaginative geography" of social relations and territorial manifestations. Students strongly identified these imaginative geographies as one of Campos' strategies, for example, how his portrayal of the U.S. and Mexico suggests that the contrasts between these countries are facts produced by human beings (policies, politicians, inequalities, capitalism).

Students particularly engaged the theme of Orientalisms in *Antorcha Guadalupana*, focusing on the depictions of UFOs and the play on illegal aliens as extraterrestrial aliens. One student noted that "Campos points out the ridiculousness of using the term ['illegal alien'] and referring to people who live just one international border away as something so foreign it's out of this world." This was echoed in a comment by a different student "The most compelling story is the 'illegal alien' imagery, expressed in hyperbole by invading UFOs and stereotypical alien invaders in prison jumpsuits, perhaps expressing the extreme fear and irrationality of many anti-immigrant activists in the U.S. immigration debate." As one student succinctly put it, "Campos seems to be recapitulating the struggles of immigrants being viewed as hostile aliens and a threat to mainstream society."

The examples above illustrate how students addressed the interlocking theoretical themes of geopolitical imaginations, the political economy of migration, and cultural Orientalisms that are present throughout the artwork. As the examples suggest, the students understood the message conveyed by Campos' artwork and sought to interpret the nuances of signs and symbols present in the paintings. Students mostly qualified these paintings as "The story of immigrants told through their struggles in the eyes of Latinos."

How Students Evaluate Campos' Work

The second part of the project asked students to go beyond textual analysis and focus on the intended audiences. While questions on content sought to get at how students interpret Campos' message, questions on spectatorship aim to get at how students evaluate this work, that is, who they think should be engaging with this artwork and why. According to the students, the following are the intended audiences for Campos' work, in ranked order from most to least popular answer: (1) Educated population (including UNC students and faculty, professionals, adult audience); (2) Elementary and middle school students; (3) Latina/os in the area.

Students were also asked about the "appropriateness" of the venue in which the paintings were exhibited (the middle school library and the Campus Y). Evaluations of the venue were split in half. Some claimed that the paintings should be exhibited in art galleries to better frame the artistic objects and that the library was a very poor choice for this sort of "political art." Others asserted that the library was an excellent space for the exhibit as it democratizes access to art and introduces important issues that all audiences should be aware of. As one student put it, "[at the library] people of all ages can enjoy Mr. Campos' talent and create their own interpretations of his art." These responses also highlight what in their view is the fundamental flaw of mounting art exhibits in art galleries: it effectively discourages the general public to visit art galleries and view paintings because of the elitist stigma these galleries engender. In the case of *Realidad Norteña*, which is exhibited in the Campus Y building, responses were unanimous and agreed that this was a good venue for Campos' art since the building already houses a series of "social justice–oriented projects." Yet a few students also pointed out that, as this is "political artwork," the university should not be spending its funds on purchasing such "biased" paintings.

In terms of the work these paintings do in depicting the migration experience, students agreed that while the artwork is complex, detailed, and emotional, above all, it is political and must be analyzed as such. Indeed, *being political* was one of the reasons students thought this art should not be exhibited in public spaces like the middle school library or even the Campus Y. Those students that were critical of its role in the middle school library (because of its overt alignment with immigration reform policies, the use of religious symbols such as crosses, or the sympathetic depiction of illegally crossing the geopolitical border) suggested that a better place to exhibit this kind of art is in an art gallery, where it is put in context as artistic interpretation and not as a representation of the real. In this sense, Campos' work produced a sense of discomfort among some students who saw it as inappropriate because it brought up political issues in spaces where politics should not be present (e.g., among middle schoolers).

This focus on "the political" brings up an important issue to consider regarding the Latinization of North Carolina communities. Debates about immigration have focused on the movement of Latina/o people into U.S. communities, their border-crossing dimensions, physical and emotional, as well as the specific practices through which this occurs (for example, through securing visas and employment documentation). What is little discussed, and what this analysis of artwork reception suggests, is that residents of U.S. communities experiencing high levels of Latina/o immigration are also experiencing a border-crossing of sorts. In other words, they are experiencing the presence of the border at home. Campos' art, by telling stories about border-crossing, becomes a border of sorts, a border that makes visual the politically volatile material on Latina/o migration to the U.S. to students (and other audiences) and questions meanings and perceptions associated with illegal immigration debates. This study asking college students to visit the venues where Campos' art is exhibited and reflect on its content and intent can offer insights into their varied engagement with Latinization. Some students tacitly agreed with the political work of Campos' art and did not describe a discomfort associated with these depictions. For them, Campos' art was a familiar border, either because they had already taken coursework that examined similar viewpoints or had attended campus events that focused on migration. Thus, Campos' art did not disrupt their political positioning with regard to immigration. For others, however, Campos' artwork about border-crossing was a more concrete (and disturbing) border. Some chose to describe their discomfort through a critique of the venue in which the art was exhibited (for example, claiming that political art does not have a place in a public school library but should be exhibited in a de-politicized venue such as a formal art gallery). Others expressed their discomfort and disagreement more forcefully, for example, criticizing Campos for telling a biased story of migration, one that only speaks of the struggle of the migration experience but does not spend enough space on the issue of illegality.

Concluding Thoughts: On Borders Being Crossed (or Not) and on Borders Crossing Us

A recent New York Times publication described the "higher profile" and "money infusion" used by cultural institutions such as the National Endowment for the Arts to create a "Latino Arts Initiative" that educates people on the growing presence of Latinos in the U.S. and to "break down barriers" and build community (Hodara 2009). While this is an important effort, this paper has demonstrated that education about borders and barriers is multifaceted and multilocational. It is important to not only illustrate the dynamics and contexts of migration, such as why people cross the geopolitical border or seek employment illegally, but also how that border is manifested in multiple locations, far from the physical geopolitical border. Indeed, work by geographers (Winders 2005, 2009; Coleman 2009) has already started exploring how geopolitical borders have emerged at more intimate scales of governance than the physical border between Mexico and the U.S. The devolution of immigration authorities to the county level, for example, has led to the development of new geographies of surveillance and security at more intimate geographic scales. Our study points to the need

> "It is important to not only illustrate the dynamics and contexts of migration, such as why people cross the geopolitical border . . . , but also how that border is manifested in multiple locations, far from the physical geopolitical border."

to better understand how borders not only can shift geographic scales but also how their re-scaling is experienced and made sense of by those that are not typically considered border-crossers, in this case, non-Latina/o individuals. Latinization, while a process that creates new hybrid spaces that reflect the shifting demographics of the South—for example, through the proliferation of Latina/o-oriented services and venues—is also a process that engenders anxieties (as well as promise) about how established communities and ways of knowing "the local" will change. Campos' artwork, which is very much geographical in its depiction of geopolitics, political economy, and cultural identities, has helped illustrate the need to consider how borders also cross people, often without their own choosing. Or as Walkerdine (2006) puts it: "It is as though crossing this anxious border is via a no man's land, the place in which you cannot go back but never fully belong, a place of extreme anxiety about the joy of belonging, the escape from restriction and pain, and the everpresent threat of being returned and found wanting" (p. 12).

As a metaphorical border, we see Campos' artistic work contributing to the process of Latinization in North Carolina in three, interconnected ways: (1) he contributes to consciousness raising by depicting what he sees are important and ignored elements of the migration experience in mainstream society, (2) his work focuses on boundaries and distinctions often articulated with the presence of Latina/os in the U.S. to question the discursive constructions that support structures of control and power and to challenge what is seen as a given, and (3) his work reflects on important aspects of the struggles over the meaning of the experience of crossing (and being crossed by) geopolitical and cultural borders. While this is not a comprehensive list of how Campos' artistic work can be conceptualized, we use this as a way of thinking about the historical and social dimensions that condition his work and his role in creating consciousness of the growing Latina/o communities in North Carolina. Concomitantly, his artwork also works as a border that its audiences are asked to recognize and cross. For audiences sympathetic with his politics, this is not a difficult task. For others, the artwork is a border that is resisted by their situated politics and lived experiences.

Notes

1. According to the U.S. Census Bureau (2006), 133,959 Latina/os have settled along the I-85 corridor in the Raleigh–Durham–Chapel Hill area (Odem 2010).

2. We do not take for granted terms such as "Latina/o art" or argue that Campos is an exemplar of such a genre (if it exists), but recognize that such categories increasingly play a fundamental role in the production of imagined communities of Latina/o immigrants.

3. The "Triangle Area" is comprised of the cities of Raleigh, Durham, and Chapel Hill.

4. Students of Latina/o backgrounds are a small minority at UNC. According to the Office of Institutional Research and Assessment, in fall 2009, 5.2 percent of the undergraduate student body was classified as "Hispanic."

5. The Mexican Muralist movement originated with the Syndicate of Technical Workers, Painters, and Sculptors, founded in 1922 in Mexico City—and is famously recognized in the works of Diego Rivera, José Clemente Orozco, and José Alfaro Siqueiros (Davies et al. 2000). When asked about artistic influences, Campos made reference to these three artists as well as Salvador Dali. Chicano art, in the form of portraiture, posters, paintings, conceptual art, and, particularly, mural paintings, focuses on Mexican workers and immigrant experiences from the perspective of a unified Mexican community and imagination (Goldman 1990; Brookman 1991; Goldman et al. 1991; Prieto, undated; Ybarra-Frausto 2006).

References

Anzaldúa, G. 1993. Border arte: Nepantla, El Lugar de la Frontera. In *La Frontera/ The Border: Art About the Mexico/United States Border Experience*, Natasha Martinez (ed.), 107–124. San Diego: Centro Cultural De La Raza: Museum of Contemporary Art.

Berelowitz, J.A. 1997. Conflict over "border art": Whose subject, whose border, whose show? *Third Text* (40): 69–83.

Brookman, P. 1991. Looking for alternatives: Notes on Chicano Art, 1960–90. In *Chicano Art: Resistance and Affirmation, 1965–1985*, Richard Griswold del Castilo, Teresa McKenna, and Yvonne Yarbro-Bejarano (eds.), 181–192. Wright Art Gallery: University of California, Los Angeles.

Coleman, M. 2009. What counts as geopolitics, and where? Devolution and the securitization of immigration after 9/11. *Annals of the Association of American Geographers* 99: 904–913.

Cravey, A. 2003. Toque un ranchera, por favor. *Antipode* 35: 603–621.

Dalby, S. 1990. *Creating the Second Cold War: The Discourse of Politics.* London: Pinter.

Davies, H., Lane, J. R., and Ballinger, J. 2001. *Frida Kahlo, Diego Rivera, and Twentieth Century Mexican Art: The Jacques and Natasha Gelman Collection.* Exhibition Catalog San Diego Museum of Contemporary Art.

Eco, U. 1979. *The Role of the Reader: Explorations in the Semiotics of Texts.* London: Hutchinson.

Frey, R. 2008. Latino Settlements in the New Century. Pew Hispanic Center, Washington D.C. Accessed 20 May 2010 at pewhispanic.org/files/reports/96 .pdf.

García, C. 2005. Buscando trabajo: Social networking among immigrants from Mexico to the United States. *Hispanic Journal of Behavioral Sciences* 27: 3–22.

Goldman, S., and Ybarra-Frausto, T. 1991. The political and social contexts of Chicano art. In *Chicano Art: Resistance and Affirmation, 1965–1985,* Richard Griswold del Castillo, Teresa McKenna, and Yvonne Yarbro-Bejarano (eds.), 83–96. Wright Art Gallery: University of California, Los Angeles.

———. 1990. The iconography of Chicano self-determination: Race, ethnicity, and class. *Art Journal* 49(2): 167–173.

Hail, S. (ed.), 1997. *Representation: Cultural Representations and Signifying Practices.* Sage: London.

Hebdige, D. 1979. *Subculture: The Meaning of Style.* London: Methuen.

Hernandez-Leon, R., and Zuniga, V. (eds.). 2000. *New Destinations: Mexican Immigration in the United States.* New York: Russell Sage Foundation.

Herrera-Sobek, M. 2006. Border aesthetics: The politics of Mexican immigration in film and art. *Western Humanities Review* 63.

Hodara, S. 2009. Turning a spotlight on Latin American music and art. December 6. http://www.nytimes.com/2009/12/06/nyregion/06artswe.html?_r=l&ref =neuberger_museum_of_art.

Hooks, B. 1990. Marginality as a site of resistance. In *Out There: Marginalization and Contemporary Cultures,* Russell Ferguson, Martha Gever, Trin T. Minh-ha, and Cornel West (eds.). New York: The New Museum of Contemporary Art.

Hyndman, J. 2004. Mind the gap: Bridging feminist and political geography through geopolitics. *Political Geography* 23: 307–322.

Katz, E., Blumler, J., and Gurevitch, M. 1974. *The Uses of Mass Communications: Current Perspectives on Gratifications Research.* Beverly Hills, CA: Sage.

Kochar, R., Suro, R., and Tafoya, S. 2005. The New Latino South: The Context and Consequences of Rapid Population Growth. Pew Hispanic Center, Washington, D.C. Accessed 20 May 2010 at http://pewhispanic.org/reports/report.php ?ReportID=50.

Lettieri, M. 2001. Cultural identity and ethnic dignity in Chicano mural art: An interview with Leo Tanguma. *Confluencia* 16(2): 136–142.

Moriarty, P. 2004. *Immigrant Participatory Arts: An Insight into Community-Building in Silicon Valley.* San Jose, CA: Cultural Initiatives Silicon Valley.

Nightingale, V. 1996. *Studying Audiences: The Shock of the Real.* London & New York: Routledge.

Prieto, A. Border art as a political strategy. *Isla Information Services Latin America.* Accessed 12 May 2010 at http://isla.igc.org/Features/Border/mex6.html.

Schmidt Camacho, A. 2008. *Migrant Imaginaries: Latino Cultural Politics in the U.S.-Mexico Borderlands.* New York University Press: New York.

Stern, M., Seifert, S., and Vitiello, D. 2008. Migrants, communities, and culture. In *Creativity and Change,* Report by Social Impacts of the Arts Project, University of Pennsylvania. Accessed 10 May 2010 at http://www.trfund.com /resource/downloads/creativity/Migrant.pdf.

Wali, A., Severson, R., and Longoni, M. 2002. *Informal Arts: Finding Cohesion, Capacity, and Other Cultural Benefits in Unexpected Places.* Chicago: Center for Arts Policy and Columbia College.

Wali, A., Contractor, N., and Severson, R. 2007. *Creative Networks: Mexican Immigrant Assets in Chicago.* Chicago: The Field Museum.

Walkerdine, V. 2006. Workers in the new economy: Transformation as border crossing. *Ethos* 34(1): 10–41.

Winders, J. 2005. Changing politics of race and region: Latino migration to the U.S. South. *Progress in Human Geography* 29(6): 683–699.

———. 2009. Placing Latino migration and migrant experiences in the U.S. South: The complexities of regional and local trends. In *Global Connections and Local Receptions,* Fran Ansley and Jon Shefner (eds.), 223–248. Knoxville: The University of Tennessee Press.

Ybarra-Frausto, T. 2006. Prologue: Immigrant imaginations and imaginaries. In *Caras Vemos, Corazones No Sabemos: Faces Seen, Hearts Unknown: The Human Landscape of Mexican Migration,* 6–13. Indiana: Snite Museum, University of Notre Dame.

Understanding the Text

1. In your own words, explain the focus and goals of Valdivia, Palis, and Reilly's study. In your response, make sure to explain the concept of the "imaginaries," which is critical to their argument.

2. According to Valdivia, Palis, and Reilly and the research they cite, what can political art and the cultural production enact? Why is this information important to the authors' study?

3. Identify the themes in Campos's political art, and provide a brief synopsis of Valdivia, Palis, and Reilly's interpretation of three of his works of art.

4. Write a brief summary of the two sections in paragraphs 26–36. What results do you consider the most significant from each section? Explain your answer.

Reflection and Response

5. Why do Valdivia, Palis, and Reilly regard Campos's art as "activist art"? Explain his two types of art. Do his art and the authors' explanation of it agree with your understanding of activism? Why or why not?

6. Summarize Valdivia, Palis, and Reilly's key points in paragraphs 37 and 38. Which ones seem most relevant to their arguments? Why?

7. Valdivia, Palis, and Reilly argue that Campos's works "illustrate the need to consider how borders also cross people, often without their own choosing" (par. 37). What do they mean?

Making Connections

8. Why did some students think that Campos's art should not be shown in public (par. 35)? Explain their reasons and Valdivia, Palis, and Reilly's analysis of the students' responses. Drawing on the ideas in this reading and at least two others in this chapter, write an essay expressing your position regarding the appropriate venue for political or activist art.

9. Valdivia, Palis, and Reilly focus on the U.S.-Mexico border and the art of Mexican artist Cornelio Campos. Conduct your own research on other artists who depict, visualize, or represent crossing borders other than the U.S.-Mexico border. Using Valdivia, Palis, and Reilly's ideas and arguments and those from John Eger's "Art as a Universal Language" (p. 218), write an essay explaining how the artist you chose crosses borders and conveys that experience through his or her art, and what we learn from this art. Remember that crossing borders does not always involve traversing a geographical barrier.

Border Fence as Möbius Strip

David Avalos

An artist, writer, and scholar, David Avalos is also a professor in the School of Arts at California State University, San Marcos, and the cofounder of the Border Art Workshop/Taller de Arte Fronterizo, a binational collective committed to creating political art, primarily about the U.S.-Mexico border. His installations and public artworks often involve multiple mediums, including video, sculpture, and photography.

The following image is a photograph of Avalos's installation *Border Fence as Möbius Strip* from the exhibit "Border Realities III," which featured art concerned with the San Diego–Tijuana border and the mixed culture of that region. Not visible in the image is the written text that the artist includes with his installation: "You try to cross the border but never reach the other side" and "You cross the fence then realize you're still on the same side." As you examine the image, consider the fence's shape and its relationship to the other installations and exhibits in the space.

David Avalos's *Border Fence as Möbius Strip.*
Courtesy of David Avalos

Understanding the Text

1. Describe what you see in the photograph. In this description, include specific symbols and images, along with their placement in the work and any compositional elements such as form, light, lines, and shapes.

Reflection and Response

2. What is a Möbius strip? Why do you think Avalos chose this shape? How does this shape relate to the shapes and purposes of traditional borders and border fences?

3. In this artwork, what do you think is Avalos's message or argument about borders? Do you agree with this message? Why or why not?

Making Connections

4. Read both Ann Marie Leimer's "Cruel Beauty, Precarious Breath" (p. 222) and Gabriela Valdivia, Joseph Palis, and Matthew Reilly's "Borders, Border-Crossing, and Political Art in North Carolina" (p. 234). Drawing on the ideas in these readings, write an essay in which you interpret and analyze Avalos's work as it appears in the photograph.

Poetry Peddler

Naomi Shihab Nye

A Palestinian American poet, writer, and educator, Naomi Shihab Nye has written or edited more than thirty books, including *The Tree Is Older Than You Are* (1995), a bilingual anthology of Mexican poetry, and *The Space between Our Footsteps* (1998), an anthology containing the work of 120 poets and artists from nineteen countries in the Middle East. Nye's poetry includes collections for both adults and children, such as *A Maze Me: Poems for Girls* (2014), *You and Yours* (2005), *19 Varieties of Gazelle: Poems of the Middle East* (2002), *Fuel* (1998), and *Red Suitcase* (1994). Her novels and children's book include *Habibi* (1999) and *Sitti's Secrets* (1994). Her work has won prestigious poetry prizes and has also garnered honors for children's literature.

Nye lives in San Antonio, Texas, but identifies herself as a "wandering poet." She crosses borders, leads writing workshops, and writes poems to remind us of our shared humanity. In her poetry, she often focuses on the "things" and small rituals of our daily lives, the small objects and mundane events that resonate cross-culturally. Nye wrote the following creative nonfiction piece for an anthology, *The Strangest of Theatres: Poets Writing across Borders* (2013). As you read, pay attention to the multiple contexts in which Nye "peddles" her poetry.

My endless wandering / becomes my language

—AMINA SAÏD, "FREEDOM'S FACES"

I was raised in a savory, slightly strange household. The walking homesickness household. I guess it makes sense that a wandering poet would be born from a father in exile and a renegade mother who defied the codes of her own strict upbringing even to marry him.

Because he had a voice, my father, Aziz Shihab—a dapper man who loved bow ties and cologne, who engaged in vigorous shoe polishing, who still liked a folded white hankie tucked into his breast pocket—embodied the hugeness of a people's suffering. He found a way to wrap his melodious, perfectly pitched voice around a room, send it out in a letter, weave it into Christmas talks about the Holy Land at local churches, without becoming shrill or arrogant. He was human size.

But his voice was bigger. He did not understand why dialogue seemed so difficult for so many people in power, but he believed humiliation would never last and arrogance could never win and someday, justice might take a deep breath again. He exercised his own voice every way he could toward that goal.

When my father died, he was still aching for Palestine, its quirky rhythms and ancient traditions, which people tried to say weren't ancient after all. "You lived here a hundred years?" they might have said. "Sorry, you're invisible."

Wherever he wandered, whichever border he crossed, he was Palestine: 5 his soft, olive-tinted skin carried almond blossoms, green fields, goat cries at sunset. He had a rich wit, a gentle sense of irony, a passion for education, pride.

Why was it so easy to downgrade, or overlook entirely, the Palestinian legacy, as if it didn't exist, as if its people would just—*pouf!*—vanish in a pollen cloud? Surely one never thinks, in the hopeful flush of growing up, "By the time I'm twenty-one, my people will be invisible."

Though I lived in Palestine in 1966–1967, only a short time myself, I felt obliged, whenever wandering, and also at home, to try to speak up about it, wherever appropriate. I wanted to make it real for people who had never considered its existence. It was not my only topic, of course, but the conditions and issues of rootedness and exile rested at the center of all my topics—respect for dailiness, mutual exchange, and simplicity.

When introduced as a "peacemaker," I'd think, well, I'm a total failure then. Because there is no peace, not for the people of Palestine. Not yet.

It was easy to feel like a failure. But I kept talking. When you feel rotten, talking and writing always help. And sometimes, such as yesterday, when I met two seventeen-year-old girls representing Hand in Hand: Center for Jewish-Arab Education in Israel and their respectful, mutual descriptions of shared life, I know with conviction that talking and writing are the only and very best things we can do.

My father believed in a better day, in human potential, in the poetry 10 of possibility, in the dignity of details. To honor him, I had to keep telling his story. Though he died frustrated, he told the hospital chaplain right before his last day he was sure things would eventually work out.

I hear an unexpected echo in this wide world from Hawaiian students familiar with legacies of occupation nodding gravely, from far-flung village Alaskans and Native Americans in Wyoming: sorrowful repetitions of injustice.

And I tried not to think too often of the chant one of my dearest writer friends used to filter his own penetrating writing—"So what?"

Those words didn't help me.

So—everything.

If a girl in Alberta, Canada, who has never been out of her own prov- 15
ince, reads a poem or story about a Palestinian girl and then asks her
mother to make her baba ghanoush,° saying, "I will never think of the
Middle East in the same way again," does that mean a poem or story has
done its humble job? How many girls like this, and the two I met yesterday, might be needed to make peace in the world?

No, I don't wish I'd gotten a regular job somewhere along the way.
Not even for benefits.

I've had my benefits. A thousand towns, beds, hotels, friends. A hundred thousand young poets with notebooks, pencils, clicking pens, far
gazes.

I think of my friend M., who said when we were twenty in a conde-
scending voice, "So what are you going to do in your life? Be a poetry
peddler?"

I stood up straighter, hurt, saying, "Yes, that's what I'll be, I'd be hon- 20
ored to be that."

The word *peddler* made me think of wheelbarrows and ragbags, two
things I really like.

So, the gift of being a poet out in the wide world, on the avenues, in the
airports, carrying scenes and voices, is immense.

I remember the worried Iranian mom who appeared in a school library
one day, wanting to read from her journals to me—is it okay to be a
writer if one has not been officially trained? To allow one's soulful longing for connection to be the flag of one's true country? I think of the
Saudi girls with covered faces who will remove their hijabs° only if we
meet in a completely enclosed space—what is it they want to talk about?
Photography! All the images they are recording on their fancy little digital cameras! Plants, doorways, tile work, light falling down onto palms!
Even two sessions with them will change entirely the sense I have of their
deep eyes, peering out, when in public, from between folds of dark cloth.

Why is it so hard for politicians to believe that people who don't
match us exactly might nevertheless harmonize with us in deeply agree-
able ways? Girls with covered heads might be visionary artists. Why are
people always picking out differences, painful contrasts, instead of making kinder links?

---

baba ghanoush: a Southwest Asian dish of cooked eggplant mixed with onions, tomatoes, olive oil, and seasonings.
hijabs: head coverings that some Muslim women wear in public.

Poetry gives these realities a place to abide: in the Asian grocery store 25
in Abu Dhabi,° in a steaming hammam° in Rabat,° in the wildly dancing,
finger-cymbal-clicking streets of Fez,° on Berlin's Ringbahn° at twilight.
I am certain that human beings think in layers and that everything
new to any one of us is simultaneously old, new, precious, passing. Talking
about poetry all over the stricken Earth, with children as well as adults,
gives us a shared, more humanized side.

The seventh grader with neatly combed black hair is crying. He's trying
to pretend he's not crying, but every time he removes his fists from his
eyes, big tears roll down.

"Speak to us," I say. "What's happening?"

We're sitting in a circle in the school library. Graceful students from
all over the planet, notebooks open on their laps, stare so quietly at him,
at their hands. They look humbled by his pain.

"I am worried about my country," he gulps. We're in Saudi Arabia, at
King Abdullah's magical liberal graduate university. Yes, it exists. Women
can drive on this campus. My head is not covered. Boys and girls are going to school together here, at King Abdullah University of Science and
Technology, aka KAUST.

I'm with the children of the university professors, students, and staff 30
at the edge of the glistening Red Sea, whose other side touches the shores
of this boy's home country, Egypt.

For days now, brave demonstrators have been gathering in Tahrir
Square,° raising their arms and voices, shouting for freedom, setting up
tents, carrying one another on their shoulders. They must be exhausted.
I've left CNN International on mute in my room for hours, watching what
happens next, even at two in the morning, thinking about the past, just a
few years ago, when I felt oddly secure hopping off the underground
metro and dashing across that very square by myself, even late at night.

"What will happen to Egypt? I don't want my grandparents or neighbors or neighborhood to be hurt," the boy says, growing more confident

Abu Dhabi: the capital of the United Arab Emirates.
hammam: a steam room or communal bathhouse in some Islamic countries.
Rabat: the capital of Morocco.
Fez: a city in Morocco.
Berlin's Ringbahn: a circular railway line running around the center of Berlin.
brave demonstrators have been gathering in Tahrir Square: Tahrir Square, a public
square in Cairo, served as the center point for the Egyptian Revolution of 2011, which
resulted in the resignation of Egyptian president Hosni Mubarak and more protests in
2013.

when no one titters. "If I were the head of the chess club and everyone said they did not want me to be the head, if everyone stood in the hallway shouting, 'Go, go, go, we want a new head! You had your turn!' I would go. I would go very fast. So why won't President Mubarak go?" Acknowledging our own essential questions helps us think about them.

This is the point my journals return to: in Bangladeshi classrooms, in Pakistani girls' schools, in the poetry salons behind a school cafeteria in India, we share our questions and dilemmas in the company of others. We may not be able to solve all our problems, but the making of analogies and metaphors, the making of poetry, feels like a possible solution, diffuses the scariness.

Here, slant of light. Now, think about this again.   35

From such abundance and raw material, from the glitter of open questioning among friends or strangers equally, poems have always gathered for me, and for so many students, bouquets of voices and scenes. Sometimes we need confirmation from one another; even if we can't solve these problems, it's helpful to speak about them across borders, cultures, religions, ages. Guiding others to try simple writing tactics and strategies is always a good reminder for ourselves too. It's all contagious—if one student witnesses another writing from a place of personal uncertainty, odds instantly grow that more will try a deeper, questioning style.

In coming months, far from one another, we'll be wondering the same things, but more urgently, about Libya and Syria. Hey, you guys in power! Haven't you had your turns? The chess club demotes you!

Tyranny will feel like a modern word again—not something from history books.

Before school every day, a studious Lebanese boy composes book reviews on an international children's website. Indian twins carefully letter a giant page with the poem they wrote together yesterday. A giggling Tunisian girl brings me wrapped gifts every morning—a shiny necklace, a tiny stitched pouch.

After I return home, a Korean girl living in Rabat who loves poetry   40 more than the whole wide world, more than skyscrapers, even, more than the ocean and the beach and the sand that stretches to the mountains, keeps writing me e-mails with yellow blinking smiley faces attached. One day her message says, "My page is empty. What if I can't write anything? Does this ever happen to you? What do you do?"

All the way across the ocean, in south Texas, where the rain has not fallen for months and the old lakes named Medina and Canyon are going dry, I stare at gray doves scrapping on a nearly empty green bird feeder hanging outside my window. When I refill it with sunflower seeds, the hungry birds gobble them within hours.

To my pen pal, pecked out carefully: "I take a walk, look at all the windows around me, and wonder who lives inside them."

When she writes back days later, her message says simply, "I tried it. It's working."

At the American School in Rabat, which has no prominent sign, on the day the fourth graders write odes, Omar is the first volunteer to read his poem. His classmates and teachers look surprised when he raises his hand. I, of course, don't know anyone's history. Not knowing who generally succeeds or fails in any classroom anywhere has always been a benefit—a visitor carries no preconceptions, welcomes all participation equally.

Tourists and travelers might wish for as much open anonymity in the markets and streets. Too often we're identified by what previous travelers have desired or spent.

Most in Omar's class wear bright-red T-shirts, the school color, but he wears what can be described only as a golden satin tunic. Omar clears his throat. He addresses his home country of Egypt, describing a "yellow flower calling to me." Across the countries between, across Libya, Tunisia, Algeria, he can hear its plaintive cry. Now he is "stuck in sad Morocco"— forced to make a new home, far from his yellow flowers. But he vows to go back someday. He has written an ode to belonging, to a better life where he felt grounded and secure.

I look around. Tears are rolling down his teacher's face.

The students seem mesmerized. They crowd around Omar after the lunch buzzer trills, begging him to sit with them at the picnic tables outside, mentioning that Morocco has lovely white flowers popping their petals open before dawn even in the schoolyard, on the soccer field, that they are happy he is here. He looks—thunderstruck.

"What's up?" I ask the teacher.

"He has been here since September," she says. "This is the first time we have heard his voice."

It is a moment that underscores what poets and poetry do.

To say something true to you and have it acknowledged, accepted, recognized as real by people around you—what better treasure? Belonging to everyone. And if that stranger in our classroom said we could talk about these things, express our love and longing—we might just keep doing it, no? Even after she leaves, even more than usual, even with the new ones, the awkward ones, even on days when it hurts to do it.

A poet walks on to the next class, the next city, the next country, fortified, knowing that all the occasions in classrooms when things didn't seem to "click" as well have just been transformed by a perfect, essential moment.

It's the same when we're writing by ourselves alone at a desk.

All those scribbles, diversions, little lost impulses and lines absorbed, 55 uplifted by the moment one line or group of lines sings.

I heard my mother say, "Be your best self, use your voice" when I stepped out onto the gravel driveway and headed up Harvey Hill to elementary school, in old St. Louis, humid city of melancholy and great architecture. It would take years of living to appreciate the challenge of that simple code.

I heard our beloved second-grade teacher, Harriett Barron Lane, age ancient, age eternal, say, "A poem can save you." Her husband had died a long time before. She had no children. We were all her children. She wore 1950s pink and green plastic bangle bracelets stacked up both arms. Anyone inattentive or reluctant received a bop on the head with those bangles. A poem can save you.

So can a window, I remember thinking, staring out the tall classroom windows in the hundred-year-old building.

Mrs. Lane felt Emily Dickinson° to be real in all our lives, more real than the school principal or the mayor of St. Louis. If we stumbled, acted ridiculous, got the giggles in the middle of a lesson—what would Emily think of that? The fact that Mrs. Lane imagined we could know was deeply compelling.

I recall reading, and feeling befriended by, the Bengali poet Rabin- 60 dranath Tagore on the day my best friend told me her family was moving away. Tagore, who had won the Nobel Prize in Literature, used to send his words out in small boats on a running stream, hoping some stranger would find and unfold them and "know who he was." Tagore knew loneliness.

Tagore would understand.

Carrying poems in one's brain is a remedy stretching far beyond the sweet meadows, ditches, and fragrant hideouts under looming pine trees where we had all wandered together, making a larger family of friends. I still hear familiar echoes guiding my steps—I'm nobody, who are you? Hope is the thing with feathers.

Emily Dickinson (1830–1886): one of America's most renowned poets. A recluse during her life, she published only a handful of the nearly 1,800 poems discovered after her death.

My first day in Berlin, the day before the Internationales Literaturfestival Berlin began, I got lost among birds at the zoo. Why hadn't I learned German? I had studied it for two years. I had attended recitation contests, speaking poems from memory in German. I had had German grandparents.

The great, complicated, multilayered city of Berlin, a city that had known true sorrow, a city that had been bombed and wrecked and rebuilt and reinvented, a city with vast empty spaces, a city still recovering, was a city whose story was inextricably linked with my father's Palestinian refugee status.

My wandering journalist father would have stood, as I did, staring at haunting memorial markers in front of Berlin homes whose Jewish inhabitants had been evicted, evacuated, massacred. He would have understood that pain.

Was this partly why he always struggled for perfect grammar and simple, strong sentences? To find a fluent home in a paragraph or a few well-weighted lines must have felt very comforting to one whose refugee family had lost its physical home and grounding.

For how many of us has poetry always felt like the genuine home? As a traveler, deficient in other vocabularies, I seem to remain on the edge, the outside, but poetry in any form—original or translated—calls me inside. *Who would I have been*, I mused, wandering among the depressed zoo bears and surly elephants of Berlin, *had I never studied Spanish or Arabic, had I not crowded my pitiful acquired-language domain with three languages? What if I had focused better?* But a poet's main concern is focus and connection—did I use my energies otherwise? Have my endless attempts to encourage students to focus and connect been meaningful in the long run? Haven't enough of them told me so for me to believe?

In one school on the edge of the city, students kept bees, bottled honey. Muslim girls in headscarfs stood in front of a large group and discussed the positive aspects of being "singled out as different." It felt refreshing, unexpected. Muslim girls, speaking fluent German, switched into English for me. They said there was power in difference—if everyone looked at you as "another kind" of person, then you were noticed, had an easier chance to shine. It reminded me of a poet's comfort in unusual perception. Seeing things "differently" always opens up possibilities of seeing the world in more intriguing, less predictable ways. I felt immediately drawn to these girls and their confidence. Speaking about poetry to students who knew intricate details about worker bees and hives also felt natural and gracious—again, the layers of thinking that poetry offers, opening wide fields.

65

One day, at a literary center on a mysterious, stony backstreet of Berlin, I helped a group of teens (Afros, striped T-shirts, a bird tattooed on a wrist) arrange wooden chairs around a big table. For hours we talked, wrote, shared entries from notebooks and sections from favorite poems, grieved, and celebrated. The words of Bertolt Brecht,° who had lived only blocks from where we gathered, stitched a seam joining us all. He wrote about doubting; going this way and that way, all at once; the inevitability of doubting; the precious legacy of doubting, which has united all artists in all places since ancient days. In our circle, we had students of many backgrounds—a German-Swiss girl with thoughtful grief etched into her face, some shy recent immigrant students from Turkey, a young man wearing a Star of David necklace, a comic French-German PUBLIC POET! (handmade T-shirt in three languages) encouraging quieter students to offer opinions too. Anyone could witness the rich sense of community possible around a table when people share poetry's immediate exchange. Later, a boy who identified himself only as "J" wrote to me, referring to that day:

I can't tell you what happened exactly. I can't tell you who said what, or which poem flipped the switch. But our time together at the lit. center gave me what I will need to live my life. And that is a big thing. Thanks.

A big thing.   70
A tiny, transportable thing.
What poetry does for us all the time.

On a crowded midnight subway in Berlin, an elderly Arab man in a baggy brown suit coat stared at me, looking startlingly familiar. We were both standing, gripping silver poles. He raised his hand and pushed across to my side of the train. "I knew your father," he said. "I am sorry he died." It seemed incredible to me. In a city of millions, running into an unnamed friend? And he handed me from his coat pocket a collection of poems by the great Iraqi poet Sargon Boulus, who, I would realize when I began reading, had died exactly the same day as my father. In exile, in Berlin.

Those about whom we hear no news
Those who are remembered by none:
What wind has swept their traces
        as if they never were?

Bertolt Brecht (1898–1956): German poet, playwright, and theater director whose work often expressed the ideologies of leftist causes.

My father and the others
Where are they?
Where?

—SARGON BOULUS, TRANSLATED BY SINAN ANTOON

They are in poems still forming, bubbling in the mist that hangs over the street right before one year slides into another, another we will have to live without him, on Earth, full of him, thanks to voices and memory.

And who was that man on the train?   75

The more we travel, the more it seems that our family members are everywhere, our poetry replete with their presences. We write out of everything we have ever read or encountered. The music is in us. The ghost signs from the sides of ruined buildings in small towns we passed through only once float in us. The succinct phrases from gravestones in the Chinese cemetery in Manoa Valley, Honolulu, are carved in us. The lilting voices of children, their pride and uncertainty, their held-out questions, are etched forever in us.

> "The more we travel, the more it seems that our family members are everywhere, our poetry replete with their presences."

I met Mahmoud Darwish° in a Philadelphia hotel lobby after years of reading his poems. I'd been carrying his voice for so long that an actual encounter seemed somehow surreal. He stared at me and said, "I thought you were much younger!"

"I was," I said. "Weren't you too?"

Tell me about your life.
It was all a bouquet.   80
In whose hand?
What would you be if you were not a poet?
Everything? Aren't we already?

No, I've replied to questions many times over, the greatest moment of a writer's life is not when a new book appears in print. The greatest moment of a writer's life is when he or she meets people like you. People in some place one never traveled to before, who wish to converse.

Mahmoud Darwish (1941–2008): Palestinian national poet whose work often centered on themes of exile and dispossession.

Understanding the Text

1. Nye begins by identifying her mixed heritage and recounting memories of her father. Why is this information important? What does she tell us about her father's voice and his beliefs about voice? Explain the significance of this information to understanding Nye's purpose and larger claim in this piece.

2. How does the metaphor of wandering or traveling, and by extension the wanderer or traveler, work throughout Nye's story to develop her perspectives on borders and poetry?

3. What, according to Nye, is poetry's relationship to borders and border crossings? In other words, what does poetry allow?

Reflection and Response

4. Choose one or two of the personal encounters that Nye recounts, identify the borders crossed (emotional, conceptual, cultural, and so on) and her perspective about poetry, and respond critically to her position. In your response, you may want to consider Nye's specific assumptions about language, power, and authority, as well as your own assumptions about these concepts.

5. Reflect on your own experiences with conceptual or physical borders, and then, like Nye's students, express them in poetic form. You can write a narrative poem — one that tells a story — or craft a poem of images and metaphors that express the fears, thoughts, ideas, or issues of borders and border crossing.

Making Connections

6. According to Nye, the language of poetry creates "a shared, more humanized side" — a place of connection. Other writers in this book address the issue of language as it relates to connection and disconnection. Drawing on Nye's ideas and those from at least two other writers in this book, explain the connections you see among language, borders, and border crossings, specifically considering the poetic or creative use of language. What place do you think language can play in border crossings and in understanding the experiences of those who cross borders of any type?

7. Revisit paragraph 67, and explain what Nye suggests about the connection among language, identity, culture, and borders. Using her ideas as a starting point, fully articulate your stance on this connection. The readings in Chapter 2 may help you develop your ideas.

danielvfung/Getty Images

5 | Can We Rethink a World without Borders?

Rethinking a world without borders is no easy task. To rethink a world without borders, we must first reexamine the nature of traditional borders and their roles in our lives. Then we must try to reconfigure our understanding of traditional borders by reimagining the related concepts of sovereignty, territoriality, and the nation-state. We must also acknowledge the existence of the various types of borders discussed in previous chapters — geographical, geopolitical, social, linguistic, cultural, and conceptual — so that we can imagine what a new, borderless world looks like.

Of course, some transborder activities, institutions, and systems already exist. The Internet, environment, art, music, entertainment, money, and diseases all routinely cross borders. However, these cross-border activities require us to think more critically about their implications in our "bordered" world and to raise questions about the plausibility of a truly borderless world. For example, what role do borders play in these transborder exchanges? Do these institutions and systems help us reconceive our world as one without borders, or do they reinforce the need for new types of borders? Do they create new boundaries that we have yet to define? Can we reenvision notions of power, difference, ownership, access, and belonging within seemingly borderless spaces? Would anyone be better off in a borderless, postnational world? These are critical questions to ask as we consider what a world without borders would really mean, both for institutions and for people.

The readings in this chapter directly address these questions. Although some of the writers seem to favor a borderless world, they all acknowledge borders' continued importance and their political, cultural, and social significance in our lives. And to varying degrees, they all suggest the need to redefine and reconceptualize borders, their roles, and our relationship to them.

Gabriel Popescu, in "Borders in the Era of Globalization," examines globalization's influence on borders and introduces the concept of "global flows" to capture the various institutions, goods, and services that cross borders all the time. He makes clear that in many areas we already operate with fewer borders without living in a borderless world. Next, David Kinkela and Neil Maher's interview with environmental historian Donald Worster takes the idea of a borderless world much further, as Worster calls for others in his field to adopt a more global perspective.

Global and transnational issues emerge as important concerns in the next two readings as well. Michael Clemens, in "A World without Borders Makes Economic Sense," and Shaun Raviv, in "If People Could Immigrate Anywhere, Would Poverty Be Eliminated?," tackle the controversial topic of international migration and fully open borders. Both writers remind us that in addition to goods, services, and money, *people* cross borders, too. Specifically, Clemens and Raviv examine how easing border restrictions could "improve the lives of millions of people from poorer nations" (p. 309). Raviv looks more closely at the open border movement than does Clemens, and in doing so, he draws attention to the moral and ethical aspects of border enforcement.

Stefany Anne Golberg also urges us to consider the ethics of living in a bordered world. In "World without Borders," she raises crucial questions regarding national, external, and internal borders, as well as war, citizenship, and home. Finally, Marilyn Chin's story "Monologue: Grandmother Wong's New Year Blessing" takes us into an ethnically diverse and colorful neighborhood in Southern California, filled with immigrants crossing diverse and numerous borders. As Grandmother Wong shepherds her twin granddaughters through the neighborhood, stories collide, linguistic borders collapse, and — in some sense — the world that Chin depicts does seem borderless.

Together, these writers begin a dialogue that reaches back to the fundamental questions about the nature of borders as it also addresses the need to ask new questions based on our increasingly interconnected world. Whether you believe that a borderless world is possible or impossible, beneficial or harmful, each of us has a stake in this conversation. As you read, ask yourself the following questions: Can *I* rethink a world without borders? Do I *wish* to do so? What is at stake if I choose *not* to do so? Whatever your answers, remember that *rethinking* allows reseeing, reenvisioning, and reimagining, all of which invite us to participate in remaking our world.

Borders in the Era of Globalization

Gabriel Popescu

Gabriel Popescu is an associate professor in the political science department at Indiana University. His work on critical geopolitics, de- and reterritorialization, cross-border cooperation, migration, and transnationalism has appeared in numerous academic journals and reference volumes, as well as in his book *Bordering and Ordering the Twenty-first Century: Understanding Borders* (2012). In this book, Popescu acknowledges the importance of the social, cultural, and political functions of borders in our lives and points to the increasing mobility of knowledge, capital, goods, diseases, and, of course, people in our increasingly globalized world.

Popescu develops these ideas in this reading, which originally appeared as a chapter in *Bordering and Ordering the Twenty-first Century*. As you read, carefully consider his main argument: does he argue for no borders or merely reconfigured ones, or is he asking us to completely rethink how borders function?

During the closing decades of the twentieth century, globalization-related developments have challenged the exclusive bundling of sovereignty, territory, identity, and borders claimed by nation-states. Increasingly, the territorial scope of economic, political, social, and cultural processes does not overlap the borders of the state. These processes are developing their own sets of borders that transcend the borders of the state. In other words, these processes are each bounded in different ways (Christiansen and Jorgenson 2000). At stake is the paramount role territorial borders play in the organization of space. The normative view of state borders as containers of social relations and regulators of interstate interaction does not account for the proliferation of global flows of capital, people, goods, and ideas (J. Anderson and O'Dowd 1999; M. Anderson and Bort 2001). These flows are transnational, nonstate phenomena that relate to space in different ways than state institutions do. They follow logics of spatial organization that diverge from the logic of the territorial container that state border lines represent. Border making works in different ways for flows than it works for fixed state territories.

The tension between state border lines and flows of exchange is not a new phenomenon. During the modern era there has always been a measure of cross-border investment, trade, and migration that raised challenges to the capacity of borders to fully contain social relations inside state territories. The need for coordination among states to achieve certain shared goals, such as participation in international organizations, regional alliances, and large-scale infrastructure projects, is in large part responsible for maintaining a certain degree of permeability for most state borders. As a result, border permeability has functioned as a regulatory mechanism for interstate exchange flows.

However, the nature of current globalization flows is generating notable departures from this traditional relationship. Past cross-border exchanges were generally intermittent, geographically specific, and selective in their nature. They did not take place twenty-four hours a day, they occurred only in certain areas, and they covered a rather limited range of products and activities. Consequently, border permeability was not a generalized condition. Twenty-first-century global flows differ in several key ways. First, the speed with which they move through space has increased dramatically with the help of new telecommunication technologies such as the internet and optic fiber and with the improvement of air, land, and water transportation networks. Second, their duration has changed as they have become constant. Third, their number and diversity have multiplied greatly, thus becoming a generalized condition in numerous societies. Fourth, their geography has shifted from primarily interstate to primarily supra-, sub-, multi- and transstate scales.

> **"Global flows have replaced interstate flows as the primary framework for organizing exchanges in space."**

Global flows tend to pass *through*, rather than simply run *between*, state territories. This is the condition that the term "global flows" attempts to capture. The institution of the state itself has been decentered as the primary locus of origin and destination of these contemporary flows (Sassen 2006). This does not mean that flows have lost their territorial grounding and that state territory has become irrelevant to them. Instead, it means that states do not exclusively organize, and their territorial borders do not exclusively regulate, flows of exchange. Global flows have replaced interstate flows as the primary framework for organizing exchanges in space.

Issues that exemplify contemporary challenges to the power of state borders to regulate social relations in space permeate numerous spheres of society, from economics, to politics, to culture. Their outcomes are wide ranging, and they have the power to produce systemic change. The following sections illustrate a series of key instances in which global flows meet border lines, and the terms of these encounters are discussed.

The Structure of the International Economy

Economic processes that span the globe constitute the leading contempo- 5
rary challenges transcending modern state borders. At the heart of the matter are profound structural changes taking place in capitalism. Capitalism
is undergoing a multifaceted restructuring of its relationship with space
that includes the readjustment of its symbiotic° ties with the nation-state.
With time, the mutually exclusive territorial logic of the nation-state system became constrictive for the internal logics of capitalist organization
of production and exchange (Harvey 2000). To the extent that capitalism
continually strengthened its position during the twentieth century as the
world's dominant economic and ideological system, state borders became
less important as mechanisms for protecting domestic markets from outside competition.

After the 1970s, neoliberal ideas of free-market economics and market-
based development welcomed worldwide competition as a new strategy
of wealth accumulation at a global scale and denounced national protec-
tionism° as an outdated development strategy. "Free trade," capitalism's
mantra for almost two hundred years, became globalization's unofficial
doctrine. State borders came to be seen primarily in terms of *costs* of exchange and *barriers* to trade that have to be overcome to allow unim-
peded trade flows essential to the existence of free markets. Thus, perceptions of borders shifted from "solutions" to "problems" for capital
accumulation. This is how the "open borders" discourse achieved promi-
nence during the 1990s to become the most important factor shaping
the creation of a new global border regime.

Financial Services

International financial markets exemplify the spatial logic of economic
activity at a global scale. Financial services, including banking, insurance,
securities, and others, have long been the leading sector of economic
globalization. They have played a central role in opening up state borders
to global trade flows. Much of the international financial system is concentrated in a few strategically located trading centers linked in a global
network by digital telecommunication superhighways (Sassen 2001). The
digital nature of global funds has turned them into extremely liquid
money. Massive, multi-trillion-dollar electronic financial flows circle the

---

symbiotic: having an interdependent relationship.
national protectionism: a set of government policies that restrict international trade
in order to protect businesses and jobs from foreign competition.

globe with the speed of light every day with little regard to state borders. The twenty-four-hour trading day starts in Tokyo, when it is evening in New York; then trading moves to London, then to New York, where it lasts until the market is ready to open again in Tokyo (Warf 1989). A series of intermediary financial centers from Hong Kong to Singapore to Abu Dhabi to Paris to Los Angeles cover eventual time lags in the trading day among financial centers. The total daily volume of electronic financial transactions is staggering. In 2010, the average daily global trade in foreign currency alone reached $4 trillion, while the average daily global trade in goods and services amounted to only approximately $30 billion (Bank for International Settlements 2010). This means that one day of currency trades on the world's financial markets accounts for over 20 percent of the trade in goods and services in an entire year.

The spatial logic of global financial flows has deep implications for the regulatory power of state territorial borders. The dazzling speed and volatility of electronic money flows profoundly affect national money supplies and inflation, interest, and exchange rates, as well as taxation revenues, financial criminality, and other issues that have long been considered components of state sovereignty. Traditionally, state borders have defined the territorial scope of these issues. In the twenty-first century, they operate on a global scale, outside the exclusive control of state governments. Massive amounts of money can be invested in a national market at a moment's notice when investors perceive favorable conditions for capital accumulation (Warf 2002). At the same time, investors can rapidly withdraw money from a national market if they perceive political instability or unfavorable economic policies. In this case, the consequences can be devastating for the local economy. National governments have relatively little control over the flow of money in and out of their economies, as demonstrated by the financial meltdowns of the 1990s in Southeast Asia, Russia, and Mexico, and by the 2008 worldwide recession that started in the United States and rapidly engulfed the entire global economy.

Manufacturing

Transnational corporations (TNCs) constitute another edifying example of the tension between state borders and global flows. They are often capital-intensive companies operating in more than one country, frequently through subsidiaries and subcontractors integrated in a global production network. During the last two decades, their number and scope have vastly increased, driven by the desire to profit from comparative advantages such as cheaper labor, lower taxes, and consumer markets, among others, that different national markets offer. In 2007 there were an estimated 79,000 TNCs employing over one hundred million people worldwide, and 790,000 foreign affiliates (United Nations Conference on Trade and Development 2008). TNCs generate over two-thirds of the world trade and foreign direct investment, effectively displacing states as the main agents of international trade. The largest TNCs, such as Walmart, ExxonMobil, General Electric, Toyota, and others have annual revenues larger than the GDP° of many countries. Thus TNC investment decisions have the power to affect a country's economy and politics. In order to make their markets attractive for TNC activities, governments often pursue economic policies that are determined by rationales originating from outside their borders.

Twenty-first-century TNCs do not organize their activities with the territory of their home nation-state in mind. Rather, the essence of their spatial logic is to think about their activities with the global space in mind. State borders remain important in this process because they induce regional differences that TNCs seek to take advantage of. However, TNC activities are not limited by these borders. TNCs' core rationale is to function above these borders, at a larger spatial scale. Low transport costs and free-trade agreements allow them to easily transcend state borders.

Generally, TNC activities reach inside state borders to exploit whatever local resources may be available there; then they transfer these resources to another country or region to process them, and then trade the final product on the global market. For example, major auto TNCs maintain their administrative headquarters in developed-world countries, while their assembly factories are spread throughout the world. Their final product can include a major percentage of parts and subassemblies produced in numerous places around the world. Thus a Volkswagen bought in the United States, for example, can hardly be called a German-made car as it may include a majority of its parts made in other locations than Germany, and it may be assembled in Mexico. To make this global spatial logic of production work, highly permeable state borders are essential.

The same global-market logic was at work in one of the first major twenty-first-century public health scares involving the United States, China, and several other countries. In 2007, a series of unexpected pet deaths led to the discovery of massive amounts of melamine-contaminated pet food supplies sold in U.S. supermarkets. Soon melamine contamination was discovered in human food supplies as well, from chicken to fish to infant milk formula (Fuller et al. 2008). Then the

GDP: gross domestic product; the total dollar value of all goods and services produced over a specific period of time within a country's borders.

Workers in a Chinese Mercedes factory assemble parts as Prime Minister Stephan Weil of Lower Saxony, Germany, and other European representatives look on. Like the German company Mercedes, many companies have their factories and headquarters located in foreign countries.
Ole Spata/picture-alliance/dpa/AP Images

debacle expanded to include toxic toys coated with lead-based paint. Massive, multi-billion-dollar food and toys recalls followed in the United States and elsewhere. The geography of this scandal pointed unequivocally toward China since the contaminated products originated somewhere inside its borders. Thus the blame fell squarely on China. Melamine, when added to certain food products, can artificially increase their protein level and make the product cheaper. Also, lead-based paint is cheaper than its alternatives. It appears that several Chinese manufacturers attempted to cut corners and used these illegal substances in order to decrease the costs of their supplies.

However, a critical interrogation of this geography reveals that the borders between China and the United States were so blurred that it is irrelevant to assign blame to any single country. This was not a classic trade situation where products made by firms in one country were imported in another and then sold in the latter's domestic market. The contaminated products did not display Chinese brand names. Instead they were sold in the global market under some of the largest and most well-established brand names in the United States, like Tyson Foods, Mattel, Fisher-Price, and numerous others. When buying these products, consumers did not pay Chinese companies but were paying U.S. companies and expected the U.S. standards of quality that these companies boast. The problem was created by the global production model that food and toy TNCs follow today. They use production facilities in countries such as China that offer cheap labor and other incentives to drive down the price. These sites can be either directly owned by a TNC, or local subcontractors can be used to supply various parts of the product. In either case the final product is made in China but bears the label of the owning TNC. The bulk of the profits resulting from the sale of the product go to the TNC that owns the label. While it is true that the contamination happened in China, the responsibility lies with the TNCs that sold the product under their name. Following the logic of nation-state borders, both Chinese and U.S. borders were equally responsible for not preventing the contamination by failing to detect and intercept the contaminated products at border-crossing checkpoints. Nonetheless, following the logic of the global market, no state border could have stopped the contaminated products since the TNCs' spatial logic purposefully transcends state borders. Ultimately, the responsibility rests with the TNCs themselves, which are expected to take on the regulatory functions that state borders previously performed.

Global Economic Institutions

International institutions such as the International Monetary Fund (IMF), the World Bank, and the World Trade Organization (WTO), to name only the most well known, are central to the structure of the global economy (Sassen 2006). The IMF and the World Bank are institutions that predate the globalization era. They function much like international investment and development banks, lending money to national governments in need, usually in the developing world. Their membership rules, which require governments to pay a quota proportional to the size of their economy, give developed countries overwhelming power to influence lending policies and strategies.

During the 1980s these institutions adopted neoliberal "free-market" 15 policies as their guiding principle. Countries that wish to borrow money are required to implement a set of austerity measures designed to structurally readjust their economies to "free-market" norms. Reducing inflation, devaluing currencies, cutting government spending on social projects and subsidies to the poor, and privatization of key public services are policies primarily intended to meet the investment needs of TNCs and finance capital headquartered inside the borders of developed countries.

In turn, implementing these changes ostensibly allows the borrowing countries to save enough money to repay their debts. Nonetheless, such policies are not designed to alleviate the effects of the crises these countries face. Cutting government spending at a time of soaring unemployment, when the government should increase spending to help weather the economic crisis, comes at great cost to the local societies and fuels widespread popular resentment.

The fact that in the last two decades the vast majority of developing countries have taken IMF or World Bank loans demonstrates the power of these institutions to reshape the international economy according to "free-market" and "open borders" principles. Recently, even developed countries such as Iceland and Britain have asked for IMF loans. In more extreme cases, the IMF has temporarily run the financial affairs of countries in crisis, as has happened in Bulgaria in 1997 and Argentina in 2002. When governments implement economic policies designed outside their borders and that are outside of their control, they implicitly endorse the unraveling of the relationship between territorial borders and state sovereignty as it was constructed during the early modern era.

The WTO was established in 1995 to provide a multinational framework for regulating global trade. Its mission is to promote "free trade" by eliminating barriers to trade such as national tariffs,° subsidies, import quotas, and other protectionist measures. The WTO includes almost all states of the world, which combined account for over 97 percent of world trade. The institution can settle trade disputes and make trade rules, and it has the power to enforce trade sanctions against noncompliant members. This also means that the adoption of WTO agreements by national governments contributes to the diminishing power of territorial borders to control trade flows.

The Environment

Environmental issues have always transcended state borders. Drought or flooding has never stopped at a state's borders. Air, water, and soil pollution, such as acid rain, toxic spills, and poisonous waste, care little for territorial borders. The idea that socially constructed border lines can contain the impact of human activity on the natural environment appears absurd. Yet modern state territorial sovereignty suggests just this — a state is free to use the natural environment inside its borders in whatever way it pleases. This conceptualization of environmental issues at a particular spatial scale limits our understanding of these issues as well

---

tariffs: taxes on imported and exported goods.

as our ability to identify sustainable solutions for them (O'Lear 2010). At the beginning of the twenty-first century there are few if any truly global environmental standards that are legally binding (Angel et al. 2007). The grid of state border lines continues to provide the primary spatial framework for addressing complex global environmental issues.

Globalization has transformed the relationship between the environment and territorial border lines in at least two fundamental ways. First, it has exacerbated the consequences of existing environmental issues and has created new ones. These developments made border lines appear even more redundant when it comes to the environment. Second, globalization has increased global awareness of acute environmental issues, which in turn has generated transnational solidarity and demands for global action. Global climate change and the Kyoto Protocol are good illustrations of these two situations.

Global Climate Change

During the first decade of the twenty-first century, anthropogenic global climate change has emerged as the most severe contemporary environmental issue and has succeeded in attracting worldwide attention. The steady increase in the average temperature of the earth's atmosphere over the last several decades has been generated in large part by human-made emissions such as carbon dioxide, methane, and other gases released through fossil fuel combustion and deforestation. The accumulation of these gases in the atmosphere has enhanced the greenhouse effect that is causing a rapid overheating of the earth's surface.

Historically, most anthropogenic greenhouse gas emissions originated from inside the borders of a relatively small number of developed countries. Since the nineteenth century, the burning of fossil fuels that release carbon dioxide has powered the industrialization process. Until recently, the United States has been the largest producer of carbon dioxide emissions. With globalization, developing countries like China and India have also emerged as major contributors to greenhouse gas emissions, thus worsening an already critical situation. In 2006, China has replaced the United States as the world's largest producer of carbon dioxide emissions. However, in terms of per capita emissions, the United States remains the largest contributor.

Deforestation is the second major contributor to greenhouse gas emissions. First, the use of fire to clear up forests releases carbon dioxide into the atmosphere. Second, the shrinking of the forest coverage deprives the earth of a highly effective carbon dioxide reservoir, as trees naturally store carbon dioxide from the atmosphere. Rampant deforestation in the tropical forests of Amazonia and Borneo is technically a Brazilian or

Indonesian domestic problem, respectively. However, deforestation inside these countries' borders exacerbates the greenhouse effect that impacts the entire globe. To make things more complex, deforestation in these places is not primarily driven by domestic consumption needs. The rising demand for lumber, beef, soybeans, and palm oil in developed countries significantly contributes to the replacement of forests by large-scale plantations and farms in developing countries.

Worldwide acknowledgment that the harmful potential presented by global climate change can be tackled only by transnational action has led to the adoption of the 1997 Kyoto Protocol under the UN framework. Although state borders still provide the spatial framework for policy implementation, this is the first international environmental treaty to provide a global road map for the reduction of greenhouse gas emissions. It includes legally binding commitments for member states to cut emissions to reach preset targets (Kyoto Protocol 1998). However, the effectiveness of the Kyoto Protocol has been crippled by the refusal of the United States to sign the treaty.

Global climate change is already having other direct impacts on state borders. Rising ocean levels are submerging low-lying islands from the Indian to the Pacific oceans, creating the prospect of mass migrations of environmental refugees from these islands to developed states like Australia, New Zealand, and beyond (Marks 2006). In the Arctic, the melting of the polar ice cap has opened up the ocean to more reliable navigation lines and to the exploitation of mineral resources. This situation has sparked an intense race between nearby states like Russia, Canada, Norway, and others to expand their sovereignty over Arctic waters by formally detemining their external borders on the continental shelf (Reynolds 2007). This point was made very clear in 2007 when a Russian submarine symbolically planted a Russian flag on the seabed right under the North Pole (Dodds 2008; Steinberg 2010).

Pandemics°

Pandemics are another example illustrating twenty-first-century dynamics between environmental factors and territorial borders. Viral outbreaks such as SARS,° the avian flu, and the swine flu have recently spread from continent to continent like wildfire. The speed and frequency of global travel and trade make such diseases difficult to contain by state borders. For example, the 2003 SARS pandemic spread within days from East Asia

25

pandemics: widespread, often worldwide, occurrences of a disease.
SARS: severe acute respiratory syndrome, a serious form of pneumonia.

to North America and Europe through air travel (Ali and Keil 2006). Similarly, the 2009 swine flu pandemic rapidly diffused from North America to the rest of the world.

Another example is the avian flu. This is a virus that occurs naturally in birds and is generally harmless to them. In 2004 the virus started to become more contagious and passed to domesticated birds such as chickens and ducks, which then passed it to humans. The virus started traveling from Vietnam and Thailand to China, and then to Russia; in 2006 it arrived in Africa and Eastern Europe, and it reached the British Isles later that year. The virus appeared unstoppable, and for good reason. The disseminating agents were migratory birds that knew no territorial borders. While avian flu–related human casualties have been very limited so far, the virus wreaked havoc on domestic birds, especially chickens. Hundreds of millions had to be culled in a worldwide effort to contain the virus.

These viral outbreaks have exposed the limited efficacy state borders provide to tackle such circumstances (Fidler 2003). The most common responses from state governments have consisted of imposing travel bans to the affected areas, reinforcing border controls, and quarantining people suspected of being affected by the viruses. At the same time, these outbreaks have revealed the need for transnational institutions capable of effectively tackling pandemics, such as the UN's World Health Organization, which provided much-needed, timely, global-level coordination in the fight against SARS, the avian flu, and the swine flu.

Human Rights

Human rights are representative of challenges to state borders in the legal realm. The UN's Universal Declaration of Human Rights of 1948 marked the beginning of the contemporary human rights regime. Its goal was to establish a set of universal norms for governing the treatment of people by their states in order to help prevent a repeat of the horrors of World War II. In the intervening period, an international human rights regime has been gradually developed through a series of international treaties and institutions that have transformed human rights standards into legally binding and enforceable state obligations. Components of this regime are located at many scales, ranging from the International Criminal Court (ICC) and the UN Human Rights Council at the supranational level, to regional bodies such as the European Court of Human Rights, to national human rights laws that claim universal or extraterritorial jurisdiction, to transnational nongovernmental organizations (NGOs) such as Amnesty International.

External Interventions

The international human rights regime is often at odds with state borders. The problem resides in the enforceability of human rights by the international community, which can be interpreted as a loss of sovereignty (Camilleri 2004). Traditionally, human rights have fallen under national jurisdiction whose spatial extent was delineated by state borders. When states ratify legally binding international human rights treaties, they are obliged to incorporate these norms into national law. At the same time, ratification also opens up the possibility of external enforcement by other parties to the treaty in case of noncompliance. Until recently, external interference has been a rare occurrence, as national governments have generally been the ultimate instance of enforcement. However, this situation changed significantly during the 1990s with the emergence of several international human rights courts endowed with jurisdiction to prosecute human rights abuses committed inside the borders of a state. The International Criminal Tribunals for the former Yugoslavia in 1993 and for Rwanda in 1994° are among the best known examples to date.

Arguably the most important outcome of the international human 30 rights regime over the last half century is the broad recognition that human rights have achieved at the individual as well as the state level (Camilleri 2004). Despite the fact that nonintervention is the central principle governing international relations, during the last two decades external interference inside the borders of a state has become more acceptable on humanitarian grounds if there is proof of massive and systematic human rights violations (Murphy 1996). At the same time, the fact that many of these interventions further aggravated human rights violations points to the risk that "humanitarian reasons" can be used by more powerful states as a facade for interventionist or neoimperialist policies (Elden 2005; Falah et al. 2006). The currency of humanitarian intervention inside state borders, with or without UN mandate, is exemplified by the numerous interventions in the conflicts in Liberia (1990), northern Iraq (1990), Somalia (1992), Rwanda (1994), Haiti (1994 and 2004), Bosnia (1995), Sierra Leone (1998 and 2000), Kosovo (1999), East Timor (1999 and 2006), Ivory Coast (2004 and 2011), and Libya (2011). Even the

---

International Criminal Tribunals for the former Yugoslavia in 1993 and for Rwanda in 1994: International Criminal Tribunals (ICT) are courts established by the United Nations' Security Council to prosecute people who violate international humanitarian laws. In the cases of Yugoslavia and Rwanda, the ICT investigated crimes against civilians, such as ethnic cleansing, removal from homes, sexual abuse, and rape.

case for the U.S. involvement in Afghanistan (2001) and Iraq (2003) was in part made on humanitarian grounds.

The principle of universal jurisdiction is a new and highly controversial outcome resulting from the incorporation of human rights norms into national law. It can allow national courts jurisdiction over genocide° and other crimes against humanity committed by anybody, anywhere in the world. Universal jurisdiction takes the conflict between the international human rights regime and bordered state sovereignty to a new level. The landmark case occurred in 1998 when a Spanish judge indicted the former Chilean dictator Augusto Pinochet for crimes against humanity committed in his own country during his years in power (Byers 2000). Pinochet was seeking medical treatment in London at the time of his indictment, and the British government arrested him in order for him to be extradited to Spain. In a compromise decision, the British government released him in 2000 to freely return to Chile, where he was indicted again, this time by Chilean judges. Eventually Pinochet died in 2006 without being convicted of any crimes. Similar cases prosecuted in Spanish courts during the last decade include former Peruvian president Alberto Fujimori and several Argentine officers involved in the juntas of the 1970s.

In a recent development, the high casualty toll among Palestinian civilians during the 2008–2009 Gaza war between Israel and Hamas° has raised questions of human rights violations by the Israeli military. Although no official indictment has been issued against Israeli military personnel, the Israeli government has expressed concerns that its soldiers can be prosecuted while traveling abroad by European courts claiming universal jurisdiction (McGirk 2009). The fact that powerful governments like Israel are taking seriously the possibility of external jurisdiction over alleged human rights crimes indicates the significant challenges the international human rights regime raises to state borders.

The International Criminal Court

The latest and most ambitious addition to the human rights regime is the International Criminal Court, established in 2002 and sanctioned by a majority of world states. The ICC is the first permanent international tribunal and represents the first ever attempt to implement justice on a global scale. The court has jurisdiction over the most severe human

---

genocide: the systematic, deliberate killing of a group of people based on race, ethnicity, nationality, religion, or culture.
Hamas: a Palestinian Islamic political organization and military group.

rights abuses such as genocide, war crimes, and crimes against humanity committed anywhere inside the borders of its member states or by a citizen of its member states (Rome Statute of the ICC 1998). In addition, its jurisdiction can extend to nonmember states if the UN Security Council asks the ICC to open investigations. However, the ICC is designed to complement national laws, not replace them. It can exercise jurisdiction only when national courts are unwilling or unable to prosecute such crimes. In addition, other human rights abuses continue to remain the purview of national law.

Several powerful states, most prominently the United States, India, and China, have refused so far to recognize or join the ICC, fearing loss of sovereignty and the possibility of politically motivated prosecutions of their citizens. U.S. reservations toward the court are representative of the nature of the encounter between globalization and territorial borders. The United States has for a long time been one of the most ardent supporters of international human rights and has praised itself for a domestic justice system that vigorously protects human rights. In appearance, there is little reason for the United States to have reservations about the ICC, as their goals with regard to human rights are similar. However, the superpower status of the United States has led to its involvement in numerous crisis situations around the world. Thus the potential that its citizens could be accused of human rights violations is significant. What U.S. leaders fear is the possibility of trading the familiarity of justice inside their national borders with the much less familiar, yet seen by many around the world as more legitimate, global justice.

The first trial at the ICC began in 2009 and deals with war crimes 35 committed by militia leaders in Congo during 2002–2003. In addition, the court has received complaints of human rights violations in numerous countries, has opened several investigations into various conflicts, and has issued arrest warrants for several people (ICC Outreach Report 2008). In 2009, the ICC indicted the Sudanese president Omar al-Bashir for crimes against humanity and war crimes committed in Darfur. This event constitutes the latest human rights regime milestone. It is the first time a sitting president has been indicted by the ICC for human rights violations in an ongoing conflict in his own country. The outcomes of such global justice still remain to be seen.

Transnational Terrorism

Transnational terrorism is primarily defined as politically or ideologically motivated violence that involves the crossing of an interstate border. From a geographical perspective, transnational terrorist organizations display a networked structure that enables them to move through borders from state to state with relative impunity. These networks have noticeable mobility-related advantages when compared with the rigidity of territorial state borders. Under these circumstances, traditional enforcement of state borders has limited effects on the overall movement inside the terrorist networks that span them.

Transnational terrorism can have multiple causes and can include state as well as nonstate actors. While state-supported terrorism has decreased considerably after the end of the Cold War,° nonstate-sponsored terrorism has significantly increased. The most spectacular terror acts starting with the 1990s have been perpetrated by self-supporting organizations that work across state borders. Their motivations are grounded in large part in religious fundamentalist ideology and are different from earlier terrorist organizations that relied mainly on political ideology or separatism. Their political goals are also more global in scope and more vaguely defined, in contrast with the more localized aims and specific political demands of earlier terrorist networks.

Islamic Fundamentalist Terrorist Networks

At the beginning of the twenty-first century, Islamic fundamentalist terrorism has become the face of transnational terrorism, effectively eclipsing other types of terrorist networks grounded in ethnic separatism, political ideology, or fundamentalist ideology inspired by other religions. Al-Qaeda is the transnational terrorist organization that has become the archetype of Islamic fundamentalist terrorism, embodying its defining characteristics. Al-Qaeda is commonly described as a "network of networks" formed by loosely associated groups, dispersed, decentralized, and without a clear hierarchy of command. It uses tools like the World Wide Web, mobile telephones, satellite telecommunications, electronic banking, and jetliners to coordinate its actions, to enable movement through state borders without detection, and to disseminate its ideology (Watts 2007). Al-Qaeda threats appear to be borderless, present everywhere at once.

However, this view is misleading due to the fact that the ubiquitous state territoriality model has largely obscured the understanding of other forms of territoriality. Al-Qaeda is not just a blend of transborder deterritorialized networks (Elden 2007). While these networks do not claim sovereignty over the territory of any particular state and have no linear borders to defend, they do need places to work as network hubs to provide operational bases and staging grounds for terror attacks. A worldwide array of

Cold War: the state of political tension between the United States and its allies and Russia and its allies, following World War II from around 1947 to 1991.

Muslim quasi-states, from Somalia and Sudan to Afghanistan and Pakistan, offers locations for territorial bases without the responsibilities of territorial sovereignty. At the same time, transnational terrorist hubs are not limited to states with tenuous sovereignty inside their borders, as demonstrated by the existence of terrorist cells in Florida, Hamburg, Madrid, and London.

State Reactions to Transnational Terrorism

The U.S. response to al-Qaeda attacks both before and after September 11, 2001, underlines the limitations of state borders in addressing global terrorism. In a world full of border lines, only comprehensive cross-border collaboration can offer an effective avenue for counteracting transnational terror networks. The problem is that the complex level of institutional cooperation this undertaking requires is virtually impossible to achieve in practice since there is no adequate global infrastructure to allow institutions in various countries to share vital information in a way that transcends the taboos of state sovereignty. Instead of working to build the necessary transnational infrastructure to overcome the segmented nature of government-to-government information sharing, the U.S. response to al-Qaeda has been marked by an inability to think outside the framework of state borders. Not accidentally, the first action taken after September 11, 2001, has been the closing of the U.S. borders, implying that these territorial lines could restore the violated sense of security many people felt. The fact that these borders were not effective in stopping the perpetrators' network in the first place was lost on many American policy makers.

The major U.S. initiative for addressing transnational terrorism has consisted in launching a "Global War on Terror" whose primary objective has been to identify states where al-Qaeda hubs are located in order to take military action against them. While the term *global* might have suggested a constructive multilateral effort to involve the global community in combating terrorism, the word *war* was reminiscent of the antagonistic power politics practices in which the powerful impose on the weak. The U.S. War on Terror has indeed reached a global scale, with U.S. troops and intelligence operations deployed worldwide. Nonetheless, this effort has been highly unilateral, falling short of building a concerted global effort to tackle the roots of transnational terrorism. The logic of this war assumed that nonstate transnational Islamic fundamentalist terrorism can be defeated by classical military might deployed against territorial states. This strategy conflated the presence of terrorist bases inside the borders of a state with the commitment of that state to supporting terrorism, overlooking the fact that in some instances central governments may not be in a position to fight the terrorists because they may not control the entire territory of the state (Elden 2007).

Afghanistan, where a clear connection between the Islamic fundamentalist Taliban regime and al-Qaeda can be documented, was an early theater in the Global War on Terror. The ousting of the Taliban from power in 2001 rid the Afghan population of a tyrannical regime but has done little to tackle Islamic fundamentalist terrorist networks. In the ten years that have followed, al-Qaeda has franchised Islamic terrorism worldwide and together with the Taliban has regrouped in neighboring Pakistan under the shelter of interstate borders. From there they have played a deadly cat-and-mouse game with U.S. troops in Afghanistan, who cannot pursue them across the border into Pakistan given that this is an allied state according to the state-by-state approach to terrorism. To compensate for the lack of military presence inside the borders of Pakistan, the U.S. military has embarked on a regular air bombing campaign of that country's northwest tribal borderlands hosting al-Qaeda and Taliban strongholds. These operations, which often come with severe costs in civilian life, are justified in military terms in order to counteract the border-transcending logic of terrorist networks. Nonetheless, the very act of a state's army bombing the territory of another sovereign state that is not at war represents a flagrant violation of the sovereignty principle. The fact that this appears to be done with the acquiescence of the Pakistani government stresses even more the quandary the bundling of territorial borders and state sovereignty faces today.

The unorthodox nature of the Global War on Terror, involving a state with fixed borders that is bound by international law to follow certain war rules, and a nonstate global organization that is not bound to follow these rules, has raised the issue of the legal status of prisoners of war. The Geneva Conventions that codify the rules of interstate war provide certain human rights protections for prisoners of war that captor states are expected to uphold. After 2001, the Bush administration claimed that persons picked up in the Global War on Terror are not entitled to the legal protections granted by the Geneva Conventions since they do not belong to the regular army of another state. Instead, the Bush administration has labeled them "unlawful enemy combatants," a designation that places these prisoners outside the jurisdiction of U.S. and international law. This has allowed their indeterminate detention without civil rights and independent judiciary oversight (Gregory 2004, 2007).

Geographically, this policy has resulted in a global archipelago° of U.S. military and CIA detention centers extending from Bagram, Afghanistan;

archipelago: a large body of water containing many scattered islands.

to Abu Ghraib, Iraq; to Guantanamo, Cuba. Among these, the saga of the Guantanamo Bay prison stands out because of the spatial logic used to select this site as the location of the main detention center in the Global War on Terror (Gregory 2006). Guantanamo Bay is the site of a U.S. Naval Base in Cuba that enjoys an ambiguous legal status. The territory has been under complete U.S. authority since 1903, but Cuba has retained ultimate sovereignty rights. Prisoners held at Guantanamo Bay are technically outside U.S. state borders and are thus outside the jurisdiction of U.S. federal courts that have the obligation to uphold human rights. In the minds of the Bush administration, this location relieved them from the responsibilities of state sovereignty despite the fact that the detainees were under effective control of the U.S. government. The first detainees arrived at Guantanamo in 2002, and soon the prison became synonymous with U.S. human rights abuses in the Global War on Terror. Guantanamo Bay is an example of how the U.S. government attempted to transcend the limitations of its own territorial borders to deal with transnational terrorism in ways it deemed appropriate at the time. The irony is that, at the same time, the same government was busy reinforcing those same borders, presenting them to the public as the ultimate protection against transnational terrorism.

"Extraordinary rendition" is another practice that has shaped the geography of the U.S. Global War on Terror. It implies clandestine operations to kidnap terrorist suspects and transfer them across borders to secret interrogation sites in other states where they can face torture (Gregory 2007). No formal records of these detainees are kept. Officially, they do not exist. Although this practice is illegal under U.S. law, it has been widely used after 2001 in the U.S. Global War on Terror. However, given its illegal nature, the procedure has never been explicitly acknowledged by government officials.

The purpose of "extraordinary rendition" is to keep detainees outside the reach of law by circumventing state borders. This is accomplished by implementing a complex geographical infrastructure to allow covert movement through state borders. Such infrastructure can include CIA-operated secret detention sites in foreign countries as well as in the United States, detention centers in various countries operated by local intelligence services, surveillance centers, transfer sites, and flight routes served by civilian aircraft to avoid suspicion (Marty 2006). These are all tied together operationally in a way that closely resembles transnational networks. In this light, extraordinary rendition practices reveal how state actors themselves are becoming more networklike in their actions in order to overcome the territorial restrictions imposed on them by border lines.

The issues discussed in this chapter illustrate several ways in which the territorial overlap between state sovereignty and the organization of social relations has become unsustainable in the circumstances of globalization. There are other forces, situated at spatial scales other than the state, that impact people's lives. State border lines do not provide a sufficiently effective framework for addressing some of the major issues affecting twenty-first-century societies. The territorial scope of these issues requires that they be regulated by different types of borders.

References

Ali, S. H., and Keil, R. 2006. Global Cities and the Spread of Infectious Disease: The Case of Severe Acute Respiratory Syndrome (SARS) in Toronto, Canada. *Urban Studies* 43: 491–509.

Anderson, J., and O'Dowd, L. 1999. Borders, Border Regions and Territoriality: Contradictory Meanings, Changing Significance. *Regional Studies* 33(7): 593–604.

Anderson, M., and Bort, E. 2001. *The Frontiers of the European Union*. Houndmills: Palgrave.

Angel, D. P., Hamilton, T., and Huber, M. T. 2007. Global Environmental Standards for Industry. *Annual Review of Environment and Resources* 32: 295–316.

Bank for International Settlements. 2010. *Triennial Central Bank Survey of Foreign Exchange and Derivatives Market Activity in 2010*. Basel, Switzerland. Available at http://www.bis.org/publ/rpfxf10t.pdf.

Byers, M. 2000. The Law and Politics of the Pinochet Case. *Duke Journal of Comparative and International Law* 10: 415–441.

Camilleri, M. T. 2004. The Challenges of Sovereign Borders in the Post–Cold War Era's Refugees and Humanitarian Crises. In H. Hensel, ed., *Sovereignty and the Global Community*. Aldershot: Ashgate. Pp. 83–104.

Christiansen, T., and Jorgenson, K. E. 2000. Transnational Governance "Above" and "Below" the State: The Changing Nature of Borders in the New Europe. *Regional and Federal Studies* 10(2): 62–77.

Dodds, K. 2008. Icy Geopolitics. *Environment and Planning D* 26: 1–6.

Elden, S. 2005. Territorial Integrity and the War on Terror. *Environment and Planning A* 37: 2083–2104.

———. 2007. Terror and Territory. *Antipode* 39: 821–845.

Falah, G.-W., Flint, C., and Mamadouh, V. 2006. Just War and Extraterritoriality: The Popular Geopolitics of the United States' War on Iraq as Reflected in Newspapers of the Arab World. *Annals of the Association of American Geographers* 96: 142–164.

Fidler, D. P. 2003. SARS: Political Pathology of the First Post-Westphalian Pathogen. *The Journal of Law, Medicine & Ethics* 31(4): 485–505.

Fuller, T., Conde, C., Fugal, and Ng, C. 2008. The Melamine Stain: One Sign of a Worldwide Problem. *New York Times*, October 12.

Gregory, D. 2004. The Angel of Iraq. *Environment and Planning D* 22: 317–324.

————. 2006. The Black Flag: Guantanamo Bay and the Space of Exception. *Geografiska Annaler B* 88(4): 405–427.

————. 2007. Vanishing Points: Law, Violence, and Exception in the Global War Prison. In D. Gregory and A. Pred, eds., *Violent Geographies*. New York: Routledge. Pp. 205–235.

Harvey, D. 2000. *Spaces of Hope*. Berkeley: University of California Press.

International Criminal Court. 2008. *Outreach Report*. ICC-CPI-20081120-PR375. Available at http://www.icc-cpi.int/NR/rdonlyres/AE9B69EB-2692-4F9C-8F08 -B3844FE397C7/279073/Outreach_report2008enLR.pdf.

Kyoto Protocol to the United Nations Framework Convention on Climate Change. 1998. *United Nations*. Available at http://unfccc.int/resource/docs/convkp/kpeng .pdf.

Marks, K. 2006. Rising Tide of Global Warming Threatens Pacific Island States. *The Independent*, October 25.

Marty, D. 2006. *Alleged Secret Detentions and Unlawful Inter-state Transfers of Detainees Involving Council of Europe Member States*. Report, Committee on Legal Affairs and Human Rights, Council of Europe, June 12.

McGirk, T. 2009. Could Israelis Face War Crimes Charges over Gaza? *Time*, January 23.

Murphy, S. D. 1996. *Humanitarian Intervention: The United Nations in an Evolving World Order*. Philadelphia: University of Pennsylvania Press.

O'Lear, S. 2010. *Environmental Politics: Scale and Power*. Cambridge: Cambridge University Press.

Reynolds, P. 2007. Russia Ahead in Arctic "Gold Rush." BBC News, August 1. Available at http://news.bbc.co.uk/2/hi/6925853.stm.

Rome Statute of the International Criminal Court. 1998. *United Nations*, Doc. A/ CONF. 183/9. Available at http://untreaty.un.org/cod/icc/statute/romefra.htm.

Sassen, S. 2001. *The Global City: New York, London, Tokyo*. Princeton, NJ: Princeton University Press.

————. 2006. *Territory, Authority, Rights: From Medieval to Global Assemblages*. Princeton, NJ: Princeton University Press.

Steinberg, P. 2010. You Are (Not) Here: On the Ambiguity of Flag Planting and Finger Pointing in the Arctic. *Political Geography* 29: 81–84.

United Nations Conference on Trade and Development. 2008. *Transnational Corporations and the Infrastructure Challenge*. World Investment Report. Available at http://www.unctad.org/en/docs/wir2008_en.pdf.

Warf, B. 1989. Telecommunications and the Globalization of Financial Services. *Professional Geographer* 31: 257–271.

————. 2002. Tailored for Panama: Offshore Banking at the Crossroads of the Americas. *Geografiska Annaler B* 84(1): 47–61.

Watts, M. 2007. Revolutionary Islam. In D. Gregory and A. Pred, eds., *Violent Geographies*. New York: Routledge. Pp. 175–204.

Understanding the Text

1. What are global flows? How do they differ from border permeability?

2. Explain how global financial flows affect the functions of borders, specifically noting transnational corporations' "spatial logic" and the traditional role of borders in the international economy.

3. What is the relationship between borders and the environment? What do Popescu's explanations and analyses reveal about the normative view of the functions of state borders?

4. How do both human rights regimes and transnational terrorism challenge our traditional understanding of borders and their regulatory functions?

Reflection and Response

5. How does Popescu's opening paragraph alert readers to the key issues of the essay and introduce the supporting topics? Explain the main idea and then note the subpoints.

6. Popescu states: "The idea that socially constructed border lines can contain the impact of human activity on the natural environment appears absurd. Yet modern state territorial sovereignty suggests just this — a state is free to use the natural environment inside its borders in whatever way it pleases" (par. 18). What is your position on this issue? Explain why you agree or disagree with Popescu, and provide sound reasons and evidence to support your position.

7. According to Popescu, why does the United States' Global War on Terror "[fall] short of building a concerted global effort to tackle the roots of transnational terrorism" (par. 41)?

Making Connections

8. Using Popescu's ideas and those of other writers in this chapter, write an essay explaining how borders both can and cannot organize social relations. As Popescu notes, issues of sovereignty, territoriality, and power are relevant to this discussion. The following readings might also prove helpful: Alexander C. Diener and Joshua Hagen's "A Very Bordered World" (p. 15), Stuart Elden's "Territory without Borders" (p. 24), Norma Cantú's "Living on the Border" (p. 58), and John Eger's "Art as a Universal Language" (p. 218).

9. Identify some of the ethical and moral questions, assumptions, and judgments in Popescu's essay. Specifically, what ethical issues emerge from privileging territorial sovereignty, enforcing border restrictions, and confronting the unorthodoxy of the Global War on Terror? In your response, be sure to note how these issues are related to borders.

Revisiting a "World without Borders": An Interview with Donald Worster

David Kinkela, Neil Maher, and Donald Worster

An associate professor of history at the State University of New York at Fredonia, David Kinkela specializes in the history of U.S. environmental politics in an age of globalization. He is also the author of *DDT and the American Century: Global Health, Environmental Politics, and the Pesticide That Changed the World* (2011), which chronicles the chemical pesticide's use and history. Neil Maher, a professor of history, teaches in the Federated History Department at the New Jersey Institute of Technology and Rutgers University. His research focuses on twentieth-century environmental and political history, and his book *Nature's New Deal: The Civilian Conservation Corps and the Roots of the American Environmental Movement* (2008) highlights both of these topics.

Donald Worster, the focal point of this interview, is a professor emeritus in the history department at the University of Kansas (KU). Prior to teaching at KU, he taught at Brandeis University, Yale University, and the University of Hawai'i. A key figure in the field of environmental studies, Worster has published several award-winning books, two of which garnered Pulitzer Prize nominations: *Rivers of Empire: Water, Aridity, and the Growth of the American West* (1985) and *Dust Bowl: The Southern Plains in the 1930s* (1979).

In this interview, Worster urges scholars to stop focusing solely on the nation-state and calls for the need to think beyond boundaries that may overshadow "nature's reality." As you read, pay close attention to the borders and boundaries that most concern him.

Few people have influenced the field of environmental history more than Donald Worster. The author of dozens of books, including the recently released *A Passion for Nature: The Life of John Muir* (2008) and *A River Running West: The Life of John Wesley Powell* (2001), Worster has also published essays that changed the course of environmental history scholarship. One such essay is "World without Borders: The Internationalizing of Environmental History" (1982), which encouraged environmental historians to move beyond a focus on the nation-state and to embrace a more transnational perspective.

With "World without Borders" in mind, the editors of this special issue of *Radical History Review* conducted two interviews with Worster in

2009. The first occurred on February 26 in Tallahassee, Florida, at the annual conference of the American Society for Environmental History, during which we questioned Worster about the writing of the essay back in 1982 and about the state of the environmental history field during those early years. Later that year, on August 6, at the World Environmental History Conference in Copenhagen, Denmark, we conducted a second interview with Worster, focusing instead on the field of environmental history today and on whether or not environmental historians have followed his recommendations for a more global approach. These interviews, which spanned six months and two continents, thus reflected Worster's call for breaking down national borders to better understand both the present and the future of environmental history as a field.

Part 1: Tallahassee, Florida, American Society for Environmental History Annual Conference

EDITORS: What was your motivation for writing your "World without Borders" essay in 1982?

DONALD WORSTER: It was given at the first environmental history conference ever held, to my knowledge, a conference organized at the University of California at Irvine, by the late Kendall Bailes. Ken didn't know much about the American Society for Environmental History at that point (ASEH was founded in 1977). He'd done great work in Russian history but decided, all on his own, that environmental history was an interesting new direction. When he discovered there was a society, he called me up, as the president of that organization, and said, "I'm working on a conference, but I could use some help." We put together a list of people to invite, and the final program included stars like Lynn White Jr. and Clarence Glacken, a historical geographer.

Ken asked me to give the final wrap-up talk. I began with a sense that we were witnessing an unusual coming together from different national histories—that this was a pioneering international, transnational, or cross-border gathering.[1]

EDITORS: It's interesting, because at this particular moment in time environmental history itself is in its infancy, yet rather than adopting a national model, there seemed to be a conscious understanding of taking the more international approach. So what was it about this particular moment in time that allowed these conversations to occur?

WORSTER: International might be too much of a claim, since we had a session here on Russian history and over there on medieval history and so on. Balkanization,° I think, was a problem from the beginning. How could it have been otherwise? Most of us did not know anything about Russian history. How could we go to a paper on that history and comment professionally? We didn't know the sources or context. We're up against real obstacles.

But much out there in the culture was pushing us to overcome balkanization. That conference was held in January 1982, a decade or so after Earth Day.° Much of the writing about environmental issues leading up to Earth Day had taken a global perspective. Even the anti-war movement didn't seem to convey that same spirit of thinking about the planet as a whole.

EDITORS: So how did you start thinking about these interconnections?

WORSTER: Not easily. I had graduated in '71 with a PhD in American studies, and my main venture outside U.S. borders was a secondary field in British history. But right after graduation I was invited to be a Mellon Fellow at the Aspen Institute for the Humanities in Aspen, Colorado, which opened my eyes to a more international set of problems. At that time I was also thinking about my next project, which would become my book *Dust Bowl: The Southern Plains in the 1930s.* Around that time there had been some huge dust storms on the Great Plains. The [grain] elevators were coated with dirt, jogging memories for me of growing up in that area and going through earlier dust storms. And now in Aspen I was talking with people about world food issues, climate change, drought, and Sahelian desertification. We worked on a white paper to present at the 1974 World Food Conference in Rome. Those conversations changed the way I thought about agriculture and erosion on the Great Plains. Reflecting that Aspen experience, my book included a photo of a woman in a desiccated Sahel. And the introduction discussed briefly the Russia dust bowl and Khrushchev's° expansionary policies. I was trying to connect U.S. history with a more global set of problems.

EDITORS: You mentioned that political ties bound people together during this moment, when that "Whole Earth" image was connecting people. And you've written in other pieces how science and the ideas of ecology flowed across borders as well as pollution. Did this help make environmental history organically transnational?

Balkanization: the splitting of a country or region into smaller areas or states, usually into hostile and ineffectual ones.
Earth Day: an annual event held on April 22, which began in 1970 to bring awareness to protecting the Earth's environment.
Khrushchev: Nikita Khrushchev (1894–1971), Russian premier of the Soviet Union from 1958 to 1964.

WORSTER: Knowledge, technology, capital, and commodities all flow across borders, making an exclusive national history too confining. Environmental historians want to bring in the nonhuman material reality, which has never observed any political boundaries and therefore has been ignored by traditional historians. It became more and more clear to me that taking nature seriously meant transcending arbitrary political lines. Why are we transfixed with the nation-state anyway? How does that perspective blind us to nature's reality and affect the questions we ask or don't ask?

> "Knowledge, technology, capital, and commodities all flow across borders, making an exclusive national history too confining."

It helped my thinking to be living in Hawaii during part of the 1970s and 1980s—on an island far from the rest of the United States, where one interacted with people from all over the world. I was more acutely aware of Australia, New Zealand, Oceania, and Asia. Simply trying to teach U.S. history there to students who had grown up in the middle of the Pacific Ocean was a challenge. How could one give the same emphasis to New England or Southern history as historians on the mainland were giving? Hawaii hardly figured into national narratives. And that led me to ask, what else didn't figure in? The Great Plains did not, nor the rest of the American West—nor soils, water, oceans, plant and animal life. I became aware that other academic fields did not go so far in making the nation-state the core theme. Even political scientists did not, nor anthropologists, nor students of literature. Nobody else was so encased in the nation-state armor.

EDITORS: Much of what you talked about [in "World without Borders"] deals with issues of scale and thinking about postnational histories. How did you deal with these kinds of scales and frameworks—the local, the regional, and the global? How did you envision these scales, operating independently from one another, and in unison with each other?

WORSTER: I have looked to ecologists for models of thinking about scale. Ecologists readily embrace the idea that their discipline has many scales: the individual organism, a population, an ecosystem, the biosphere. Ecologists see themselves working on any one of these levels, but also all of them. Pick up a textbook in ecology and it's often divided in terms of scales, but they form a cohesive whole. Students are trained to think about all those different scales.

We don't do that in history. What if we were to write a textbook that was based on scales? We would see history as a hierarchy ranging from biography to the world. Each scale would be valid and important to pursue.

Right now we are debating whether we should be doing national or world history. Neither is sufficient. The remedy for national history is not that everybody should do international or world history. Each can be an oversimplification. Take that picture of Mother Earth hanging on the wall: it, too, can become a way of simplifying the earth. If you stand in outer space, you may think you can easily encompass the whole planet. You can talk grandly of "world systems." But when you get down to the level of a single individual, the world may look different—more complicated than you ever imagined. Working at the biographical scale can teach us that all of our explanations or theories rest on simplifications. That's why I think we need to have historians working at different scales, so that we can understand different levels of complexity, different kinds of questions and so on.

Part 2: Copenhagen, Denmark, World Environmental History Conference

EDITORS: In this interview we're going to focus on more contemporary issues within the environmental history field and want to begin that discussion by asking, how good a fortune-teller were you in your "World without Borders" essay? Has environmental history succeeded in moving across national boundaries towards, as you call it, a postnational history?

WORSTER: I am amazed at how far we have lately come in crossing national boundaries towards a transnational, if not postnational, history. We certainly have not abandoned the concept of the nation-state. It's still important, but we are thinking about new shapes and boundaries for the past. Look at the opening sessions here [in Copenhagen]: the keynote address is titled "The Anthropocene: Humans as a Force in Global Environmental Cycles," and the very first session of papers is on "Trans-National Environmental Science." And on it goes: "Global Foresters," "World Environmental History," "The Ecology of Wartime Nature." There are a few sessions focused exclusively on a single country, but for the most part it is all quite mixed up.

EDITORS: While you suggested postnational history provides a way to 20 consider a borderless world, as editors of this special issue we also take the position that borders do matter for a variety of reasons. So what role do you see borders now playing in this new transnational or global environmental history?

WORSTER: The main reason why they are still significant is in policy making. There is a whole new dimension of international law and policy making going forward, but in terms of resource consumption, conservation, environmental protection, and antipollution legislation, the primary focus is still on the nation-state.

EDITORS: Do you see a danger in the field branching out so broadly, way beyond the nation-state? Will it result in environmental historians writing these very thin transnational or global histories that are not very deep?

WORSTER: Thick and thin are relative concepts. You can go quite deeply into a local place but remain very thin on ideas. The new transnational history may be thick in a new direction. Here in Copenhagen we are seeing a lot of very detailed studies about very specific places, but usually they are put in a context where everybody has to ask, "Why is this important? What am I learning here that's useful to me someplace else?" So I don't at this point feel that we're moving into a more superficial kind of history. Rather, we're moving into a much more difficult kind of research to visualize and pursue, which is quite exhilarating.

EDITORS: Let's shift to politics within the field of environmental history today. In your 1982 essay you wrote that the field in the U.S. was overly focused on the political movements of conservation and environmentalism. How has the field as a whole broadened its political history methodology beyond these narrow movements that are often associated with environmental history? In other words, how has environmental history engaged political history in a broader way?

WORSTER: Nobody quite seems to know what the concept or entity of the state is. It's not defined simply by politics in the old sense. Rather, the state seems to be a process of centralizing power, trying to catalogue, control, and exploit resources, to serve as an intermediary between people and landscapes. One of the sessions I chaired was on how the state has influenced the evolution of species. That wouldn't have been considered part of the old political history. Now we're talking about the role of the state in determining genetics, or what we use and consume, or the ecological impacts of all that.

EDITORS: Do you think that environmental history is naturally conducive to studying political history? You mentioned material nature, and how that's very important for getting at the politics of power. But do you think environmental history is more ready to engage political history than other types of history because of what we're looking at? Because of the material nature?

25

WORSTER: Our goal should be to bring a new dimension to political history, just as social history has changed what we meant by political history. We have come to see how categories like race and class enter politics, or how gender analysis gives us a radical new way of seeing politics. We have been forced to look more at the culture of different groups, as well as differences in power. Power thus became a more complicated concept, not just the power of dominant parties, but the power of identity groups and so forth.

Environmental history can have some of the same revolutionary consequences. We're beginning to acknowledge that the state can be influenced by its environment. Power is still the issue here, but what are the limits on state power in dealing with different environments? And how does the state respond to or modify deserts, forests, et cetera?

EDITORS: Now a lot of environmental historians seem to be looking at political history and trying to bring the two fields together, but we don't see as many political historians looking to nature. Why aren't political historians including nature as a fourth category, along with race, class, and gender, in their approach? Why don't they naturally think about nature? What have we done wrong to not get through to those historians?

WORSTER: I think they're just slow in catching on. We can, however, 30 look to people in political science, if not political history, for innovative thinking — James Scott is one example. He's beginning to have an impact by asking, "How is what we're doing in the natural world parallel to what we're doing in the human world?"

EDITORS: In your responses, and in much of your written work, you seem to be emphasizing economics and ecology over politics. Even today you've talked a lot about political economy. Do you agree with this statement? If not, what role did politics play in your call for a new postnational environmental history?

WORSTER: I believe that environmental history ought to be focused primarily on the material world, the changes taking place in it, and not simply on what's in our heads or culture. The material world of economy is where we interact with the material world of nature. So, bringing economic analysis into the picture — the interaction of economics and ecology — should be at the core of the new history.

EDITORS: Lastly, back in 1982. you also wrote that more biographies of John Muir° will not take environmental historians very far towards a

---

John Muir (1838–1914): naturalist and conservationist; founder of the Sierra Club, an organization devoted to the wilderness and environmental issues. Muir is often called the "father of our national park system."

less national, more global history, and an international consciousness. But then you went and wrote a wonderful biography on John Muir. So what gives?

WORSTER: A foolish consistency, Emerson° said, is the hobgoblin of little minds. I'm as inconsistent as anybody. Back in 1982 I was still under the influence of my graduate professors, many of whom thought that biography was beneath their dignity. So maybe I was too dismissive of biography and have since learned better.

In writing about John Muir and John Wesley Powell° I had to ask   35 how environmental history operates at the individual scale. That's been a useful corrective to my thinking.

EDITORS: You went back to Scotland [where Muir was born] and did some research there, correct?

WORSTER: I did indeed go to Scotland, three times. I went to all the places I could go that John Muir knew. I didn't go everywhere he went in his life, but I did try to gain a sense of what he was seeing and feeling. After all, nature wears many faces, and they all have an influence on human life. Nature influenced the path John Muir took—for example, a mosquito gave him malaria on his way to Florida, which slowed him down, forced a change of plans, altering the direction he took in life. Instead of going on to South America, he decided to go to California. And the impact of the California landscape at a particular moment in time had a profound effect on him. I had to see and try to imagine those places as much as possible.

EDITORS: And do you think that biography is a good way to approach transnational or global history now? You just mentioned that you went back to Scotland, and Muir is a transnational person, and in some ways you can trace people across places.

WORSTER: Yes, we tend to think of people as having a social identity but no place identity, and thus we dismiss the power of places. John Muir became a famous American conservationist. But if you look at his whole life, he was an international figure. His family were migrants from Scotland, he spent a critical period in Canada, and he traveled around the world. He went to South America and Africa; he traveled the Siberian railroad from Moscow to Vladivostok and took a boat from there to China. He saw India and Egypt, Australia, New Zealand, and the Philippines.

Emerson: Ralph Waldo Emerson (1803–1882), American essayist, poet, and philosopher. **John Wesley Powell** (1834–1902): geologist and scientific explorer. He led the Colorado Expedition through the canyons of the Green and Colorado Rivers in the Grand Canyon.

All of that travel reflected changes in transportation technology 40 and personal affluence. Those places helped Muir gain a more global sense of the declining condition of forests, for example. And people around the world looked to him for vision and insight. He was astonished to find some of his books in libraries way up the Amazon River. Or in New Zealand at botanical gardens, where the local naturalists knew who he was. We tend to forget how much internationalizing of life was going on even in the nineteenth or early twentieth centuries and how much influence a figure like Muir had on the whole planet, not just on the United States.

EDITORS: It's funny because one thinks of him as so connected to the Sierras, and one doesn't really think of him beyond that.

WORSTER: Well, in some ways, he was never really a dyed-in-the-wool American Yankee. He was always, because of his strong connections to Scotland and the world, a man whose identity was multinational.

EDITORS: That's a great way to end two days of conversations on two different continents. Thanks.

Note

1. The conference proceedings, including Worster's essay "World without Borders," were subsequently published in Kendall E. Bailes, ed., *Environmental History: Critical Issues in Comparative Perspective* (Lanham, MD: University Press of America, 1985).

Understanding the Text

1. In paragraphs 12 and 13, Worster presents two key ideas for his argument regarding the need to move beyond "arbitrary political lines." Identify and explain those ideas. Why does Worster believe we need to transcend these national boundaries?

2. What does Worster mean by "scales" (pars. 15–17)? How does this concept relate to his response about the "danger" of the field of environmental history "branching out so broadly" (pars. 22–23)?

3. Explain what Worster means when he claims that people have a "place identity" (par. 39). Why is place identity significant to our understanding of John Muir?

Reflection and Response

4. According to Worster, environmental historians must consider issues of power when they study political history (pars. 27–28). What evidence does he present to support this view? Do you agree? Why or why not?

5. Do you think Worster is advocating for a borderless world? Support your response with specific examples from the reading.

6. Kinkela and Maher ask Worster about his shift to writing biographies. How does Worster respond? Do you think what he learned from the experience fits with some of the ideas he expresses earlier in the interview? Explain your answer.

Making Connections

7. Read Gabriel Popescu's "Borders in the Era of Globalization" (p. 273) and synthesize Popescu's and Worster's ideas. What does your synthesis help you understand about the role of borders and border issues in the twenty-first century?

8. Do some additional research about the field of environmental history and "postnational history" so that you can provide your own answer to the question in paragraph 18: "Has environmental history succeeded in moving across national boundaries towards . . . a postnational history?" Explain the significance of your findings. Other readings from this chapter and Chapter 1 might prove helpful.

A World without Borders Makes Economic Sense

Michael A. Clemens

Michael Clemens is an economist and an expert in migration, development, economic growth, aid effectiveness, and economic history. Currently he is a senior fellow at the Center for Global Development, where he leads the Migration and Development Initiative as its research manager. In his studies, Clemens focuses on the effects of international migration from and in developing countries. His work has appeared in such journals as the *Journal of Development Studies*, the *Journal of Globalization and Development*, the *American Economic Journal*, and the *Economic Journal*.

In the following reading, which first appeared in the *Guardian* in 2011, Clemens argues strongly against policies restricting international migration. As you read, consider how Clemens uses various rhetorical appeals, and note which ones seem most effective.

What is the biggest single drag on the beleaguered global economy? Opponents of globalization might point to the current crisis, which shrank the world economy by about 5%. Proponents of globalization might point to the remaining barriers to international flows of goods and capital, which also serve to shrink the world economy by approximately 5%. That sounds like a lot.

But the truly big fish are swimming elsewhere. The world impoverishes itself much more through blocking international migration than any other single class of international policy. A modest relaxation of barriers to human mobility between countries would bring more global economic prosperity than the total elimination of all remaining policy barriers to goods trade—every tariff, every quota—plus the elimination of every last restriction on the free movement of capital.

I document that remarkable fact in a new research paper. Large numbers of people wish to move permanently to another country—more than 40% of adults in the poorest quarter of nations. But most of them are either ineligible for any form of legal movement or face waiting lists of a decade or more. Those giant walls are a human creation, but cause more than just human harm: they hobble the global economy, costing the world roughly half its potential economic product.

The reason migration packs such economic punch is both simple and mysterious: a worker's economic productivity depends much more on location than on skill (see Figure 5.1 on p. 306). A taxi driver in Ethiopia's capital, no matter how talented and industrious, cannot earn more than a few thousand dollars a year. The same person doing the same job in New York City can easily earn $35,000 a year. The reason people will pay him that much is that his driving adds more than $35,000 of value to the New York economy, more value than his actions can add to the Ethiopian economy.

This has puzzled economists since Adam Smith in the eighteenth cen- 5 tury. It is related to international differences in legal systems and geographic traits, and to pure proximity to other high-productivity workers. But regardless of the reason, the fact remains that simply changing a worker's location can massively enrich the world economy. And stopping such movement massively impoverishes it.

> "The world impoverishes itself much more through blocking international migration than any other single class of international policy."

Stopping movement particularly impoverishes people born, through no choice of their own, in countries with little economic opportunity. The large majority of Haitians to emerge from destitution did so by leaving Haiti, not by anything they or any development agency did within the country. A low-skill male Cambodian can earn a living standard six times higher in the US than in Cambodia, for similar work. No act within Cambodia can reliably and quickly create so much opportunity for the industrious poor. And the benefits need not be limited to a tiny handful. In the late nineteenth century, roughly one third of Sweden's labor force permanently emigrated to opportunity; today, about half of Guyana has left Guyana.

How can the benefits of this—the world's greatest arbitrage° opportunity—be reaped? There are numerous clear and sound proposals for more economically sensible migration policy. These include Lant Pritchett's proposals for bilateral guest-worker agreements, the ideas of Pia Orrenius and Madeline Zavodny for raising permanent economic visa allocations, and the proposal by Jesús Fernández-Huertas and Hillel Rapoport for tradable immigration quotas. I suggest using migration policy as one tool to assist people in poor countries struck by natural disaster. Each approach has advantages and disadvantages, but they have in common a drive to generate triple-wins for migrants, destination

---

arbitrage: the simultaneous purchase and sale of securities, currency, or commodities in different markets in order to profit from price discrepancies.

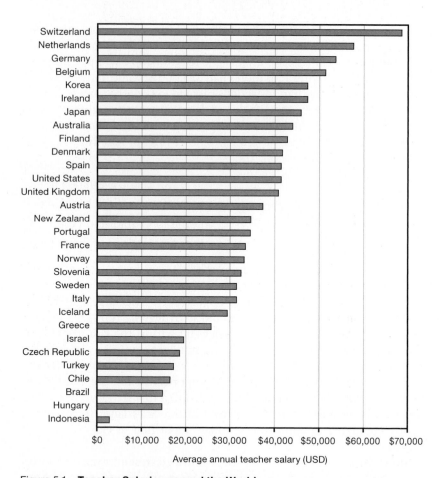

Figure 5.1 **Teacher Salaries around the World**

Global salaries vary widely depending on where you work. This graph shows the average teacher salary by country. Data from GEMS Education Solutions, "Education Efficiency Index Report" (2014), p. 19. Salaries adjusted according to purchasing power parity (PPP).

countries and origin countries, taking advantage of what Pritchett calls "the cliff at the border."

Many people fear that even a minor increase in international migration will wreck their own economies and societies. Those fears deserve a hearing. They are old fears, of the kind that filled US newspapers a century ago. The US population subsequently quadrupled, largely through immigration to already-settled areas. Today, even in crisis, America is the richest country in the world. History, too, deserves a hearing.

Of course, history is often the brooding and ignored stepchild of policy debate. Political constraints may make it impossible in the short-term to realize the gains from greater geographic worker mobility, just as political constraints blocked other forms of worker mobility in the past. But that can change. All the economic and social arguments against immigrant entry to the workforce could be—and were—deployed decades ago against female entry to the workforce. ("But men built those companies! Why should we allow women to work when there are qualified, unemployed men? Why should a man pay taxes for a woman's unemployment insurance? Will female employees assimilate and act just like men as we all wish? And what harm will be wrought in the homes they abandon?")

Now these arguments sound worse than ridiculous. Society decides 10 who is or is not a member of the relevant club and, beyond the short-term, that decision can change massively. Though our fears will likely continue to impoverish us for some time, they need not do so forever.

Understanding the Text

1. In your own words, explain Clemens's claim in paragraph 5 and how he develops it.

2. Summarize the arguments opposing Clemens's position, as he presents them. How does Clemens respond to each argument?

3. What argument does Clemens make regarding history's place in ongoing debates about migration policies? Identify both his stated and unstated assumptions on this issue.

Reflection and Response

4. In paragraph 8, Clemens writes, "Many people fear that even a minor increase in international migration will wreck their own economies and societies." Extend this statement and identify specific fears that you or others may have. In what ways might more open borders adversely affect your society?

5. Clemens uses several elements from classical argument — such as ethos, logos, and pathos — to appeal to his readers. Identify at least three of these rhetorical appeals, and locate a passage from the text that you think best illustrates each one. Explain your choice and how it functions in the reading.

6. As you read this piece, how did you react to Clemens's tone? To the information he presents? To his claims, reasoning, and evidence? Did you want to know more? What questions did you have as you read? Did you "talk back" to him as you read? Write a detailed description of how you responded to this reading.

Making Connections

7. Locate several of the proposals for economic migration policies to which Clemens refers in paragraph 8. Choose one proposal to summarize and explain; then argue whether you think this proposal should be implemented or not. Support your argument with textual evidence from the proposal, Clemens's piece, or other readings from this chapter or elsewhere.

8. Do some research on the global economy and the status of international migration. Using your research, extend, support, or challenge Clemens's ideas. Shaun Raviv's "If People Could Immigrate Anywhere, Would Poverty Be Eliminated?" (p. 309) provides a good starting place for your research.

If People Could Immigrate Anywhere, Would Poverty Be Eliminated?

Shaun Raviv

An American journalist based in Ghana, Shaun Raviv moved to Swaziland in 2010 on a Fulbright Fellowship for playwriting. During his time there, he began sending stories on Swaziland, Africa, and migration to the *Atlantic* magazine, which now frequently publishes his work. He has also written articles for *Foreign Policy*, *Mosaic*, and *The Big Roundtable*, including his narrative nonfiction piece "The Killers of Swaziland," which tells the story of serial killer David Simelane.

The following essay first appeared in the *Atlantic* in 2013, and as the title suggests, it considers the socioeconomic consequences of reimagining a world without borders. As you read, think carefully about the implications of this reconfiguration, and note the advantages and drawbacks of completely eliminating border restrictions.

What if there was a program that would cost nothing, improve the lives of millions of people from poorer nations, and double world GDP? At least one economist says that increased mobility of people is by far the biggest missed opportunity in development. And an informally aligned group of advocates is doing its best to make the world aware of the "open borders" movement, which suggests that individuals should be able to move between countries at will.

Vipul Naik is the face, or at least the voice, of open borders on the Internet. In March 2012, he launched Open Borders: The Case, a website dedicated to the idea. Naik, a Ph.D. candidate in mathematics at the University of Chicago, is striving for "a world where there is a strong presumption in favor of allowing people to migrate and where this presumption can be overridden or curtailed only under exceptional circumstances." Naik and his two primary co-writers, Nathan Smith and John Lee, parse research into immigration impacts, answering claims by those they call "restrictionists"—people who argue against open borders—and deconstructing writings on migration by economists, politicians, journalists, and philosophers.

The theory they espouse is that border restrictions of almost any kind are wrong, that they are antithetical to the fundamental human right of self-determination. To see their point, imagine an American in rural Mississippi being told she cannot move to New York City to seek a better career. That is exactly what the U.S. and other developed nations are telling the millions of foreigners who are denied access to their rich labor markets.

> "What if there was a program that would cost nothing, improve the lives of millions of people from poorer nations, and double world GDP?"

The moral case for open borders has perhaps been most eloquently described by Michael Huemer, a philosopher at the University of Colorado. In a blog post, he recounts the story of the young boy Starvin' Marvin, named after the skeletal *South Park* character. Speaking over the phone, Huemer told me Starvin' Marvin's hypothetical tale of woe:

> *[Marvin] is very hungry and is trying to travel to the marketplace to buy some food. Another person, Sam (Sam has a large number of nephews and nieces, so we'll call him Uncle Sam), decides to stop Marvin from going to the marketplace using coercion. He goes down there with his M16 and blocks the road. As a result, Marvin can't trade for food and, as a result, he starves. So then the question is, did Sam kill Marvin? Did he violate his rights? Almost anyone would say yes, Sam acted wrongly. In fact, if Marvin died as a result, then Sam killed him. It wouldn't be that Sam failed to help Marvin. No, he actively intervened. . . . This is analogous to the U.S. government's immigration policy. There are people who want to trade in our marketplace, in this case the labor market, and the government effectively prevents them from doing that, through use of force.*

Marvin's story leaves open many questions that writers on the Open Borders site spend hours deliberating on the site's blog. If Uncle Sam doesn't prevent Marvin from coming to the market, won't Marvin take jobs from Sam's nieces and nephews? What if Marvin is a criminal or a terrorist? Will Marvin learn English and assimilate culturally? Won't Marvin just take advantage of the marketplace's welfare system? Can the marketplace even sustain more Marvins?

George Mason economist Bryan Caplan, whose writing at EconLog 5 inspired Naik's interest in open borders, has offered "keyhole" solutions as a substitute for black and white, yes-or-no questions on immigration. "If immigrants hurt American workers, we can charge immigrants higher taxes or admission fees, and use the revenue to compensate the losers," Caplan wrote last year. "If immigrants burden American taxpayers, we can make immigrants ineligible for benefits. If immigrants hurt American culture, we can impose tests of English fluency and cultural literacy. If immigrants hurt American liberty, we can refuse to give them the right to vote. Whatever your complaint happens to be, immigration restrictions are a needlessly draconian remedy."

While Caplan advocates for keyhole solutions over the status quo, he would pull the trigger immediately on open borders if given the chance: "My conscience wouldn't allow anything else." If people are so afraid of what might happen with open borders, says Caplan, then we should just implement it gradually. "But it's very easy for you to say that when you're in the first world living a comfortable life," he told me. "If you are living in abject poverty in Haiti, on the other hand, this go-slow attitude seems rather callous."

Though he generally disagrees with the standard arguments against increased immigration (that immigrants take jobs from native workers, increase crime, take more out of the system in welfare than they put back in taxes, and hurt their countries of origin due to so-called "brain drain"), Caplan understands that some developed-world workers could see a minor decrease in real pay. But whatever downsides there may be, he wrote in a 2011 post, "the upside of open borders would be the rapid elimination of absolute poverty on earth."

To prove the economic power of open borders, supporters often turn to the work of Michael Clemens, a development economist and one of the strongest voices for loosening border restrictions. Clemens is not an open borders advocate, but his research and writings make it very clear that movement of people across international borders should be a much higher priority than it is now. He is, he told me, "in favor of a vastly more sensible way of regulating movement," if not "a utopia of completely free movement." Based out of the Center for Global Development, a think tank in D.C., he has spent much of the past half-decade compiling international labor mobility statistics that are, as he says, "gasp-inducing."

Barriers to emigration may—according to Clemens's paper—"place one of the fattest of all wedges between humankind's current welfare and its potential welfare." Though he affirms that the research on migration's effects is far from complete, what Clemens has found "suggests that the gains from reducing emigration restrictions are likely to be enormous, measured in tens of trillions of dollars." Remove all remaining barriers to trade, says Clemens, and all remaining barriers to capital flow, and it still wouldn't compensate for the inefficiencies created by current global labor mobility restrictions. His research indicates that allowing free movement of all people across international borders could double world GDP.

According to Clemens, we are all victims of an epic intuition fail. "Development is about people, not places," he has said many times over, and often the best way to make a person richer is by allowing them to move to another place. We don't really care about helping poverty-stricken Liberia, we care about helping poverty-stricken Liberians. It sounds almost too simple at first: A very large percentage of people who have gone from extreme poverty to relative financial stability have done so by moving across borders. So why don't we just let more people move?

In 2008, Clemens and his frequent co-writer, Harvard economist Lant Pritchett, came up with a new statistic called "income per natural." Their goal was to show "the mean annual income of persons born in a given country, regardless of where that person now resides." They found that large percentages of people from Haiti, Mexico, and India who live above international poverty lines don't actually reside in their home countries. "For example, among Haitians who live either in the United States or Haiti and live on more than $10 per day—about a third of the U.S. "poverty" line—four out of five live in the United States," Clemens wrote. "Emigration from Haiti, as a force for Haitians' poverty reduction, may be at least as important as any economic change that has occurred within Haiti."

The trillions of dollars are lost by not maximizing human potential. Workers in the developing world can be much more productive when they are not locked in places with crumbled infrastructure, poor academic institutions, and mass corruption. "It's the biggest arbitrage opportunity in the world," Clemens told me. "It's hard to find a cell phone or pair of jeans that sells for a thousand percent price difference in two different countries, and yet the labor of a McDonald's worker, the labor of a child care worker, the labor of a construction worker, does sell for thousand percent differences between Haiti and the United States."

If wealthy nations open their borders, won't native workers lose their jobs or see their pay shrink? Not so, according to Clemens. He and his co-authors, through study of all the available economic literature, have found that decades of immigration of tens of millions of people to the United States has reduced real wages for the average American worker by fractions of a percent, if at all. Meanwhile, immigrants to the U.S. from developing countries can increase their income by 100 percent, or 1,000 percent. "Immigration is very, very far from being a zero-sum game of 'their poverty or ours,'" Clemens wrote in 2010. "Within ranges that even slightly resemble current migration levels, it is rather simply 'their poverty or their prosperity,' while we remain prosperous."

Clemens's research also challenges the notion that immigrants take away jobs from Americans. In agriculture, for example, he has estimated that for every three seasonal workers who are brought in, one American job is created across all sectors. Directly, workers need managers, and more often than not those managers are Americans. Indirectly, workers buy things, which means more Americans are needed to sell and produce those things. And yet, Clemens told me, "when a bus of 60 Mexicans is coming up from the border, nobody looks at it and says 'Ah, there's 20 American jobs.'"

But some immigration restrictionists have far bigger worries than   15
workers losing small percentages of their salaries. There are many possible negative consequences of open borders. Naik points out that "political externalities" may be a major drawback of allowing anyone who wants to move to stable, wealthy nations to do so. Gallup polls have found that 700 million people would like to permanently move to another country, many of them from developing nations with failed political systems. If the U.S. or another wealthy nation were to see a sudden large increase in immigrants from these countries, it's possible that the new populace will vote for bad policies in their new home. As Naik puts it, some people believe that "if you're coming from a place that has a problem, you are probably part of the problem, and if you move to a new place you might bring the problem with you."

But if loosening border restrictions really is the key to a much richer world, what does anyone do about it? I asked John Lee, a regular contributor to the Open Borders site, what someone with unlimited money should do if they want to convince people to support open borders. Mark Zuckerberg,° for example.

"The four words, 'I favor open borders,'" Lee told me. "That would be the biggest thing he can do. You really need to de-radicalize the idea." When I spoke to Lee, it was several weeks before the leaked announcement that Zuckerberg, along with other Silicon Valley leaders, would be forming a political action group, officially called Fwd.us. The group will focus much of their attention and $50 million on immigration reform, particularly high-skill immigration, a fairly uncontroversial issue that Zuckerberg has spoken out on in the past.

But the goals of the group are still small in scope compared to the changes championed by Clemens or the open borders advocates. The first principle stated on the Fwd.us site is "comprehensive immigration reform that allows for the hiring of the best and brightest." That "best and brightest" qualification makes this goal the opposite of comprehensive. It is not the type of Earth-altering change that Zuckerberg is known for. If the group makes the U.S. an easier destination for the world's best programmers, designers, and thinkers, it will certainly be very helpful to those who need help the least. But it won't drastically change the direction in which the world is headed. It won't, as Zuckerberg says in his *Washington*

Mark Zuckerberg: cofounder, chairman, and chief executive of Facebook.

Post op-ed, "ensure that all members of our society gain from the rewards of the modern knowledge economy." And as Nathan Smith of Open Borders writes, "If it's the common good of mankind he's after . . . he ought to try to open the world's borders generally, not to help America win some competition for talent."

Lobbying his unparalleled audience, the largest online community the world has ever known, to create an army of open borders supporters—that is the kind of connect-the-world change that Zuckerberg has already created with Facebook. Perhaps not this year, or even five years down the line, but Zuckerberg might eventually use his clout to start a global debate about the borders that keep Marvin from the marketplace. The lure of trillions of dollars for all, the potential elimination of world poverty, and a solid moral footing preached by Naik and Clemens probably won't convince a majority without backing from major business leaders.

"Open borders will become a reality when the public stops believing that immigrants are a threat," sociologist Fabio Rojas recently wrote, comparing the open borders movement to the gay rights movement. "Even if a pro-immigration referendum fails to pass, it will still serve the function of forcing the issue onto the public stage. These actions won't change the minds of those strongly committed to anti-immigration policy. Instead, they will make immigration seem 'normal' to a later generation of people." 20

Understanding the Text

1. Define and explain the following terms: *open borders*, *self-determination*, and *keyhole solution*.

2. Raviv presents what he identifies as the moral case for open borders. Fully explain the arguments and reasons that support this position.

3. Identify and explain the keyhole solutions proposed by Bryan Caplan, whom Raviv quotes. Discuss the advantages and disadvantages of these solutions (pars. 5–7).

4. In paragraph 10, Raviv quotes Michael Clemens, who insists that "[d]evelopment is about people, not places." Explain what Clemens means and how Raviv develops this idea.

Reflection and Response

5. Raviv presents ample and varied evidence to support the claims regarding the need for open borders. He also appeals to readers by using elements of classical argument. Whether or not you agree with his position, what evidence, examples, and rhetorical elements do you find the most persuasive? Explain why.

6. When asked how to go about "loosening border restrictions," John Lee stressed the "need to de-radicalize the idea" (pars. 16–17). What does de-radicalizing involve? Do you see it occurring today? If so, offer an example and explain where and how. If not, explain why.

7. Choose one of the arguments regarding open borders that Raviv presents about which you feel most strongly, and critically respond to it. In your response, clearly identify the issue and the terms of the debate.

Making Connections

8. What is your position on open borders? Write a fully developed essay staking out your position, using sound reasoning, evidence, additional research, and examples to support and develop your claims and explanations.

9. Read John Eger's "Art as a Universal Language" (p. 218) and Ann Marie Leimer's "Cruel Beauty, Precarious Breath" (p. 222). Explain how these authors' ideas extend or support the arguments that Raviv presents.

World without Borders

Stefany Anne Golberg

Stefany Anne Golberg is a multimedia artist, composer, and writer. After earning an M.F.A. in music/sound from the Milton Avery Graduate School of the Arts at Bard College, she co-founded the Flux Factory art collective and currently writes for *The Smart Set* magazine. Her writing has also appeared in the *Washington Post*, the *Arkansas Gazette*, the *Pittsburgh Post-Gazette*, and *3 Quarks Daily*.

In "World without Borders," which originally appeared in *The Smart Set* in 2013, Golberg profiles international peace activist Garry Davis, whom Golberg calls "a man out of time." Throughout her essay, she also channels Davis and confronts long-held notions regarding conflicts and borders. As you read through the multiple contexts that frame her arguments, consider the various borders Golberg addresses as you identify her main argument.

The world looks a lot more unified on old maps. Maps of today look more like mosaics, like the fragile Earth fell off a shelf and had to have its broken bits pieced back together. You can forget sometimes how new these lines and borders are.

The United Nations headquarters in New York City displays two maps in its lobby. One map is called "The World In 1945." This is the year the UN was founded. The map is a rainbow of colors. Big chunks of blue represent the few nation-states that belonged to the UN at the beginning. Bits of red and tan and yellow and green spread around the map represent places that did not belong to the UN. Many of these non-blue regions were classified as dependent: "Territories administered under a League of Nations mandate"; "Territories which by 1949 were under the United Nations Trusteeship System." Others were not even countries. "The World In 1945" was a world of empires.

The other map is called "The World Today." The World Today map, by contrast, is all blue. Only a bare handful of non-member red and yellow spaces remain, most of them faint specs that float around in the open space of sea. Since 1945, the number of people around the world who have been able to call themselves citizens of independent countries has increased exponentially. As a result, the UN maps have gotten bluer and bluer. It is the dream of the United Nations that "The World Today" could, one day, be entirely blue—a world of independent sovereign nations, united under a single hue.

The UN map of member nations vexed Garry Davis to his dying day (which happened to be July 24). This is to say that Garry Davis was vexed not only by the UN but by nations. Davis was no fan of empires either. But borders were his enemy of choice. Garry Davis was a lifelong promoter of the One World movement, which sought to unite all humanity under one universal set of laws that would be based on fundamental human rights. Garry Davis did not invent the One World movement. Philosophers and poets and emperors alike have imagined an Earth united. "As long as there are sovereign states possessing great power, war is inevitable," wrote Albert Einstein in a letter to World Federalists° in 1949. "There is no salvation for civilization or even the human race other than the creation of a world government."

When, in 1948, Davis walked into the American Embassy in Paris and publicly renounced his American citizenship, he became the One World Government's most prominent modern advocate. In this, Garry Davis was a man out of time. The twentieth century—especially after World War II—was the century of the nation-state. Of everything that will come to define the twentieth century in the books of tomorrow, this fact may be the most lasting. It's a fact that Garry Davis thought about, and railed against, for 65 years. "We are born as citizens of the world," Davis wrote in *Passport to Freedom: A Guide for World Citizens*. "But we are also born into a divided world, a world of separate entities called nations. We regard each other as friends and yet we are separated by wide artificially created barriers. Whatever we may think of one another, each one of us on this planet is designated as 'alien' by billions of his or her fellow humans. The label applies to everyone who does not share our status as a 'national citizen.' And many millions of us, despite our religious, ethnic or racial kinship, are forced to wear another label: 'enemy.'"

During the Second World War, Garry was a bomber pilot. By the time he walked into the American Embassy in Paris in 1948, ready to renounce his American citizenship, Davis had had enough of nations and their antics. "How many bombs had I dropped?" Davis later wrote in his memoir. "How many men, women and children had I murdered? Wasn't there another way, I kept asking myself?" Garry Davis told the newspapers that, from now on, he considered himself a citizen of the world.

In November 1948 Garry Davis stormed a session of the United Nations General Assembly with 20,000 supporters in tow, calling for the UN to recognize the rights of Humanity. The following day, the Universal

5

World Federalists: members of a post–World War II movement promoting a loose federation of the nations of the world.

Declaration of Human Rights was passed. "How very much better it would be," wrote Eleanor Roosevelt° in her *My Day* column, "if Mr. Davis would set up then and there a world-wide international government." Garry Davis agreed. In 1953 he announced the formation of the World Government of World Citizens from the steps of the city hall in Ellsworth, Maine. No longer would people be citizens of this or that country. With one world government all people would be citizens of the world. It would be a place where people could travel freely, citizens all. A place that had eradicated the "plague of war." With one world government there would be peace at last. Indeed, the very survival of humanity depended on it. Davis created a World Passport and before he was done issued over 750,000 of them. Albert Camus,° E. B. White,° and Albert Schweitzer° were among his supporters.

On Davis' World Government website there is a quote attributed to U Thant, former Secretary-General of the United Nations. "Last year for the first time humans could see our planet from the moon. They show no borders, no nations, no races, no ideologies and no political systems. They show vast oceans and seas, a few great land masses, precious atmosphere of air and clouds without which there would be no life on earth."

It is a moving quote. When pictures of the Earth from space circulated to human beings around the world in the 1960s, it was as if the people of Earth were being shown an Ur-map of their planet. This, thought Garry Davis, was how the Earth ought to look from the inside too.

Though it may seem ideologically fanciful, anyone can understand   10
how Garry Davis came to the conclusion that the path to world peace was the creation of one nation. Like the old maps show, national borders are artificial lines drawn in the sand of an otherwise unified planet. Ostensibly, national governments defend the people inside their lines against those living outside the lines. Yet if the borders were erased, wouldn't the reason for the borders go away too? The group of people who once called themselves Americans would not be worried about the people who once called themselves Mexicans crossing into their neighborhood. They would not feel a need to arm themselves against the threat of visitors because there would be no more "visitors." It would be like shooting the woman

Eleanor Roosevelt (1884–1962): First Lady, married to President Franklin D. Roosevelt. A politician and diplomat in her own right, she worked in the areas of human rights and children's and women's issues.
Albert Camus (1913–1960): French writer, philosopher, and Noble Prize winner.
E. B. White: Elwyn Brooks White (1899–1985), American writer and well-known author of the children's books *Charlotte's Web* and *The Trumpet of the Swans*.
Albert Schweitzer (1875–1965): Alsatian-German theologian, concert organist, medical missionary, philosopher, lecturer, and writer.

A young Garry Davis with his "World Passport" in 1961.
© Bettmann/Corbis

who sat down next to you on the subway for invading your territory. "Invasion," "immigration," "tourism"—these categories for how we move around our world would die. Space would be intrinsically shared.

Except that borders don't just define the outsiders, they define the insiders too. Each person living inside a nation calls that nation home. A person without a nation is considered homeless upon Earth. Garry Davis understood this. Over the years he sent or sold World Passports to refugees and dislocated peoples, hoping that the passports would allow them to defy immigration laws and travel freely. In 2012, Davis sent a World Passport to Julian Assange, the founder of WikiLeaks, who has been living in the Ecuadorean Embassy in London since last year. It is a beautiful subversion, this distribution of One World passports. And also, it is puzzling. Because if Planet Earth is the natural home of man, man shouldn't need a passport at all. According to the logic of the World Government, these passportless people are already free.

Garry Davis' many opponents have objected to his "crackpot" path to peace for mostly practical reasons. People, it is argued, are as inherently violent as they are peaceful. Without representative governments there would be no way to protect people from each other. This leads to a deeper, more existential question. What causes war in the first place? If we define war simply as conflict that happens between nations, then erasing nations erases war. But erasing nations doesn't erase conflict. Conflict existed long before nations. It exists not just between groups of people; conflict is inseparable from life. Conflict exists between people and the beasts, between people and the plants, between insects and the plants, between the insects and themselves. Inside each living thing, cells and microorganisms are battling it out for survival. And, of course, the battle is not just biological. Within each individual person is a mysterious invisible force—the soul or psychology or will—battling against itself, turning man into a being at war with Being, a being who lives inside the world and a being who lives outside the world too, because she cannot stop thinking about living in the world. Within each individual are internal borders—borders that are bravely crossed, cannily outsmarted, unbridgeable. There are internal regions with their various points of entry and walls armed by sentries. Externally, a person might have a nation to call home. But inside, a person rarely feels at home, no matter where she is. She is always caught up in the battle of the will, the mind, the soul. It is this internal war within each individual that creates external war. Erasing national borders would not end war for this simple reason: National borders don't cause war any more than they prevent them.

> "Erasing national borders would not end war for this simple reason: National borders don't cause war any more than they prevent them."

The pledge of allegiance to the World Government of World Citizens defines a world citizen as such.

A World Citizen is a human being who lives intellectually, morally and physically in the present. A World Citizen accepts the dynamic fact that the planetary human community is interdependent and whole, that humankind is essentially one. A World Citizen is a peaceful and peacemaking individual, both in daily life and contacts with others. As a global person, a World Citizen relates directly to humankind and to all fellow humans spontaneously, generously and openly. Mutual trust is basic to his/her lifestyle. Politically, a World

Citizen accepts a sanctioning institution of representative government, express-
ing the general and individual sovereign will in order to establish and maintain
a system of just and equitable world law with appropriate legislative, judiciary
and enforcement bodies. A World Citizen makes this world a better place to live
in harmoniously by studying and respecting the viewpoints of fellow citizens
from anywhere in the world.

Why did Garry Davis advocate for One World Government rather
than No World Government? Perhaps because, in the end, Davis did not
trust individual people to act peacefully any more than his opponents.
A World Citizen is still a person looking out, looking to others to feel
whole. As Davis wrote, "every human [is] an inalienable member of humankind itself living on home planet Earth." But living on home planet
Earth does not mean that every human being *feels* at home on Earth. On
the surface, his definition of a World Citizen is an inspiring image of
man, a vision of how people could live in harmony and peace with each
other. But it is missing an essential component—namely, how individuals can live in harmony with themselves.

Pliny the Elder° was bewildered by people's desire to wage war against 15
each other. He wrote in *The Natural History*: "Other living creatures live
orderly and well, after their own kind: we see them flock and gather together . . . the lions as fell and savage as they be, fight not with one another: serpents sting not serpents, nor bite one another with their ven-
omous teeth: nay the very monsters and huge fishes of the sea, war not
amongst themselves in their own kind: but believe me, man at man's
hand receiveth most harm and mischief." Man, Pliny observed, did not
feel comfortable even in the world of men. But Pliny also proposed a solution: "Home," he wrote, "is where the heart is." Did we miss the meaning of his words? The phrase is not about the location of home. It is about
the location of the heart. A person at peace with herself is a person at
home in the world. A person who can make her heart into a home
doesn't need a passport and already lives beyond nations. She is a map
without borders.

Pliny the Elder: Gaius Plinius Secundus (23–79 CE), ancient Roman naturalist and
author of *Natural History*.

Understanding the Text

1. Explain the One World movement, noting Garry Davis's role in that movement and his perspective on nations and borders.

2. What does Golberg find "puzzling" about Davis's creation of World Passports? Explain her reasoning.

3. What is Golberg's main argument in this piece? Locate where in the text she makes her position clear, and explain how she develops it.

Reflection and Response

4. Golberg opens her essay by drawing attention first to maps in general and then to specific ones (pars. 1–3). Explain why you think she begins her essay this way. What characteristics of maps are significant to the development of her argument?

5. Reread paragraph 13, which defines a "world citizen." What is your understanding of a world citizen? Do you think that someone can be both a world citizen *and* a national one? Why or why not?

6. Do you agree with Golberg's claim in paragraph 12 that "[e]rasing national borders would not end war for this simple reason: National borders don't cause war any more than they prevent them"? Explain your position, addressing the reasons and evidence that Golberg offers for her position.

Making Connections

7. Imagine a conversation among Garry Davis, Grandmother Wong (p. 323), Naomi Shihab Nye (p. 258), and Sherman Alexie (p. 104) about the One World Government's definition of "world citizen" (par. 13). Create this conversation using whatever format you wish (interview, roundtable discussion, and so on). Intertwine quotes from each reading with dialogue you create based on what you imagine Davis, Wong, Nye, and Alexie would say. Conclude by explaining what this conversation might teach us about the possibilities of a world without borders.

8. Read Gabriel Popescu's "Borders in the Era of Globalization" (p. 273). Explain how the concept of global flows complicates, challenges, or supports the One World movement.

9. How would Gloria Anzaldúa (p. 55, p. 143), Heewon Chang (p. 94), Sherman Alexie (p. 104), Manuel Muñoz (p. 157), or Karla Scott (p. 181) respond to Golberg's claims in paragraph 12 regarding internal borders, crossing those borders, and external wars? How would they respond to her closing arguments in the last paragraph?

Monologue: Grandmother Wong's New Year Blessings

Marilyn Chin

Marilyn Chin — feminist, activist, poet, and author — was born in Hong Kong and grew up in Portland, Oregon. She earned an M.F.A from the University of Iowa and taught at San Diego State University for many years. As a teacher she has conducted workshops internationally and nationally, and as a writer she has published four collections of poetry and one novel, translated works by Chinese and Japanese poets, and edited anthologies of Asian American writing. Her most recent poetry book, *Hard Love Province* (2014), won the Anisfield-Wolf Book Award for literature, which recognizes work that confronts racism and examines diversity. Chin currently serves as a mentor on the international faculty of the City University of Hong Kong's low-residency M.F.A. program, the first of such programs in Asia.

In the following story, which is an excerpt from Chin's novel *Revenge of the Mooncake Vixen* (2009), her characters cross and blend many cultural, racial, and linguistic borders. As you read, note the specific ethnic/racial communities that Chin depicts, the histories that she evokes, and the cultural experiences that her characters represent.

I say Moonie, you drive me to my friend's house. Mei Ling, you come to translate. Mei Ling say, but Granny, I writing paper on *Moby Dick*. Moonie say, I memorizing Declaration of Independence for speech class.

I say, *Moby Dick*? No worry big fish story. Chinese girl have good memory: life, liberty, hirsute happiness. Easy. We go to my friend's house. Give them New Year presents. We do every year. If we don't, for all year, we have bad luck. You too stupid, you don't know about this.

Moonie say, don't call us stupid. That's child abuse.

I say, okay smart turtle egg, call big lawyer put me in jail. Forget it, I don't need you drive me. I go a hundred buses, two hundred transfers. I walk ten thousand miles!

They good girls, do homework, get straight As. But I have to teach re- 5
spect. Only I do, because their mother and father too busy make money. They open restaurant at 4 a.m. Go to sleep at one. They get three-hour sleep. All my son do is swear . . . fuck this, fuck that . . . and Mei Ling mother, all she do is cry . . . She say, I go back to Hong Kong! I go back to

Hong Kong! In Hong Kong she use to ride rickshaw to teahouse. Now, in America, she work like slave. Her hand use to be white and soft. Now rough like sea cucumber. I say, don't you know? This what you suppose to do in America? Work day and night. You think Jesus or Buddha give you free money? All they do work work for money then fight fight about money. Money never enough. They always keep big eyes on cash register. I say, your daughters grow breasts! You can't see? You don't care, grow breasts or snakes!

Little peapods, I say, you don't want to be like that. You get straight As, go work high in the sky in glass building, be king of office. Lawyer, doctor, president, I don't care, close restaurant if you want, just don't dance at Pink Pussycat. I don't want you cook if you don't want cook. My Moonie hates to cook. And I say that's okay. She won't get husband, but who needs husband, end up like my son, useless, spit in wok, hate this, hate that.

So we load up presents in van, Drive and drive. Moonie say, Granny, we're lost, where we going? I say, what the matter, you suppose to know your way. We drive in circles. Don't you know the way to black town?

Mei Ling say, not black town, Grandma, don't you know, not political correct to say "black town"? Say Watts.° Say, Little Sudan. Say, hood. Say, crib. Don't say black town.

Chinatown, black town, yellow town, brown town, white town, I only speak truth. What color people in this neighborhood, you tell me. Not white people. White people won't live here. They live up white people hill where white people live.

"Chinatown, black town, yellow town, brown town, white town, I only speak truth."

Moonie say, I don't like to go to Mrs. Faith house, she always cry. I say,   10
silly piglet. She always cry because she has sad story: You know why she here? Salama and Bobo parents were killed by Janjaweed.° Don't you know Janjaweed? So, if she cry, she has something to cry about, not like you cry because you skateboarding with Coolio and break your tooth.

Watts: a roughly two-square-mile neighborhood in South Los Angeles that is predominantly Hispanic and black.
Janjaweed: a Sudanese militia, particularly active in Darfur, Sudan. Starting around 2002, the Janjaweed became a counterinsurgency group and in the following decade began a campaign of ethnic cleansing in the Darfur region, killing hundreds of thousands and displacing millions.

Mei Ling say, why don't she move? She lives next to giant power station. Mrs. Roberts science teacher say it cause cancer. I say, don't say cancer, unlucky it's New Year. Mrs. Faith too poor to move. Spoiled girl, you give her million dollars. Then she move.

Mrs. Faith grandbaby Salama is shy, watch behind curtain with thumb in mouth. I say, girls, go play with Salama, I want to talk to Mrs. Faith. She open door in bright purple dress with yellow flowers on it. She laughs and she cries loud and give me big hug with big breasts.

She say, here I am, twilight of life, suppose to lie in big pillow chair, watch lions dance; instead, I watch grand babies . . . day, night, we never safe. I say, Mrs Faith, Janjaweed can't kill your grandbabies, you in America now. She say, I worry, nightmare every night, can't sleep, carry big machete. I tell Moonie, bring my bag, and I pull out big China cleaver. I say, this better than big machete. It's biggest cleaver . . . I tell Auntie Wu to buy. Auntie Wu say there's no bigger cleaver in China.

She smells it, kiss blade and say, thank you, Mrs. Wong, I can kill lion and twenty hyenas. I say, yes, you chop chop Janjaweed, lion, hyenas, demons—boil in big soup. Eat for New Year. Nobody bother you.

I say I pray to great Buddha that your grandson don't become gang- 15
ster. Mrs. Faith say, I pray to Jesus your girls don't dance at Pink Pussycat. She give me a big necklace, string of big orange beads. I say, thank you, I think it's ugly, but I will wear all New Year week. Then, she give me big dish of goat. I say, goat, I hate goat . . . it taste too strong. She say, it suppose to be strong, like how God will it. I say, okay, I give to Mei Ling. She love goat.

She give me big breast hug and not let me go. She has big strong arms. I say 2008 will be good year. It's Rat year. Rats will come out to play and kill the mean cat. I promise, I say. She cry, laugh, cry, and kiss me goodbye.

Then, we stop for gas, so Mei Ling get Diet Coke. I say, you thirsty for eating too much goat. Hurry, we go Mrs. Gonzalez house in Mexican town. Mei Ling say, bar-ri-o,° we going to bar-ri-o, Granny. Moonie say, I hope Mrs. Gonzalez don't cry too; old ladies cry, yuk, gross! I'm tired of old lady crying.

We go to Mrs. Gonzalez house. We have to climb four flights of stairs. Moonie complain because I make her carry two big jugs. What's in these things, she say, they weigh a ton! I say, don't complain, you have strong shoulder from kung fu. Good practice to carry.

---

barrio: Spanish word for "neighborhood." In the United States, this term refers to a community inhabited mostly by Spanish-speaking people.

Mrs. Gonzalez shout from upstairs, Señora, Señora Wong! I hear her fast walk. I tell Mei Ling to translate, "Don't walk down, we come up, don't hurt lumbago!" (No-anda-abajo-señora. Subimos-ahora. No-ofende-su-lumbago, por-favor!)

I tell her many years to move in apartment downstairs and she say, no, addicts crawl through window. I say, put wire around window then make wire in plug. Moonie know how. Moonie genius with electricity, got first prize in science fair. She fry him like chicken. Mrs. Gonzalez say, no, that's illegal and not nice. I say, why be nice to drug addict? They nice to you?

Look at cute, fatty Gonzalez girls. How you pronounce name, Mei Ling. She say So-phi-a, Sa-bin-a, Sol-e-dad, Se-ren-a. They are little dolls. Pigtails. Fluffy dress. Like little cakes. Who spend hours curling pigtails and fluffing up dresses and put bows in hair? Their grandmother Maria Gonzalez, not their mother, Maria Romero. Their mother, Maria Romero, work all morning waitress at the Big Sombrero Restaurant, then, work at Hilton in afternoon as receptionist; all night she go college to become accountant. She good with numbers, I say to Moonie. Hardworking, good with numbers and you get good future.

Mrs. Gonzalez bring us em-pan-ad-as. I say, Mei Ling slow down with translation. I can't pronounce. She say, oh just call them Mexican dumplings. I say, why Mexicans like corn more than rice. Mrs. Gonzalez say, we like corn, rice and beans like one perfect family, father son and holy spirit. I say I don't understand bean, it taste dirty, maybe I put soy sauce and garlic or maybe I put sugar . . . make sweet bean paste.

We laugh and laugh . . . she say, why you have good skin for old lady. Mei Ling translates and roll eyeballs. I say, my secret, I bring umbrella everywhere I go, rain or shine, I don't want get wrinkled or too dark. She say, yes, everybody want be white face lady, no matter Mexican or Chinese . . . I too dark, this why husband run away. I say, I too dark, this why husband die heart attack. We laugh and laugh.

Then, she start crying. Hand Moonie a big basket of Mexican dumplings. She say, there is sweet ones and salty ones. Yam and bean, bean and cactus, Mei Ling translates. I give her big jugs of tiger-bone wine from China. She hit her heart with little fist and cry loud, Mrs. Wong, estoy-consada,° estoy-consada, estoy-consada! I hit heart, cry with her, I estoy-consada, too!

In car, Mei Ling say, Granny, you give her tiger-bone wine. It's 100 proof. Like drinking fire. I say, mind your business, little worm—she need fire

estoy-consada: mispronunciation of *estoy cansada,* or "I'm tired" in Spanish.

to keep her heart burning. Don't you know she wake up at three, make one thousand Mexican dumplings to sell at market. You don't see dumplings all over kitchen? We old, but we need take care of grandbabies and make money. We never sleep. What will happen when all grandmas run out of fire? We can't die. We die, nobody take care of you.

Mei Ling shut up. Then, we drive up the hill to rich people houses. Every New Year, I bring phoenix web to Mrs. Goldstein, and I bring her extra sauce on side. Moonie say, Mrs. Goldstein is your BFF because she likes to suck bones out loud then spit them on floor like Chinese. I say, she no spit on floor, she ladylike and spit in napkin. Moonie say, we don't like Benny, all he do is sit in closet, play dungeon and dragon. Mei Ling say, yes, he strange, he talk to nobody. He'll grow up, become shooter.

Mrs. Goldstein say, phoenix web not salty enough this time, Mrs. Wong. I say, Benny's Grandmother, I should bring pork ears, they're crunchy and more salty. She say, we Jewish and can't eat pork ears . . . how about ox ears? I say, ox ear no taste good . . . but ox intestines taste good with curry and scallion. She say, why you call phoenix web; are they really made of phoenix? I say, no they not made of phoenix, funny lady, no such thing phoenix, but we Chinese try make sound better, "phoenix web" sound better than "duck web," no? She say, no, you must tell TRUTH; people expect phoenix and get duck. Mei Ling say, enough chicken and duck debate . . . you old ladies think you're Plato!

Then, I say, speaking TRUTH, what happen to Benny's parents? Why Benny living with you? Divorce, she say, my son left good wife and married shiksa.° I ask Moonie, what is shiksa? She say, the yellow-hair bimbo, you saw them kissy at restaurant remember? I say, that shiksa! I say, men too stupid, my boy like gamble, yours like shiksa.

Then we talking about Germans and Japanese . . . Moonie say, oh, no, here come ancient history lesson. Make it short, Granny! I say, Chinese proverb "Small nation like small men with big ambition." She say, they killed six million of us. I say, I guess twenty million of us. She say, like killing cockroach, like killing lice. I say, cockroach, lice, we okay, we survived! What is killing American children? she say. Too greedy, I say, stomach bigger than brain. She say, my son not wise, he like money and shiksa more than Benny. I hear her son, Mr. Goldstein, in back room yelling into phone.

She say, I have bad news, Mrs. Wong, I have cancer, not long to live . . . 30 Will you remember to watch Benny, make sure he does homework? She give me white envelope with words "Open When I'm Gone." I say, you not die, don't say that on New Year, bad luck. I hate white envelope: it

---

shiksa: a non-Jewish girl or woman; often a derogatory term.

means immigration lawyer and funeral. Always bad news. Then, she give girls big gold box of Godiva chocolate. Mei Ling claps. Moonie jump up down like monkey. I say, not polite! I pinch, make her stop.

In car, Mei Ling say Mrs. Goldstein survive Buchenwald—we study Holocaust and went to survivors' museum on field trip . . . she real survivor. I say, she survive Holocaust, but will die of broken heart. Because her son like shiksa and money and don't take care of Benny.

We run out of New Year presents. Mei Ling say, can we go home now? All this old lady stuff depressing. Moonie say, I won't grow old. I commit suicide before forty, so I won't have to grow old. Mei Ling say, you give me rat poison, kill me first when I'm thirty-nine so you can suicide at forty. Moonie say, cyanide pill faster, we use cyanide pills. Then they rip up big box of chocolate and stuff mouths.

I say, go home and memorize "life, liberty, and hirsute happiness." Read *Moby Dick*. Someday, you open eyes, TRUTH not in books, stupid girl poop!

Moonie say, you not suppose to say stupid no more. Say "in-tel-lect-ual-ly challenged."

They put on earphones, eat chocolates and pretend I'm not in car. I 35 don't care, I talk loud. I talk to ghosts.

Mrs. Gonzalez, when you die, I burn incense and little pink dumplings and pretty ribbons so you have something good to eat, and you can put bows on all dead children in heaven. I also send tiger-bone wine. You drink, breathe fire like dragon, barbeque bad people who crawl through window.

Mrs. Faith, when you die I burn ten thousand paper cleavers. Janjaweed ghost won't kill you, you kill them first. Chop off their heads. Cut up their livers. Stir-fry in big wok. Then, you have peace in heaven.

Mrs. Benny Grandmother, when you die, I burn phoenix web for you, almond cookies, veggie eggroll, all your favorite food . . . Then, I burn ten thousand soldiers of Qin.° They knee down with magic bow and arrow, they protect you. Nobody hurt you, no Germans, no Japanese.

I write names of all our grandbabies: Mei Ling, Moonie, Benny, Salama, Bobo, So-phi-a, Sa-bin-a, Sol-e-dad, Se-ren-a. See girls, I can pronounce, I write on red paper, then burn them, make names—*poof*—all smoke. Girls, grandbabies, study hard, make happy life. No worry, demons can't kill you if they don't know your names!

---

ten thousand soldiers of Qin: refers to the terra-cotta army—soldiers, weapons, and horses—buried with Qin Shi Haungdi (259 BCE–210 BCE), the First Emperor of China during the Qin dynasty (221 BCE–206 BCE).

Understanding the Text

1. In paragraphs 1–6, what insights does Chin provide about the experiences and expectations of many Chinese Americans?

2. As Mei Ling and Moonie take their grandmother to visit each of her friends, they encounter multiple racial/ethnic identities and cultural experiences. Identify and explain these identities and experiences.

3. Describe Grandmother Wong and her interactions with her granddaughters and each of her friends. What does she offer her friends and granddaughters, and why? How does Chin express the theme of the story through her characterization of Grandmother Wong?

Reflection and Response

4. The full title of Chin's piece in her book is "Monologue: Grandmother Wong's New Year Blessings or They Can't Kill Us If They Don't Know Our Names." What connection do you see between the story and its title? In your response, consider the immigrant community or communities that Chin depicts here.

5. How did you react to Grandmother Wong's language? Why do you think Chin chose to narrate her story in this voice? Do you agree with her choice? Why or why not?

6. Identify and explain the multiple border crossings that occur in this story. How or when do these crossings take place? Who engages in them?

7. How does this story relate to the possibility of a borderless world? Do you think this story reinforces or challenges the plausibility of a world without borders? Explain your answer and support it with examples from the story.

Making Connections

8. Using Gabriela Valdivia, Joseph Palis, and Matthew Reilly's ideas about migrant "imaginaries" (p. 234), explain what Chin's story adds to your understanding of what it means to live as a border crosser in the United States.

Acknowledgments (*continued from page iv*)

Omar Akram. "Can Music Bridge Cultures and Promote Peace?" by Omar Akram from *The Huffington Post*, June 12, 2013. Copyright © 2013 by Omar Akram. Reprinted by permission of the author.

Sherman Alexie. Excerpts from *Bill Moyers Interview with Sherman Alexie on Living Outside Cultural Borders*, April 12, 2013. Copyright © Public Affairs Television, Inc. All rights reserved. Used by permission of Nancy Stauffer Associates.

Leslie R. Alm and Ross E. Burkhart. "Canada-U.S. Border Communities: What the People Have to Say" from *Association for Canadian Studies in the United States*, Volume 43, Issue 1, March 1, 2013. Reprinted by permission of the publisher, Taylor & Francis Ltd. http://www.tandfonline.com.

Sinan Antoon. Excerpt from poem "Akhbar 'an la ahad" by Sargon Boulus, translated by Sinan Antoon, which appears in "Poetry Peddler" by Naomi Shihab Nye from *The Strangest of Theatres: Poets Writing Across Borders*. Reprinted by permission of Sinan Antoon.

Gloria Anzaldúa. "How to Tame a Wild Tongue" and "To Live in the Borderlands Means You" from *Borderlands/LaFrontera: The New Mestiza* by Gloria Anzaldúa. Copyright © 1987, 1999, 2007, 2012 by Gloria Anzaldúa. Reprinted by permission of Aunt Lute Books. www.auntlute.com.

Elizabeth Bishop. "The Map" from *The Complete Poems 1927–1979* by Elizabeth Bishop. Copyright © 1979, 1983 by Alice Helen Methfessel. Reprinted by permission of Farrar, Straus and Giroux, LLC.

Norma Cantú. "Living on the Border: A Wound That Will Not Heal" from *Smithsonian Festival of American Folklife Program Book*, edited by Peter Seitel (1993). Courtesy Center for Folklife and Cultural Heritage, Smithsonian Institution. Copyright © 1993 by Norma Cantú. Reprinted by permission of the author.

Heewon Chang. "Re-examining the Rhetoric of the 'Cultural Border'" was published by Heewon Chang in *Electronic Magazine of Multicultural Education* (1999, Vol. 1, No. 1). Reprinted by permission of the author.

Marilyn Chin. "Monologue: Grandmother Wong's New Year Blessing" from *Revenge of the Mooncake Vixen* by Marilyn Chin. Copyright © 2009 by Marilyn Chin. Used by permission of W. W. Norton & Company, Inc.

Michael Clemens. "A World without Borders Makes Economic Sense" by Michael Clemens from *The Guardian*, September 5, 2011. Copyright © 2011 by The Guardian. Reprinted by permission of Guardian News & Media Ltd.

Alexander Diener and Joshua Hagen. "A Very Bordered World" from *Borders: A Very Short Introduction* by Alexander Diener and Joshua Hagen from pp. 1–18. Copyright © 2012 by Oxford University Press. By permission of Oxford University Press, USA.

John Eger. "Art as a Universal Language" by John Eger from *The Huffington Post*, May 25, 2011. Copyright © 2011 by John Eger. Reprinted by permission of the author.

Stuart Elden. "Territory without Borders" from *Harvard International Review*, August 21, 2011. Reprinted by permission of the author.

Kate DeVan Filer. "Our Most Famous Border: The Mason-Dixon Line" from the *Pennsylvania Center for the Book's Literary and Cultural Heritage Map of Pennsylvania* by Kate DeVan Filer, Fall 2008. Reprinted by permission of Pennsylvania Center for the Book.

Stefany Anne Golberg. "World without Borders" from *The Smart Set*, August 22, 2013. Copyright © 2013 by Stefany Anne Golberg. Reprinted by permission of the author.

François Grosjean. "Change of Language, Change of Personality? I and II" by François Grosjean on the *Psychology Today* blog "Life as a Bilingual." Reprinted by permission of the author.

Index of Authors and Titles